D0982487

A NATION IN THE MAKING

Harvard Studies in American-East Asian Relations 4

The Harvard Studies in American-East Asian Relations
are sponsored and edited by the
Committee on American-Far Eastern Policy Studies
of the Department of History at Harvard University.

A NATION IN THE MAKING

The
Philippines
and the
United States,
1899–1921

Peter W. Stanley

Harvard University Press
Cambridge, Massachusetts
1974

To My Mother and Father

Preface

This is a history of the formative years of an imperial relationship. Its premise is that the peculiar character of Philippine history prior to the American conquest—specifically, the partial stultification of social, cultural, and economic life by the Spaniards—and the nature of the United States as industrially the most developed and psychologically the most ambivalent of imperial powers gave the Fil-American encounter an explicitly developmental and consensual aspect. To establish this point, I have dealt at some length with Philippine history in the Spanish period, a subject with which most American readers understandably will not be conversant. My aim in doing so has not been to uncover new details, but rather to interpret what is already known to specialists in such a way as to improve our perspective upon the years that followed.

I am aware, of course, that the drift of modern scholarship concerning Southeast Asia has been to emphasize that cultures in transition often look more integral and feel more satisfying and supportive from within than an outsider might imagine. This is a point well taken. All cultures have their absurdities, their non sequiturs, their atavisms; and there is no reason to suppose *prima facie* that syncretistic religion, for example, would appear stultifying or illogical to people who had grown up with it. By extension, therefore, one might doubt that they would seek development and modernization as a resolution of their dilemma. This would raise questions about the validity of the imperialism of suasion I have described. In the case of the Philippines, however, the penetration of commerce and westernization during the nineteenth century exposed the limitations and dysfunctions of the existing hybrid culture, identifying them as the result of earlier Spanish rule and the tactics of present Spanish control. To seek change in such circumstances was not to disown one's roots, but to burst an alien bond.

This is not to say that Filipinos welcomed American sovereignty as an alternative. The record of their resistance is clear. For too long, however, historians have been mesmerized by the high drama and base ethics of the initial political and military encounter at the turn of the century. What is striking in retrospect is that the conflict itself and the issues informing it gave way so quickly to what Filipinos of our own time call binationalism. That is the story I have tried to tell.

I want to thank the people who have helped me. I am grateful to my teacher, Ernest R. May, for all manner of things technical and informational, and even more for his example, his boundless generosity, and his liberality in allowing me scope and initiative to be myself. Theodore Friend generously read and criticized the manuscript. His supple, probing critique and his ongoing interest have stimulated me and improved the book. Thomas R. McHale, James C. Thomson, Jr., Glenn May, and two anonymous critics have also read all or part of the manuscript and given me their counsel. Carlos Quirino and Serafin D. Quiason befriended my wife and me in Manila. I am grateful to Dr. Quiason for permission to quote from the Quezon Papers and to Mr. David C. Forbes and the Harvard College Library for permission to quote materials in the Forbes Papers. I appreciate, as well, the assistance of the staffs at the National Library of the Philippines, the Manuscript Division of the Library of Congress, the National Archives, the Houghton Library at Harvard, and the Massachusetts Historical Society. Our good friend Sheila Driscoll organized the preparation of the original manuscript, and my wife Joan helped with the revised version.

The final draft of the book was researched and written while I taught at the University of Illinois at Chicago Circle. I want to acknowledge the stimulation provided by my graduate students and the personal and professional support given me by Edward C. Thaden, chairman of the Department of History. A number of colleagues offered encouragement; and my friend Burton J. Bledstein, who has little use either for the concept of modernization or the practice of diplomatic history, kept me honest.

Above all, my parents and my wife have sustained me. Individually and ensemble, they gave me their interest, their criticism, and their faith at every stage of the project. No one could have asked for more or for better.

Contents

ONE

The Philippines,
1565–1898

1

Society

and

Culture

To take the measure of the imperial encounter earlier this century between the United States and the Philippine Islands one needs to begin a great deal earlier, with *datus, encomenderos,* and the Manila galleon. For it was the three and a quarter centuries of Spanish rule from which the Philippines emerged in the 1890's, as well as the traditions and history of the United States, that gave the relationship between the two countries its special character and tone.

We know surprisingly little about Philippine life in the pre-Hispanic period. In fact, several key documents having recently been exposed as forgeries, historians are in the anomalous position of knowing less now than they formerly thought. Nevertheless it is clear that when the Spanish arrived in the Philippines in the sixteenth century they found a culture which, however primitive it may have appeared to the European eye, was vital and in some respects sophisticated. It was, for one thing, a culture of developed skills in fields as diverse as pottery, weaving, jewelry, boat building, and metalworking, one in which the ability to smelt iron and make glass had been learned more than 1,500 years earlier. Moreover, by comparison with Spain's colonies in the Western Hemisphere, it was a humane culture that eschewed human sacrifice in its religion and prescribed customary formulas for saving face and avoiding hostility when dealing with strangers. It was, in addition, literate. There was a written alphabet, which with regional variations was shared by inhabitants in much of the low country and hill regions; and early Spanish chroniclers agree that the ability to read and write was widespread, especially in the Tagalog and Ilocano speaking regions of Luzon. There literacy was so well established that early Spanish missionaries had the Belarmino catechism translated and printed in the native alphabet for distribution. "They are of a happy disposition," reported the first Jesuit mission among the Tagalogs, "candid, loyal, simple and sociable. . . . They have a lively wit, and easily learn Christian doctrine and how to read and write in our alphabet; most of them read and write in their own."[1]

Patterns of political, social, and economic life were decentralized. The basic unit was the *barangay,* a community of thirty to one hundred families generally interrelated by ties of blood, marriage, or dependency. Each barangay was ruled by a *datu,* a traditional leader whose position was ordinarily hereditary but might be won by wealth, wisdom, or force. Economically, these barangays were largely self-sufficient, and a certain tension seems to have existed in their relations with each other. But in a number of places—Pampanga, Mindoro, Samar, Leyte, Cebu, Bohol, and especially the region around Manila Bay—there had emerged settlements of unusual size that carried on extensive trade both within the archipelago and with China, Indochina, and possibly Japan and Indonesia abroad. Apart from textiles and occasional handicrafts, the principal exports appear to have been raw materials, in return for which the islanders imported such refinements as Chinese porcelain, silk, lacquerware, and wine, Javanese cloth, and the locally rare metals tin, brass, and lead. It was a brisk trade. By the sixteenth century, Chinese porcelain had become so commonplace as to be used by some for storing unhusked rice and by others for carrying off the trinkets and gewgaws presented them by the Magellan expedition.

The Spanish impact upon this culture was considerable. The islands were conquered with relatively little bloodshed; and the basic tax, the tribute, was not in itself ruinous. In addition to the tribute, however, the government exacted forced drafts of labor and produce under its *repartimiento* system. Early accounts speak with particular force of the "ruin and death" brought upon natives by labor drafts for cutting and transporting timber and for building ships. Gangs of six or eight thousand were removed from their fields and subjected to poor food, bad pay, and the discipline of the lash, while their villages were taxed to pay for their support. The church, however beneficent its intentions, added to the burden. Natives served as rowers, porters, and domestic servants, furnished food, and constructed buildings for the clergy without pay. Like Christians in many other parts of the world, they also paid stole fees and gave alms. With large numbers of men

4

withdrawn in these ways from the fields, shortages of food began to appear. This might well have occurred in any case, but it was rendered inevitable because the sudden influx of Spanish conquerors attracted thousands of additional traders and artisans to the islands' Chinese community. Neither the Spanish nor the Chinese engaged in the production of food, and their presence threw a considerable burden upon the subsistence agriculture of the archipelago. In 1586, according to the Jesuit Hernán Suárez, a public assembly held at Manila to discuss the plight of the islands concluded that the needs of unproductive foreigners and the abuses of officials who extracted native goods under conditions which offered the natives no incentive to increase production had brought the islands to the brink of disaster. Prices were rising, food was scarce, and Spaniards as well as Filipinos were sinking into ruinous poverty. By the end of the century the productive capabilities of the natives had increased sufficiently to ease the strain upon the islands' food supply; but in the seventeenth century, under the pressures of wars against the Dutch and the Moros, the government increased its exactions and fell into arrears in its payments both for labor and for food. Finally, there were the profiteering and abuses of *encomenderos*. An *encomendero* was the recipient of an *encomienda,* a quasi-feudal grant of the tax revenue from the inhabitants of a certain region given in return for the encomendero's undertaking to defend his region against internal or external disorders and to support the missionary efforts of the clergy. Early accounts of the encomienda system speak of robbing and murder, of arbitrary quotas of produce and gold, and of *indios'*, as the natives were called, being provoked into attacking superior forces of Spaniards who coveted their lands. Encomenderos charged with such abuses responded that they had no alternative: isolated among a people accustomed to subsistence agriculture, they could support themselves only by committing the excesses of which they were accused. "We thus have a heavy load on our souls which we are unable to shake off by reason of our great poverty, and because of this we go about in great confusion of mind."[2]

What this means in human terms is not easy to say with certainty at this distance from the events. It would appear, however, that considerable personal suffering and cultural disruption occurred. In 1583 Philip II wrote in a cédula:

> We have been informed that the native inhabitants . . . are being gradually consumed by the ill treatment inflicted upon them by the encomenderos; that their numbers have declined to such an extent

that in certain regions the population has been reduced by more than one-third; that the full tribute is being demanded of them when they are only obliged to pay one-third of it; that they are treated worse than slaves, many of them being sold by certain encomenderos to others; that some have died under the lash, and even women perish under the heavy burdens laid on them, while their children are taken away from others for labor in the encomienda estates; that these women sleep in the open fields and there give birth, give suck, and die bitten by poisonous vermin; that many hang themselves or starve themselves to death or take poison; that there are even mothers who kill their infants at birth saying it is to free them from the sufferings to which they themselves are subject; and that the natives have conceived such great hatred of the Christian name, looking upon the Spaniards as deceivers who do not practice what they preach, that whatever they do, they do only by compulsion.[3]

Others, living in the islands, remarked upon the disruption of traditional patterns of authority and the resultant disorder in the countryside; there are reports of a return from the villages to the hills and of deliberate neglect of agriculture in the hope of discouraging Spanish interest. The early seventeenth century Spanish chronicler Antonio de Morga remarks upon the loss of certain skills; and in the nineteenth century, José Rizal, drawing largely upon his study of Morga and of Gaspar de San Agustin, concluded that at least in Pampanga, Mindoro, and Panay there had been serious depopulation of once prosperous regions.

We know about the abuses of encomenderos and the dislocations caused by taxation and requisitions of food and labor largely through the clergy who defended the natives' interests. They had on their side the best colonial theories of the time, and they enjoyed peculiar access to the monarchy. The classic formulations of Spanish colonial theory, worked out in the course of the sixteenth century and well understood by those who directed the conquest of the Philippine archipelago, derived the justification for acquiring and ruling pagan lands from a divine commission to convert their inhabitants. The regnant Dominican theory articulated by Francisco de Vitoria and Bartolomé de las Casas recognized the right of pagans to develop their own social, economic, and political arrangements and warned that it would be unjust to disrupt any aspect of an indigenous culture that did not interfere with the fulfillment of the commission to evangelize. Considerations of wealth, strategy, and national pride entered into the decision to take the Philippines, it is true; but from the very beginning the Dominican principles shaped the monarchy's attitude toward the pursuit of secular gains. They inform Philip II's instructions to Legazpi; they underlie the royal cédula of 1597, establishing indirect government wherever traditional local rulers would assent to Spanish sovereignty and Christian evangelization; and they provide the conceptual basis for the declarations of the Philippine clergy in the Synod of Manila. That synod, meeting between 1581 and 1586, when Spanish control of the archipelago was already a fact, affirmed in the face of those who sought profit and glory in the islands that the justification for Spanish temporal rule in the Philippines was simply that the safety of Christian missionaries and the receptivity of the society to their message could be guaranteed in no other way.[4]

This in itself need not have prevented economic or social change, since the theory precluded coercion of natives but not persuasion through example. The Synod of Manila, in fact, urged the government to encourage travel and trade, hoping this would not only facilitate the provisioning of the new towns formed by missionaries to bring the people closer to the churches but also increase understanding between Spaniards and natives by increasing the amount of contact between them. But given the existence of a predatory group of military captains intent upon supporting themselves by abusing native laborers and drawing off whatever surface wealth could be found, the emphasis of the clergy and of the government in Madrid quickly focused upon the protection of the indios against exploitation by Spanish laymen. Abuses of the repartimiento system could be and were moderated; but the system itself, modified somewhat over the years, remained in effect for as long as the Spaniards ruled the Philippines. Inevitably, the clergy concentrated their attack upon the other, easier target, the encomenderos. One aspect of their attack upon encomenderos' abusive treatment of the indios was to force acceptance of the responsibility to maintain order by withholding the sacraments from those who failed to do so. The second, far more important for the subsequent economic history of the Philippines, was to oppose penetration of the Philippine countryside by Spanish laymen and to combat economic development because of its harmful effect upon the indigenous population. There was to be no Philippine parallel to the mines of Mexico and Peru. By the time Morga wrote his *Sucesos de las islas Filipinas* in 1609, lay Spaniards were forbidden to enter the villages of the natives except for the collection of taxes; even government officials were required to change their residence from time to time so as to avoid lengthy contact with the inhabitants of any one place. The indios, for their part, were forbidden to leave their villages for trade without permission of the government or the clergy. A century and a half later in 1768, Simon de Anda y Salazar, the anti-clerical reformer and Governor General who had led the Spanish defense against English invaders of the Philippines in 1762–64, wrote that the priests had been known not only to discourage travel but even to whip and humiliate travelers who reached their villages. Their defense, which Anda considered merely a cover for their wish to preserve the arbitrary power they enjoyed in the isolated villages, was that the laws against contact still stood in the *Recopilación,* and that contact with the Spaniards could only result in the corruption of the indios.

The success of the Spanish clergy in preventing the penetration and economic development of the Philippine countryside reflects not only their ideological and political strength at Madrid, but also the burden of economic realities in the Philippines. The islands were a long way from Spain and lacked either a highly developed civilization or obvious forms of surface wealth. Few Spaniards migrated to the archipelago, and those who did were discovering by the last decades of the sixteenth century that nothing in the countryside could compare in profitability with the Manila galleon trade to Mexico.

The Manila galleon, at its inception, was conceived of primarily as the means of communication between the government in the Philippine Islands and its overlord, the Viceroy in Mexico. Once a year, a government-owned galleon made the round trip to Acapulco and brought back the only news, orders, and personnel to arrive in the colony. Commercial space allotments were made by a government *junta de repartimiento* (after 1769 by a *consulado* of merchants, acting under government supervision) to persons associated with the government and others thought to deserve well of it. These allotments in the form of *boletas,* or tickets, were transferable and could be amassed in the hands of wealthy persons. From the very beginning the eastbound cargoes were composed primarily of Chinese silks brought to Manila in the junk fleet each spring and, in lesser measure, of Indian cotton goods and spices. In return, Mexican merchants shipped silver, the only Spanish product the Chinese would regularly accept. Manila thus became a point of trans-shipment in an exchange of silk and silver, and the Spanish merchants of the Philippines middlemen to whom each of the principals consigned his product. So great was the profitability of the trade that it came to absorb almost the entire attention of the Spanish commercial element. The galleon *Santa Ana,* captured by Thomas Cavendish in 1587, was carrying a cargo valued in Manila at one million pesos and expected to bring twice that amount in Acapulco. In 1593, in an attempt to limit a trade which was embarrassing to peninsular Spanish merchants with whose goods the Manila cargoes competed in the Western Hemisphere, the Spanish government restricted the size of the galleons to 300 tons and the Manila value of the cargo to 250,000 pesos, with a maximum return cargo of 500,000 pesos. These limits were raised from time to time, but there is very little reason to believe they were seriously adhered to, whatever the level. Already by 1614 there had been galleons of 1,000 tons; and in 1616, when the tonnage limit remained at the level of 1593, a galleon of 1,600 tons is known to have existed. In 1698, when the value of cargoes was still ostensibly limited to 250,000–500,000 pesos, the galleon *San Francisco Xavier* brought home 2,070,000 pesos.[5]

The determination of the friars, the profitability of the galleon trade, and the rugged topography and decentralized population pattern of the archipelago separated the Spaniards' society and economy from those of the natives for most of the first two centuries of Spanish rule. In effect, there were three economies in the archipelago. The Spanish economy was centered in Manila, concentrated upon speculation in the galleon trade and unconcerned with the development of indigenous Philippine production. There were exceptions to this general rule: certain encomiendas lasted into the eighteenth century, harassed both by the government and the clergy; and the *alcaldes,* or provincial governors, profiteered at the expense of native producers by demanding payment of taxes in kind and undervaluing the produce thus received. But before the middle of the eighteenth century, when the silk-silver exchange began to lag and Philippine produce was drawn upon to fill out cargoes shipped from Manila, this marginal contact was the principal Spanish involvement. The native economy away from the fringes of Manila and several lesser settlements of Spaniards remained primarily one of subsistence agriculture. The Chinese economy was symbiotic to the other two. The Chinese dominated the carrying trade with China; and within the islands they were the artisans, the middlemen in what commerce took place between Spaniard and indio, and the provisioners of the Spaniards. During the seventeenth century, those who had converted to Christianity were given the privilege of living in the provinces by permission; and by the eighteenth century, Chinese, converted and unconverted, were living in many parts of Luzon, in Panay, and wherever else the Spanish economy touched that of the natives. Compromising, as they seemed to, the religious purity of Spanish rule, and ordinarily outnumbering the Spaniards, the Chinese became objects of fear and suspicion among the Spanish population. They were needed, however; and they were tenacious. In spite of discriminatory taxation, illegal labor drafts, deportations, and occasional massacres, the Chinese remained and, along with the friars, provided the indios' principal contact with the outside world. The tumultous impact of Spanish conquest was followed not by centuries of exposure and exploitation but by two hundred years of deliberate, planned isolation.[6]

The history of those years merges with the history of Philippine Catholicism. Throughout the period, the friar priest was the principal agent of government and the only European in most Philippine communities. The friars, members of regular orders each with its own rule for internal discipline, accepted the unusual burden of administering isolated missions in order that the paucity of secular clergy not retard the conversion of the Filipinos; but in doing so they in no sense surrendered their privilege and duty of obeying only the will of God and the Church, as set forth in the rule of each order and interpreted by the order's superior. As early as 1598, the superiors of the four chief orders served notice upon the government that any attempt on the part of the government to enforce upon friars the rights of examination and approval it exercised over the appointments and transfers of secular clergy would necessitate the complete withdrawal of the friars from all missions. In the 1620's royal instructions in accordance with the will of the papacy that the friars in missions submit to episcopal visitation in connection with their parish ministry ("en lo tocante al ministerio de curas y no en más") were rejected by the orders and quietly abandoned by the government after renewal of the threat to resign. The pattern was set. Although neither the government nor the archdiocesan officials at Manila conceded the point and many more efforts were made, the friars administered their mission charges without responsibility either to the state or the church in its broader sense. The degree to which the government relied upon these clergy whom it could not control is suggested, hyperbolically perhaps, by the lament of an eighteenth century critic, Francisco Leandro de Viana, onetime fiscal of the Audiencia of Manila: "The despotism of the ministers of the doctrinas is absolute, so that they are almost the only ones who command in these islands; and . . . they govern at their own will the villages and provinces." In 1766 Viana calculated somewhat impressionistically that the royal government received in tribute 250,000 pesos, of which 187,229 pesos 6 tomins was spent in subsidies for the ecclesiastical establishment in the islands. He calculated that the clergy received another 245,400 pesos from the indios directly. His figures, however inexact, represent the informed opinion of the legal officer of the government: 432,629 pesos 6 tomins were drawn from the economy to support the religious establishment, while 62,770 pesos 2 tomins were drawn for support of those government functions not performed by the clergy. Simon de Anda complained in the same period that local officials were punished if they executed royal orders without first securing the priests' approval; and in 1768 and again in 1801 the government at Manila ordered the alcaldes to protect lower officials against personal abuse, humiliation, and physical punishment at the hands of the friars.[7]

By the nineteenth century, although Europeans were once again allowed to dwell in the provinces, the pattern of domination by the friars had become fixed. For one thing, matters of corruption and the shortcomings of individual friars aside, many Spaniards seem to have become convinced that Catholic Christianity as administered by the Spanish clergy was the principal support of Spanish rule. "Between the Philippines and Spain," as Mas put it, "there is no other bond of union than the Christian religion." For another thing, the friars were more effective agents of government than most civilians. Almost alone among Europeans the priests spoke the native dialects; and, since they held their parishes for long periods of time, often for life, their knowledge of the country and the people ordinarily surpassed that of royal officials serving a short assignment. This was true even at the highest level. Sir John Bowring computed that during the period when there had been 78 governors of the Philippines, there had been 22 archbishops; and that between 1835 and the time of his visit in 1858–59 there had been 5 provisional and 11 formal appointments to the governor-generalship, but only 2 archbishops. The reliance of the government upon the clergy at the end of the Spanish period is wonderfully revealed in the testimony of Father Juan Villegas, provincial of the Franciscans, before the Taft Commission of 1900:

The following may be mentioned as among the principal duties or powers exercised by the parish priest: He was inspector of primary schools; president of the health board and board of charities; president of the board of urban taxation . . . inspector of taxation; previously he was the actual president, but lately the honorary president of the board of public works.

He certified to the correctness of the cedulas, seeing that they conformed to the entries in the parish books. They did not have civil registration here, and so they had to depend upon the books of the parish priest. These books were sent in for the purpose of this cedula taxation, but were not received by the authorities unless viséd by the priest.

He was president of the board of statistics because he was the only person who had any education. . . .

He was the president of the census taking of the town. Under the Spanish law every man had to be furnished with a certificate of character. If a man was imprisoned and he was from another town, they would send to that other town for his antecedents, and the court would examine whether they were good or bad. They would not be received, however, unless the parish priest had his visé on them. The priest also certified as to the civil status of persons.

Every year they drew lots for those who were to serve in the army, every fifth man drawn being taken. The parish priest would certify as to that man's condition. . . .

By law the priest had to be present when there were elections for municipal offices. . . .

He was the censor of the municipal budgets before they were sent to the provincial governor.

He was the president of the prison board and inspector (in turn) of the food provided for the prisoners.

He was a member of the provincial board. . . . Before the provincial board came all matters relating to public works and other cognate matters. All estimates for public buildings in the municipalities were submitted to this board.

He was also a member of the board for partitioning Crown lands. . . .

In some cases the parish priests in the capitals of the provinces would act as auditors. . . .

He was also counselor for the municipal council when that body met. . . .

The priest was the supervisor of the election of the police force.

He was the examiner of the scholars attending the first and second grades in the public schools.

He was the censor of the plays, comedies, and dramas in the language of the country, deciding whether they were against the public peace or the public morals.

By threatening to withhold his signature from certain of the documents referred to by Father Villegas, the friar could control any aspect of local government. He could and did secure the banishment of people without trial. All this, moreover, was in addition to the power the friar exercised over the native in his priestly role.[8]

The power of the friars derived not only from a logical extension of Spanish colonial theory and from the reality of Catholicism as a cultural force in the archipelago. It was said by their opponents (and it ought not to be inferred from the foregoing that they lacked opponents among either Spaniards or indios) that the friar orders were able to control the government of the archipelago by using their great wealth and their influence at court to win offices for those who would cooperate with them and to remove those who would not. In any case, it is clear that the Philippine friar benefited from the paucity of other Europeans who might contest his position. In 1810, according to Comyn, there were no more than four thousand Spaniards and Spanish *mestizos,* including military and religious personnel, in the Philippines. As late as 1848 it was estimated that but 293 Spaniards who were neither military nor clerical lived outside of Manila and Tondo. At Naga (Nueva Caceres), seat of a bishopric and provincial capital of Camarines Sur, where in the early seventeenth century almost one hundred Spaniards had lived, Jagor in the 1850's found "hardly . . . a dozen." He considered the change typical of the withdrawal of Spaniards over the intervening years from provincial centers settled in the first decades.[9]

Partly for this reason—though also because the Dominican rationale for Spanish sovereignty favored by the monarchy prescribed indirect rule wherever the islanders were compliant—the Spanish administration relied upon traditional native leaders to fill local offices below the rank of alcalde. From among the village elders, their status traditionally defined by the possession of a number of personal dependents, one was appointed (after the mid-eighteenth century, elected) to fill the office of *cabeza de barangay.* The cabeza collected taxes and brought out the labor drafts in what was still the basic sociocultural unit; he was unpaid. The past and present cabezas of the barangays in a pueblo, or township, comprised its *principalía.* Their representatives under the guidance of a friar elected its *gobernadorcillo,* or captain, in whose office were fused many local administrative powers such as the enforcement of laws, the settlement of disputes prior to their reaching the courts, and the supervision of the cabezas in their col-

13

lection of taxes. Preserved in at least some measure of their traditional role, the principalía had a strong interest in maintaining the status quo and were in no sense a challenge to the priests. An element of continuity in Philippine society and culture, they mediated between the Spanish and a population too large and diffuse to be governed directly.[10]

In somewhat circular fashion, this priestly and indirect rule born of the shallowness of westernization encouraged the continuation of a static, insulated society. It would have been inimical both to their hopes for the indios and their ambitions for themselves for the friars to have permitted any significant introduction of secular ideas or any considerable development of hopes for mobility and change. That the Philippines had been deliberately isolated "both intellectually and physically" was one of the chief indictments of the old order made by the Filipino revolutionaries. By the end of the nineteenth century, it is true, travelers in the countryside seldom encountered hostility from the resident friars. But in Manila a board of censorship, half of whose members were friars, continued to exercise jurisdiction over all written matter, whether imported or printed in the Philippines. According to James A. LeRoy, onetime secretary to the Taft Commission and America's first scholarly authority on nineteenth century and revolutionary Philippine history, the policy of the censors was "to keep the few Filipino readers of inquiring minds, so far as possible, from excursions into the bibliography of modern thought, scientific, religious, philosophical, or political."[11]

Perhaps the most persuasive indication of the insularity of provincial life under the Spaniards is the continued strength of tribal uniqueness. At the time of the Spanish conquest the tribes had shared, with some variations, a common language and had been engaged in trade. The Spanish seem to have disrupted both. For many years, there were sharp restrictions upon a native's freedom to leave his village; and even after these restrictions had been lifted in the eighteenth century geographic movement was discouraged both by fear of the friar's displeasure and by fear of Moros and bandits. In the 1850's Bowring found Tagalog and Visayan so broken up into dialects that inhabitants of different islands and districts frequently could not understand each other, even though their dialects had been derived from a common source. In keeping with the requirements of rule through traditional elites, Spanish administrative units had originally corresponded to tribal groupings; and it is revealing to find that after more than three centuries of rule by the same power these groupings remained valid in the overwhelming majority of cases. The census of 1903 found that of 950 municipalities (omitting those in largely uncivilized regions such as Benguet, Lepanto-Bontoc, and the *comandancias*), 620 had populations in which at least 99 percent of the males 21 and over were from the same tribe, and 820 had populations in which at least 90 percent of such males were from the same tribe. Of the provinces, 24 out of 41 had populations 98 percent or more from the same tribe. Where members of a tribe lived outside the province dominated by that tribe, there was a tendency for them to live together in villages separate from those of the region's dominant tribe. Only the Ilocanos regularly migrated beyond the bounds of their traditional homeland. In 1886, when 2,200 miles of telegraph line linked provincial capitals, the Japanese visitor Minami Teisuke remarked upon the little use to which the line was put; apart from government officials, almost no one had an occasion to communicate with people in a distant province.[12]

Well into the nineteenth century the Spanish government relied heavily upon a form of indirect rule, using traditional elites in an isolated, tribally oriented countryside. But indirect rule, to be effective, requires a viable traditional culture through which to work. In fact, the Spanish had in varying degrees disrupted the traditional culture of the Philippines during the period of conquest and the first decades thereafter. They continued to weaken it for the rest of their rule through the imposition, at least in part, of their own religion and law and the diffusion under the guidance of friars of religiously inspired education. Given the sparsity of western settlement, however, and the fears of the friars, Hispanic civilization could not itself replace the traditional forms it weakened. What emerged from the deliberate isolation through priestly and indirect rule of a people whose traditional institutions had been uprooted was a highly eclectic and often internally contradictory cultural fusion.

The character of Philippine Catholicism is illuminating in this respect. Conversion was the primary cultural effort of the Spanish period, and pagan religion was the aspect of Filipino civilization most deliberately and persistently disrupted. Filipino paganism incorporated two levels of divinity: a beneficent and essentially unknowable First Cause called in Tagalog Bat-hala Meikapal and in Visayan Laon, and a host of spirits, called *anitos* or *diwatas,* which controlled the good or bad fortune a man might encounter in the normal things of life. These

15

spirits, which a man associated with his ancestors and their friends or enemies, inhabited or employed the dangerous and mysterious parts and processes of nature. Certain locations, certain trees, caves, and wild animals, were peculiar to them and were to be treated with respect. The anitos themselves were propitiated by sacrifices, normally performed privately. The Christian god could fit easily into this scheme in place of Bat-hala without, from the native's point of view, requiring any renunciation of the anitos. The Spanish clergy were, of course, aware of this danger; and because of it they insisted upon presenting Christianity as an alternative rather than as a reformation or revision of traditional beliefs. Forewarned by their experiences in the Western Hemisphere, they aspired under normal circumstances to administer baptism only to those who had repudiated paganism, owned a belief in the efficacy of baptism, and, in the case of adults, memorized the Lord's Prayer, the Creed, the Ave Maria, and the Ten Commandments and displayed at least some comprehension of the importance of the other sacraments and of attendance at Mass and Confession. They deliberately refrained from translating many Christian concepts into native dialects, lest a confusion of the pagan with the Christian result.

Nevertheless, in their catechistic technique the early friars stumbled into precisely the trap they were seeking to avoid. All the orders were short of clergy in the Philippines; and for this reason they fell into reliance upon expedients such as seeking the conversion of communities through the example and authority of the local chief and using bright converts to teach the new religion to their neighbors. In addition, the very process of presenting Christianity as an alternative encouraged the drawing of parallels to the functions of the existing paganism. Consider the case of the early Jesuit missionaries. Since the indios learned their paganism in youth, through rote memorization of traditional chants, the Jesuits deliberately took over this cultural form, commencing their evangelization with the children and short-circuiting them into Christianity, so to speak, by substituting basic Catholic prayers and the Creed for the traditional stories. Pedro Chirino, one of the earliest, had the children sing these Christian prayers to the rhythms of traditional chants, thus using the very vehicle of the existing paganism. Anxious to saturate native culture, the Jesuits deliberately drew parallels between religion under their new dispensation and the cultural forms of religion under the old. Thus, in place of the sacrifices formerly made to solicit the spirits' good will toward crops, the friars introduced the blessing of the seed, the first green blades, and the harvest. The erection of crosses in the fields to ward off locusts presumably bore some parallel in the indios' minds to the evocation of the spirits' protection and gained in this from the crosses' having specific physical location.

The indios resiliently acknowledged the Christian God, kept their anitos, and translated much of Catholic symbolism and the cults of the saints into a language and thought derived from the world of pagan spirits. Miracles abounded in Hispanic Philippine Catholicism; and, significantly, few of them were recognized by the church. From the very beginning, baptism was sought by many because of its alleged power to heal physical illness. Later on, aberrational uses of holy water and of the rosary appeared, the latter, for example, being absorbed into the traditional pagan ritual for determining a criminal's identity. When necessary, aspects of Christian practice were used as fronts to disguise a continued belief in the reality of the pagan spirits. Accustomed to gather in the house of a dead person on the third day after death to await the return of the spirit, indios continued to do so during the Christian period, telling the friar that they were there to recite the rosary. The priests were under few illusions. As late as the middle of the seventeenth century prominent Jesuits admitted that, although readily received, Christianity had not yet been understood.[13]

By the nineteenth century it was clear that there had developed in the Philippines a highly syncretistic folk Catholicism. Scapularies were used in some places to discover thieves; and rosaries and medallions of the Virgin were worn by bandits as *anting-anting*, a protection against harm. A popular belief had it that crimes committed during Easter week were outside the scope of the law, in view of Christ's having pardoned the thief on the Cross. Spurious shrines abounded and were thronged; hawkers sold in the streets the privilege of kissing small boxes containing a religious picture or image. Yet at the same time the ancient belief in the spirits of the forest continued to exert a strong influence, and visionaries claiming supernatural powers commanded enthusiastic followings. Grotesque self-flagellation in public, though opposed by the friars, was far from unknown. On a subtler plane, the celebration of holy days and patronal feasts had acquired carnival aspects, with towns competing under the aegis of religion in the extravagance of their displays, their merriment, and their hospitality. Bursting from the bonds of the satirical form he had chosen for his first novel, José Rizal put a savage and heartfelt indictment of the entire system into the mouth of Elias: "You say that [Spain] snatched us from error and gave us the true faith: do you call faith these outward forms, do you call religion this traffic in girdles and scapularies, truth these miracles and wonderful tales that we hear daily? Is this the law of Jesus Christ? For this it was hardly necessary that a God should allow Himself to be crucified or that we should be obliged to show eternal gratitude. Superstition existed long before—it was only necessary to systematize it and raise the price of its merchandise."[14]

How are we to explain the continued existence three centuries after the Spanish conquest of this syncretistic mélange of traditional paganism, secular opportunism, and Hispanic Catholicism? It resulted in part from the difficulties encountered in deriving from Hispanic Catholicism with its powerful strain of mysticism and its predelection for miracles and the cults of the saints, a compellingly integral alternative to paganism. It resulted also from the human shortcomings of the men who served as friar priests during the long, boring centuries which followed the heroic period of evangelization. Many of the friars during the nineteenth century were ignorant men, drawn from the Spanish peasantry and educated under one or another charitable endowment. In a remote Philippine pueblo, powerful but alone, friars of this sort often proved incapable of preserving the clarity of their faith and the perspective of a European Christian. There is no question that the friars were responsible in some measure for the profusion of costly holy day celebrations and for the simple faith of the indio in the nearly boundless magical powers of the tangible things of religion. Spectacular tales concerning them blanket the literature of the period: here a friar operates a spurious shrine, there a friar announces raffles for his own profit from the pulpit of his church; another friar arranges to have the arms of an image move while he preaches and its head nod assent to what he is saying. In some, ignorance and arrogance are combined with devastating effect; in others, cruel and lustful behavior is common. The tales are too numerous to be entirely without foundation, but they tell only part of the story.

Just as the isolation of the clergy stimulated the growth of personal idiosyncrasies and distortions of Catholic practice among the friars, so also it ensured the indios the freedom to improve the aberrations learned from the friars and to preserve in one degree or another the pagan folk-lore of the past. For not only were there too few European laymen and secular priests to provide a broad perspective for the indios and a corrective for wayward clergy, there were not even friars enough to minister in any depth to the majority of Filipinos. Their number in the seventeenth century varied between 254 and 400, to serve perhaps 600,000 newly converted Christians spread sparsely over much rugged terrain; and at the end of the Spanish period, with 6,559,998 Catholics on the parish registers, there were only 1,124. Of these, many were devoted and intelligent priests, men with a keen awareness both of the shortcomings of their brethren and of the syncretistic character of the islands' Christianity. The English businessman Frederick Sawyer remarks upon clerical efforts to restrain excessive penitential zeal and to discount rumors of miracles and visions whenever they seemed questionable. As for friars' abuses, "There was," wrote Sawyer, "the certainty that any open scandal would be followed by punishment from the provincial and council of the order." And even John Foreman, from whom we have the story of the friar whose preaching vitalized the limbs of an image, admits that the abuse, when made known, was terminated by order of the archbishop himself. But there was little one could do where the abuses of friars remained unknown and the real beliefs of indios camouflaged. In a very real sense, syncretism was the price paid by the friar orders for their success in sealing off the Filipino from contact with others.[15]

What was true of religion, the primary cultural interest of the Spaniards, was true also of other aspects of Hispano-Philippine culture. Consider the response to the introduction of Spanish law. Deliberately and humanely, the early Spaniards preserved Philippine traditional law in civil cases of many types. On the other hand, where there was no custom, where traditional law seemed barbarous according to Christian standards, and in all criminal cases Spanish law was introduced. As in their reaction to Spanish religion, the indios acknowledged the new system, preserved many of their old practices, and adapted the forms of the western import to suit traditional functions. Complaints begin very early in the Spanish period that indios were learning Spanish codes and processes so as to legalize violence, vengeance, and robbery. By bringing suit and presenting false testimony natives covered illegal abuses with the gloss of perfect propriety. In time, of course, western law came ostensibly to replace traditional practice; and in the years 1887 to 1889 Spanish law was formally extended to the colony. But established cultural patterns did not give way easily, and even in the nineteenth century some indios continued to use the law in ways which seem to have been derived from the opportunistic eclecticism of their ancestors. According to the conservative Spaniard Manuel Bernaldez Pizarro, writing in the early part of the century, "There is nothing more discredited than the evidence presented by Indian and mestizo witnesses, who are not restrained from perjury by either an intimate acquaintance with the obligations of religion or by sentiments of conscience, honor, and reputation. It is very common to see, in court cases, that witnesses of that sort will swear, and then contradict their own testimony, according as the witnesses [are affected by] either their own interests or the influence of the litigant who presents them." And at the end of the century Pizarro is echoed in part by the far more liberal and open-minded Frederick Sawyer: "They are unscrupulous about evidence, and many will perjure themselves or bring false witnesses without shame."[16]

As with the case of religion, this aberrant use of Spanish legal forms seems likely in many cases to have resulted from imperfections that grew up in Spanish practice in the isolation of the Philippines. Procedure in the courts of the islands was such that justice was unreliable and the outcome of cases frequently turned upon arbitrary or unpredictable elements. Prior to the reorganization of Spanish colonial justice in 1869, the court system was highly specialized (there were special courts, for example, for ecclesiastical, naval, military, commercial, and treasury matters), and a multitude of distinct law codes overlapped each other. Cases tried under one code could be appealed under another. Even in the late nineteenth century it was possible, according to Foreman, for a case begun under the Civil Code to run in due course through appeals under the Criminal Code, the Law of the Indies, Roman Law, or any of the extant royal ordinances from the entire period of Spanish rule. Moreover, the principle that executive and judicial powers should be separate was not established. This was evident, formally, in the union of the two sorts of powers in the office of the alcalde of each province and, informally, in persistent intervention by officials to manipulate or circumvent the law in court cases. Apart from these structural considerations, the entire system was pervaded by ignorance and malpractice. At the local level, for example, many gobernadorcillos and attorneys, minimally educated and in some cases unable even to read Spanish, had only the sketchiest notion of the laws with which they dealt. And everywhere, clerks and other poorly paid subordinate employees of the courts added to the uncertainties of justice by shaking down litigants and forging, substituting, or losing documents. Contemptuous of such vagaries, the Guardia Civil of the nineteenth century took to murdering certain well known criminals before they could get into court. But to people who lacked the power to take independent action the whole system must have seemed what the visiting British Liberal Bowring disdainfully called it, "a farrago." Jagor comments upon finding accused robbers who had been imprisoned "a couple of years" and were still awaiting trial; Foreman tells of a tenant held eighteen months in jail without trial, who was subsequently released and three months later made a gobernadorcillo. Who can wonder that men failed to respect the majesty of such a system? The forms of an alien system of justice had been imposed upon them, but its substance proved elusive.[17]

Such was the outcome of the Spanish attempt to evangelize and to hispanize selectively while insulating the islands against development and exploitation. It was in many respects a remarkably humane policy, characterized by tolerance and self-restraint. It accomplished the conversion of the Filipino people (with certain exceptions in the highlands and the southern islands) and established a Spanish presence economically and strategically in the Western Pacific; and it did so, prior to the nineteenth century, without the horrors of plantation and mine, or the psychological oppressiveness of regular and multiple encounters between "superior" foreigners and "inferior" natives. There was a cost, however. The Spanish had intended to allow scope for Filipinos to adapt the historically derived practices of their society to the new demands that Catholic evangelization and a thin layer of Spanish political administration placed upon them. Unintentionally, they also allowed scope for Filipinos to adapt to their own pre-existent expectations, wherever these survived, the few Spanish institutions that were imported.

Social institutions and practices are culturally specific; they develop out of the historical experience of a people. Their adaptation to changing circumstances and needs, therefore, depends upon the perceptions of the society doing the adapting. The cultural context that informed Spanish structures such as the church and the courts was never transmitted compellingly or integrally to Filipinos because of the shallowness and sparsity of intercultural contact. On the other hand, certain key institutions and practices of traditional Filipino society that survived the Spanish conquest had been divorced by it from the values and goals that had originally informed them. Accordingly, there evolved an ad hoc Hispano-Philippine culture that was not simply hybrid or eclectic, but often quite specifically dysfunctional, using the

2

The Turmoil
of
Change

In the second half of the eighteenth century, a new economic pattern began to emerge in the Philippines, breaking down the islands' isolation from the outside world. As a result, Filipinos were exposed to the challenge of ideas and practices more liberal, secular, and capitalist than any they had previously known. As the new wash of foreign influence penetrated Philippine life, the dysfunctional character of the Hispano-Philippine compromise, previously a logical abstraction in the absence of alternative models, was perceived as a reality and protested by growing numbers of people. For reasons of their own, however, the Spanish responded to these changes only haltingly and, for the most part, within the parameters defined by the structures of priestly and indirect rule. In effect, they attempted further to prolong Filipinos' suspension part way through the process of cultural transition. Tension mounted along the fault-lines of Hispano-Philippine culture. A tremor was building.

The process began shortly after mid-century with two contemporaneous disruptions of the status quo. The first of these was of the Spaniards' own doing. In 1755 the non-Christian Chinese of the islands were expelled; and in the late 1760's, following their cooperation with British invaders who had occupied Manila from 1762 to 1764, many Christian Chinese were compelled to leave as well. In their place a group of Chinese-Filipino *mestizos,* well situated in the provinces to corner the cash crops of the archipelago at their point of origin, took over the role of economic middlemen and provisioners of the Spaniards. Simultaneously with this change in the distribution system of the archipelago, there grew up a significant foreign demand for

24

Philippine produce. During the British occupation of Manila Philippine commerce had been opened for the first time to Europeans from outside Spain, and after the British withdrawal the commercial interest which had begun under their administration remained. Bribing and smuggling when necessary, Europeans from outside the peninsula entered the market for Philippine agricultural produce and pushed up land values by making it profitable for landowners to specialize and produce for the export market. Exportation of Philippine sugar in significant quantities, for example, began in the aftermath of the British invasion.

Partly in response to this challenge and partly as an outgrowth of the new efficiency of the government at Madrid under the rule of Charles III (1757–88), Spain itself launched a program of economic development. To encourage trade with the mother country, direct voyages to Spain (the first in Philippine history) were opened up by Spanish naval vessels. Under Governor José de Basco y Vargas in the 1780's a variety of initiatives were undertaken, among them the institution of prizes for increases and innovations in production, the founding of the Economic Society of the Friends of the Country, and the inauguration of a government tobacco monopoly. Under the tobacco monopoly system, the cultivators in large parts of northern Luzon were required by law to produce a certain quantity of tobacco and sell it at fixed prices to the government. The production was carried on under the supervision of government inspectors in order to insure proper cultivation and a high level of quality. Tobacco production in other parts of the islands was outlawed but not in fact eliminated. Although the original goal in establishing the monopoly was simply to create a source of government revenue, tobacco subsequently became one of the principal exports of the Philippines; and its cultivation by men who had formerly carried on subsistence agriculture led to specialization in the production of rice in neighboring provinces. In 1785 the Royal Company of the Philippines was established by royal decree. Chartered, among other reasons, to subsidize the development of indigo, sugar, pepper, cotton, silk, and cinnamon in the islands as one of the bases of a worldwide commercial system, the company quickly concentrated upon more promising fields and actually accomplished relatively little in the Philippines. One result of its creation, however, was that in 1789 foreign ships were for the first time legally permitted to trade with the Philippines. They could import only Asiatic goods, the government's intention being to facilitate the trade of the Royal

Company by increasing its supply of Chinese and Indian goods for the European market. But exports of Philippine products were permitted, and the networks of foreign economic involvement already begun in the years after 1762 were strengthened. There are indications that by the end of the century European and American cargoes were being imported in foreign ships without official opposition. The first foreign commercial house, an English concern, was opened in Manila in 1809; and in 1814 the Spanish government officially sanctioned the new involvement of foreign merchants in the Philippine economy by opening the port of Manila and permitting the settlement there of European aliens.[1]

The growth of foreign involvement, centering upon the cultivation of Philippine products for export, suited the need of the Spanish government. The Manila galleon, its profits dried up by the competition of European smugglers and merchants engaged in direct trade between China and the Western Hemisphere, made its last eastbound voyage in 1811 and its final westbound crossing in 1815. And in 1820, Mexico, which almost from the beginning of Spanish rule in the Philippines had sent an annual subsidy to help finance the islands' administration, won its independence from Spain. Pressed for revenue, the government revitalized the lagging Economic Society, eliminated the import duties on agricultural machinery, levied new tariffs to protect Philippine textile production, set in motion a program to construct highways and expand postal service, and even authorized regional officials to draft unemployed indios for work (at a fair wage) on any estate that might require labor.

The local Spanish merchants, disconcerted by the collapse of traditional entrepot patterns, financially embarrassed because of losses suffered during Mexico's revolutionary disorders, and inexperienced in competitive enterprise, were unable to adjust to the new opportunities. The major role in the nineteenth century development of the economy was played by foreigners. Established originally as commission houses, firms such as Ker, McMicking & Co., Wise & Co., George W. Hubbell (which later became Peele, Hubbell & Co.), and Russell & Sturgis branched out in the course of the century into widely diversified activities. According to Benito Legarda, Jr., "They . . . traded on their own account; were agents for marine, fire and life insurance companies; were agents or consignees of shipping lines, or shipowners; owned shares in such enterprises as cordage works, banks, and slipways; owned real estate, including plantations; engaged in foreign exchange operations; and, most interesting of all, received funds at interest and made advances." The measure of their value to the economy is suggested by the govermnent's extension of privileges to foreigners. Once restricted to Manila, they were permitted to trade directly at Zamboanga, Iloilo, and Sual in 1855, at Cebu in 1860, and at Legazpi and Tacloban in 1874. In 1863 access to all occupations and the right of ownership and inheritance of land were granted; in 1870 the right of ownership and inheritance was extended to movable property.[2]

The growth of the economy under foreign tutelage is clear. The value of domestic Philippine produce exported rose 45 percent between 1810 and 1818 and doubled in the years from 1818 to 1828. Total annual exports, which had fallen off sharply at the end of the galleon trade, hovered around the figure of ₱1,000,000* in the early 1820's and rose to approximately ₱3,000,000 in the early 1840's; they were over ₱6,000,000 in 1855 and reached ₱36,655,727 in 1895. The value of imports rose from ₱4,235,814 in 1855 to ₱25,398,798 in 1895. For much of the nineteenth century sugar was the principal export. In 1855, 48,237,169 kilos worth ₱2,100,458 were exported, comprising 34.31 percent of all Philippine exports; forty years later, the figures were 341,469,556 kilos, worth ₱11,808,688, amounting to 31.34 percent of all exports. In the early and middle parts of the century sugar was grown primarily in Central Luzon, in Pampanga, Pangasinan, Bataan, Bulacan, and Laguna provinces, and in lesser quantity on the island of Cebu; subsequently Negros, particularly its western half, became the principal sugar producing region of the archipelago. The opening up of Negros, the land held largely by mestizos, indios, and Spaniards and the production of sugar financed by English and American houses at Manila, shows the effect of foreign capital infusions at its most spectacular. At mid-century, its European population, aside from clergy, was said to have consisted of one Spaniard and one Frenchman; and Jagor in 1857 found not a single iron sugar mill on the island. By 1864 there were twenty-five Europeans, seven steam mills, and forty-five animal-powered mills in three towns alone; and exports of sugar were twenty-five times their volume only eight years before. Over the period from 1850 to 1893 the population of Negros increased tenfold and its exportation of sugar multiplied 600 times. Abaca (Manila hemp), which was the second-ranking export for much

---

* Pesos indicated in this way are Philippine currency issued after the currency act of 1903.

of the century and the leader after 1887, was first developed commercially under the stimulus provided by advances of American capital. The first commercial shipment from the Philippines arrived in the United States in 1820, and by the end of the decade Russell & Sturgis at Manila were receiving orders to "purchase all that can be got, and even got half, or a dollar higher than the old prices to obtain it." Hemp throve in many parts of the Philippines: being essentially a jungle plant, it was easily cultivated on crudely and imperfectly cleared land and withstood competition from other plants sharing the same soil. It was immune from attack by locusts or blight. By 1855, 12,258,419 kilos were being exported, at a value of ₱1,399,724; by 1894 the figures had risen to 96,497,799 kilos worth ₱14,516,717. The principal regions of commercial production were in southeastern Luzon, especially the provinces of Camarines Norte, Camarines Sur, Albay, and Sorsogon; and in the Visayas, on the islands of Leyte and Samar. With the population of the Philippines growing rapidly (estimates are faulty, but it would appear that it quadrupled in the course of the nineteenth century) and agricultural production tending in large parts of the archipelago toward specialization in sugar, abaca, or tobacco, increasing amounts of food and clothing were imported in the second half of the century. The value of textile imports rose ninefold in the half-century before the revolution; and rice, the cultivation of which was abandoned by some in order to concentrate in the more profitable export commodities, began to be imported with regularity around 1870.[3]

The foreign commercial houses in Manila were linked to provincial producers and consumers in several ways. Two were of special importance. Prior to the middle of the century, the principal contact seems to have been that made through indio and mestizo wholesalers living in the provinces. Located close to the sources of production, they brought export crops to Manila in their ships and returned with foreign imports to be sold through itinerant peddlers who visited periodic markets. After the 1840's this pattern increasingly gave way to a new distribution system dominated by the Chinese. As part of its program to revitalize the Philippine economy the government had in 1839 removed its rigid eighteenth century occupational and residential restrictions upon the Chinese; and by the 1850's they were returning in considerable numbers and fanning out into the archipelago. In contrast to the mestizo wholesalers, the Chinese *cabecillas*, or wholesale merchants, established themselves in Manila and created a network of agents in the provinces. The Manila cabecillas, often united in ad hoc syndicates to deal with European importers, provided a volume and regularity of purchase which suited the needs of the foreign houses. Wherefore, they received support from importers in the form of extensive credit. The Manila commercial houses advanced goods to the cabecilla, who advanced them to his agents, who in turn sold them to the Filipinos either for produce or for a lien on a future crop. The produce received by the agent was turned over to the cabecilla and eventually through him to a foreign house. As other ports were opened to direct foreign trade, cabecillas appeared in them as well, often specializing in exports, since the overwhelming majority of imports continued to enter through Manila.

This is only a schematic outline of a system very much less tidy in practice: some cabecillas specialized in either imports or exports; some agents had agents of their own; certain Chinese retailers in the provinces and at Manila had direct contact with foreign houses. But as Edgar Wickberg observes: "The cabecilla-agent system was the characteristic, and in some ways the most efficient, method of handling imported goods and export produce." The advantages were numerous. The foreigners secured not only a wide network for the distribution and sale of their imports, but also a complementary mode of access to the exports produced in the provinces. The Filipino profited from the fact that, unlike the itinerant indios and mestizos, Chinese agents in the provinces typically set up permanent stores in the market towns and readily extended credit. The cabecilla, for his part, was able either to avoid or to turn to advantage many apparent obstacles to successful business activity. There was both a shortage and a confusion of currency during the last decades of the Spanish period in the Philippines; by conducting their trade on credit and exchanges in kind the Chinese escaped having to cover in currency the value of the goods they handled. Moreover, because of the vagaries of the Spanish tax system, which after 1852 taxed self-employed Chinese by the size and character of their shop rather than their income, the cabecilla, a middleman without a shop, secured a way of doing business without paying taxes. Finally, because the parties to a relationship between a cabecilla and an agent were kept secret and because the agents ordinarily were boys under the age of majority and hence not legally responsible for their debts, the sytsem was quite effectively ensured against legal action should local operations in the provinces become overextended. Measurements as to the Chinese share of the distribution traffic of the archipelago do not exist, but there is abundant testimony from the late years of the century that they were the indispensable dynamic element.[4]

The economic expansion of the nineteenth century introduced unsettling elements into a society and culture suited to isolation and stagnation. Manila, which had always been somewhat more westernized than the rest of the archipelago, grew in size and became subject to external modernizing influences with the coming of a foreign colony and the expansion of commerce. After the middle of the century, steam navigation, the opening of the Suez Canal, and the inauguration of cable service brought the city into closer contact with Europe and America; and the opening of provincial ports to direct foreign trade, the creation of a cable network within the islands, and the movement of Chinese and westerners into the provinces extended many of these influences to other parts of the archipelago. Moreover, in the provinces the opening of new opportunities in export commerce had been stimulating social change ever since the last years of the eighteenth century. As the economy continued to grow, greater numbers of people were exposed to new ideas and incentives. Production for market encouraged the spread of materialism, and newly acquired wealth made possible travel and even study abroad.

One result was the emergence of a new group of social and economic leaders with no vested interest in preserving the status quo of cultural isolation and indirect rule. Implicit in this was a change in consciousness and self-definition. For whatever their racial backgrounds, those most positively affected by the spread of commerce came to share immediate interests and goals that bridged the social and ethnic divisions informing traditional Hispano-Philippine culture. Rooted economically in the soil and products of the islands, they identified themselves with the Philippines more intensely than had the Spaniards, Creoles, and Eurasian mestizos. Relatively wealthy, worldly, and capitalistic—taking their cue from mid-century Spanish liberals and the foreign agents and merchants around them—they sought westernization and secular liberalism more forcefully and knowingly than had the indios or even the Chinese mestizos. Inadequately described simply as Spaniards, indios, or mestizos, they were Filipinos in the modern, inclusive use of the term.

The overall effect of these developments, when taken in conjunction with certain governmental reforms such as the ending of the alcaldes' trading privileges in 1844, the separation of the judicial from the executive power in provincial government, and the attempted secularization of education in the 1860's and 1870's, was to set in motion gradual evolution toward a more mobile and liberal society and a culture patterned upon that of the West. Powerful groups in Philippine life opposed these changes, however; and the existing institutions of the islands, some of them larded with two centuries of inertia, provided no adequate channels for constructive, peaceful adaptation to the new forces.

Ideally, education might have provided such a channel for adapting Philippine society to its new economic environment. But education in the Philippines was a product of its culture and was incapable of providing definition and coherence as if from without. Prior to the reforms of 1863 education was the province of the friars and its content was almost exclusively religious. The school day began and ended in the church and was punctuated by chanted prayers sung in procession behind a crucifer. The curriculum emphasized study of the catechism, the church calendar, the local dialect, and moral precepts. At the beginning of both the morning and the afternoon sessions, students were inspected for personal cleanliness and suitable attire, and discipline was meted out to those who were found deficient in either respect or who had been disrespectful. The government supported education with as much vigor as it could, and partly because of its interest there was by the nineteenth century a school in almost every civilized township; but because of the smallness of its resources and the extent of its reliance upon the clergy, it could do little to secularize education. Repeated attempts to enforce the requirement that indios be taught Spanish failed, since the friars feared that access to western literature might expose the provincial population to unhealthy thoughts.

Educational reforms in 1863 attempted to break through this pattern and establish in the Philippines the same sort of education available in Spain. The Jesuits, who had proven their interest in improving education, were placed in charge of training male Filipino teachers; and three normal schools for women were established somewhat later under the direction of the Sisters of Charity and the Augustinian Sisters of the Assumption. Local school boards of a civil character were ordered established. Reforms in the curriculum were decreed, and the requirement to teach Spanish was stiffened by a provision that after fifteen years no one should be eligible for the principal offices of local government unless he could read, speak, and write Spanish. As a

31

result, the number of schools seems to have grown and the curriculum to have broadened. This was especially true in the most westernized parts of the archipelago, the Tagalog, Pampangan, and Bicol provinces in Luzon and the regions near Cebu and Iloilo. But it is doubtful that the social effect of education changed greatly in regions not already opened to outside influences. Almost everywhere the friars remained, in fact if not in theory, inspectors of the schools; and religion continued to dominate the actual instruction in the schools, whatever may have appeared in formal curricula. Instruction, as before, was characterized by rote memorization from exceedingly limited sources. Where Spanish was taught, it was not always understood: "They read, write, and memorize selections, and sometimes whole books in Spanish, without understanding a single word," said Rizal's fictional schoolmaster. "Padre Damaso . . . said to me in Tagalog: 'Don't try to shine in borrowed finery. Be content to talk your own dialect and don't spoil Spanish, which isn't meant for you.'" Where buildings existed, they were not always used: "In the town of Kalamba two masonry school-houses . . . were constructed at the people's expense," wrote Rizal in an essay. "Yet the children have no school, for these buildings are now used as barracks and town hall." The Schurman Commission calculated that only 1,914 teachers had served a total civilized population of 6,709,810 in the concluding years of Spanish rule. And the census of 1903 found that 55.5 percent of the population ten years of age or older could neither read nor write in any language or dialect.[5]

Secondary, but not higher, education was of a somewhat different character. The Dominican secondary schools, San José and San Juan de Letran, were indeed archaic places, in which, according to Felipe Calderón, students were taught Latin and philosophy without learning Spanish. But there were alternatives. Private secondary schools, perhaps ninety to one hundred of them, existed in several parts of the archipelago; and the government ran several secondary schools providing instruction in technical and vocational subjects. The most modern and comprehensive school in the islands was a secondary school, the Jesuit Ateneo Municipal de Manila, which had been founded as the Escuela Municipal in 1859 upon the return of the Jesuits to the Philippines. The Ateneo taught an eight-year program which included in addition to Christian doctrine and manners, Spanish, basic arithmetic, algebra, geometry, trigonometry, elementary science, geography, poetry, history, rhetoric, philosophy, Latin, and Greek. After 1768, however, the only university in the archipelago was Santo

Tomás, a Dominican institution of almost medieval character. Until well after the middle of the nineteenth century, its curriculum was composed of theology, canon law, civil law, scholastic philosophy, and grammar. In the 1870's under pressure from the government to modernize, the university added chairs in medicine and pharmacy and began, additionally, to provide training for notaries, midwives, and surgeons. Even then, however, it so thoroughly ignored science, technology, engineering, and both business and civil administration that the government was forced to rely almost exclusively upon Spaniards and foreigners to staff its fledgling professional and technical bureaus. In 1887, in connection with the Philippine displays at the Exposition of Madrid, the Dominicans characterized the university as follows: "Its organization is simple without being rudimentary. Having for a basis religious education, at the same time that it avoids the danger of professors expounding more or less advanced theories, which in practice sooner or later are reduced to moral ruins, both public and private, it contains the pupil within the circle of a severe discipline, in which, if some apparently see oppression and a suppression of spirit, this apparent oppression is softened by the paternal affection which the priests in charge of the instruction know how to bestow upon the natives of this archipelago." Spanish conservatives in the Philippines considered that only those who took their higher education in Europe were likely to become *filibusteros,* agitators for change.[6]

While Hispano-Philippine education, with the exceptions noted above, was continuing its time-honored task of preparing men for life in a static, isolated society dominated by traditional religion, economic changes were in fact altering the islands' social structure. Ironically, the first to feel their impact in a critical way were the Spaniards. The Spanish community of the Philippines was subdivided into three groups, *peninsulares* born in Spain, *creoles* born in the empire, and mestizos of mixed Spanish and native parentage. At the beginning of the nineteenth century as at the beginning of the seventeenth, most of the laymen lived in Manila and occupied themselves in the government or the entrepot trade. The early decades of the century dealt them a succession of blows.

For one thing, the demise of the galleon trade and the influx of European and American foreigners to develop a new commercial system based upon the exportation of Philippine produce broke down the traditional three-part economy of the archipelago and disrupted what had been, so to speak, the Spanish sector. Unable to challenge the

Chinese mestizos' control of production and trade in the countryside and lacking the capital, experience, and foreign connections necessary to compete in international commerce with British and American rivals, Spaniards suffered relative decline in the importance and profitability of their commerce. They were never driven under altogether. Spaniards remained active in shipping, in some aspects of the retail trade (especially books, metalwork, and tobacco), and even in foreign trade; at the end of the century Foreman mentions the existence of fourteen Spanish commercial houses "of a certain importance." But they lost control and even eminence in the economy of what ostensibly was their colony, and in consequence their bitterness and frustration grew to dangerous proportions. Just how dangerous became evident in 1820. During a smallpox epidemic that year, envious Spaniards circulated among indios the rumor that white foreigners had deliberately brought the disease to the islands and were at that moment administering poison under the pretext of giving medical aid. Their "jealousy and envy," reported the Russian Consul, were directed "against all strangers, and particularly those who resided or intended to form establishments in the country." In the ensuing massacre a large part of the European population of the Philippines was murdered and much property destroyed, but Spanish life and property were left conspicuously inviolate.[7]

The effect of this economic decline was intensified by the arrival in the islands of a wave of immigrants who increased the size of the Spanish population and accentuated its internal divisions. The loss of Spain's colonies in the Western Hemisphere brought to the Philippines many opportunists, adventurers, and politicians whose predecessors in balmier days would have scorned so distant and impoverished a possession. Beginning as a trickle in the 1820's and 1830's, this migration grew considerably after the opening of the Suez Canal and the inauguration of direct steamer service to the Peninsula. Some of the newcomers entered commerce; others entered one of the professions, took up journalism, or acquired land. But given Spain's declining role in the islands' economy, a very large number were forced into dependence upon government jobs, for which they competed with Spaniards already resident in the Philippines. Even at mid-century the government could employ less than half the applicants. And although as the century progressed the bureaucracy was rapidly and arbitrarily expanded, raising taxes and increasing inefficiency, the gap between the number of positions available and the number of Spaniards seeking them was never closed.

The result was a peculiar demoralization. Competition for jobs and status divided the already vulnerable Spanish community into contending factions. Proud and bitter—presuming their metropolitan birth made them more purely Spanish and therefore more cultured, more loyal, and more deserving—the newly arrived peninsulares disdained resident creoles and mestizos and, wherever possible, displaced them from the government and the leadership of society. As justification, they adduced the lesson of New Spain: that the loyalties and cultural affinities of such as these ran to the place of their birth, making them latently—some would say inherently—seditious. In retrospect, one perceives this to have been a self-fulfilling prophecy. For as early as the Novales uprising of 1822, disaffected creoles and mestizos began to fight back. Increasingly, they responded to peninsular pretensions by turning the tables and asserting special claims of their own based upon identification with the islands. By mid-century, frustrated both in commerce and government, their resentment was becoming openingly seditious. As Juan Manuel de la Matta observed in 1843:

> In general there is to be seen considerable indifference, and even disaffection, to Peninsular interests. Ideas of emancipation are sheltered in many bosoms. Discontent swarms in all places. It is given utterance with effrontery, and is developed and fomented in various manners. Since the beginning of the colony, boldness, deceit, and acrimonious speech have had a foremost seat, but greed is today the dominant passion in the white people. Their needs are many and there are few means of satisfying them. The hot climate especially contributes to captiousness, and the development of vehement passions. A multitude of jealous, complaining, and evil-intentioned men foment the discontent, to which also pusillanimous persons contribute by their indiscreet and excessive fear. Although by means of different passions, there is a manifest tendency to constantly discredit the dispositions of the government, to attack maliciously the authorities who represent it, and to foment rivalry and discord among them, to which both the complexity of the legislation and the burning climate lend themselves.

In practice, however, there were built-in restraints upon the scope of creole sedition. Given the creoles' numerical insignificance and alienation from the indio masses, a revolution on their own terms was simply out of the question. For all their animosity toward peninsulares

35

and the insular government, they remained dependent upon Spanish sovereignty and their own identification as Spaniards for the maintenance of their prestige and status. Wherefore there ensued between them and the mestizo members of the Spanish community much the same pattern of competition and captious hostility that characterized peninsular-creole relations. "Life in the city proper cannot be very pleasant," wrote Feodor Jagor of Manila: "Pride, envy, place-hunting, and caste hatred, are the order of the day; the Spaniards consider themselves superior to the creoles, who, in their turn, reproach the former with the taunt that they have only come to the colony to save themselves from starvation. A similiar hatred and envy exists between the whites and the *mestizos*."[8]

Vulnerable and defensive because of its declining fortunes, the Spanish community was, in a sense, redefining itself by the restrictive process of excluding peripheral members. By a variety of means—some as bald as discriminatory sumptuary legislation—it eventually drove many mestizos and some creoles to a revolutionary perception of Filipino nationality. In this there is painful irony, for ideas as well as men had come to the Philippines since the 1760's. Spain itself had been a source of liberal and secular impulses during the reign of Charles III in the eighteenth century and its republican and Carlist interludes in the nineteenth; and the prospect of reform and modernization within a Spanish context had at times seemed quite real. There were Spaniards in the islands, for example, who opposed the continued hegemony of the friars—the friarocracy, as it has been called —and supported the liberal, reforming governors general de la Torre and Terrero. But the insecurity and internal division of the Spanish community as a whole deprived it of resilience to change. Outside the Spanish community, the leaders of the drive for reforms and the chief beneficiaries of any liberalization that might be enacted were men whose new affluence and independence posed a serious threat to the status of many Spaniards. And for this reason the friars and the reactionaries like Rafael Comenge were able consistently to arouse broadly based opposition within the Spanish population to even the mildest of reforms simply by exaggerating to their nervous and all too receptive compatriots the dangers involved in gratifying the driving ambition of those they called "brutes laden with gold."[9]

These "brutes" were the leaders of the emergent Filipino society; and their rise to affluence, like the decline of the Spanish merchants, reveals much about the social effect of the nineteenth century's economic expansion. The membership of the new elite cut across two of the basic divisions in the traditional Hispano-Philippine social structure—that between indigenous ethnic groups and that between hereditary traditional leaders and the rest of the native population—and in so doing set up cultural tensions of great force. The formation of such a group had first become apparent in the last years of the eighteenth century when the subsidies, prizes, and credit advances of the Royal Philippine Company and the Economic Society permitted a certain number of indios and mestizos, possessed either of good luck or of land or capital, to profit from the dawning commercialization of agriculture. Since it was entirely possible for a small landholder to rise in this way on the strength of credit advances (there being no significant large-scale productive units to compete with him), there was no necessary correlation between economic success in the new order and membership in the principalía or traditional leadership corps in the old order. As foreign houses replaced the Royal Company and pumped increasing amounts of capital into the production of export crops, there grew up what has been called a "third class" of Filipinos. Of these, a considerable proportion were Chinese mestizos who, having been displaced as provincial wholesalers and retailers by the Chinese in the middle of the nineteenth century, had retreated with their capital into land acquisition. In time, this agricultural wing of the new elite was complemented by an urban wing. Indios and mestizos were able to rise socially and economically into what has been called a Philippine middle class by supplying the skilled services needed in the railroad, some parts of the cigar factory, and the offices of commercial houses and the government. Some went beyond this to become doctors, lawyers, or journalists. Detached from provincial culture by their new wealth and responsibility, and often stimulated by education or travel abroad, the members of the new elite were the dynamic, westernizing element in Hispano-Philippine civilization.[10]

To such men the traditional Spanish policy of governing the Philippines through indirect rule and division according to ethnic character was at the least irrelevant and at the most threatening. Spanish practice had organized the local government of the islands around the ethnic groups in any given place: indios, mestizos, and Chinese each, wherever their numbers were sufficient to justify it, had their own *gremio*, or municipal corporation, with their own cabezas and gobernadorcillo. This system of overlapping ethnic jurisdictions within the same geographical province reflects the shallowness of Spanish settlement and control and the essentially static conception of society which to some degree still informed Spanish government well into the nineteenth century. The new elite would have none of it. Ethnic isolation ran directly in opposition to their aspiration to hispanize themselves; and this, along with governmental reforms which stripped gobernadorcillos and cabezas of much of their authority and left them only onerous responsibilities, caused the new de facto leaders of indio and mestizo society to shun election to office.[11]

Once the principalía of a community could no longer claim in fact to be the social, cultural, or economic leaders of their people there was no rationale whatever for continuation of the forms of indirect rule. In a sense, the Spanish governmental reforms alluded to above recognized this fact: there is a somewhat circular relationship between the refusal of the new elite to accept the traditional offices of leadership and the transfer of important judicial and financial powers from those offices to agencies of the central government. Nevertheless, Spanish practice continued to assume the viability of a considerable measure of indirect rule. Even the celebrated Maura Law of 1893, which attempted to rationalize the administration of local government by increasing the measure of local autonomy, reducing the role of the priest, and extending the electorate to include some large taxpayers as well as the traditional principalía, left the balance of power in the electorate with those who had already served as cabeza or gobernadorcillo. (The Maura reforms had not yet been put into effect in most places when Spanish rule ended.) However, since the cabezas and gobernadorcillos received only nominal pay and yet were personally responsible for the full tax quota of their communities, since most communities were in reality still dominated by their parish priest, and since those filling the offices were frequently not the social and economic leaders of their communities, the result of continued indirect rule for the nineteenth century gobernadorcillo or cabeza was often unpopularity and financial ruin. Many actually found profiteering and abuse of office indispensable to their financial survival. In effect, the offices became immense and unrewarding burdens upon men ill-equipped to cope with them; they demoralized the traditional leaders of the country and alienated the rising class. The personal strains involved are suggested by Rizal: the gobernadorcillo, he wrote, was "only an unhappy mortal who commanded not, but obeyed; who ordered not, but was ordered;

who drove not, but was driven. Nevertheless, he had to answer to the alcalde for having commanded, ordered, and driven, just as if he were the originator of everything."[12]

The movement of the new elite and its middle class allies toward western culture and the example they set in rejecting not only the traditional offices of local government, but also the values and assumptions underlying the whole scheme of indirect rule through ethnic gremios created strong currents in the rest of Philippine society. There has always been in modern times an informality in Philippine class divisions, especially in the rural parts of the archipelago. Members of the upper and lower classes are frequently linked by strong dyadic ties, the powerful accepting a responsibility to support the little man in economic misfortune or to patronize his child, and the little man repaying this noblesse by becoming in a limited way a retainer, magnifying the political or social importance of his patron. To this must be added in the nineteenth century the freedom derived from proximity, from the everyday mingling of rich and poor in market or church. For this reason, cultural change at the highest levels of Philippine society had direct and immediate effects upon large numbers of people in the lower strata. One sees this process at work in the Chinese mestizos' abandonment of the traditional, ethnically oriented structure of local government. The mestizos were economically the most dynamic ethnic group in Philippine society, if one excepts the Chinese because of their being, as we shall have occasion to show, essentially a foreign group. When the gremios had possessed real power, the mestizos had been engaged in wholesale and retail commerce; and a local government separate from that of their indio clients had been a useful form of insurance. But with the decline in the importance of the gremios and the movement of mestizos from commerce into landholding, clerical work, and the professions, the advantage in their maintaining community institutions separate from those of the indios all but vanished. Informally, in the course of the nineteenth century mestizo gremios in most parts of the Philippines simply dissolved, their members merging into the regional indio gremios. The Spanish government in effect recognized this melting of indio and mestizo into Filipino by abolishing ethnic tax categories when it instituted the *contribución industrial* in 1878 and the *cédula personal* (a compulsory identification card, purchased according to a graduated scale of payments adjusted to one's tax category under the contribución industrial) in 1884. By the end of the century the use of the term mestizo to designate offspring of a union between Chinese and indio was anachronistic in most places. The Chinese mestizo of old now became either Filipino or Chinese, and the term mestizo itself was transfered to Eurasians. Significantly, however, the meaning of mestizo in its traditional sense survived during the late Spanish period in a few areas where identification as a mestizo signified that a man possessed a greater than usual degree of westernization. In Manila and Central Luzon, in Cebu, and in certain other places where mestizos had achieved wealth and led in the movement of the new elite toward westernization, indios of wealth reversed the customary pattern and joined mestizo gremios.[13]

In the late nineteenth century there appeared, also, signs that the new economic conditions and the changing social structure of the Philippines were affecting attitudes of ordinary Filipinos, men of no special wealth or skills. The indolence and childlike irresponsibility of the Filipino are constantly recurring themes in the eighteenth and nineteenth century literature concerning the islands. Robert Mac-Micking, a perceptive and sympathetic observer, wrote in the middle of the nineteenth century that "the greatest defect in their character is their indolence and dislike to any bodily exertion"; Foreman, forty years later, marveled that the native never tires "of sitting still, gazing at nothing in particular." He is portrayed as unreliable at work and irresponsible with money. Typically, he will not work until given his pay in advance, but upon receiving the money or goods he may vanish. Where he stays in good faith, his work is often slow and insufficient to cover the advances already made. Surrounded by lush forests which freely provide most of his basic needs, and ennervated by the heat of the tropical sun, he had found in the static social and economic life of the first centuries of Spanish rule not incentives to individual or group initiative, but discouragement. Wherefore he has an aphorism. "Do not adventure much until you are certain of the issue." There is no end (even now!) to these complaints about indolence, scarcity of labor, and abuses of advances in pay, but evidence does appear to suggest that by the end of the Spanish period natives in the most urbanized, westernized, and commercially advanced parts of the archipelago were beginning to seek work. In 1886 a petition with 5,000 signatures urged the government to switch from the use of Chinese labor gangs to the use of native labor in its public works projects at Manila. Moreover, we are told by men well placed to know, Frederick Sawyer among them, that given decent incentives natives were proving to be reliable and dogged workers. Horace L. Higgins, general manager of the railway built from Manila to Dagupan in the years 1887–91, testified before the Schurman Commission that natives had undertaken work rejected by Chinese coolies and had proven themselves preferable to the Chinese not only in building, but in operating his line.[14]

The changing tone of economic and social life, both for Spaniards and for Filipinos, shows clearly in the renewal of anti-Chinese agitation in the 1880's and 1890's. The Chinese penetration of the Philippine economy after the middle of the nineteenth century had not been limited to the wholesalers and retail merchants of whom we have already spoken. Using credit skillfully and pressing into parts of the archipelago thought by others to be too inaccessible to be of commercial importance, Chinese became major producers and marketers of abaca and tobacco. They also refined sugar, milled rice, and cut and marketed timber. They were artisans, especially in carpentry, shoemaking, and food preparation; urban laborers; and monopoly contractors to the government, especially with regard to cockpits and opium. Chinese dominated retail trade in Manila. The ambiguities of the Chinese position, as seen by others, were considerable. As the Spanish chargé d'affaires in Japan put it: "Chinese in the Philippines represent work and activity; they promote commerce . . . and lower by means of competition the prices of merchandise. On the other hand . . . they do not take root in the country, leaving soon for home, they do not consume their winnings . . . and what is worse and more detrimental is that on account of their greediness they adulter the products and thus prostitute the bona fide commerce." Armed with such complaints, those who had been displaced by the rise of Chinese economic activity—indio and mestizo traders, artisans, and monopoly contractors; indio urban laborers; and Spanish businessmen— acted to secure government protection. The mass petition of 1886 complained that competition from Chinese labor and Chinese monopoly contractors was ruining the middle and lower classes; it requested that the government cease to employ Chinese in either capacity. A memorial by Spanish merchants and manufacturers in 1896 called upon the Madrid government to suspend Chinese immigration and ban resident Chinese from carrying on trade or manufacturing anywhere outside the ports open to international trade. The opposition covered the entire archipelago, a tribute to the extent and effectiveness of Chinese economic endeavor; and by the 1890's the Chinese were being hit not only by government legislation designed to close the legal gaps which had shaped their distribution system but also by psychological pressures and widespread vandalism against their property.[15]

Wherefore the Chinese community—homogeneous in its geographic and cultural background in China—began in this period to turn inward and separate itself from Philippine society by creating separate institutions and fostering the growth of ethnic cultural awareness. Cultural relations with China were strengthened, and a program was launched to block the assimilation of the community's mestizo children into Filipino society. Chinese newspapers and a Chinese school came into being. The existing Chinese cemetery and hospital grew in importance. Catholicism declined among the Chinese, its attraction having been weakened not only by cultural tensions but also by the end of Spanish favoritism toward Catholics in matters of taxation, land grants, and residence. At the same time, an existing unofficial community body, the Gremio de Chinos, headed by the wealthiest men of the community and the gobernadorcillo, was replacing the traditional governmental unit, the Catholic-oriented Gremio de Chinos de Binondo. In the 1880's the gobernadorcillo won recognition of his right to participate in all cases involving Chinese, and in the same decade the Gremio de Chinos petitioned for recognition as "the sole spokesman of the interests of the Chinese community." By the 1890's the Gremio and the gobernadorcillo were hiring lawyers to represent, and filing petitions in support of, individual Chinese. Thus, as anti-Chinese pressure mounted, the Chinese turned away from assimilation and became in effect a foreign group living as if under consular protection within the Philippines.[16]

The growth of a westernizing elite and the proliferation of at least some of its values and attitudes generated social tension and led to a direct confrontation between leading groups in the freshly defined Filipino and Spanish communities. Many Filipinos had been exposed to the inadequacy of static Hispano-Philippine life and were actively seeking economic and social change. Beyond this, they were reaching out for westernization (specifically, hispanization, since that was what was available and known) as a means of affirming the new dignity which some of them felt and to which others of them aspired. In so doing they threatened Spaniards with the loss of that socio-cultural uniqueness which, in the decline of material fortunes, was for many their principal remaining distinction. As we have already seen, this tended to solidify among conservative Spaniards and the friars a potent will to defend the status quo; it was almost certainly a factor in their ability to rally broad support in the community in opposition to the liberalizing reforms of de la Torre and Terrero. The new currents in motion among the natives and particularly the appearance of a Filipino people combining the "brains" of the mestizos with the "numbers" of the indios were considered by some to present a challenge not only to resident Spaniards, but indeed to the very continuation of Spanish government in the islands. As early as 1842, Sinibaldo de Mas had warned that if Spain wished to retain the islands as a colony it must curtail education, avoid teaching Spanish, encourage friar control of the villages, frustrate the rise of native priests to positions of authority, end social distinctions for indios other than the traditional principalía, and keep the mestizos and the indios "separated and at swords' points." We have already seen in the case of Rizal's fictional teacher a suggestion of the brutal opposition encountered by many Filipinos who attempted to hispanize themselves and their countrymen in the last years of Spanish rule. A Filipino physician, speaking to the Schurman Commission, put the problem concisely:

> The Filipino, as a general thing, is very fond of imitating the people whom he believes are his superiors in culture; and as they are fond of culture they are desirous of obtaining it. When a priest met a man who had any education, any culture at all, in towns where there was very little culture, and got him before a great many people, he would say, "O! You are a Spaniard now, I suppose. You will very soon be a Protestant and a heretic, and soon you will be excommunicated"; and of course it exposed the man to great shame. And the friar would say, "You are a very ugly person to try to imitate the Spaniards; you are more like a monkey, and you have no right to try and separate yourself from the carabaos."

Given, as Rizal said, "that continual alarm of all from the knowledge that they are liable to a secret report, a governmental ukase, and to the accusation of rebel or suspect, an accusation which, to be effective, does not need proof or the production of the accuser," it becomes evident that this opposition could be not merely humiliating, but crippling.[17]

Two issues in particular epitomized the conflict: clerical nationalism and the ownership of landed estates by the friar orders. Both pitted leaders of the new elite against the embodiment and arch defenders of the old order, the friars.

The desire to replace Spanish friars with Filipino secular, or diocesan, priests in the parish ministry reflects both the rise of Filipino aspirations and the centrality of the parish priest's role in Philippine life. A potentially explosive issue even under the best of circumstances, it was supercharged in the nineteenth century because of past experience. In the eighteenth century, royal and diocesan officials attempting to end their reliance upon the friar orders had used inexperienced and ill-trained Filipino priests as their pawns. In the almost total absence of European diocesans, for example, dozens of indios and mestizos had been appointed to parishes formerly held by friars, following the expulsion of the Jesuits in 1767; others were used to replace friars who died. The friars having done nothing in the preceding years to educate native priests for this type of responsibility, the results of these appointments were often disastrous; and Filipino priests became easy targets for friar counterattacks, often broadly couched in racial terms and reflecting scornfully upon the capacities of the Filipino people in general. One witticism had it that the ferries on the Pasig River would have to stop running, the Archbishop having ordained all the boatmen. Spanish conservatives joined the fray, alleging that the loyalty and moral tone of the colony had been compromised. In 1826, by royal decree, most of the parishes in question were returned to friar control and their native priests demoted to curates. With the return of the Jesuits in 1859 the cycle was complete.

But the question was far from settled. The social and economic changes of the nineteenth century enabled members of the new elite to improve upon traditional insular education and broaden their perspective. As a result, there emerged in time a Filipino intelligentsia, the *ilustrados,* or enlightened ones. The failings of individual Filipino priests notwithstanding, the appearance of the ilustrados destroyed the legitimacy of the friars' argument of native incompetence. Indeed, it increased the offensiveness of their aspersions. By the mid-nineteenth century clerical nationalism—the demand that Philippine parishes be manned by Filipino priests—had become an issue of unusual force. Individually, many ilustrados considered the parish priesthood the most prestigious, pivotal, and appropriate employment available; accordingly opposition from incumbent friars and their Spanish supporters led to immediate, personal frustrations for the most articulate members of the new elite. By extension, since the friars and their allies were Spanish, the fight for control of the parishes focused and intensified both the racial and the political content of Filipino discontent and further polarized the two communities. Availing themselves of the insecurity and defensive conservatism of the Spanish community, the friars attacked these disturbers of the status quo as a threat to the very survival of Spanish sovereignty. At times, indeed, that seemed the only identity willingly conceded them in the torrent of abuse and scorn. "The *indio* priest," one conservative publicist wrote, "is a real caricature. . . . He is a caricature of the Spaniard, a caricature of the *mestizo*, a caricature of everybody. He is a patch-work of many things, and is nothing. I put it badly; he is something, after all; more than something . . . he is an enemy of Spain." In 1872, during the conservative reaction that followed de la Torre's removal, the leaders of the movement, the Filipino priests José Burgos, Jacinto Zamora, and Mariano Gómez, were tried by court martial and exe-cuted on the spurious charge of implication in an uprising at the Cavite arsenal. Dozens of prominent ilustrados and native priests were arrested; and many of them, including the young T. H. Pardo de Tavera, were exiled or deported. It proved a pyrrhic victory. To Filipinos, the three priests became martyrs. Even the Spanish arch-bishop, believing them innocent, refused to excommunicate them and ordered the tolling of church bells to mark their death. Forty thousand people gathered to witness the execution.[18]

In some places, moreover, contention between the new elite and the friars was intensified by specifically economic disputes over land policy. It was in the Tagalog regions around Manila that hatred of the friars was most intense and most widely spread. There, in the prov-inces longest exposed to foreign commerce, the landholdings of the friar orders were concentrated. Typically, the lands were leased to *inquilinos,* usually mestizo members of the new elite, who worked them with the labor of *kasama,* or share-crop tenants. By the end of the nineteenth century members of both these groups were alienated from the friars, the inquilinos because they coveted control of the lands which were the economic basis of their prominence and for which already they were charged with much of the responsibility, and the kasama because they had been forced by the inquilinos to absorb the rent increases of the nineteenth century and were reacting to the friars as the source of the problem.[19]

Thus the contention between conservative Spaniards and friars on the one hand and the new Filipinos on the other was grounded both in principle and in self-interest. The continuation of Spanish rule as it had been known up until then, vital for the economic and social interests of the Spaniards as they perceived them, was incompatible with the aspirations of the Filipinos and the resolution of the cultural tension inherent in their growing sophistication. By the end of the century, Filipinos were appraising their lot with a bluntness and candor verging upon open disavowal of the Hispano-Philippine past. Rizal's novels and the assumptions underlying the formation of his *Liga Filipina* in effect admitted the childishness and irresponsibility charged against Filipinos by Spaniards—and laid the blame with the latter: "What we are, you have made us." "In our country where there is no society, since there is no unity between the people and the government, the latter should be indulgent, not only because indulgence is necessary but because the individual, abandoned and uncared for by it has less responsibility, for the reason that he has received less guidance." "The tendency for betterment or progress is a necessity or law found in all creatures, whether individually or collectively," wrote Apolinario Mabini somewhat later. "When a government produces a stagnation of a people in order that it may perpetuate its own interests or that of a definite class . . . a revolution is inevitable." We have seen already, however, that although Spanish theory and policy at Madrid made allowance for the need for change and secularization in the Philippines, Spanish practice in the islands themselves remained more or less rigid. It is true, of course, that administrative reforms were introduced to rationalize the structure of government. But the results were uneven at best and, given the continued dominance of friars and local conservatives, had little or no effect upon attitudes or values.[20]

Inflexible to the end, the government responded to gradualism and reform as to sedition. Under the prodding of friars and frustrated Spanish conservatives, it alienated and suppressed even relatively conservative reformers such as Rizal and the landed and professional members of the new elite. For less patient and cerebral Filipinos, and for men with less to lose, the moral was clear. Following the arrest of Rizal in July 1892, a Manila clerk, Andres Bonifacio, founded a revolutionary secret society, the Katipunan. Rejected by the elite because of its radicalism and latent class orientation, the Katipunan grew rapidly among the lower and middle classes of the Manila region. In August 1896, betrayed to the Spanish authorities, Bonifacio fled to the suburb of Balintawak and proclaimed the revolution. The Spanish struck back not only at the Katipuneros but at the reformist elite, arresting more than five hundred of them and torturing many. John Foreman, standing at quayside in Manila, watched as prominent

Filipinos from a peaceful district, "bound hand and foot, and carried like packages of merchandise," were unloaded from the hold of a steamer "with chains and hooks to haul up and swing out the bodies like bales of hemp." Many of the "brutes laden with gold" who were thus apprehended were shamelessly despoiled through the profiteering of officials, or through outright confiscation or pilferage. The vengeance of the Spanish community upon those who might ideally have presided over a peaceful transition from traditional to somewhat more modern ways epitomizes the bankruptcy of the old order.[21]

The Spanish period in the Philippines defined the problem Americans inherited, by fusing economic growth, socio-cultural change, racial assertion, and political independence into a single complex and emotion-charged issue. This is not to say that all Filipinos saw it as such, or that the component parts were equally important to the people as a whole or to any individual among them. It is to say that these were widely desired goals, logically symbiotic, not identical; and that each of the components was charged with both tangible implications and emotional overtones concerning one or more of the others. Economic penetration of the islands had led to increased production and trade; with these had come foreign merchants and more intimate ties to peninsular Spain. Ideas tinged with secularism and even a little Enlightenment political thought became known here and there. A new elite composed primarily of mestizos appeared, challenging both clerical dominance and the empty forms by which traditional leaders had been drawn into an impotent collaboration. Urbanization began, a tiny middle class appeared, professional men increased in number and status; European furniture and manners penetrated parts of the countryside; Filipinos and their sons began to travel and even to study abroad. The provincialism of Hispano-Philippine culture became evident to the wealthy, and they attempted in faltering ways to acquire the cultural repertoire of worldly nineteenth century men. Rizal—scientist, physician, linguist, historian, poet, and novelist—was their pre-eminent exemplar. In the Spanish empire in the Philippines, however, acculturation had always been in disfavor; and the developments that had produced the new elite—indeed the very existence of such a group—intensified opposition. The Spanish community of the nineteenth century, watching in helpless outrage as its economic status declined and the colonial government began first to experiment with liberalism and then to totter toward its fall, fell back on racial and cultural pride and froze the mestizos and their allies out of the limited social goal they most sought, the dignity of being a Spaniard. An assertation of their pretensions to worldliness, culture, and economic power became, therefore, an assertion of race. Proud and sensitive themselves, most of them sought to maintain a distinction variously depicted as one of class, culture, learning, experience, and sometimes race, toward the bulk of the Filipino people. Yet as their pretensions and frustrations grew apace, both they and their Spanish "betters" saw what was happening as a struggle to define the dignity and worth of Filipinos. Wherefore, in the end, there was a revolution against Spain, in which ilustrados nervously collaborated with and attempted to dominate men of the working class, peasants, and a few ideological radicals.

It is tempting to think of revolutions as if they were great chasms, dividing two pieces of land and breaking the continuity of terrain. There is no need to enumerate the ways in which the Philippine Revolution has proven a dividing point in the islands' history. It is important to remember, however, that the revolution did not succeed in any but a very restricted sense. Something of the explosive configuration of the late Spanish period survived the revolution and the transfer from Spanish to American sovereignty. In 1901, after five years of intermittent but savage fighting, and a great deal of social turmoil and economic dislocation, Filipinos found themselves possessed not of independence, but of a new and apparently inextinguishable foreign sovereignty. Further economic growth was all but inevitable; and social and cultural change would now proceed as corollaries to economic development and as the natural result of the removal of a longstanding and partly discredited network of social, political, and religious institutions and practices. Since the revolution had in a political sense failed, these changes in the life of the people, so intimately a part of their hopes for nationality and self-respect, would occur in a setting dominated by a professedly superior, alien people of a different race. As they did so, the course of their evolution would both reflect and shape the tone of racial and political relations between American and Filipino. The future course of Philippine life turned upon the success Filipino and American leaders had in isolating, defining, and balancing the component parts of the complex issue before them.

TWO

The Philippines and
the United States, 1899–1912

3

Conciliation

The Philippine Revolution against Spain went forward in two stages, the first of which ended in a stalemate formalized in the Truce of Biyák-na-Bató in 1897, and the second of which, coinciding with the Spanish-American War in 1898, ended in victory. By August of 1898, Filipinos were in possession of most of their country except for Manila and its environs. There Spaniards gave way directly to Americans, who prevented Filipino forces from entering the city. The revolutionary government established itself in Malolos, Bulacan, 45 kilometers to the northwest, and a standoff ensued, with Filipino and American forces facing each other around the perimeter of Manila. During this uneasy but peaceful period decisions were made in Washington and at the peace negotiations in Paris between the United States and Spain, which committed the United States to acquiring Spanish sovereignty in the islands and remaining to govern them. This, of course, was not what Filipinos had fought for. Predictably, as the American purpose became clear, tensions and hostility rose between the two camps in the islands. In February 1899 a minor incident led to general war between American and Filipino forces, which dragged on through successive stages, punctuated by almost countless atrocities on both sides, until 1902.

There was never any doubt that the American army could prevail by force. But given the rugged geography, crude transportation and communications systems, and decentralized population of the Philippines, it was less clear that a peaceful government could be established successfully after Filipino armies and the principal guerilla units had been defeated. The highest officials in the United States

51

government shrank from both the moral and political implications of maintaining a protracted military government, however; and some method had to be found of creating a government that could win the support of the Filipino people. As it happened, a key group in Filipino society had been alienated from the revolutionary leadership by the end of 1898. This group, potentially of as great political significance as the revolutionists themselves, needed a means of coming to power and was willing to combine its own ends with those of the United States. From these circumstances there arose what William Howard Taft was to call "the policy of attraction."

The most unstable element in the Filipinos' revolutionary front against Spain during the years 1896 and 1898 was the ilustrados, the class of educated and generally affluent men whose frustration and resulting alienation from the government had contributed greatly to undermining Spanish authority. Their attitude toward the revolution was ambivalent; and their politics, as a result, were often erratic or opportunistic. Their prominence and attainments naturally predisposed such men against radical social or economic changes, and their exposed position in society made them especially vulnerable to Spanish vengeance. For these reasons they tended to be wary of becoming involved, and few took an active role in the events of 1896. Nevertheless, they emphatically desired reform, particularly guaranteed civil liberties, decentralization of government, separation of church and state, and recognition of their position as leaders in Filipino life. A combination of military successes by the revolutionaries and vindictive repression of their class by the Spaniards led some of them in time, therefore, to side openly with the revolution. Those who did so were welcomed as the natural leaders of society. Between 1897 and 1898, however, when General Emilio Aguinaldo and his lieutenants were in voluntary exile in Hong Kong, prominent ilustrados gravitated back into cooperation with Spanish authorities. Certain of them—including Pedro A. Paterno, Cayetano S. Arellano, Trinidad H. Pardo de Tavera, Gregorio Araneta, and Benito Legarda—were appointed by Governor General Augustin to the Consultative Assembly formed in May 1898 to promote Filipino cooperation in repelling the United States. In spite of this, Aguinaldo, who by that time had returned to the Philippines with American encouragement and resumed the revolution, pointedly sought out supporters among the ilustrados both for their acknowledged talents and also for the prestige his leadership would

derive from their adherence. At one or another time Arellano, Pardo de Tavera, Paterno, Araneta, and Legarda all were named to cabinet posts.

There were, of course, differences within the ranks of the ilustrados. Most of them, however, brought to their offices a proud determination to assert and legitimize through the new government the role of leadership that Spain had denied them. In this, their interests opposed those of Aguinaldo and his principal adviser, Apolinario Mabini. Mabini was himself an ilustrado; his prominence in the new revolutionary government epitomized Aguinaldo's efforts to broaden its base. But he was different from the others. His background was lower class, and his social goals were at least relatively radical. Convinced that discipline and unity were essential, and wanting from the ilustrados as a whole no more than sanction and advice, he and Aguinaldo designed a government with a strong executive and a merely consultative congress. They were overruled, however, by the congress itself, which, after electing Paterno, Legarda, Araneta, and Pablo Ocampo its principal officers, appropriated the power to draft a constitution for the new government, and in so doing aggrandized its own powers and restrained those of the executive. The principal architect of the constitution, Felipe G. Calderón, explaining the significance and motivation of the action, later wrote: "Being fully convinced . . . that in case of obtaining our independence, we were for a long time to have a really oligarchic republic in which the military element, which was ignorant in almost its entirety, would predominate, I preferred to see that oligarchy neutralized by the oligarchy of intelligence, seeing that the Congress would be composed of the most intelligent elements of the nation."[1]

To this concern with the balance of power within the new government, some added a fear that the Philippines could not succeed as an independent nation. Belief in the desirability of an American protectorate was strong in the cabinet in September and October 1898; and Pardo de Tavera, then Director of Diplomacy, told Aguinaldo that he should write to President McKinley "asking him under no circumstances to abandon the Philippines." Florentino Torres, another prominent ilustrado, later wrote that the educated and propertied men of Central Luzon had been "convinced that . . . the only possible way of saving these islands from anarchy in the interior, from the ambitions of certain powers, or from some other colonial system similiar to that of Spain . . . was the frank and loyal acceptance of the sovereignty of

America." There was, however, no consensus on this point. Pardo's recommendation, for example, was opposed within the cabinet by Felipe Buencamino and Pedro Paterno and probably never had the support of a majority of the congress. In fact, during the weeks after adoption of the Malolos Constitution Aguinaldo and Mabini were able to rebound from their defeat precisely by playing upon the threat of continued American presence in the islands. By December their position was strong enough for Aguinaldo to propose a constitutional amendment giving him power to govern by decree "during the time the country may have to struggle for its independence." The issue of future relations with the United States had become fused with that of control within the revolutionary government.[2]

Recognizing its defeat on both counts, the group around Pardo and Legarda began in November to separate itself from Aguinaldo. In the meantime, American policy was evolving in a way that must have confirmed their feeling that the interests of the Philippines and their own group would be safe in American hands. Almost simultaneously with Aguinaldo's proposal of the amendment authorizing dictatorial powers for himself, McKinley instructed his commander in the Philippines, General Elwell S. Otis: "The earnest and paramount aim of the military administration [should be] to win the confidence, respect, and affection of the inhabitants of the Philippines by assuring them in every possible way that full measure of individual rights and liberties which is the heritage of free peoples, and by proving to them that the mission of the United States is one of benevolent assimilation." By the end of the year, Filipinos who had withdrawn from the Malolos government, joined by others who, living in Manila, had never adhered to the revolutionary cause, were in frank communication with American authorities. Embittered by their inability to dominate compatriots whom they considered ignorant and socially inferior, they confirmed Americans in the opinion that the revolutionary leaders were dangerous, self-serving men, incompetent to guide their country through a difficult period. Some transfered their allegiance totally, maintaining contact with the Malolos government at Otis' request, to assist him as intermediaries or informants.[3]

Grounded as it was in the conservative ilustrados' resentment of the leaders of the Malolos government and desire for American guidance and protection, this association with American authorities survived the outbreak of the so-called Philippine Insurrection on February 4, 1899. A month to the day after the beginning of hostilities, moreover, there arrived in Manila the First (or Schurman) Philippine Commission, which institutionalized and amplified consultations between Filipinos and Americans. The Commission—which consisted of Jacob Gould Schurman, president of Cornell University; Dean C. Worcester, a zoologist from the University of Michigan, who had twice previously visited the islands and had written a book about them; Charles Denby, formerly United States minister to China; and the ranking naval and military authorities in the islands, Admiral George Dewey and General Otis—was investigatory in character and had power only to report to the President and make recommendations. The decision to send it had been made prior to the outbreak of war; and its original mission—to adjust amicably the growing differences between Americans and Filipinos and to gather and collate information on the islands and their peoples, so as to give officials in Washington reliable materials on which to base future policy and legislation—had been complicated in the interval. Finding in Manila "a reign of terror," in which "Filipinos who had favored Americans feared assassination, and few had the courage to come out openly for us," the Commission naturally drew heavily for its information and guidance upon the educated and propertied men who had separated themselves from Malolos and joined their interests to those of the United States. In doing so, it implicitly recognized the ilustrados with whom it dealt as legitimate leaders and spokesmen for the Filipino people and granted them, at least indirectly, participation in shaping the islands' future.[4]

Out of their testimony before the Commission there emerged an analysis which was to be of great influence in the early years of the American government. Felipe G. Calderón, principal author of the Malolos Constitution, who was a lawyer in Manila and a property owner in Batangas and Cavite provinces, put it in this form:

> The archipelago as a whole is composed of three classes of individuals: The rich and intelligent element; the poorer element of the country—the element that is willing to devote itself to work—and an element that may be called intermediate, made up of clerks and writers, who have a habit of stirring up the town. The first of these elements, the wealthier class, and the diligent class, that by its work produces sugar, tobacco, etc., [wish] by whatever means, peace and quiet. They have certain wrong ideas which result from their complete ignorance of the character of the Americans . . . . The third, or intermediate class, do not wish for peace under any circumstances, because it goes against their individual interests . . . .

The first and second classes wish peace by any means whatever, because they are weary of the state of anarchy which exists, but they are disturbed as to the conduct of America in the future. The most important thing is to show them actual deeds. The common people now lack confidence in the Americans because there [have] in the past been enacted laws which have never been carried out. The Spaniards made them promises which have never been fulfilled.

Calderón's view that the insurrection was the work of a class of discontented men on the make, whose interests differed from those of both the established leaders of the people and the mass of common men, perpetuated into the American period the ilustrado response to Bonifacio and the Katipunan. His testimony was supported not only by other ilustrados but also by Americans and Europeans who appeared before the commission. Frank S. Bourns, Commissioner Worcester's colleague on his two zoological expeditions to the islands, confirmed and amplified it:

The great mass of the people here are ignorant. They have a very vague idea either of independence or liberty as such. I think it is more or less a matter of indifference to them what their government is so long as it is not oppressive . . . .

The second class, the highly educated class, the wealthy class, I think are clearly desirous of peace here—that is, those who have money—because they wish to continue in their business and make more money; also those of education . . . because they appreciate the fact that an American government here would be greatly to the benefit of the country, and they know that they themselves are not as yet fitted for self-government. The middle class is the class that is opposed to us . . . . This class is made up at the present time of the military leaders, and, to a considerable extent, of the class known under the Spanish rule as the empleados del gobierno . . . . In this middle class, I think, are found to-day . . . those who declare that the Filipinos are to-day fitted for self-government.[5]

No doubt this view sprang in part from wishful thinking: faced with an ugly war against Filipino armies and guerillas in the countryside and a "reign of terror" even behind American lines in the capital, Americans and Filipino ilustrados must have found it comforting to postulate a potential majority in favor of peace and stability. One suspects, however, that certain of their premises were sound. Modern sociological studies of the Philippines suggest that in rural regions notions of class identity and class interest have developed only slightly. Local magnates and the little people around them typically encounter each other not in conflicts of interest, but in reciprocal dyadic relationships such as *compadrazgo*, a form of ritual co-parenthood derived from the Catholic institution of god-parenthood. This enables them to articulate their demands upon each other through a network of usages informed by sensitivity to honor or "face" on both sides and to the reciprocity of obligations. Sensitively adhered to, these usages tend to align society in vertical rather than horizontal patterns, in roughly parallel and often competing alliances of richer and poorer, stronger and weaker parties, based upon family, extended or ritual kinship, and mutual obligation. Under such conditions, it is easy to imagine a shared response to war incorporating the dependence of elites upon law and order and the typical yearning of peasants for peace and personal security.[6]

However, these patterns may be broken or compromised in a move from the land to a major city, and they may be challenged if one of the parties acquires new obligations or gains new knowledge or experience of other forms of social organization. It is plausible that in the social and cultural disruptions of the 1890's the sudden prominence of issues of racial dignity and economic status loosened up the customary relationship of leaders and the led so as to allow the spread of a revolutionary fervor which many among the leaders considered dangerous. James A. LeRoy, who was for several years secretary to Worcester and later became the foremost American student in his day of the history of the insurrection and the American military government of the islands, considered that at the outbreak of hostilities with the Americans in Central Luzon "the great mass of the people . . . their natural racial sympathies stirred by the events of three years past and aroused more than ever by the terrible colors in which the Americans had been painted to them by their radical . . . leaders," had passed temporarily out from under the sway of propertied and established leaders. This he traced partly to the vacillations of the latter. In the long run, the Malolos government could not maintain its hold upon the people without them; and conversely were they to be rallied to the side of the Americans and their allies among the conservative ilustrados a dynamic would have been found for reaching the common people and depriving the insurrection of at least some of its popular support.[7]

There followed from this analysis four conclusions: that the mass of Filipinos were near-ciphers, or perhaps children, whose interests were minimal and who could be led or manipulated; that ordinary patterns of leadership and social organization had been weakened, even broken, but not permanently destroyed by a confluence of dramatic events, emotional and relevant issues, and vacillation among established and therefore exposed and vulnerable leaders; that an insurrection grounded in so anomalous and presumably tenuous a social organization, and deriving its appeal partly from the exhilaration of having overthrown a third party, Spain, and partly from simple ignorance and misconceptions of America was not legitimate or representative of a national will or interest; and that the United States, in order to act upon these presumed conditions—to attract the wavering leaders, detach from the insurrection the simple masses, and thereby tumble the unsteady revolutionary polity and obtain a more conservative alignment of society, responsive to an American program of "benevolent assimilation"—had to offer tangible evidence of good faith, not merely promises.

Under its instructions, the Schurman Commission was incapable of providing tangible evidence—of showing the people "actual deeds," as Calderón had put it. On April 4 it issued a proclamation, drafted by Schurman himself, which warned of stern suppression of rebellion against American sovereignty but promised to govern in the interests of the Filipino people. Specifically, the proclamation pledged a discreet amount of home rule, economic development without exploitation, the protection of civil liberties, the creation of an honest civil service, the construction of public works, and the spread of education and an effective system of justice. The proclamation, however, had no force in law. On April 21, Pardo de Tavera, by then already a trusted associate of the commissioners, brought before them a delegation of Manila business and professional men, who asked for something concrete to communicate to Aguinaldo's government in order to promote peace. Later that month a representative of that government, Colonel Manuel Arguelles, hinted to the commissioners that the proclamation might be an acceptable basis for ending hostilities, if only its provisions could be guaranteed and the form of government to be established in the Philippines made clear. Neither Pardo nor Arguelles got what he was looking for, and the war continued.[8]

The proclamation is important, however, as an early and tentative definition of "benevolent assimilation," an attempt to bring together McKinley's vague abstraction and the realities of Philippine conditions. In its subsequent report to the President, the Commission went further. Filipinos, it argued, had launched a rebellion for limited

58

ends within the structure of Spanish sovereignty. The United States had fallen heir to an existing struggle, the terms of which had become blurred partly by the rhetoric of independence (put out, it insisted, for foreign consumption, to justify rebellion but never a popular rallying point among Filipinos), partly by the ambitions of insurgent leaders, partly by the confusion attendant upon the destruction of Spanish power and the transfer of sovereignty. Abstracting from a Tagalog manifesto circulated in July 1897, the Commission listed the aims of the revolution of 1896–97:

(1) The expulsion of the friars and the restitution of the lands held by them to the townships or to the original owners; (2) the recognition of Filipino priests in filling the incumbencies vacated by the friars; (3) absolute religious toleration; (4) the equality of all persons—Filipinos as well as Spaniards—before the law; the assimilation of the laws of the archipelago to those of Spain, and the equality of Filipinos with Spaniards in the civil service; (5) the freedom of the press; (6) the establishment of representative institutions; (7) home rule; (8) abolition of deportation and other unjust measures against Filipinos; and (9) the continuance of the war as a means to coerce Spain into granting these rights.

Here was a platform upon which American and Filipino could agree: "The very thing they yearn for is what of all others our Government will naturally desire to give them—religious liberty, fundamental personal rights, and the largest practicable measure of home rule." Events since 1897 had not basically altered this happy circumstance. It was true that Filipinos now desired ultimately to become "self-governing and independent"; but witnesses before the Commission had been "uniform in their testimony that in view of the ignorance and political inexperience of the masses of the people, the multiplicity of languages, the divergencies of culture and mode of life, and the obstacles to intercommunication, an independent sovereign Philippine state was at the present time neither possible nor desirable." Having in mind not only this testimony, but also the Malolos Constitution, the report concluded: "The political ideal of the Filipinos coincides with the political practice and traditions of the Americans . . . . As in their bill of rights, so again in their demands for provincial and municipal autonomy, there is a complete harmony between the aspirations and needs of the Filipinos and the desire and capacity of the Americans to satisfy them." The Commission recommended establishment of a civil government under American control, with a legislature in which "at least" the lower house would be elective, and, at the provincial and local levels, self-government through elected Filipino officials who would be advised by American resident commissioners.[9]

At this point, initiative in defining America's Philippine policy shifted to a new group of men. The Schurman Commission, whose usefulness had been compromised by internal dissension and by the resentment felt toward its civilian members by the military, was disbanded after it had submitted its report. In the meantime, on account of the outbreak of hostilities, responsbility for the Philippines had been transfered from the State Department, where McKinley had originally wished it to reside, to the War Department. In the summer of 1899, Elihu Root, a brilliant New York attorney, with a rigorous mind, elegant manners, and a puckish sense of humor, was appointed Secretary of War to preside over the establishment of the new governments in the Philippines, Cuba, and Puerto Rico.

The appointment took Root by surprise. Hoping to define his responsibilities, he accumulated a library of books about the English colonial system. He read until their cumulative weight and detail threatened to overwhelm him. Then, standing back, he decided that the precedents of other countries were less important than the legal rights and moral traditions of his own. He concluded that although the Philippines were "subject to the complete sovereignty" of the United States, "controlled by no legal limitations except those which may be found in the treaty of cession," and had therefore no claims upon the United States, there were moral restraints inherent in the nature of American government which must necessarily apply to the government's dealing with any people, regardless of their legal status. Reminiscing to his biographer thirty years later, he said: "I came to the conclusion that there are certain things the United States Government couldn't do because the people of the United States had declared that no government could do them—the Bill of Rights." This did not mean, as Root conceived the relationship of the two peoples, that Filipinos had a right to self-determination. "Government does not depend upon consent," he argued in a campaign speech the next year. "The immutable laws of justice and humanity require that people shall have government, that the weak shall be protected, that cruelty and lust shall be restrained, whether there be consent or not." Drawing his information from civilian and military subordinates on the spot, he was convinced that "the great mass of the people" were "but little advanced from pure savagery," childlike in their "lack of reflection, disregard of consequences, fearlessness of death, thoughtless cruelty, and unquestioning dependence upon a superior." It would be ludicrous to apply the doctrine of the consent of the governed to such as these.[10]

Out of these premises there came a policy of tutelary retention that was firm, even unbending, in its central conception of the Philippine problem, but fluid and on occasion solicitous in its particulars. Having mapped out this policy in broad strokes, Root was content to give responsible authorities on the spot free rein to work out its precise meaning and application. This willingness proceeded not only from pressures of time, difficulties of communication, the detailed and intimate knowledge possessed by men on the spot, and Root's high opinion of them, but also from a desire to adapt what America created in the islands to the character, capabilities, and expectations of the Filipinos. McKinley's instructions to the Second Philippine Commission, which were written by Root, are an eloquent statement of both aspects of Root's attitude:

> In all the forms of government and administrative provisions which they are authorized to prescribe, the Commission should bear in mind that the government which they are establishing is designed not for our satisfaction or for the expression of our theoretical views, but for the happiness, peace, and prosperity of the people of the Philippine Islands, and the measures adopted should be made to conform to their customs, their habits, and even their prejudices, to the fullest extent consistent with the accomplishment of the indispensable requisites of just and effective government. At the same time the Commission should bear in mind, and the people of the islands should be made plainly to understand, that there are certain great principles of government which have been made the basis of our governmental system, which we deem essential to the rule of law and the maintenance of individual freedom . . . ; that there are also certain practical rules of government which we have found to be essential to the preservation of these great principles of liberty and law, and that these principles and these rules of government must be established and maintained in their islands for the sake of their liberty and happiness, however much they may conflict with the customs or laws of procedure with which they are familiar.[11]

The dominant figure of this commission, as indeed of the first half decade or more of Philippine history under the American civil government, was William Howard Taft. Son of a prosperous, self-made Cincinnati lawyer, Taft had been raised in a home where earnestness, sobriety, and moral rectitude set the tone of life. He was no carbon copy of his parents, for from the beginning he seems to have had an infectious, almost boisterous sense of humor and limited ambition. As a youth in Cincinnati and later at Yale, he struck people as obviously intelligent and sensible, but placid and plodding rather than creative. He wanted to be a judge; and in that desire one sees not only a natural extension of his father's legal career, but also something consistent with the puritanical tradition of moralism personified by his New England-born parents. His biographer, describing him in his youth, calls him "almost too perfect" and suggests that he would have been "obnoxious" had it not been for his good nature; a college contemporary remembered that "he towered above us all as a moral force." This powerful streak of moralism, combined with a temperamental affinity for the judgmental and an emotional set which made him on occasion both erratic and stubborn, could when engaged render him opinionated and combative. "Mr. Roosevelt," Archie Butt observed, "once said that Mr. Taft was one of the best haters he had ever known, and I have found this to be true." Notwithstanding his courage, warmth, and obvious mental capacity, Taft lacked perspective and self-knowledge. He was not precisely self-righteous, but he had an unblinking certainty of the location of orthodoxy. It is from him, and the colleagues whom he dominated on the Second Philippine Commission, that there came into the language of official Philippine correspondence and reports those confident phrases that echo through the first thirteen years of civil government: "the best students of the question are agreed"; "no one who has studied the question carefully doubts"; "intelligent observers"; "the best opinion."[12]

Taft had not sought a post in the Philippines. He, like Schurman before him, had opposed acquiring the islands. What he wanted from the McKinley administration was a place on the United States Supreme Court. When the President summoned him to Washington in January 1900 and asked him to be a member of the new Philippine Commission, Taft had explained his feelings about acquisition and candidly told the President that he was reluctant to interrupt his judicial career. In response to this, Root, who was also in the room, had told him bluntly: "You have had an easy time of it . . . . This is the parting of the ways. You may go on holding the job you have in a humdrum, mediocre way. But here is something that will test you; something in the way of effort and struggle, and the question is, will you take the harder or the easier task?" McKinley then assured him that his judicial career would not suffer because of his having taken the appointment. Taft went home to Cincinnati and pondered the question. Although opposed to acquiring the islands, he did not believe the Filipinos could govern themselves; and he did not think that the United States would debauch its own principles by administering the islands. His wife and his brother Horace urged him to accept. On February 2 he wrote to Root saying he would accept if he was to be president of the Commission, a possibility at which the President had hinted. The job would be that of creating a new government, a lawyer's job as Taft conceived it; if he went, he wanted real responsibility.[13]

The Taft Commission arrived in the Philippines in June 1900 and assumed legislative power over the islands on September 1. During the interval, the members familiarized themselves with conditions, dividing the subjects of inquiry according to personal talents and interests. Taft, the president, reserved for himself potentially the most explosive subjects: friars, the civil service, and the public lands. Dean C. Worcester, the only holdover from the Schurman Commission, had no legal training but was a scientist and had traveled widely in the archipelago; he took forestry, agriculture, mining, public health, and municipal corporations. Luke E. Wright, a gold Democrat from Tennessee, a former military officer and state attorney general, and a prominent corporation lawyer, studied internal improvements, franchises, militia, police, and the criminal code. Henry C. Ide, Vermont attorney and former judge of the United States Court in Samoa, examined the code of civil procedure, the courts, banks and currency, and the registration of laws; Bernard Moses, a professor at the University of California and a historian of Spanish America, studied schools and taxation. In addition, the three lawyers, Taft, Wright, and Ide, jointly studied the civil code; and the whole Commission studied the form of central and provincial governments. On August 21 they cabled Root, their immediate superior, their preliminary findings and recommendations: The Filipino people—"ignorant, superstitious, and credulous in remarkable degree"—had been misled into hostility toward the United States by "absurd falsehoods of unscrupulous leaders," most of them Tagalogs from Central Luzon. Now, however, the insurrection had been broken by military action and reduced to sporadic guerilla operations; peace was widely and intensely desired, and the majority was willing to accept American sovereignty. Should McKinley be re-elected and American policy confirmed, the "remnant of insurrection will disappear within sixty days by surrender of leaders and fading out of rank and file." Turning the government of the islands over to a "coterie of Tagalog politicians"—Aguinaldo and the leaders of the insurrection—would ruin the chance of developing the Philippines economically by rendering "life and property, secular and religious most insecure," and thereby driving out both capital and conservative Filipinos. The United States, therefore, should proceed to organize a civil government—should create a Filipino constabulary, establish an efficient civil service open on an equal basis to Filipinos and Americans, reform the judicial system and codes, establish a sound currency on the gold standard, reform the tax system so as to end discrimination against the poor, spend the islands' surplus customs revenues on public works, promote investment of capital, grant railroad franchises, and promote education and the use of English as a *lingua franca*.[14]

Important parts of the analysis found in the Taft Commission's cable of August 21, were present in the mind of its president even before he left the United States. In a letter to a friend, which suggests familiarity with the Schurman Commission's report and the thinking of Filipino conservative ilustrados, Taft had written:

> The situation as I view it, is that until the Presidential election, and it is settled that McKinley is to be re-elected, the radical insurgent leaders, who are unscrupulous plotters and desperate men, will resort to every expedient to give the American voter the impression that the task of settling that country is hopeless. They have no doubt that if Bryan is elected he will let the Islands go at once, and that they will then be able to overawe the more peaceably inclined inhabitants and the better educated class, and make themselves the head of an oligarchy. The mass of people themselves, generally are in a sullen condition, and until we are able to do something the value of which they can estimate by the fruits, they are not inclined to welcome us.

His ideas about the insurrection were largely confirmed and his views of the incapacity of the people amplified after his arrival in Manila by repeated contact with conservative ilustrados, particularly Arellano and Legarda. "The great mass of them are superstitious and ignorant," he wrote only a month after reaching the islands, "and their leaders do not recommend universal suffrage, but quite a high qualification for it . . . . The idea that these people can govern themselves is as illfounded as any proposition that Bryan advances. They are cruel to animals and cruel to their fellows when occasion arises.

They need the training of fifty or a hundred years before they shall even realize what Anglo-Saxon liberty is."[15]

It followed from this attribution of a pivotal role to the American election that little could be hoped for other than simple military successes until McKinley had been safely re-elected. Benevolent assimilation would have to wait. Repeatedly during the months up to November, Taft insisted that the insurrection, while militarily all but defunct, was holding on as a guerilla and terrorist movement in the hope of winning from Bryan what it had no right to either by force of arms or of law. This in turn, he held, intimidated Filipinos who might otherwise have cooperated with the Americans. For one thing, they stood the risk of being assassinated by guerillas, and for another, they too wondered what would happen if Bryan should win. "Fear of being too sympathetic with the American cause when there is a reported danger that the Americans are going to withdraw immediately after the election has kept some people who would ordinarily come into our public meetings away . . ." Taft wrote to Root. Their conduct seemed to him understandable, and for the time being forebearance on the part of the Americans was justified.[16]

On the other hand, once the election was past and the insurrection had been left exposed in its futility and alleged viciousness, decisive steps would be warranted to consolidate American authority. To this end, Taft conceived and subsequently effected a carrot and stick policy. Convinced that the leaders of the insurrection were unscrupulous and their followers terrorists and assassins, he was determined to stamp out the movement by a rigorous policy of suppression. "It is necessary after the election," he wrote, "and after the people shall have spoken in favor of retaining these Islands . . . to depart from the policy of leniency which up to this has been pursued by the American forces and authorities, and give the men in arms an opportunity to come in, and if they do not accept it, declare them outlaws and either hang or transport them as they are captured. This is entirely justified . . . . The resistance to American authority is nothing but a conspiracy of murder and assassination." Taft's fame as the benevolent patron of his "little brown brothers"—the man who replaced oppressive military rule with participatory civil government—notwithstanding, this prescription for suppression was too iron-fisted for the Military Governor, General Arthur MacArthur. For almost two months after the election he continued his practice of pardoning both leaders and followers whenever possible, and refused the Commission's requests that he confiscate the property of *insurrectos* and speedily execute or deport those captured. Finally, in January, 1901, he succumbed to the extent of ordering several deportations. Taft was exultant: "Everything is looking better here," he wrote to Root on January 13; and again, five days later: "The situation is becoming more and more favorable every day . . . . The deportations have had a wonderful effect."[17]

The principal aspect of Taft's strategy, however, was not the heroic cure applied to the insurrection itself, but a policy of attracting those Filipinos who were willing to separate themselves from it. In this respect, of course, he and his colleagues drew upon the ideas of the Schurman Commission and its ilustrado advisers. But they brought to these ideas a quite different attitude from that which had originally informed them. The ilustrados who had argued for a policy of attraction before the Schurman Commission had desired to bring about not only an end to warfare and violence, but also a restoration and recognition of the social and political organization of the countryside which had grown up de facto in the last century of Spanish rule. It was an essential part of their argument that the natural leaders of the people, taken together, possessed a reasonable amount of intelligence and responsibility and enough self-knowledge to realize that their interests were in the final analysis conservative. Taft, who shared their low opinion of the capacities of ordinary Filipinos and proposed to follow their recommendation to attract the leaders of the countryside, did not accept the premise that the leaders whom the policy of attraction would benefit were, on balance, intelligent and responsible. Wherefore there came into the policy over whose symbiotic and even altruistic qualities Schurman had effused, a kind of opportunism that was in later years to cause disillusionment on both sides.

Charged with opportunism, Taft should be allowed to speak for himself. The people, he wrote to Root,

> are easily influenced by speeches from a small class of educated mestizos, who have acquired a good deal of superficial knowledge of the general principles of free government, who are able to mouth sentences supposed to embody constitutional law, and who like to give the appearance of profound analytical knowledge of the science of government. They are generally lacking in moral character; are with some notable exceptions prone to yield to any pecuniary consideration, and are difficult persons out of whom to

66

make an honest government. We shall have to do the best we can with them. They are born politicians; are as ambitious as Satan, and as jealous as possible of each other's prefern nt..

Again, amplifying the theme in a letter to a close friend: "Of the educated ones among them, most . . . have not the slightest conceptions of the practical questions . . . . Their liberty is a kind of liberty that entitles the speaker to complete license and the person who differs with him to imprisonment or the loss of limb or head. The possibility of a majority rule in which the minority has indefeasible rights is something that is hard to bring to their minds." The social authority of such leaders seemed to Taft nothing more than "a kind of quasi slavery called caciquism." Daniel Williams, the Commission's secretary, complained that for this reason the people lacked the stuff of free government: "The average Filipino accepts as gospel any doctrine laid down to him by the select few . . . . and [is] easily influenced by these so-called leaders to take up any scheme, however absurd or chimerical."[18]

Yet these were precisely the men and the channels of social organization Taft proposed to use, first to end the warfare, and later to form a new government in the Philippines. It is true that he felt respect and even affection for a few prominent Filipinos, such as Arellano, Pardo, and Legarda, and true also that one can find more discriminating comments than those quoted above, in which he attempts to distinguish between types of ilustrados. But his recognition that some Filipinos stood out from what he considered the general run of corrupt, ignorant, and pretentious leaders does not alter the fact that he intended to use the latter. Pedro Paterno, a prestigious ilustrado, formerly president of Aguinaldo's cabinet, he branded "a great deal of an ass"—"but," he added, typically, "he seems to have a good deal of influence in certain circles among the Filipinos. . . . If he is not trusted in any way he may be useful hereafter." The letter describing "educated mestizos" as "difficult persons out of whom to make an honest government," goes on to propose that after two years, during which time the Commission could pass fundamental legislation unimpeded, a lower house composed of just such persons be added to the legislature. The policy of attraction, as it had evolved by late 1900, then, transcended the interests of any particular group of ilustrados or established caciques: it was a pursuit of the loyalty of the Filipino people by the only means available.[19]

For a while, attraction proceeded haltingly. It was necessary to wait out the American election before expecting real results, and in any case no vehicle had been developed by which leaders could be involved and the masses reached. These obstacles were removed almost simultaneously by the re-election of McKinley and the formation in the Philippines of a political party dedicated to promoting pacification and the annexation of the Philippines to the United States. This party, the Partido Federal, arose because a considerable number of prominent Filipinos had become convinced by the last months of 1900 that the insurrection had been defeated and could survive only through a kind of guerilla warfare and sporadic violence which they, as men of property and standing, found abhorrent. The time was ripe, therefore, for risking an attempt to organize the countryside. Doubtless they were also impelled by recognition that the United States would shortly elaborate its government in the islands and fill at least some posts with Filipinos. Members of an established party that had demonstrated its ability to mobilize and lead Filipinos would stand a better chance of garnering these places than would isolated individuals.

In October 1900 a brother of Felipe Buencamino, Aguinaldo's one-time Secretary of Foreign Affairs, had been captured on a public highway by insurgents. Buencamino was not part of the circle around Pardo de Tavera and Arellano; he had opposed Pardo's recommendation that Aguinaldo ask McKinley not to abandon the islands. He had never been a warhawk, however: in 1899 he had served in the cabinet formed by Paterno, which had displaced Mabini from power and attempted to make peace with the Americans on terms giving the Philippines autonomy, but not independence. For his efforts, he had been slapped in the face by a volatile Filipino general. He had come to Manila when the advance of American armies caused the collapse of the Malolos government. Now, with the capture of his brother, he had had enough. Surrounding himself with a group of former civilian and military supporters of Aguinaldo, he went to Taft and asked permission to launch a counter-revolution. The counter-revolution they proposed was eminently nonviolent and bore all the marks of a bid to establish a political party. There would be a central headquarters in Manila, provincial committees, a press, and a policy on the part of the Americans of favoring adherents of the counter-revolution in appointments to offices. On November 4 Taft cabled to Washington a petition from the group urging that the war be brought to a speedy conclusion and American sovereignty be definitively established. To fail to do this, they affirmed, would be "to hand over the government to the robbers, assassins and abductors of the honest and peaceable people."[20]

The only Filipinos whom Taft actually respected were Pardo, Arellano, Legarda, and certain of their associates. Buencamino's movement had to be shaped around this reality, and in the end it cost him control. His party platform, drafted with the assistance not only of his original colleagues, but also of Ambrosio Flores and Tomás G. del Rosario, who had good relations with Pardo's circle, was submitted to Arellano, Pardo, Florentino Torres, and Frank Bourns for approval. They, in turn, passed it on to the Commission, which discussed it at meetings on December 12 and 16. Somewhere in this process both the concept of a counter-revolution and the primacy of Buencamino's circle were irrevocably lost. On December 23, 1900, the party was promulgated by a meeting of 125 prominent ilustrados, gathered under the presidency of Torres. Pardo de Tavera was elected president of the party, to serve with a directorate consisting of Arellano, Torres, Bourns, Flores, del Rosario, and José Ner, only the last a member of the original Buencamino group. Buencamino himself was named to a 25-member Council of Government of the party. The platform, adopted at the same meeting, envisioned a two-stage progress for the Philippines: in the first stage, American sovereignty would be accepted, disorders put down, personal liberties guaranteed, education encouraged; representative, autonomous local governments, and provincial governments subject only to loose supervision by the central government, established; and the separation of church and state made definitive. In the second stage, the "constitutional period," the Philippines would achieve representation in the United States Congress, and, at home, an elected assembly and a senate, half of whose members would be appointed by the Governor General and half elected by the mayors of the islands' municipalities. The following year in November 1901, after Aguinaldo's capture, the platform was clarified at a convention of the party, which petitioned the United States government for annexation as a state.[21]

Statehood to these Federalistas was not an end, but a means to an end. (It was not even that for some, who simply wanted peace. Pedro Paterno, for example, joined the party to help promote pacification. He continued to believe that neither independence nor annexation but rather an autonomous protectorate was the best goal for Filipino statesmen.) Recognizing that their country had little choice but to accept American sovereignty, and desiring that the relationship between the United States and the Philippines should be so shaped as to assure American tutelage and protection and effect economic growth, modernization, and the spread of education, they seized upon full annexation into the union as the best available way to obtain these ends without having to accept secondary citizenship or the types of social inequality typical of colonial relationships. Pardo de Tavera, who accompanied the Commission on its trips to inaugurate civil provincial governments, told the people that independence was impossible, because the islands' social disorganization would lead inevitably to anarchy; annexation, on the other hand, would secure the essential goals of the revolution.[22]

Pardo de Tavera has had a bad press. Filipino nationalists resent the position he espoused and are inclined to attribute it, at least in part, to his having been largely of Spanish descent and having lived for many years in Europe. Among Americans, those sympathetic toward Philippine independence have loved him no better than their Filipino counterparts, and retentionists have been soured toward him because of Cameron Forbes' revelation that he was an intriguer, the author of an "insidious cabal" that secured the removal of Governor General Luke E. Wright by means of a "campaign of unjust vilification." It is all true: he was vain, back-biting, and Europeanized; and he despised the Filipino people, because he considered them indolent. But these ought not to be the only things one remembers about him.[23]

Pardo was a man of unusual attainments, a distinguished bibliographer and historian, a physician, a landowner, and a firm believer in modernization. His experiences in Europe had persuaded him that the cultural forms of Hispano-Philippine life at the end of the nineteenth century were nothing but "miserable vestiges of a worn-out and incomplete civilization." This he considered the basic fact of Philippine life, and to it he attributed a stagnation of social energies. The masses of the people were illiterate and fatalistic; men of capacity squandered their talents in pursuit of glory in politics or the church. Yet this was the age of commerce and industry, and it was not politicos or churchmen who held the key to progress and modernity:

> The men who are at the head of banking, agricultural, manufacturing, and commercial institutions; who devote their activity and intelligence to the management of financial concerns; who manage railway lines, navigation lines, and all other industries like those which now exist or can be operated in this country; who direct the

agricultural development that makes the land fertile and extracts therefrom the elements of wealth which are the basis of national prosperity; who address themselves to the distribution and exchange of domestic and foreign products; and those who work and give work of any kind, and by their creative activity take over and transform the latent energy found in coal and in the metals, and the productive energy of the land by the application of man's voluntary labor; all these men constitute a *power* in the community, and it is by such men, and no others, that the power of a nation and the height of its civilization are measured.

"The most urgent question," he argued, "was a social one, because the solution of our political problem necessarily, and as sure as fate, depends upon the solution we give to our social problem." He rejected independence because it would have thrown the people back upon their own resources; and owing to the Spanish experience these were inadequate to the most important task facing them, reshaping their society and culture.

Pardo was a nineteenth-century liberal, a believer in individualism, in laissez-faire, and in progress; and he was convinced that the remedy to the problem he had perceived lay in education—the kind of education that takes place in schools and the kind that comes from the guidance and example of those who have already achieved that to which one aspires. "My wishes," he wrote,

> have nothing to do with the question of whether the sovereign power shall reside in foreign hands, as now, or in our own, as we aspire: I want to prepare the people so that they can not be oppressed by Government, so that they can not be exploited by the authorities, and in order that they may not look upon office as the only thing worth striving for and possessing. That is my ambition, an ambition for a transformation in our society without which any political change would be factitious and never capable of subserving the true interests of the people. . . .
>
> Confidence in the virtue of politics and politicians is one of the most evident signs of an inferior type of society. Political independence does not make a people safe from slavery: the law can not protect the individual of inferior capacity from the native or foreign individual of superior capacity. . . . It is only a social transformation that can shield us from this danger.

Annexation to the United States was the means whereby the Philippines might be effectively modernized and their society transformed; and this was the rationale, at least in part, for Pardo's devotion to the goal of statehood. This, and a peculiar sense of obligation which is the

71

little-noted counterpoint to his contempt for the ordinary Filipino. "The enlightened class in the Philippines," he said, after his political career had ended and when he had nothing to gain from dissimulation, "represents its own interests and the interests of the masses who confide in it. This sort of trust places upon us a tremendous responsibility."

Wherefore, Pardo pursued Americanization with a vengeance. "After peace is established," he wrote to General MacArthur, "all our efforts will be directed to Americanizing ourselves; to cause a knowledge of the English language to be extended and generalized in the Philippines, in order that through its agency the American spirit may take possession of us and that we may so adopt its principles, its political customs and its peculiar civilization that our redemption may be complete and radical." He predicted that once public education had been organized throughout the islands and the administration of justice reformed so as to protect the people's rights, Filipinos would lose their fears and suspicions and become receptive to America's tutelary presence. Moreover, he intended that this tutelage should apply to himself as well as to the unenlightened. "I want them [his sons] to be educated in America so that they may be Americans," he wrote to Taft in January 1902. "I, also, wish to pass some time in the U.S. to learn American principles, to know their social and political customs, to meet their men and to be able, *el día que vuelva a mi país,* to be more useful in advancing the civilization and the progress of the Philippines."[24]

Taft thought that Pardo's ideas about annexation and statehood were visionary, and he doubted that many Federalistas would have approved of them if the issue had been thought real and present. On the other hand, the party's potential for bringing about effective pacification was obvious; and, convinced as he was of the shortcomings of both the people and their leaders, combining attraction with reform appealed to him. He felt that Pardo "on the whole has a better and more common sense view of the situation than any Filipino I know." Therefore, he made the Federal Party a quasi-official organ. As civil government unfolded, the Commission chose Federalistas for its Filipino appointments. Arellano became Chief Justice of the reformed Supreme Court and Torres an associate justice in 1901; Pardo, Legarda, and José R. Luzuriaga, a wealthy Federalista from the island of Negros, were added to the Commission itself; and Buencamino was appointed first Director of Civil Service. Moreover, acting partly under authority of the sedition laws and partly through the exercise of his prestige as governor, Taft prevented the formation of opposition parties. Willingness to attract the corrupt and the vapid had not softened his judgment of the advocates of independence. To spokesmen for a proposed Partido Democrata, whose platform recognized American sovereignty but called for early autonomy and eventual independence, he wrote that such a party would become a "nucleus . . . for the gathering into one movement of all the lawless, restless, lazy, and evil members of society." Political parties, then, were acceptable as a means whereby the government might obtain pacification of the country and cooperation from its people, but not as a channel for expression by the people of desires the government found inconvenient. Casting himself not only as the representative of American power but also as the guardian of Filipinos' interests and well-being, Taft informed the would-be Democratistas: "The error of your attitude is that you . . . seem to regard it as entirely proper for you to continue an agitation which has devastated your country and injured your people by dressing it up in a slightly different form."[25]

All this, of course, was grist for the mill of the Federalistas. By May 1901, according to Taft, their party had "spread into every part of these islands and the people are all helping us to find insurrectos and to bring them in or to shoot them down." An apparently conservative estimate credits the Federal Party with 150,000 members and 290 provincial or local committees by May. Eventually, after peace and civil government had been achieved, the party lost some of its impetus and began, as we shall see, to waver on the issue of annexation. But for some time, Taft continued to give it the whole-hearted support of the government. In 1903 he attempted unsuccessfully to get $20,000 from the Republican Executive Committee for the Federalistas; and, in fact, the Commission did appropriate $6,000 for the party's ailing newspaper, La Democracia, candidly specifying that $1,800 was for advertising such as was purchased in other papers and $4,200 for financing the creation of a Tagalog edition.[26]

If Americans wanted to win the cooperation of Filipinos, Calderón had told the Schurman Commission, they would have to demonstrate their good will by deeds rather than words. In this respect, little could have been more to the point than rapid extension to Filipinos of participation in local governments. Calderón himself drafted a plan during the Schurman Commission's visit and submitted it to Arellano, who revised it. The plan, which closely followed the Maura Law of

1893, provided for a municipal council, composed of the president of the municipality and the headman of each of its barrios, with extensive legislative powers. Acts of the council were, however, subject to the approval of the senior American military officer in the municipality. Recognizing that the United States Army was unsuited to governing small units of Spanish- and Tagalog-speaking Filipinos, senior American officers backed the plan and gave it a trial in communities on the outskirts of Manila. This proved successful; and the plan, denominated General Order No. 43, was put into effect in a number of municipalities in Bulacan along the railroad from Manila to Dagupan and, subsequently, in Pampanga. In March 1900 it was replaced by General Order 40, a municipal code drafted by a board headed by Arellano, which extended the powers of the municipal council and restricted suffrage in local elections to adult males who could meet requirements based upon education, wealth, or previous experience of office-holding. Whichever code was used, of course, real authority resided for the time being in the local military commanders; but an important step had been taken. The extension of local self-government—a conciliatory gesture of genuine appeal—had been made a vehicle for strengthening the control of local communities by the established elite. The Commission, building upon these foundations, replaced the earlier forms with a municipal code of its own in January 1901, retaining the limited franchise and providing for an elected municipal president and council with power over almost all local aspects of government, including preparation of the municipal budget and collection of municipal revenues. Municipal ordinances were subject to review by provincial authorities, however.

After the Taft Commission's assumption of legislative power, steps were also taken to establish civil governments at the provincial level. On February 6, 1901, the Commission enacted a Provincial Government Code, under which each province was to have a governor elected by the members of the municipal councils in the province, and a provincial board or legislature consisting of the governor and two appointed officials, the provincial treasurer, and the provincial supervisor of public works. (Later, in 1906, the supervisor was replaced by another appointed official, the division superintendent of schools; this arrangement lasted only until November of that year, when the superintendent was replaced by an elected "third member.") This was a carefully balanced measure: its provision for indirect election of the governor, especially when seen in the light of the limitations placed upon suffrage even in the election of the councillors who chose the governor, favored the interests of ilustrados and caciques of established reputation. The code was, in this respect, perfectly consistent with the logic of the policy of winning the people by attracting their more conservative leaders. Even so, little was risked. Control of finances and contracts, the sort of power Taft thought Filipinos' ethic unsuited to, was safely lodged in appointive offices; and, as with municipal government, the whole operation was subject to review, in this case by the executive secretary of the insular government, an American.[27]

Immediately after passing the code, four of the five commissioners, accompanied by Filipino, American, and Spanish reporters and prominent members of the Federal Party, traveled northward from Manila, organizing the first city governments, in Pampanga, Pangasinan, and Tarlac. Open sessions were held, at which the Provincial Government Act was explained and special amendments were enacted in order to suit the general act to the conditions in the province in question. Arellano, Pardo, and Flores would then speak to the people, explaining the goals of the Federal Party and encouraging cooperation with the Americans. Finally, the Commission would announce its appointments to provincial offices. Late in February, Bataan and Bulacan were similarly organized, and in March the Commission sailed southward to organize provinces in the Visayas. That these steps did indeed meet with the approval at least of that part of the population entitled to vote became evident in the first provincial elections, a year later in February 1902. In the thirty provinces then under civil government, almost two thirds of the Commission's gubernatorial appointees were elected to remain in office; in five cases the Commission's choice was replaced by their appointee as provincial secretary; and in one instance where the Commission's appointed governor was replaced, the new governor elected was an American.[28]

In this organization of local and municipal governments there was a happy confluence of American and Filipino ideals. The decision to organize from the bottom up was a pragmatic one: the islands as a whole needed a military governor after many parts of them had been sufficiently secured to warrant establishment of civil and participatory government. In this case, however, pragmatism and principle complemented each other. Filipinos, their basic social and political loyalties turning upon local and familial considerations, had resented the centralization of political power under the Spaniards in the persons of the

Governor General and a few other key officials in Manila. (It is paradoxical that in some cases they also argued for a strengthening of the Governor General's secular power as a means of controlling the influence of the friars over government.) Both ilustrado reformers and the working and middle-class members of the Katipunan had stressed decentralization and the importance of local units in their thinking about government. The creation of municipal and provincial governments, even though they were circumscribed and restrained in various ways, was therefore a pertinent and gratifying step from the standpoint of Filipinos. It was also one which conformed with American thinking about both the nature of government and the nature of a proper Philippine government. Both because they took our own federal system for a model and also because they were mightily impressed by the existence of tribes with different languages or dialects in different parts of the Philippines, Americans felt that the formation of local governments ought to antecede that of a central civil government, and that the local governments thus established ought to possess important independent powers. Thus in McKinley's famous instructions, the Commission was enjoined: "The general principle to be followed in distributing powers between the various government units is to be somewhat after the pattern of the states and the national government of the United States. Hence the central government is to have no direct administrative control except in matters of purely general concern and its supervision over local governments is to be limited to securing and enforcing faithful and efficient administration by local officers."[29]

The Commission did not stop with the creation of local and provincial governments but pressed vigorously for an end to retention of the central executive power by the military and early organization of a fully civilian government. So long as the President governed the Philippines under his powers as commander-in-chief of the armed forces, this would be of questionable legality; but during the winter of 1900–01 Congress had before it legislation introduced by Senator John C. Spooner recognizing the President's previous actions in the islands and establishing a basis for future civil government. In January 1901, looking ahead to passage of the Spooner bill, Taft wrote to Root that following installation of civil governments in the major provinces a "central civil government" should be organized, with "a Governor General and a legislative body, consisting of the Commission and possibly one or two reliable Filipinos to act as a provisional legislature for eighteen months or two years and until we can establish a government very like that of Puerto Rico or the one described in the plat-form of the Federal Party." His own desire, expressed three months later in reply to a request from Root, was a legislative council of eleven members, five of them Filipinos, with the Governor General sitting as president. The existing American commissioners, who would sit in this council, would also hold executive portfolios; and one of the proposed Filipino members, Torres, would hold the portfolio of Secretary of Justice. This partial merger of the executive and the legislative powers would maximize the Americans' tutelary role, and would also reduce the possibility of friction between the two branches of the government: "We are all agreed that it is much better that the Governor General should be a member of the legislative body and thus in sympathy with it, and should not be brought by the exercise of the veto power in a natural opposition." Taft showed this plan to his fellow commissioners, who revised parts of it, reducing the size of the council first to nine (five Americans, four Filipinos) and later, when Wright, Ide, and Moses insisted that there be an American majority large enough to survive the absence of one member, to eight (five Americans, three Filipinos). The Filipino executive portfolio was eliminated, on grounds that the salaries paid to American commissioners were higher than those that would be paid to Filipinos and that this could be rationalized by giving the Americans additional responsibilities. The overlap of executive and legislative functions and the omission of a veto power for the chief executive, however, were retained.[30]

Taft always argued that Filipinos passionately desired an end to the military government of their country, and that completion of the transfer to civil authority would be a major step toward attracting the people. It is unlikely, however, that Filipinos' longings in this respect were any more ardent than those of Taft himself. Difficulties between American military and civilian authorities had been present from the outset. The Military Governor, General MacArthur, had pointedly snubbed the Taft Commission upon its arrival in Manila, and when finally he did receive the members, told them bluntly that they were "an injection into an otherwise normal situation" and that Filipinos would need military supervision and discipline for at least a decade. He assigned the entire Commission one small room for office space.[31]

There was more than personal pettiness involved in this. MacArthur's view of Philippine conditions differed from Taft's in two fundamental ways: he took seriously the extent and intensity of support for the revolution among the Filipino people even in 1900 and 1901, and he believed that the United States' primary obligation was to prepare the Philippines for independence. While Taft was writing, in the Commission's report of November 1900, that "a great majority of the people long for peace" and would be "entirely willing to accept the establishment of a government under the supremacy of the United States" were it not for their fear of insurrectos, MacArthur in his own report, dated one month earlier, painted a vastly more complex picture.

> Most of the towns [organized under the Commission's municipal code] secretly organized complete insurgent municipal governments, to proceed simultaneously and in the same sphere as the American governments and in many instances through the same personnel— that is to say, the presidentes and town officials acted openly in behalf of the Americans and secretly in behalf of the insurgents, and, paradoxical as it may seem, with considerable apparent solicitude for the interests of both. In all matters touching the peace of the town, the regulation of markets, the primitive work possible on roads, streets, and bridges, and the institution of schools, their open activity was commendable; at the same time they were exacting and collecting contributions and supplies and recruiting men for the Filipino forces, and sending all obtainable military information to the Filipino leaders. Wherever, throughout the archipelago, there is a group of the insurgent army, it is a fact beyond dispute, that all contiguous towns contribute to the maintenance thereof.
>
> The success of this unique system of war depends upon almost complete unity of action of the entire native population. That such unity is a fact is too obvious to admit of discussion. Intimidation had undoubtedly accomplished much to this end, but fear as the only motive is hardly sufficient to account for the united and apparently spontaneous action of several millions of people. One traitor in each town would effectually destroy such a complex organization.

Believing this to be the case, MacArthur opposed transfer from military to civilian government as a farce. It would be an injustice not only to Filipino patriots, but to the United States Army that had so bitterly fought them, to suppose that so determined a people could be duped into peaceful cooperation. Realism required that the struggle be fought out openly until the Americans had definitively triumphed.[32]

The point of this triumph, however, was not to be imperial conquest but regeneration of the people and early progress toward viable independence. For this reason, MacArthur was more restrained than Taft in his ideas as to punishment of those whom he sought to defeat. Their advocacy of independence did not strike him as ludicrous or contemptible. When Aguinaldo was captured in March 1901 MacArthur received him courteously at Malacañan Palace and pardoned him in return for Aguinaldo's taking an oath of allegiance to the United States and issuing a proclamation urging his followers to support the Americans. Taft, who was in the southern islands when the news reached him, was horrified. Aguinaldo ought to be deported to Guam, he wrote to Root, for he was a born conspirator and would join with "fools" in both the Philippines and the United States to carry on the struggle for independence in peaceful form. "MacArthur," he continued, "has some definite views which he once expressed to me that we are here only to prepare these people for independence. Whether this be true or not, it is most unwise to foreshadow any such purpose in any public document given to the world with the consent . . . of the American government by one who has acquired the prominence in the insurrection of Aguinaldo."[33]

It is difficult to reconcile Taft's alarm over peaceful agitation for independence with his repeated assurances that only the threat of violence kept most Filipinos from dissociating themselves from the opposition to American sovereignty. Nonetheless, as we have seen in connection with his reaction to the rise of opposition political parties, he considered the danger from this source real and shaped his policies accordingly. The creation of civil government at the insular level reflected this concern. Taft was inaugurated Civil Governor on July 4, 1901, and, unhampered by MacArthur, set in high gear his program of attracting Filipinos through the Federal Party. On September 1, the first anniversary of the Commission's accession to legislative power, Pardo, Legarda, and Luzuriaga were added as legislative members, and the new governor took the occasion to praise the wisdom of their party's course. The Commission, he said, recognized the legitimacy of political parties as channels for expression of the people's sentiments, and it welcomed advice or amendments designed to correct flaws in the methods it had set up for reaching its goals. It would not, however, respect criticism of the goals themselves. It was engaged in creating a new, viable, modern government, an eminently practical task in which it needed the cooperation of all; and the aptitude of Filipinos for self-government would be shown not by their "dreaming" about "theories of government," but by their participating in the work of strengthening and perfecting the government then a-building. Later on after the new government had been established and elaborated, there would be plenty of time for thinking about their ideals for the future.[34]

Political attraction and the extension of participation in the government to Filipinos, then, were policies derived in the first instance from Elihu Root's understanding of the nature of American government and in the second instance from the need of Taft and his colleagues to pacify an insurrectionary people and consolidate American control of the islands. They were, among other things, tutelary in intention; and the members of the Commission were fond of saying that out of this sort of measured, supervised participation there would emerge a new and more responsible attitude toward the uses of government. As to the ultimate question whether Filipinos in the fullness of time would be their own men or America's creatures, such policies were professedly neutral and open-ended. Obviously, attraction and participation might be steps toward self-government and eventual independence; and this surely was implicit in Taft's motto, "the Philippines for the Filipinos." On the other hand, they might amount to nothing more than co-optation, a subtle way of stutilfying Filipino nationalism by absorbing its energies in structural and institutional activities premised upon American functional definitions. The ambiguity was fruitful: it suited the need to allow for the vagaries of the American electorate and its Congress, and it gave the Commission the widest possible leeway in its dealings with Filipinos. By extension, the characteristic Taft approach, not just to insular politics and aspirations, but to Philippine problems of all sorts, became an emphasis upon pragmatic reform and reconstruction, coupled with a plea for cooperation in good faith to meet short-term problems and a warning against premature consideration of long-term and philosophical interests.

4

Nation Building

By common consent, there were almost countless aspects of Philippine life at the turn of the century in which reform, revision, or modernization were badly needed. Filipinos themselves had felt this in the last decades of Spanish rule; and the testimony before the Schurman Commission is filled with appeals for secularization of the state, reform and extension of education, improvement of government services, and development of infrastructure. Americans, if anything, felt these needs even more. Daniel Williams, the Commission's sometimes arch secretary, wrote to his family that the tasks at hand were enormous: "Not only did we inherit an insurrection, and a church problem upon which [the Spanish] government was wrecked, but the whole administrative machinery is so antiquated and disorganized as not to admit of patching or repair. Questions of municipal and provincial law, of revenue and currency, of courts, sanitation and police, of education and transportation, of land titles, forestry and mining—of everything in fact essential to organized society—are clamoring for attention and must needs be solved with few, if any, precedents to guide."[1]

Meeting these needs was critically important not only to Filipinos, but to the United States. To the latter, it was important partly for basic reasons of administrative coherence and efficiency and also because this was a means by which to provide what Calderón had called "actual deeds." Rectification of the inadequacies, anachronisms, and corruption of the Spanish governmental structure complemented political conciliation by demonstrating American good will and solicitude and drawing Filipinos into cooperative endeavors from which a recognition of shared interests might emerge. Americans in the insular

81

service approached these challenges with an almost evangelistic fervor. Ten months after writing the passage quoted above, Williams surveyed the progress achieved in the interval and added: "I doubt if in the world's history anything similar has been attempted . . . . The whole fabric is being made over; scarcely anything is left as it was. Having started to mend the machinery, we have found that all the parts must be replaced in order to make the thing move." He exaggerated, of course; but in a very real sense Americans in the Philippine government during the first decade of this century conceived of themselves as engaged in building the foundations of a modern nation. Few, however, had any sympathy for the notion that the result would be an independent Philippine nation; and many hoped that what they were doing would extend the process of conciliation well beyond anything needed simply to pacify the people, so that in the end Filipinos would wish not only to cooperate with American tutors, but to form permanent bonds with them. In this context, American efforts at reform and development became retentive political acts, amounting to a policy of nation building without regard to nationality.[2]

Perhaps the most fundamental reforms carried out by the Americans were the secularization of the government and of education. With the blessing of liberal American Catholics, the near identity of church and state was ended. Separation was proclaimed and, more important, secular schools were established and protestants and schismatic Aglipayans tolerated. That such a change was inevitable under American government did not in the least detract from its potency as a political act in the Philippines. "The fact that Aglipai has been permitted to proclaim himself as Archbishop Maximus and to parade the street in that garb," wrote Taft, "has taught them more of the real principles of American government than any one thing. As a consequence, the agitation about independence etc. seems to be largely settled." At the same time, the Roosevelt administration undertook politically hazardous direct negotiations with the Vatican to acquire the friar estates and secure the removal of the Spanish orders from the islands, if possible. In December 1903, after months of irritating and often evasive exchanges, 410,000 acres on which there lived approximately 60,000 tenants, were purchased for $7,239,000. The Commission subsequently surveyed the estates, appraised the tenants' holdings, and instituted a program leading to ownership after 25 years.[3]

At the same time, the government was moving to meet Filipinos' wishes for reform and expansion of the islands' schools. Compulsory education and creation of a system of free public schools under secular control had been provided for in the Malolos constitution; and even while fighting for its survival, Aguinaldo's government had both maintained its schools and begun plans for extending and modernizing them. American military authorities, impressed by this appetite of the people for education, had allowed local officers to detach soldiers from their commands to help establish and run schools in the areas behind American lines. General Otis himself selected and ordered some of the textbooks to be used. By the arrival of the Taft Commission, the Army had organized in Manila 39 schools, with a total daily attendance of between 4,500 and 5,000 pupils; in the islands as a whole, it opened approximately 1,000 schools before giving way to civil government in 1901. Recognizing the value of such steps as an aid to pacification, the military nevertheless had found itself engaged by more pressing matters and had left major planning and curricular reforms for the period after the insurrection should have been suppressed. The Commission, entering, as it believed, when the military phase of the insurrection had all but passed, quickly took up where the Army had left off. Its first act aside from basic organizational measures was to appoint a civilian superintendent of public instruction; and on May 8, 1900, even before reaching the islands, Taft wrote his new appointee to read Trevelyan on education in India.[4]

The reference to India is suggestive, for the commissioners had Britain's experiences there and in Egypt much in mind. Aware of the risks involved in arousing ambitions and introducing a subject people to modern western thought, they found themselves impelled by Filipino desires and by their own logic of tutelary retention to embark upon a program of educational reforms that would have important social and cultural effects upon Philippine life. A government conceiving itself to be acting for the best interests of the Filipinos, and believing the people "ignorant, superstitious, and credulous in remarkable degree" and their society "a kind of quasi slavery"—a government advised by its most respected Filipino associates that the previous educational system had been a cruel farce and that social regeneration was essential—could do no less. Accordingly, modern education came to the Philippines with an aura of *noblesse oblige* and goals that were frankly reformist. It sought to dignify the *tao* of the fields, to spread skills, and to instill democratic and bourgeois values; and by so doing to break through traditional patterns of dependence, promote individual initiative and mobility, and reduce the economic imbalance between rich and poor. Popular, constructive, and reformist, education served actually to strengthen American control by conciliating Filipinos and weakening established patterns of social organization. In this one sees once again the ambiguities of attempting to attract the populace through established leaders. For having once used the networks of elitist influence for its own ends, the Commission was intent upon denying them to others. "On political grounds alone, without reference to general humanitarian considerations," wrote a later commissioner and justice of the islands' supreme court, "the new government felt justified in . . . giving the Filipino people a common-school education which would render them less liable to be led by political leaders into insurrectionary schemes."[5]

The proper tasks for education in these circumstances seemed to be to end illiteracy and spread English as a *lingua franca;* to provide all schoolchildren with enough basic arithmetic to enable them to defend themselves in the market place and in making credit arrangements or disposing of their labor; to teach at least a little history and geography as an aid to developing less parochial and tradition-bound attitudes than currently existed; to develop healthy bodies through programs of instruction in health and physical training; and to teach the dignity of labor and develop vocational skills. Primary emphasis would be placed upon reaching the largest possible number of children, and elementary schools would take precedence in the allotment of teachers and funds over intermediate and secondary schools. It was a program calculated to bring at least a little of the modern, secular world to the mass of Filipinos and effect certain changes in attitudes and social relationships, while minimizing the risk of promoting assertive nationalism.[6]

For at least a decade after establishment of this curriculum in the years 1901–03, the Commission was agreed that its central features were instruction in English and vocational training. The use of English as a *lingua franca* for the islands followed logically from the reality of American sovereignty and from the lack of alternatives. (Spanish, the language of the past, was known by few people; and those who knew it best were the people from whose control education was supposed to emancipate the average Filipino. The Filipino dialects were regionally exclusive, inconvenient to Americans, and impoverished of modern literary or scientific works.) However, the Taft Commission, directly contradicting its instructions, went farther and introduced English not just as a subject, but as the language of instruction. In doing so, it was concerned in part to ease the job of American teachers and supervisors in the schools; but its primary design was to intensify the exposure of Filipino children to the English language. From this there would follow two benefits: English, the natural vehicle for conveying American ideas about government and society, would acquaint Filipinos with values and a literature that would simultaneously stir them to social reforms and increase their receptivity to the relationship with America. "If we can give the Filipino husband-man a knowledge of the English language," wrote the superintendent of public instruction in 1903, "and even the most elemental acquaintance with English writings, we will free him from that degraded dependence upon the man of influence of his own race which made possible . . . insurrection." The vocational training program was designed to have two cultural effects beyond the obvious economic one of creating skills: it was hoped that among children of the upper classes and others with aspirations in that direction compulsory vocational training would break down the inherited Spanish contempt for manual labor; among ordinary folk, it would break through indolence and establish habits of industry. These cultural goals, having about them an aura of democratization, seem to have been more important to most American officials than any direct economic results. Years later, the Monroe Survey Report of the 1920's revealed that for some time the vocational programs had been an end, not the means to an end, and had in fact been creating skills for which there was little demand. The commissioners and educational officials of the first decade of civil government, were they here, probably would not resent our concluding that vocational training was a counterpoint to expanding horizons, a moral lesson in the virtue of working in one's calling.[7]

The development of public education was one of America's most notable achievements in the Philippines, a nation-building act which by honoring the wishes of Filipinos did credit to the United States. In keeping with the notion of tutelage, however, not only the curriculum, but also the values and goals of the schools were defined by Americans; and the interests and justifiable pride of the Americans involved were transmitted to Filipino students. As with the case of religion, the reform of insular education became at least indirectly a political act. Manuel Quezon doubtless exaggerated several years later when he wrote that American teachers had "endeavored to instil into the mind of their pupils the belief that it is the destiny of the Filipino people to

banks, he peppered Washington officials with incitements to early action. "If the bill which bears your name has not passed when this letter reaches you," he wrote to Spooner at the end of November 1900, "for Heaven's sake press it to a passage. It is this which we need now to assist us in the development of this country and make these people understand what it is to have American civilization about them."[11]

Taft and his colleagues were disappointed. Consideration of Spooner's bill was put off for months in the Senate owing to Republican leaders' fear of a Democratic filibuster; and when the measure finally was called up, as an amendment to the Army appropriation bill of 1901, Senator Henry Cabot Lodge, chairman of the Committee on the Philippine Islands, inadvertently delayed passage still further by introducing a controversial resolution to prohibit the importation and sale of intoxicating liquors in the islands. Moreover, the administration had more limited desires than those of Taft and Spooner. Secretary Root considered it America's moral obligation to develop the Philippines economically, but as a lawyer he had qualms about doing so under the authority of the President's war powers. The Spooner bill, though it would if passed afford Congressional sanction for the President's actions, was not an organic act; and until such an act should have passed, Root insisted on caution. Consequently, he wrote into the Spooner bill as it finally appeared before the Senate prohibitions upon the sale or lease of public lands or of mining and timber rights on them, and qualifications of the power given the Commission to grant franchises. They were to be awarded only with the approval of the President, in cases where "great public mischief" would result from postponement, and in any event were to terminate one year after the establishment of permanent civil government (that is, under a Congressional organic act) and to be subject in the interval to amendment or repeal. Root's changes struck a responsive chord in Congress. Anti-imperialists and most Democrats approved them in principle; some congressmen backed them on the ethical grounds that it was improper to speed up the granting of franchises at a time when some members stood to profit personally. The bill passed with the reservations in it.[12]

This outcome was a blow to the Commission in Manila. Daniel Williams complained that it "effectively ties the hands of the Commission so far as developing the resources of the islands is concerned." Taft, while acknowledging that exploiters of various sorts were eyeing the Philippines, wrote to Theodore Roosevelt that "the danger on that side cannot outweigh the fact that the happiness of these people and their prosperity are dependent on a tremendous investment of capital here in railroads, steamship lines, agriculture and in manufacturing and mining." Lodge's management of the bill struck Taft as bungling and cowardly, and this impression of the chairman of the Senate committee seems never thereafter to have left him.[13]

Actually, the episode may have been a blessing in disguise for the commissioners; for out of it there came a clear shift in the location of initiative in legislative matters from Washington to Manila. In the months that followed passage of the Spooner bill, both Lodge and Root decided—apparently independently—that the forthcoming organic act for the islands should be drafted by the Commission. In response, Taft, believing that the commissioners' informed opinions had been given insufficient attention in the past, not only outlined their wishes for the new act, but also traveled to the United States to argue the case personally before Congress.[14]

Taft's aims were of two sorts. Politically, he sought continuation of the Commission and the structure of government elaborated around it during the past year, and the early addition to this government of a popularly elected assembly as lower house of the legislature. Economically, he wanted a variety of powers for the Philippine government: power to grant franchises and dispose of the public domain, to reform banking and coinage, and to control the Philippine tariff. He also wanted—and very urgently—a reduction of from 50 to 75 percent in the American tariff upon imports from the Philippines. By 1902, however, tutelage and development in the Philippines were no longer good politics in America. Accounts of brutality and tortures by both Filipino and American forces during the insurrection had spread widely and dimmed the luster of benevolent assimilation. For five months from January to June 1902, during the time when it was considering the Organic Act, the Senate Committee on the Philippines was also holding secret hearings to determine whether Americans had been guilty of duplicity, aggression, and atrocities in their conduct toward Filipinos. To the opponents of American presence in the Philippines—the anti-imperialists of principle, and those worried over competition from Philippine imports or immigration of Filipino laborers—were now added others who were defensive or cautious. Some Republicans such as Lodge and Albert J. Beveridge remained proud and unabashed imperialists. But the tenor of the times was shown by the decision of other members of the administration's party to back setting a low limit upon the size of landholdings in the islands and cite this as evidence of their party's and nation's purity of motives.[15]

Harried on all sides, Taft concentrated his efforts upon the assembly and tariff provisions, both of which he thought crucial to attraction and pacification, and both of which Lodge opposed in the Senate. His success was limited. As we shall see, the Organic Act did provide for an assembly, though not at so early a date as Taft had desired; and a separate act on March 8 lowered the Dingley tariff rates in the case of imports from the islands, but only by 25 percent. Moreover, the economic powers granted the Commission were sharply restricted. Although given power to dispose of public lands, it was prohibited from leasing or selling them in amounts greater than 40 acres in the case of individuals and 2,500 acres in that of corporations. The sale of timber lands was restricted and various reservations imposed upon the disposition of mineral lands, including a provision that no party be permitted to hold more than one claim on the same vein or lode. The power to grant franchises, which was finally awarded to the Commission, was qualified by Congress' reserving to itself the power to alter or repeal them. Under the influence of domestic progressivism, stock watering was outlawed and, in the case of public service corporations, provision was made for regulation of rates, government access to books and accounts, and payment of an earnings tax to the government. Conservative limits were placed upon the borrowing power of both insular and municipal governments. So much debate arose over provisions affecting currency and banking that they were put over to the next session as the price of getting action on the rest of the bill.[16]

Much of what was done within these limits had about it more the air of correcting past inadequacies than that of building a new nation. At the Commission's insistence, a census was taken in 1903, providing the first reasonably reliable and inclusive compilation of hard data concerning geography, resources, and population in the islands' history. That same year, direct cable service to the United States was inaugurated, breaking down the Philippines' awkward dependence upon Hong Kong for communication with the outside world. The islands' code of civil procedure, which the Commission had characterized scathingly in its first report, was withdrawn and replaced by one based upon the state codes best known by the commissioners; and the courts themselves were reorganized. (The code of criminal procedure had been rewritten under the military government, and the liberties in the American bill of rights—except for trial by jury and the right to bear arms—had been extended to the islands by McKinley's instructions.) By its Act No. 98 (March 9, 1901) the Commission equalized the rates of common carriers, thus acting against the extortionate and irregular character of inter-island shipping; and by acts 829 and 1090 (August 7, 1903, and March 22, 1904, respectively) it went further, authorizing government vessels to carry private passengers and freight. Subsequently, it rejuvenated private inter-island shipping by awarding subsidies to lines willing to adhere to government standards as to rates, frequency and punctuality of service, and maintenance of vessels.

In the same spirit, the Commission acted to improve the islands' major harbors. Conditions in Philippine ports at the turn of the century were primitive. At Manila there was no sheltered anchorage for vessels drawing more than 13½ feet of water forward. Ocean steamers lay at anchor in the bay, two or three miles off shore, loading and unloading by lighters. Handling cargo in this way was hazardous in rough weather and impossible in the typhoon season; and many lines refused to call at Manila. At the end of the Spanish period only one, the Compañía Transatlantica, had provided direct scheduled sailings to Europe on a regular basis. Of Iloilo, the second-ranking port of the archipelago, one observer wrote: "The port has neither wharves, cranes, moorings, or lights. The coasting steamers drawing up to 13 feet enter a muddy creek and discharge their cargo on the banks as best they can, whilst the ocean going ships lie out in the bay and receive their cargoes . . . from lighters."[17]

One result of these conditions had been the development of a captive carriage trade in Philippine imports and exports between the islands and ports of transhipment that was risky, time-consuming, and costly. The Commission discovered that "freight rates from Manila to Hong Kong, a distance of about 700 miles only, are as much and sometimes more than from San Francisco to Hong Kong, a distance of about 8,000 miles." Having inherited from the Spaniards an incomplete sea wall at Manila, the Commission promptly appropriated $1,000,000 to speed the work forward. In due course, three large breakwaters were built and the sheltered area inside them dredged to a depth of 30 feet. A new commercial district with deep-water piers was created south of the Pasig River. At Iloilo, a breakwater was constructed and a channel dredged; 1,300 feet of reinforced concrete wharf replaced the mudbanks at which steamers had previously tied up. At Cebu, harbor improvements provided almost 2,400 feet of wharfage, dredged to a depth of 22 feet, and ten acres of reclaimed land, upon which a new commercial district was built, complete with railroad tracks to the water's edge.[18]

Some reforms, such as that of currency, proved difficult. Familiar for generations with Mexican currency, Filipinos preferred large silver coins to small gold ones. At times during the nineteenth century gold currency had circulated in the islands at up to 33 percent discount from its face or exchange value. In 1857, attempting to regularize the currency of the archipelago, the government had authorized the establishment of a Philippine mint. The mint, which commenced operation in 1861, produced a Philippine currency consisting of gold coins of one, two, and four dollars, and silver coins of less than a dollar's value. Foreign silver coin, which had theretofore circulated freely, was called in and purchased for reminting into Philippine fractional currency. The archipelago theoretically adopted the gold standard. But there remained a shortage of silver coins, especially in the provinces, where they continued to be preferred. Therefore, in 1876, at a time when the value of the Mexican silver dollar or peso was very nearly the equal of a gold dollar in international exchange, the government had permitted the importation of Mexican silver coin and authorized its circulation at parity with Philippine gold coin. By the late part of the 1870's, however, silver was already beginning its long decline in international exchange value. From the beginning in 1876, and in increasing measure as time went on, Mexican silver imported into the Philippines was used to buy Philippine gold at its artificially maintained parity. The gold thus acquired was then shipped out of the country at a profit, leaving the Philippines with coin significantly less valuable in foreign exchange. In 1883, restrictions had been placed upon the importation and use of silver coins, and in 1886 all foreign coin had been called in. But it was too late. By 1884 gold currency had virtually vanished from the islands, and the government's decree of 1886 was unenforceable in the absence of gold coin with which to redeem the foreign coins called in. For the remainder of the Spanish period the Philippines, nominally on a gold standard and with foreign silver barred from entry, had functioned de facto on a silver standard, dependent for its circulating medium upon coins theoretically withdrawn from use in 1886 and upon regular infusions of foreign silver smuggled into the country at a premium of perhaps 10 to 15 percent.[19]

Such conditions discouraged investment in the islands from outside and accentuated the element of risk in all business dealings. As Benito Legarda, identifying himself as "a capitalist," said to the Schurman Commission, "there is no security in business." In addition, the de facto reliance upon silver benefited exports at the expense of those who produced them. Filipino producers, preferring the less valuable silver to the more valuable gold coin, accepted Mexican silver at its face value; and exporters found themselves able to pay for the products of the country in depreciated silver and have it accepted on a parity with gold. Thus little or no increase in commodity prices resulted from the depreciation of the islands' currency. (There was, apparently, a rise in prices attributable to a growing demand in the market for Philippine produce, but witnesses agreed that it was not large.) For this reason, exporters, selling overseas in the much more valuable gold coin, were able to price Philippine products low enough to ensure them a large world market. Conversely, the price of imports purchased in gold overseas and sold in silver in the Philippines rose markedly. The testimony of Edwin H. Warner, a Manila merchant, before the Schurman Commission on the subject of imports is suggestive.

Q. You buy for gold and sell for silver?—A. Yes.
Q. You can't sell it at the same price in silver you buy for gold? —No. Suppose a piece of stuff costs you 25 cents a yard, then you sell it for 50 cents a yard silver plus the duties.
Q. Imports are diminished?—A. Imports are diminished, but you must take into account that this is a country where there is a large balance in trade in favor of the country itself.

. . . . .

Q. The former wages he [the native] received in gold would purchase more for him in the way of food and clothing than the same wages would purchase for him on a silver basis at present? —A. Just about the same, because the native has taken to wearing a cheaper quality of clothing than he did before.
Q. Then, as a matter of fact, in quality of the clothing or in some respects, he is getting less in the way of wages on a silver basis than he did get on a gold basis?—Yes.

Economies of production and of transportation served no doubt to ease this situation with regard to European imports; and of course China, another major source of Philippine imports, was itself on a silver standard. Nevertheless, it is notable that for the last thirteen years of the

Spanish period for which we have complete and reliable statistics, 1883–95, there was an unbroken surplus of exports over imports. This was precisely the time when the growing number of Filipinos drawn into the exchange of exports for imports typified in the Chinese distribution system was looking to imported goods to meet needs such as clothing which had formerly been met locally.[20]

To almost everyone's surprise, the configuration of the currency problem briefly reversed itself in the first years of American control. Rising demand for Mexican silver in China, and a sudden increase in its use in the Philippines owing to the needs of the American Army, pushed up the value of silver relative to gold. In August 1898 the military government authorized the islands' three principal banks to import Mexican silver free of duty in return for their agreeing to defend a ratio of 2:1 between the Mexican silver dollar and the American gold dollar. In July 1900 only a month after the Taft Commission's arrival, this ratio broke. The banks began to exchange American gold dollars at $1.98 Mexican. Panic and speculation promptly drove the price lower still, until in some places the value of American dollars amounted to only $1.50 Mexican. Early in August the military government, acting to bolster confidence, announced that it would accept United States currency at 2:1 in payment of taxes or customs duties and concluded an agreement with the Hongkong and Shanghai and Chartered banks to reimburse them in Mexican silver at 2:1 for all the American gold currency they would accept at that rate. The Commission, for its part, ordered payment of the civil service in United States currency. All this came to nothing, however, since the banks refused to accept deposits or checks in any currency other than Mexican and used the silver they received from the government not to strengthen their future ability to maintain the 2:1 ratio but rather for export to China for profit. Between August 27 and November 1 the two banks in agreement with the military authorities exported $2,087,500, while, as the Commission angrily reported, "the deposit of Mexican money belonging to the Government in those two banks was, during that same period, depleted nearly the same amount."[21]

As if this were not sufficient to convince the commissioners of the need for action, an easing of the demand for silver, which began in November and December 1900, was followed within the next year and a half by a return to conditions of the late Spanish period. The price of silver fell rapidly, and the 2:1 ratio (banks were now cooperative about maintaining it) began to cause an export of gold. At the end of May 1902 Acting Governor Wright was compelled to cease making contracts payable in United States currency. In November Taft raised the ratio of gold to silver to 1:2.60 and in January 1903 increased it again to 1:2.66.[22]

"It is apparent," the Commission wrote in its first report, "that as long as the principal currency of the islands is Mexican money, the ratio of exchange between it and the United States money will be subject to constant fluctuations, not only as the market value of silver changes, but . . . [as the] demand for Mexican dollars may increase or decrease in the great contiguous Chinese markets." To solve this problem, it appealed to the Japanese model, recommending the creation of "a theoretical United States-Filipino gold peso" valued at $0.50 American as "the standard of value" and a circulating silver peso "receivable in business transactions as the equivalent of 50 cents in United States money" but having an actual silver content marginally less than that of the Mexican dollar. Such a coin would not be exported, since its intrinsic value would be less than that of Mexican coin, but would be unimpaired as a medium of domestic transactions because of its convertibility to gold. Foreign trade would be figured and transacted in gold. Initially confident that this plan could be effected under the authority anticipated from the Spooner bill, the Commission quickly shifted to the view that only specific authorization by Congress and a guaranty of support from the United States Treasury would make the new currency workable. Two American experts—Charles A. Conant, a prominent New York banker and propagandist for the importance of Asian empire and trade, and Jeremiah W. Jenks, an authority on economic conditions in the British and Dutch colonies in Asia—refined the concept of a dual peso; and with their plan in hand, Taft set out to secure currency legislation as part of the Organic Act in 1902.[23]

He failed. While the House passed a bill establishing the gold standard in the Philippines, the Senate, influenced by members from silver-producing states and by the arguments of conservative easterners that maintenance of a gold reserve would prove very difficult at that time, favored creating a Philippine silver dollar coined freely on private account from American silver. Anxious to avoid imperiling approval of a legislative assembly, Taft considered accepting the Senate plan but held out in the end. "When you strike coinage or banking," he wrote to Wright, "you strike the territory of a lot of cranks and are likely to encounter discussion." In the end, legislation on currency was put over to the next session in order to facilitate passage of the rest of the Organic Act.[24]

Meanwhile, conditions in the Philippines were worsening. By autumn 1902 Taft had determined that there could be no compromise. "A large majority of the business transactions between these islands and the rest of the world is in gold," he wrote to Congressman Henry A. Cooper, "and with the fluctuations in silver the merchants never can know at what price they will be able to sell their goods in silver; they mark them up to the highest rate possible and the effect is to increase all the expenses of living to the poor of these islands." Existing conditions were also a grave discouragement to investors. By unanimous vote, representatives of the English, Spanish, and American banks of Manila, the merchants' association, and the Manila Chamber of Commerce decided to support the campaign for a gold standard and a ratio of 2:1, and petitioned Congress to that end. At the same time, Charles Conant passed the word to silver men in American banking circles that with silver bullion declining in price, another year's delay in establishing the Philippine currency would be harmful to their interests. By act of March 2, 1903, a dual system was at last established, with a gold peso of 12.9 grains, 900 parts fine, as the unit of value and a circulating silver peso of 416 grains, 900 parts fine. An elaborate dual reserve fund was simultaneously created—a reserve of token silver pesos to back paper currency issued against them and a reserve of gold to ensure convertibility of the token silver peso at 2:1. Cumbersome it all was, and slow in coming; but the system worked, and for the first time in decades the islands had a stable currency of predictable value.[25]

By the time this had occurred, it was already clear that America's role in the economic life of the Philippines would necessarily involve much more than the mere correction of past inadequacies and righting of structural imbalances. Years of warfare, the disruption of the distribution system and sudden contraction of established Spanish markets, and then, after the turn of the century, severe epidemics of cholera among humans and rinderpest among carabaos had devastated the economy. By October 1902 it was estimated that 75 percent of the carabaos in the islands had died; and at the end of November Taft himself placed the figure at 90 percent. With a famine approaching, the Commission imported both animals and rice for sale at cost, put its laboratories at work on a crash program to develop a serum effective in combatting animal diseases and in December passed a law requiring the *presidentes* of municipalities to promote the planting of quick-growing nutritious crops such as corn and sweet potatoes, the seeds for which the government provided free. In a personal letter to President Roosevelt, Taft urged a congressional relief appropriation of $3,000,000. For a time, it seemed nothing would work. The serum, once developed, proved unreliable; newly imported animals caught the disease and died. An extraordinary drought decimated the special planting of food crops; and locusts appeared and destroyed much of what did grow. The congressional relief fund was not voted until March 1903. By that time, ladronism and general disorder had begun to spread. Coming when government officials were convinced that even vestigial political and military opposition to the United States had finally died, this economic convulsion altered American priorities. For economic concerns thrust themselves most terribly to the attention of the government just when attraction and tutelage through politics had lost their urgency. Receptive anyway to the idea that the political progress of the Filipino people would be both slow and risky, American officials upon whom responsibility fell during 1902 and the next several years shifted their primary attention to a full-scale economic regeneration of the Philippines.[26]

The central thrust of this overt concern with nation building was a determination to open the country through extension of roads and railroads. Here, too, there was an element of reform, for transportation facilities had been notably deficient under the Spaniards. The islands had but one railroad, a narrow-gauge line from Manila to Dagupan built by British capital in the years 1887–91; and their roads, few in number, were often impassable. Sir John Bowring, writing in the 1850's, had put the point eloquently: "The seasons bring their floods, and the mountain torrents create their gullies; but the water escapes into the sea, and the labourer brings his produce, as best he may, amidst the rocks and sand and mud which the cataracts have left behind them. I have seen beasts of burden struggling in vain to extricate themselves, with their loads, from the gulf into which they had fallen, and in which they were finally abandoned by their conductors. I have been carried to populous places in palanquins whose bearers, sometimes sixteen in number, were up to their thighs amidst mire, slough, tangled roots, loose stones and fixed boulders." Forty years later, in the last decade of Spanish rule, John Foreman estimated that of the roads in existence 20 percent could not take a vehicle at any time and 60 percent could not do so in the wet season.[27]

The inadequacy of land transportation distorted the Philippine economy. Prices varied widely throughout the islands, and famine is said to have occurred in provinces quite close to regions having a surplus of food. Land near Manila yielding an average of twenty-one tons of sugar cane per acre was accounted nearly four times as valuable as land in Nueva Ecija yielding thirty-five tons per acre. Gold, coal, and copper mines, some of them promising, stood abandoned for lack of transportation; and Max Tornow, himself involved in the German import-export trade at Manila, pronounced that lack of such transportation would probably prevent the successful establishment of any other form of large-scale rationalized production. It is suggestive of the economic potential being frustrated by lack of transportation, that the opening of the railroad from Manila to Dagupan was said at the time to have doubled the production of rice in the great central valley of Luzon.[28]

What had most concerned the military authorities in this was that it made many parts of the islands all but inaccessible to modern armies, creating de facto sanctuaries where Filipino insurrectionary forces held sway and from which they sortied. By General Orders No. 15 (March 25, 1901), the Army command directed quartermasters throughout the archipelago to report upon roads, bridges, navigability of rivers, and availability of labor in their districts with an eye to creating a system of transportation that would facilitate the Army's task. Beyond this, it was felt in some quarters that the condition of transportation in the islands was an effectual barrier to the further civilization of the Filipino people. The Taft Commission, mindful both of the military's need for access to remote parts of the islands and also of its own interest in breaking through regional isolation and reaching the people with its tutelary and pacifying message, adopted a road program designed to link provinces and open up new country. It is indicative of the importance the Commission attached to these goals that its first legislative act was an appropriation of $1,000,000 for roads. In the meantime, however, existing Spanish roads in the more developed, commercially active parts of the islands fell into disrepair.[29]

With the passage of time and the consolidation of American rule, priorities shifted. As organized opposition faded and education replaced the Army as the cutting edge in America's contact with ordinary Filipinos, the importance of physical inaccessibility declined. The new agents of the American government—one or two teachers, a constabulary officer with a platoon of Filipino policemen—did not need roads suitable for the movements of units of a regular army. And as with other aspects of the American-Philippine encounter, so with roads: once the urgency of political attraction and pacification had passed, emphasis turned to economics.

The great figure in the history of Philippine road building—as indeed in the history of many other aspects of the United States' efforts to rebuild the Philippine economy—was W. Cameron Forbes. A multimillionaire accountant and investment banker, grandson of John Murray Forbes and Ralph Waldo Emerson, Forbes served as insular Secretary of Commerce and Police from 1904 until 1909 and as Governor General from then until 1913. He was a complex figure. A bachelor, intensely loyal to his family, his friends, and his widowed mother, he had a precarious temperament, driving and authoritarian on the surface and warm almost to the point of sentimentality just beneath. He cherished nature, books, and the poetry of Rudyard Kipling; unwound through strenuous athletics, stiffened in light society, and revelled in the camaraderie of vigorous and purposeful men. Forbes seems to have felt a compulsion to measure up in his own time to the dynamic pattern set by his ancestors. Although his business career had been successful, it apparently had not been fulfilling. He had sought in the government service constructive work of large scope that he could make his own. A post in the Philippines, although it had not been his first choice, suited him perfectly. Forbeses and Perkinses had been partners in Russell & Sturgis and active in oriental trade for decades; in a sense, he would be part of a great family tradition. On the other hand, the work before him would be altogether new, not a mere extension of the labors of great forebears. Moreover, it would be work appropriate to his interests, for Forbes was very much a man of the age of steel and machines. He was a man who valued getting results, who believed unquestioningly that things modern were things progressive and would work toward the amelioration of man's lot. His journals abound in celebrations of the new, the speedy, the mechanical, and, perhaps above all else, the efficient. Returning from the Philippines in 1913, he paused briefly in India and noted in his journal: "If I wanted to see the sights of India I'd go on the great irrigation works, the schools and the colleges, and see things doing and growing, and leave out the temples and historic spots where people did things creditable or otherwise many years ago."[30]

Predictably, Forbes was impatient with the frailties of man. Although he was a generous and affectionate man with some, and showed on occasion a delightful wit, he suffered fools badly. One infers that he had a tendency to view man at his highest as a unique type of machine, splendidly equipped for getting results in fields as varied as polo, architecture, and high finance, and conversely to see those who couldn't get efficient results as misfits in the modern world. The standards he set himself are suggested in his jubilant descriptions of "slashing away," "crashing through," and "blasting out of the way" problems of government. "I have been messing things by being in too much of a hurry. . . ." he confessed a few months after reaching the islands. "They aren't used to people who do things any how and find out if they're right afterward." His difficulty reconciling such values with a respect for the dignity of opponents and fools—they were often equated in Forbes' mind—was great. In 1905, at Governor Wright's request, Forbes headed a committee that studied the organization and operations of the insular government and recommended reforms. Its work was a striking success in reducing expenses and increasing efficiency but made Forbes so unpopular as to jeopardize his continued membership on the Commission. Recounting at the time one of the committee's sessions, he wrote: "Oh, what a raking down we gave the Auditor! . . . Barre, assistant auditor, felt dazed and said he felt as though something had hit him when we finished today. We ripped him up and down and raked him fore and aft. The Property Auditor Smith came in, and after he'd been on the rack about two hours, he owned up that there was a flaw in the system. He was told that the flaw was so big that the system had got lost inside of it. I said if I had a floor as big as that in my house, I shouldn't be able to find a billiard table on it."[31]

Intelligent, energetic, intolerant, and paternalistic, Cameron Forbes in a real sense adopted the Philippines. As he wrote years later, "I considered one of my most important functions in this world to be looking after the interests of the Philippines wherever found and in the manner that I felt was best for them, regardless of whether they liked it or not." Originally, he had asked for a post on the Panama Canal Commission. That had fallen through. But Roosevelt, who had told Forbes candidly that he liked young businessmen of family and status to enter the government service, remembered this prematurely bald, but superbly conditioned former Harvard football coach. In 1904, when Taft informed him that the Philippines needed a business-man with experience in railroads to succeed Governor Wright as Secretary of Commerce and Police, the President summoned Forbes to the White House and offered him the portfolio. "I don't like to in-trude advice," he concluded at the door, "but I advise you to take this place; it is doing some of the world's work; it is more important work than you can get otherwise."[32]

Family and business responsibilities prevented Forbes from giving a prompt acceptance, but from the beginning he knew this was what he'd been looking for. To test his judgment, he called upon prominent Boston business and professional men and sounded out their opinions. Henry Lee Higginson, at first lukewarm, reconsidered and sent a messenger after Forbes with a note urging acceptance; Richard Olney said that while he disapproved of the country's being in the Philippines and thought the government's position probably illegal, the Philippine Commission was a vastly better position than canal work and Forbes shouldn't think of declining it. Another strode his office, exclaiming "You asked him for bread and you got a plum pudding," then added that he regretted America's ever having mixed in Philippine matters. A cousin, who hated Roosevelt, "shook with a rather scornful laugh-ter," but agreed with the observation of a visitor: "Of course it's all very un-American; but it's rather good fun to be one of the five despots." Amid all this ambivalence mixed with class and family pride, only William James expressed concern. "You are showing the highest patriotism in going," he wrote to Forbes, "as well as philanthropy. But nurse no extravagant ideals or hopes, be contented with small gains, respect the Filipino soul whatever it prove to be, and try to educe and play upon its own possibilities for advance rather [than] stamp too sudden an Americanism on it. There are abysses of crudity in some of our popular notions in that direction which must make the Almighty shudder."[33]

Like Taft, Forbes formed his ideas of the Philippines and Filipinos quickly and largely from second-hand information. On the long voyage out he read the past reports of the Commission and Milner's *England in Egypt*. He arrived in Manila, August 8, 1904, moved in with Secretary Ide, and took dinner that night and the next with Ide and

Governor Wright. Then he sat down and confided to his journal a lengthy indictment of Filipino agitation for independence, complete with examples of ingenuousness, credulity, and opportunism.

> They want independence [he concluded], but they want it very much as a baby wants a candle because it is held out for him to seize at. People who tell them they should have it are doing the same kindness they would do by holding a flame to a baby and telling him to take it. The intelligent men who want it all modify the statement by saying that they want it under American protection. What they want is the honor, the patronage, and the salaries, while America goes to the expense of keeping an army here to suppress the wild tribes, the Moros, and the insurrections, to keep off the Japanese and Germans, and generally to do the work and they to get the pay.

Governor Wright had an amusing story he enjoyed telling, about a committee of Filipinos who had come to him demanding independence and, when asked by Wright how long they thought an independent government would last after the Americans had left, replied that they wanted an independent government under American control. Forbes heard the story on one of his first two nights in the Philippines and never forgot it. From time to time over the years he would cite it as epitomizing Filipino ambivalence toward independence. Twenty-four years later, he included it in his book. A month to the day after his arrival, Forbes had settled into the new economic emphasis. "The problem instead of being very complex is comparatively simple," he wrote to Olney. "The islands are peaceable, the people are pretty well content, and, as far as I can see, unusually well governed. . . . The real demand here is for a commercial revival, and 50 or 100 first-rate American business men with ample capital coming in and developing the transportation, manufacturing and agricultural interests of the Islands would do more toward real civilization than I can express."[34]

By November 1904 Forbes had become convinced that an entirely new road policy was necessary. No system of maintenance existed, and one by one the hastily constructed roads built into the back country in the early years were becoming impassable. This raised two questions: whether the government could afford to build cheaply, with poor designs and low-grade materials (as, for example, in bridges), and whether it ought to continue to place its emphasis upon long-distance, interregional highways. Forbes answered both in the negative. Mortified that American public works were proving less durable than those of Spain, and disgusted with the treadmill effect of redoing projects at short intervals, he pushed through the Commission a policy of using only permanent building materials for public works and secured the creation of a systematic program of maintenance. Simultaneously, he developed a new, economic, rationale for road building.

Conceiving of roads as wealth-producing, he insisted that the government should give its first attention to those that would stimulate the stricken Philippine economy. Under Forbes' direction, a technique was devised whereby

> The number of wheels passing over a road in its unimproved state was counted, and a value placed upon the road of two cents per kilometer traversed by each cart per day. It was thus easy to compute the value of the road and from this figure the annual cost of maintenance was deducted and the resulting figure was assumed to be the annual income earned by the road to the community. This figure was taken to indicate four per cent of the capital value of the road. This was compared with the cost of building the road, and, if the estimated service which the road could perform justified the cost, it was undertaken.

Highest priority was given to roads carrying most traffic. This meant, in effect, shifting emphasis away from inter-provincial roads with their great length and low density of traffic, and concentrating instead upon creating intra-provincial networks of short or intermediate length roads linking key population or market centers with regions already commercially active. Roads of proven usefulness, many of them neglected since before the revolution, were restored or improved. Mileage of first-class roads increased from 303 in 1907 to 1,303 in 1913, Forbes' final year in the insular government. Total mileage of first-, second-, and third-class roads (that is, all improved roads) grew from 3,476 in 1910 to 4,505 in 1913. New territory was still opened up— when its commercial potential was such as to promise economic benefit commensurate with the cost or when pressure was applied by an important local politician—but the conception behind road building had changed from one informed by goals of pacification and tutelage to one shaped to intensify economic development.[35]

Roads built in this way were to be complemented by the construction of long-distance railroads linking the various regional centers. It would be difficult to overemphasize the importance the commissioners attached to this. Thus, Luke Wright, in a cable of April 1904, began by pronouncing the construction of railroads "especially necessary to prosperity and development of Filipino people," and then, warming to the topic, continued:

> Will open up and furnish market to large areas of Luzon now practically inaccessible. More valuable in educating people even than schools. Will increase taxable values and thus enable us to reduce rate of taxation. At the same time will furnish increased revenues and enable us to reduce if not completely break down tariff barriers to trade between United States and the Philippine Islands which we earnestly desire. Will furnish needed employment at fair wages. Will end chronic ladronism which has existed for centuries, thereby enabling us to reduce number of American troops and native constabulary.

Apparently, the commissioners were not alone in their enthusiasm. Later that same year, Forbes observed: "The people I meet of every station ask immediately for railroads; they are crying for them, and from all sides I am pressed with questions as to their probability, how soon they can have them, etc."[36]

As early as 1901 the Commission had mapped out systems of 1,000 miles in Luzon and 500 miles in Mindanao to be built by private parties with a government guarantee of 3 percent return upon capital invested. All such plans stumbled over the existence already in the islands of the narrow-gauge line from Manila to Dagupan. Poorly and expensively built, subject to repeated wash-outs during the wet season, it excited little admiration. "Truly Spanish," was Forbes' verdict: "ponderous stations and light rails." Moreover, it had been badly damaged by warfare, and for several years after the American annexation was not capable of meeting even its own low standards of operation. Nevertheless, there it was, an existing railroad on the most valuable route in Luzon, right up the length of the central valley. Any comprehensive system of the future had either to duplicate it or absorb it. Taft's first impulse was toward the latter course, which involved a commitment to narrow gauge and to dealing with the English owners, who at the time were pressing large claims for war damage upon the government. But the attractions of new ownership and better engineering were manifest. In December 1902 Root and Wright sounded out Sir William Van Horne, American-born builder of the Canadian Pacific, who was then constructing a line in Cuba. Van Horne was enthusiastic. He thought that an integrated network of railroad and steamer lines could be built, tapping all the major islands, and was confident that such a system would generate enough traffic to be profitable.[37]

At Van Horne's request a survey was made by trained engineers in 1903. They reported favorably on four lines in Luzon, but warned that Filipino labor would have to be supplemented by Chinese. The War Department's Bureau of Insular Affairs circulated this report privately to prospective backers of Philippine railway construction, and at one or another time received expressions of interest from E. R. Harriman, J. P. Morgan, James J. Hill, the Guaranty Trust, and Lee, Higginson & Company. Belgian investors offered to build without any guarantee at all. One by one, however, these prospects faded. Van Horne lost interest as time stretched out, Morgan after discovering that stock watering would not be allowed. In the meantime, Clarence R. Edwards, the garrulous chief of the BIA, jestingly told another prospective investor, one of the Speyer brothers, that if he wanted to get a franchise for new lines he should buy the old ones first. Speyer took him up on it, acquiring an interest not only in the existing railroad but in its numerous claims against the United States government. Whatever system was built would have to have a Manila to Dagupan link, and Speyer was on the spot with one. Anyone else would have to duplicate its existing trackage.[38]

By the Cooper Act of February 6, 1905, Congress empowered the insular government to guarantee 4 percent interest on first lien bonds of railroads authorized to build along routes approved by the Manila authorities. The guarantee was applicable only in the case of corporations organized under the laws of the Philippines, the United States, or a state of the union; and the total obligation of this type was limited to $1,200,000 annually. A prospectus was issued in June 1905 and bids were called for. It was already clear, however, that the bidders would be Speyer Brothers for lines in Luzon, and a group headed by J. G. White & Company for lines in the Visayas. The Commission in Manila, which would have preferred not to deal with the Manila & Dagupan for future railroads, was won over by the Speyers' willingness to build at least some additional lines on Luzon without a guarantee of interest, thereby increasing the mileage which the government could potentially hope to obtain with its limited resources. As we shall see, this was a period when the insular government was experiencing a revenue shortage and when two of the three Filipino commissioners were intriguing for removal of three of the five American commissioners largely on grounds of their advocacy of increased taxes. Economy had a strong appeal. As it happened, the insular government found itself so embarrassed for funds that it accepted no bid for Luzon railroads, except the portion of the Speyers' bid for which no guarantee was required. A bid from the White syndicate was accepted for lines on the islands of Cebu, Negros, and Panay, with full guarantee.[39]

This was in some respects an inauspicious beginning. Besides the White and Speyer bids only one other was received, and it was later withdrawn. The total mileage of the routes finally awarded was roughly 725, on four islands, as opposed to estimates of 1,500 miles on two islands in the beginning. It was all a far cry from Van Horne's idea of an integrated rail and water system covering the archipelago. Nevertheless, even this was a notable advance. Between 1907 and 1913, operational railroad mileage grew from 122 to 608.

The programs that have been described—pacification, political attraction, religious and educational reforms, regeneration of the economy—were demanding upon those who conceived and executed them. Inevitably, one asks why they did all this, what their goals were for themselves and their nation. The answer, of course, is that their goals and motives were various. Some wanted to secure the Philippines as a trading base for American penetration of the China market. Thus Senator Beveridge, predicting that "our largest trade henceforth must be with China," called the islands "a base at the door of all the East." And years later, in 1921, Governor Forbes noted in one of his scrapbooks: "I always considered the great argument in favor of our retention of the Philippines was the control it gave us of the approach to China and the Chinese markets, a future asset of inestimable value." Some were interested in the Philippines for their own economic potential. Lodge, in a superbly Hobsonian mood, informed Taft: "It has been my firm belief that the Philippines would not only become an important market to us for our finished goods but what is still more important would furnish a large opportunity for the investment of surplus capital, and thus reduce the competition of accumulated capital at home, which is tending to lower very much the rates of interest and to create, in many places, needless competition by the establishment of plants which cannot hope to earn any decent return." And James J. Hill, the railroad and shipping magnate, filled the young Forbes with apocalyptic predictions of "a war (possibly bloodless) between capital and labor," after which the Philippines in particular and the Orient in general would be the nation's "refuge." After returning from a trip to the Philippines, where he was the object of intensive evangelization by retentionists in government office, William Redfield, a Democratic congressman from New York who was later Wilson's Secretary of Commerce, went up to the Lake Mohonk conference and told an applauding throng: "Ten years ago it might be said our great productivity was sufficient only for our own needs; today it is no longer true. . . . We must have markets abroad—we shall wither in our industrial life without them. Amid great contending forces it is absolutely necessary that some kindly, generous, strong power shall hold as precious a prize as the Philippines lest it become prey to the wolves of the world."[40]

To others, economics of all sorts were beside the point. Frank Carpenter, the executive secretary of the insular government for years and a personal confidant of governors Smith, Forbes, and Harrison, confessed in later years that he had been concerned with building a Philippine model of occidental values, in order to effect "the political reconstruction of Asia upon the basis of our institutions, the saving of the world to Occidental civilization and thereby, we may hope, the survival of our race." The Right Reverend Charles H. Brent, Episcopal bishop of the Philippines, and an intimate friend of Taft and Forbes, was worried over "the dawn of nationalization" among Oriental peoples and pointed out that Filipinos, already partly westernized, might by an act of "moral regeneration" be made a bulwark of western civilization in a region otherwise pregnant with threats.[41]

Others, more bullish about the future of western civilization, felt a responsibility to progress and world order. Latin America was a negative model for them. Protecting the independence of such governments, according to Taft, was "protecting nothing but chaos, anarchy and chronic revolution." A government under the control of some enlightened power such as England "would be vastly better for the people there." In its grosser forms, this was an idea very popular among the American residents of the islands. Wrote the editor of the *Cablenews:* "All of us who have lived in the Far East know that in practice these yellow and brown peoples must be guided and often driven in a forward direction so that they do not obstruct the progress of the world nor infringe on the rights of other nations. . . . [I]f a race, through ignorance or perverseness, will not heed the advice of civilized nations about, it must be cared for as is a child by its stepmother or a wild beast by the keeper who cages it but treats it humanely." Forbes, who also was given to invoking Latin America as a negative model for the Philippines, worked out a near science of stewardship. Positing something vaguely akin to Alexander von Humboldt's isothermal zodiac, and crossing this notion with the traditional American belief in the westward course of empire, Forbes predicted that in time the United States would overflow and form a "sister republic" in Siberia. "With England, this would make a belt right round the world, at the dominant latitude as though a hand were placed over the top of the world. . . . One can thus imagine the control extending in parallel lines south as though the fingers stretched south —Philippines and Australia one, India another, Egypt and Africa a third, South America." The ideal society of nations would be like the society of individuals: one could enjoy independence so long as one adhered to the rules of the community. Or, better yet, nations would be like corporations: "I think a nation, whether large or small, ought to have some sort of a franchise to do business such as is granted to corporations. They must conform with certain rules, pay their debts, fulfill certain obligations, maintain their property so that it shan't be a menace and nuisance to the world. If the corporation does these things the state does not interfere. If it doesn't do these things . . . the management of the thing is taken out of the hands of the people who made a failure of it."[42]

Above all, the major participants felt a sense of responsibility for the well-being of Filipinos. It was, of course, the official faith. The martyred McKinley had spoken of an "unsought trust" to provide "fostering care" for "the wards of the nation." And his successor avowed that "the justification for our stay in the Philippines must ultimately rest chiefly upon the good we are able to do in the islands." But it went much deeper than that. As vice-president Roosevelt had written privately to Taft that the nation "should count itself fortunate, because of the chance to do well its share of the great world work." The commissioners agreed. In 1901 Taft wrote to a friend: "The position that it would have been better for the United States not to come out here, I have never given up for I think that the United States can invade the world with her trade without further territorial aggrandisement, but I must recognize a responsibility which has been thrust upon us by circumstances and must hope that there may be found no restrictions in the constitution which will prevent us from being . . . a blessing to the people of these islands." Shortly thereafter he grumbled to Root about foreign capitalists who were merely "investors of money" and lacked interest in "the uplifting of the people."

Forbes, in a letter to former President Eliot of Harvard, exulted: "We are of the belief that we are doing God's work here; that we are giving the people the benefits of a century or so of experience of free institutions, and of those measures which are necessary to secure a real freedom in a normal manner for the future." Writing his impressions of the islands for the *Boston Evening Transcript,* the Harvard historian Albert Bushnell Hart put things in a nutshell. "You cannot stay in the Philippines a week," he wrote, "without realizing that the Insular Government is in reality a big mission, the bishop of which is the governor general."[43]

Diverse and even ambivalent as the men who held them, these motives were alike in their long-range character. Whether it was a trading base for China or a social reformation within the islands, the ends sought by the early makers and executors of American policy were intended to be lasting. Their goal was to implement permanent changes of their own definition in at least certain aspects of the Philippines and Philippine life. Accordingly, their conception of reform, development, and nation building contained built-in restraints upon the scope of self-determination permissible to Filipinos. This, of course, was the essence of tutelage. Complemented by discretion, sensitivity, and countervailing restraints upon Americans' freedom of action, as Root had originally prescribed, it was potentially a sophisticated and discriminating way to transmit what was universally relevant in the American experience without unnecessary cultural paraphernalia. In practice, this determination to assure permanence and fidelity to American definitions reduced in many American minds to a need permanently to retain formal sovereignty and at least some measure of active political control. A common denominator because it seemed the requisite means to various ends, permanent retention became the pivot of American Philippine policy—an end in its own right.

Circumstances led to the adoption of indirect tactics to achieve this end. In Congress, where an issue of this sort would normally be fought out, a stand-off of retentionist and antiretentionist forces prevented action of any kind on the issue of Philippine independence until the Wilson administration had come into power. On the one hand, there was no possibility of precipitate withdrawal from the islands. The question of annexation had been decided in 1899, and since then a dreadful war had been fought to make good America's claim to sovereignty. Possession of the islands was the status quo; and the Democratic minority, despite the help of anti-imperialist Republicans, was unable to challenge the existing order of things even to the extent of enacting a promise that independence would ever be given. On the other hand, Congress showed little inclination to improve upon simple possession. As we have seen, the administration had great difficulty securing approval for its economic programs, and sometimes failed. Having already the mandate it needed for indefinite retention of the Philippines, it would have been rash indeed to provoke a major Congressional battle of uncertain outcome by asking for a definitive statement that the acquisition was to be permanent.

Making the best of an ambiguous situation, influential and intelligent retentionists like the first five civil governors of the Philippines decided simply to do their job well, and to do it if possible in such a way as to leave open the option of permanent association. In effect, having ruled out the possibility of obtaining a quick decision for retention in America, they pinned their hopes upon producing slowly and in due course a decision to the same effect in the Philippines. For if the Philippines were to be governed well and their exposure to America made profitable and beneficial, it was conceivable that Filipinos themselves might come to recognize something of value in the relationship. It might be that they would be the ones to seek retention of at least some links with the United States. And if such were to be the case, perhaps Americans, freed from the pangs of conscience, would agree.

Since the turn-of-the-century antagonism between the two peoples was political in character and expression, hopes for such an outcome depended upon the Commission's de-emphasizing politics and accentuating other forms of contact. This, in a sense, it did. It ended armed conflict, placed the control of insular politics in the hands of friendly conservatives, and established local and provincial governments in such a way as to ally to itself natural leaders among the men of property and standing in the countryside. Having acted in these ways to pacify and attract the people, and to establish, as the commissioners hoped, a conservative political order, the Commission had turned to ostensibly apolitical matters. It had embarked upon a program of attractive reforms and undertaken to renovate the economy; and in so doing it had drawn attention to the beneficent potential in American sovereignty and dramatized the power, the wealth, and the technological sophistication of the United States. It has been suggested since, that actions such as these made Filipinos psychologically dependent, presumably by filling them with awe for American power and knowledgeability. Certainly one is tempted to feel that in some measure they diverted Filipinos' attention from political questions and were meant to do so. Professedly neutral and open-ended as to Philippine independence, they were intended to bind Filipinos ever more closely to the United States and dissuade them from seeking an independent existence.[44]

"When we shall have made a successful government," Taft wrote to the Episcopal bishop of Massachusetts; "when we shall have developed and educated the people, when we shall have created an independent public opinion—then the question what shall be done may well be left to both countries; for if America follows her duty, as I am sure she will ultimately, I do not think that the Filipino people will desire to sever the bonds between us and them." Several months later, in an unusually detailed statement, he told the Harvard College Alumni Association:

> Our policy in the Philippines must be "The Philippines for the Filipinos." This duty we have assumed and it is the duty which we shall doubtless discharge. It is fortunate that this policy is also the best policy from a selfish standpoint, for thus we have additional assurance of its being maintained. The more we develop the islands, the more we teach the Filipinos the methods of maintaining well-ordered government, the more tranquility succeeds in the islands, the better the business, the greater the products, and the more profitable the association with those islands in a business way. If we ultimately take the Philippines in behind the tariff wall . . . it will have a tendency to develop that whole country, of inviting the capital of the United States into the islands, and of creating a trade between the islands and this country which can not but be beneficial to both. Now, under these circumstances, is it impracticable, is it wild to suppose that the people of the islands will understand the benefit that they derive from such association with the United States and will prefer to maintain some sort of bond so that they may be within the tariff wall and enjoy the markets, rather than separate themselves and become independent and lose the valuable business which our guardianship of them and our obligation to look after them has brought to them.

Representative Peter Hepburn of Iowa—brought to Manila at the Commission's expense by Taft in 1905—addressing a banquet in Manila, denied that "sordid ideas or motives" had led to acquisition of the islands and pledged his support for Filipino participation in the government and for ultimate independence when the people were capable of maintaining it, then added: "When that time will come, I do not know; but I believe that whenever it does arrive, the Filipino people, learning our principles, will love our government, will believe that there is nothing better under the sun, nor ever has been, and they will be as loth to sever their relations with it as some of them, I am told, now are to join their forces more closely with it."[45]

Hepburn's formulation—the attractive power of the excellence of American institutions—was less common than Taft's. Most of the Americans who were active participants in the American-Philippine encounter during its early years seem to have felt that the great influence in promoting receptivity to the retention of links with the United States would be economic. John Hord, who was insular collector of internal revenue and had contributed to the authorship of Philippine tariff legislation, epitomized this point of view in a 1908 speech on the value of free trade with the Philippines: "The familiar thought that a bloody war of occupation is usually succeeded by a more enduring conquest through the peaceful arts of mutual beneficial commerce appeals with peculiar force to those who have lived any length of time in countries . . . new to Western civilization." The most persistent advocate of this approach, after Taft himself, however, was Forbes. Identifying himself with economic development and the spread of infrastructure, he ostentatiously refused to discuss the islands' political future and urged Filipinos to devote their energies to creating prosperity. Questioned about political privileges while visiting a region still under military government, he replied:

The real problem before the Philippine people is not their political status; that is fixed both here and in other parts. The real problem is the industrial development and by industrial I mean agriculture, manufactures, and commerce. What we want to do is to increase the product of the Islands, and my advice to . . . people who have been thinking about political changes, is to get busy and devote their attention to the practical questions confronting us— things where there is something to be done. I have come here to do what I can to help the people to better their conditions, to increase the products, of rubber, hemp, coconuts, sugar, tobacco, lumber, and other things, by which money can be made. I want to have, when I come again, Filipinos crowd 'round me and present suggestions of ways to enable the people to live better, have better houses, better food, and better clothes. No change in the civil status of the government will do that. The government is good enough now, it is all right.

112

To which the semi-official *Manila Times* added, "Personally we have always been for more rice than reasons, more meat than manifestoes, more hemp than harangues, more potatoes than politics." In 1913, Forbes candidly advised Woodrow Wilson's personal emissary, Henry Jones Ford, that "a temporary form of government may be better for the present than a more permanent one, as the economic relations between the two countries have not yet developed to a point where we can get an ultimate line on their magnitude and nature, and it has always been my belief that the political relationship should follow and conform to the economic necessities."[46]

In effect, Taft, Forbes, and their colleagues abandoned simple, unitary notions of imperialism as control and distinguished between types of control, segregating overt political imperialism, on the one hand, and what mid-century man calls cultural and economic neoimperialism, on the other. Primarily interested in retention simply as a means to other ends, they perceived the irony that certain of those ends, considered good in themselves, might be construed in such a way as to promote retention. Needless to say, so circular a proposition did not originate as a philosophical premise. It was a pragmatic response to Philippine conditions and, in its implicit merging of means and ends, a reformist stance broadly characteristic of domestic American progressivism.[47] Coming on the scene after the decision to annex had already been made, these officials had been appalled by the backwardness, as they saw it, of both the country and the people. This led them to assume, whatever their other interests, an obligation to themselves, the Filipinos, and the world to enlighten and uplift the people. Doing this would require modernizing and developing the economy, which in turn, they realized, would bring profit to Americans. Conceived in this light, the American-Philippine encounter was mutually beneficial; and many Americans had difficulty discerning what there might be in the appeal of nationality that would justify terminating this symbiosis at some future date. Therefore, finding themselves required by Root's formulation of America's mission in the islands to work through the people and involve Filipinos promptly in the government, the commissioners improved upon this for their own ends, using politics in such a way as to neutralize Filipino opposition and facilitate economic and cultural reforms, in order that, having established their credibility, they could pursue the goal of retention by means of building a Philippine nation.

5

Alliances

To a greater degree than is usual in imperial encounters, the future of the relationship between the United States and the Philippines turned upon what happened in the possession, rather than what happened in the metropolis. In the first instance, to be sure, the islands' political status had been imposed by external force. By conceding political participation and local self-government, however, the United States had voluntarily renounced further attempts at shaping the Philippine future by unilateral action. It had chosen instead to effect its plans largely through suasion. This was evident at the conceptual level, where, as a result, it was sometimes difficult to tell ends from means: annexation and retention were necessary in order to reform and develop; reform and development were necessary in order justifiably and permanently to retain. It was also evident at the pragmatic level of day-to-day government and tactics. For once there was a political system legitimately in operation, all important matters had to be dealt with in terms of this reality. The evolution of Philippine politics was, therefore, of the greatest importance to the American commissioners and their superiors in Washington. The success of the program outlined by Root and Taft—indefinite tutelary retention, combined with social reform and economic development, looking to the promotion of permanent, mutually beneficial links between the United States and the Philippines—depended upon the ability of the insular government to shape Philippine politics in such a way as to avoid repeated or intensive agitation of the independence issue and, instead, to channel the energies and aspirations of the Filipino people, and particularly

114

their articulate leaders, into the pursuit of prosperity and socioeco-
nomic change and growth.

At the beginning, the Commission had hoped to do this through the
Federal Party. Devoted to the encouragement of peace and cooperation, and informed by Pardo de Tavera's vision of social and economic
modernization culminating in statehood, the party had seemed an
excellent vehicle through which to extend participation in the government to Filipinos. In fact, however, it proved a weak reed. Within
five years of its founding, the party was a shambles, its platform
reversed and its relations with the government precarious.

Taft had been right to doubt that the members of the Federal Party
necessarily agreed with Pardo de Tavera's goal of statehood. In large
measure, the party's attraction had been its advocacy of peace and
participatory government. Once the insurrection had ended, it began
to show signs of degenerating into primarily an agency for gaining
office. This tendency was aggravated by the essentially local and
provincial nature of Philippine politics, which turn in the first instance
upon the voters' loyalty or obligation to a locally prominent figure and
subsequently upon his power to deliver their votes to another figure
at a higher level of government with whom he has the same sort of
relationship. Accordingly, the higher one's position in government and
the broader one's constituency, the less ability one had to affect voters
directly and the greater one's dependence upon local power brokers.
Based apparently upon the social and familial structures around it,
this political system was dyadic. Power in the form of allegiance flowed
up; and power in the form of patronage, public works, and the like
flowed back down as a reward. The Schurman and Taft commissions
had banked on the system's capacity for influencing large numbers of
people through the medium of a limited number of identifiable leaders;
and the Federal Party had been the vehicle through which, in the
event, this had been attempted. But the party proved to be federal
in more than one sense. Once peace and patronage had been assured,
its impulse toward united action weakened, and the centrifugal forces
inherent in the local character of its power base made themselves
felt. By 1903 the party already showed signs of disintegration; in that
year its directorate sought out the Commission's help to invigorate
the party organ and attempted through Taft to obtain financial support from the GOP in the United States. Frank Bourns, the Commission's liaison man with the Federalistas, warned Taft that "all sorts

of chimerical schemes and recommendations" were being urged upon the party by its local committees and that there was a danger of the leaders' losing control.[1]

In these circumstances it proved impossible to maintain the party's advocacy of statehood. Pardo, Legarda, Bourns—the prestigious figures at the center of the party—remained committed to the original goal. But from the party at large there came increasing pressure for change. We cannot be sure precisely why—whether the electorate itself, small and privileged though it was, preferred independence to statehood as its ultimate goal, or whether its members felt pressures from the voteless masses around them: for some reason the statehood plank had become an embarrassment to the party. Its members could not afford to be complacent about the matter. The sedition law's ban on advocacy of independence had become legally inoperative after President Roosevelt's amnesty proclamation of July 4, 1902, and it was foreseeable that eventually there would be a rival party that would take possession of the issue. In June 1904 the annual convention considered a resolution calling for eventual formation of "an independent republican government, maintaining, if necessary, such political relations to the government of the United States as both countries may adopt by mutual agreement." By this time even such major figures as Arsenio Cruz-Herrera and Juan Sumulong agreed, and the resolution was defeated only after Governor Wright himself intervened. Then, in the summer of that year, prominent Federalistas visiting the United States as part of the Honorary Commission to the St. Louis Exposition discovered what Taft had always known, that Americans didn't want colored and allegedly backward Filipinos as compatriots. That did it. Pardo de Tavera attempted to save the day by offering an "evolutionary" program, under which Filipinos would petition Congress to postpone action as to the future status of the islands, but commit itself to consult Filipino opinion when it did act. In the period of grace thus assured, Filipino energies could be devoted wholly to "the questions of the day"—"the present development of the commerce, agriculture, manufacturing, public instruction, and other matters of interest to the material life and morals of the Philippine people." Predictably, Taft considered this an ideal policy. But its pessimism as to the current capacity of Filipinos for self-government showed too plainly for the electoral purposes of Pardo's fellow Federalistas. Presented at the party's 1905 convention, Pardo's plan was

116

thoroughly defeated, after which the members went ahead, Pardo alone dissenting, and pronounced the party in favor of eventual independence.[2]

At the same time, a disastrous change was coming over the Federal Party's relations with the insular government. In part, this resulted from the change in governors that took place when Taft returned to the United States in December 1903 to become Secretary of War. His successor, Luke Wright, was in many respects a natural choice. A dignified, candid, good-natured man who was also a respected lawyer, he had served from the beginning as Secretary of Commerce and Police, in which capacity he had presided over the construction of public works and the organization of the Philippine Constabulary. He had been acting governor during Taft's absence from the islands from November 1901 to August 1902 and won encomiums for his conduct of the government. However, Wright was different from Taft in important ways. As a former Army officer and corporation lawyer, he was closer to the resident American military and business community; as a southerner who believed in the superiority of the white race, he was less close to Filipinos. His relations with some Filipinos were further complicated by his wife's Catholicism, which led to suspicions that he himself was insufficiently opposed to the hierarchy and the friars. Finally, as Theodore Roosevelt put it, "Luke Wright is no politician." Sincerely convinced that economic development would be beneficial to the Filipinos, and no more cynical than his predecessor as to the likely political effect, he was inept enough to place alongside "the Philippines for the Filipinos" a new motto of his own, "Equal Opportunity for All," and to qualify Taft's famous slogan by adding, "but our business now is to see that the Philippines are worth something to the Filipinos."[3]

Wright's relations with the Federalista leaders had been strained for some time. He had tangled with Bourns over the appointment of an additional government liaison man with the party and had upset Pardo by discouraging anti-friar agitation. In April 1903 when Wright, returning from the United States, was honored at a large reception, Pardo conspicuously absented himself. Legarda, who attended, credited the size of the turnout to Filipinos' desire to please Taft. Upon learning of Wright's appointment, Worcester, who had very close relations with the Federalista hierarchy, wrote pointedly to Taft: "I trust that under the new régime there will be no deviation from the established policy of recognizing the Filipinos wherever it is possible to do so, and of opposing the attempts of the American colony where they look toward the exploitation of the country."[4]

Despite these omens, Wright's administration began on a note of harmony. In his inaugural, true to form, he sounded the new economic emphasis and did so straightforwardly: "Up to this time we have been going through what may be aptly termed a period of political reconstruction. . . . From this time forward our labors must mainly be toward the consolidation, elaboration, and making permanent that which we have established and the building up and developing the natural resources of the Islands. Our first and most obvious need is an improved method of inter-communication among the people." But he added to this a pertinent warning: "We have assumed control and government of these Islands without consulting the wishes of their inhabitants. Are we not then in conscience and honor bound to offer them the best we have to give? . . . We can not ignore the truth that in our relations with this people the Americans here are quite as much on trial before the civilized world as are the Filipinos." The Federalista hierarchy was pleased. The speech had been "excellent," Pardo wrote to Taft; it had "caused an exceedingly favorable impression among the Filipino people," seconded José Alemany. This was only a lull, however; within a year, Wright and the Federalista leaders had all but broken relations.[5]

The cause of the break was disagreement over taxes, and in this one sees something far more important than simply the erosion of the Commission's original political base in the Filipino polity. At bottom, the dispute over taxation was a confrontation of differing views concerning the nature of economic development and the future of the Philippine economy. From the American point of view the issue was clear. The Taft Commission considered the Spanish internal revenue system it had inherited utterly unacceptable. Consisting of numerous small and sometimes illogical taxes—as, for example, on the size of a shop rather than the amount of business transacted—but lacking any land tax whatsoever, the system had seemed both complicated and discriminatory against the poor. Wherefore, the Commission had reformed it in various ways. The effect of these reforms and of the agricultural depression that struck the islands in the early years of American rule was to reduce markedly the revenues of the government. Whereas in the fiscal year 1896–97 the Spaniards had collected approximately ₱12 million from internal revenue, in 1902–03 the

United States obtained slightly less than ₱4½ million. Everyone considered it desirable that the Philippines be self-supporting; and therefore it followed that unless the government were to reduce its expenditures very greatly, new revenues would have to be found. Sharply limited by Congress in its ability to borrow money, the Commission could not reduce expenditures without sacrificing its infrastructure and other economic development programs. Moreover, as we have suggested and will subsequently have occasion to discuss at greater length, it was determined to secure from Congress reciprocal free trade between the United States and the Philippines; and this, when it occurred, would still further reduce the revenues of the government and increase its reliance upon internal revenue. By contrast, it seemed perfectly clear that the Philippines could afford to pay more in domestic taxation. Even Filipinos had said as much. Florentino Torres, for one, had told the Schurman Commission: "There will be no difficulty over the question of money. . . . [T]he enlightened people will be content if their aspirations are fulfilled, even if they spend more or less. The complaint of the people was not that Spain took the money, but it was that the employees took their money and spent it. There are many towns which are able to pay taxes to an intelligent and moral government."[6]

In the spring of 1903, while Secretary Ide was home in Vermont on leave, he and John Hord prepared a wholly new system of internal revenue for the Philippines. Ide was in a foul mood; he had been suffering for over a year from various illnesses, including an immobilizing and painful back ailment. Hord had just joined the Philippine government and had no personal knowledge of the islands. He had formerly served in Puerto Rico and was anxious to duplicate in the Philippines the revenue structure he knew from his previous post. Together, they prepared a bill designed to set the government's existing finances aright and also prepare for the eventual loss of customs duties on American products. It taxed everything in sight, including businesses previously exempt. "I am tired and sick of it," Ide wrote from Vermont, "and never want to see it again until it has been enacted in the proposed form or in some other."[7]

This bill, coming on top of the Commission's earlier institution of a land tax, jolted the Federalista leaders. Many of them were large landowners and some were interested in business. Both Pardo and Legarda, for example, had investments in the tobacco industry; and Legarda was perhaps the islands' largest manufacturer of alcoholic beverages.

119

Under the old system, neither industry had been taxed. Predictably, both men protested the proposed change. Raising taxes upon businesses and manufacturing, Legarda argued, would discourage new investment and prevent the modernization of the islands' few industries. If this were combined with the introduction of free trade with the United States, these industries would be overwhelmed. Instead of more revenue, he favored governmental economy. From St. Louis, Missouri, 36 members of the Honorary Commission under the chairmanship of Pardo and Legarda wrote to Taft, charging that the new taxes were opposed by "all social classes," and urging prompt creation of an elective assembly in order to give the Filipino people a voice in such matters.[8]

One can scarcely overestimate the importance of their challenge. Taft's closest associates among the Filipinos had perceived that modernization and economic development might hurt as well as help and that links with the United States might as easily dampen as invigorate Filipinos' energies and individuality. This was not what they had had in mind when they signed on for tutelage and retention. Secure, as they supposed, in their own enlightenment and relative progressiveness, they had asked that others be reformed and that structures be rebuilt; now, suddenly, it had become apparent that there would be a price to be paid. Their discomfort was, if anything, increased when widespread opposition forced redrafting of the bill. Recognizing that a depression was the wrong time for increasing taxes and broadening their applicability, Wright had Ide and Hord alter their bill so as to reduce its impact on the economy and give the government no more money than was absolutely essential to stay out of debt. They did this by eliminating most of the new or objectionable taxes except for those upon the manufacture of tobacco and alcoholic beverages. "It will possibly cut in somewhat on their profits," Wright informed Taft, ". . . but they can stand it for they have all been doing a tremendously profitable business and have practically escaped taxation."[9]

Faced with the alternatives of cutting back its development program and temporarily dooming free trade or flying in the face of two of its own members, the Commission chose the latter course and passed the revised bill in July 1904, while Pardo and Legarda were in the United States with the Honorary Commission. Briefly, it appeared that the Commission might be able to have its cake and eat it, too. *La Democracia*, the Federal Party's newspaper, resigned itself to the altered bill; and such Federalista stalwarts as José Alemany and Gregorio

Araneta expressed approval. The important role of Spaniards and Spanish *mestizos* in fomenting opposition to the revenue act became known, as did the fact that the honorary commissioners' protest to Taft had been prompted by a cable from Francisco Reyes exaggerating the opposition in Manila; this complicated and to some degree compromised the issue. Then, however, Pardo and Legarda counterattacked.[10]

Legarda had been urged by his friend Taft to give the law a chance. Doubtless it would be a burden at first, but its long-term effect might well be to benefit established manufacturers like himself by forcing out "fraudulent and unsubstantial" competitors. Apparently, Legarda was impressed. Two days after returning to Manila, he had a lengthy interview with Wright and Ide. They informed him that the government faced a deficit of ₱2,500,000 for the current fiscal year and simply could not remain solvent without new taxes; like Taft, they expressed confidence that the taxes would not hurt well-established businesses. Legarda, repeating his objections in principle to taxing infant industries, admitted that he lacked first-hand knowledge of conditions and agreed to examine the situation personally before reaching any final conclusions. What he saw in this examination, however, convinced him that his original view had been correct. In producing regions such as Bulacan and Capiz, there was unemployment and distress. Instead of benefiting established manufacturers, the taxes were driving consumers into the hands of bootleggers. In Manila, the sales of his own distillery and that of the Zobel family had fallen to one-third of what they had been prior to the act. In the case of tobacco, he and Pardo estimated that annual production of cigarettes under the tax law would be 2,750,000,000, as compared with 4,800,000,000 in the calendar year 1903. Conceding the need for increased revenues, they argued that it could be met better by a lighter tax upon a higher volume of sales.[11]

The Commission's majority disputed them at every point. There was distress in Bulacan and Capiz; but it had come about not because of the new taxes, but because middlemen had taken the occasion to put a squeeze on producers. The remedy, accordingly, was not revision of the tax schedule but the use of relief funds to tide over the producers. The consumption of distilled beverages had indeed declined, but not for the reasons given by Pardo and Legarda. Determined to keep the same percentage of profit as before the tax (Hord informed the Commission that the profit ranged from 270 to 300 percent), the distillers and their retail outlets had raised prices by an amount greater than that of the tax; in effect, they took a profit from the tax as well as from the product. The first step toward improving the volume of sales, it was argued, ought to be a reduction of these inflated profit margins. Even their percentages and statistics for the decline in business were challenged. The figures used by Pardo, Legarda, and the businesses in question for the normal output of distilled beverages in a typical year prior to 1904 were higher than those given in the sworn statements of industrial capacity filed by the distilleries with the Bureau of Internal Revenue. "Clearly the capacity of a manufactory might exceed its output, and very often does," Hord wrote sarcastically in a rebuttal to the arguments of Pardo and Legarda, "but the output of a manufactory can never exceed its capacity." In the case of cigarettes, the use of the calendar year 1903 as a norm was disputed. If the twelve months prior to institution of the tax were used instead, the figure for annual production of cigarettes was only 3,200,000,000.[12]

This escalating conflict over taxation was intensified by the emergence simultaneously of other important irritants. Publication in Manila of a personal letter from Wright to Roosevelt, commenting upon the demoralization of the Federal Party and blaming its foreseeable abandonment of the statehood plank upon a cowardly rush to "join in the general cry," humiliated the party's leaders. So did the tactics used by the Constabulary while attempting to quell outbreaks of disorder that occurred in Batangas, Cavite, and Samar. Capricious and occasionally brutal, the Constabulary, in effect, terrorized the population in the hope of preventing it from cooperating with the guerillas. Objections to such a course were clearly in order; and Pardo de Tavera, in particular, opposed it bluntly. Let the Constabulary protect the people against *pulajanes* and *ladrones*, not terrorize them for having collaborated while they were defenseless. There was special point to this; for the Constabulary, feeling the obligation to be consistent in its treatment of the rich and the poor, arrested and prosecuted prominent Federalista collaborators, including a member of the Roxas family. Tension rose. Wright, the former Secretary of Commerce and Police, defended his men. Caught in the middle of an exchange between Pardo de Tavera and General Henry Allen, chief of the Constabulary, he asked Pardo to make specific charges, not sweeping indictments. Pardo, still smarting from having been called by a Constabulary officer "Mr." instead of "Commissioner," took Wright's request as a veiled challenge to his veracity and replied coldly that the people were more inclined to tell the truth to him, a Filipino, than to those whom they didn't trust. Never again, he wrote to Taft, would he expose himself to such "idiosyncracies which I cannot bear to stand nor have I the nature to suffer them."[13]

Whatever the merits of these cases, it was clear that the Filipino Commissioners could not go on in this way without acute loss of face. Their position was well known. In September rumors that Pardo and Legarda had threatened to resign were said to be of greater interest to the public than the effects of the taxation itself; and in November Alemany, scurrying for cover, frankly based his new opposition to the law in part upon its having been made a party issue. There was much more than economic interest at stake, therefore; the dignity of two proud ilustrados and, by extension, the role of Filipinos in the government had been placed in question. The attitude of the Americans on the Commission, Pardo wrote to Taft, suggested that Filipinos had been brought into the government simply as window dressing, to applaud policies over which they had no control and to be disowned if they dared voice opposition. To Pardo, in particular, it seemed like a partial return to the evils of the Spanish regime. The Constabulary was behaving like the Guardia Civil, abusing the people and at the same time so coloring the attitude of the American community by its reports as to prevent reform or change. Behind all these conflicts, he perceived racial arrogance, an assumption that a Filipino was not the equal of an American as a commissioner, as a victim of police brutality, as a man of honor. As in the conversation with Wright, he began to fall back upon that sense of racial identity—of being a Filipino, of being one with the people of the islands against a common foe, the foreign, white rulers—that had briefly appeared in some ilustrados during the centripetal press of forces that created the revolution against Spain. Urgently, he wrote to Taft that the regeneration of the Philippines hung in the balance: "You left here before leaving your work consolidated, and the symptoms which I notice, which are as clear to me as the light of the sun, indicate that the purpose of our redemption will crumble."[14]

By 1905, then, the Commission's ability to influence Philippine politics through the Federal Party had been gravely compromised. Americans had never considered the party's statehood plank important, and taken in itself, its loss was easily borne. But the substitution of an independence plank, however conservative, was altogether another matter. It bespoke a new trend in insular politics. Once the

Federalistas had come out for independence, it was inevitable that other independence parties would arise, presumably to their left. This suggested that if the government proposed to act through Filipino politics and with the cooperation of the Filipino people, at the least it would have to recognize independence as a legitimate political goal, and possibly it would soon have to bring into its own ranks outright *independistas*. The open-endedness of its Philippine program—the insistence upon refusing to define the ultimate relations of the two countries, so as not to foreclose the possibility of evolution into permanent association—had thus been placed in jeopardy. At the same time, the attractiveness of economic development and social reform had been questioned by the party's ostensible leaders, the Commission's ilustrado advisers and associates. Whether they considered reform and development ends or means, Americans had always assumed that Filipinos considered them desirable. Now Pardo, Legarda, and their supporters had challenged this assumption. For them, infrastructure and free trade were less desirable than low taxes and the protection of domestic industries; and reform, if it meant equalizing the tax burden or treating ilustrados the same way one treated ordinary folk, was anathema. In a word, it was no longer clear who spoke for the Federal Party, what support the party commanded among the people, or what aspects of American policy might be acceptable to its members in the future.

Taft, receiving Pardo's and Legarda's agitated complaints, recognized that something had gone radically wrong and decided to make a personal visit to the islands in the hope of re-establishing his old equation. With the benefit of hindsight, one perceives that the questions facing him were of a fundamental character: whether his original policy for dealing with the Philippines could still be pursued through the Federal Party in the altered circumstances of 1905 and, if not, whether the policy or the government's established alliance should be changed. However, this does not seem to have been Taft's impression. So far as one can tell, he never questioned the continued applicability of the policy but instead concentrated his attention wholly on the surface irritants. These were easily disposed of. Investigation showed that the taxes in question were inconvenient, but not ruinous, and that the Constabulary had indeed been heady and iron-fisted in its behavior. At Taft's order, steps were taken to confirm the former and reform the latter.[15]

Having dealt with these matters, Taft addressed himself to the question of independence. In the principal speech of his visit, delivered at a banquet given in his honor by prominent Filipinos in Manila, he laid out American policy toward the Philippines in a rigorous and definitive form. The American public, he began, was divided into three parts on the question of the Philippines: outright imperialists, advocates of immediate independence, and dutiful tutors. Filipinos should be under no illusions concerning the second group; it had been "twice defeated in national elections on this exact issue" and did not represent the views of the American people as a whole. The majority of Americans, including President Roosevelt and himself, belonged to the latter group. Observing the poverty of the islands, the ignorance and indolence of most of their inhabitants, and the prevalence of caciquism, this majority had accepted the unsought obligation to become "the instrument for the gradual education and elevation of the whole Filipino people into a self-governing community." The United States would govern in the best interests of the Filipino people, but no American official would "permit his sympathy with their courage and high ideals to blind him to the necessity of ignoring their wishes in best shaping the future of the Filipino people and in realizing the great end to which the government of the United States has devoted its energies, its treasure and so many of its people in these Islands." The task would take at least a generation, probably longer. For the present, it would be "absolutely impossible to say just what form of self-government the American people and the Filipino people will agree upon for the Philippines, when they have reached the condition in which they shall be competent to determine what form of government is best for them. Whether they shall become an independent nation or whether they shall prefer by reason of mutual benefit to maintain the bond between the two peoples, as is done between the United States and Cuba, or between England and Canada, England and Australia, or what the form autonomy may take may well be left to the future, and to the circumstances and to the individuals who shall be in control of the two nations at that time." What then should well-meaning Filipinos do? They "should devote their attention to the present Government and to its support." They should "institute movements to encourage industry among the people, to encourage the learning of trades by manual training schools, and to teach the people the immense opportunity for production and wealth which these islands afford . . . ." This and the help the American government hoped to provide through free trade and the introduction of new railroads and additional investment would lead to prosperity; and then "the great body of the common people will be well on their way to self-govern- ment." There was no use whatever in wasting energies agitating for independence now or for a declaration that independence would neces- sarily come later. Nothing of that sort would meet the Americans' definition of capacity for self-government.[16]

That left only the question of the government's future political alliances. Wright and Forbes, among others, wanted a change. Ad- mitting that the Federalista leaders had been alienated from the government, they asserted that this was of little importance. The Federal Party was dead, Wright argued; and its commissioners had no constituency other than a hot-house clique of self-serving agitators and status seekers. Conditions had changed. For the time being no orga- nized political body either supported or opposed the government. It followed from this that the government ought to take a flexible atti- tude and preserve the option to deal with whatever forces might sub- sequently appear. Above all, it ought not to tie itself so closely to any one party, especially a dying one, that opponents of that party would wind up running against the government. To this end, Wright had acted unilaterally to terminate the Federalistas' monopoly of patronage by appointing talented men of other parties or no party to government posts. Evidently these efforts to broaden the government's political base were at least partially successful. Wright proudly reported that Archbishop Aglipay, discounting the embittered Federalistas as mere agitators, had told him that his own following, 1,500,000 strong, was reasonably well satisfied with the government. Pardo himself indirectly testified to Wright's effectiveness by attempting to discredit him with the charge that independence agitators approved of his administra- tion.[17]

This analysis had no appeal to Taft. He had always believed that a political base in Philippine society was essential and he could con- ceive of no such base but the one he himself had created. The appar- ent alternatives—infiltration of the Philippine polity by Americans or reliance upon Filipino advocates of independence—seemed obviously impossible: the first because it ran afoul of Root's instructions and in any case was unlikely to attract Filipinos' support, and the second be- cause advocacy of independence was inconsistent with a policy of indefinite retention and open-ended reform. However precarious the Federal Party, and however obvious its ostensible leaders' recalcitrance towards parts of the government's policies, the party remained, in

Taft's view, the only group likely to cooperate with a program looking to long-term, tutelary retention. Moreover, within the Federal Party, the most plausible allies for Taft's policy were the ilustrado leaders he knew best. They had always been his advisers, his link with the Philippine polity; and even in 1905 their dissent from his policy was less fundamental than that of the provincial committees. They had not dissociated themselves from permanent retention. It was plain, however, that these men could not continue to work with Wright and Ide. Taft satisfied himself of this during his visit; and had he entertained any doubts, they would have been removed by the blunt letters sent after him by both Pardo and Legarda, urging Wright's removal. Wright had abused "people of all classes," Legarda wrote, and was a bad administrator, as well. He had shown "profound contempt for Filipino public opinion," according to Pardo. Perhaps the crowning blow was a letter sent directly by Pardo to Congressman H. A. Cooper, Taft's special ally in the House. Wright and Ide, wrote Pardo, "despise" the Filipino people, who in turn "detest" them.[18]

Reluctantly, Taft concluded that Wright, Ide, and possibly Forbes would have to go. To his wife, he wrote that Wright had "managed now to get the government into a condition where it is supported by no party and where the Filipinos of Manila having social aspirations are setting their faces like flint against him." At the end of the year, he summoned Wright home to the United States, where Roosevelt gracefully named him America's first ambassador to Japan. Vice Governor Ide was given a face-saving appointment to succeed him until April 1, 1906, or such time as his successor should qualify. In fact, he lasted until September when James F. Smith, who had formerly been Secretary of Public Instruction and appealed both to President Roosevelt and to the Federalista commissioners, was inaugurated. Faced with a challenge of a fundamental character to both his strategy and tactics for the Philippines, Taft had elected to ignore the roots of the trouble and attempt a restoration of the status quo of three years before.[19]

While Taft was reinforcing the government's alliance with the Federalistas, the foreseeable rise of independence parties to their left went ahead unabated. In 1905, the year the Federalistas opted for eventual independence, President Roosevelt, acting upon the Commission's certification that a "condition of general and complete peace with recognition of the authority of the United States" existed in the so-called Christian portions of the islands, ordered a general election two years hence for the establishment of an assembly. These two actions, that of the Federalistas and that of the President, were followed by the formation of several parties committed to early or immediate independence. For a time, there was much confusion. An attempt to organize a united movement in 1905 failed in a welter of conflicting views and rival ambitions. In January 1906 the professedly more radical members of the movement—among them Justo and Vicente Lukban, Alberto Barretto, Fernando Ma. Guerrero, Sergio Osmeña, and Manuel L. Quezon —formed the Partido Independista Inmediatista, with a platform demanding immediate independence and the negotiation through the good offices of the United States of an international treaty of perpetual neutrality. Later that year, two other independence parties, professedly more conservative, merged to form the Partido Union Nacionalista. This body—led by Dominador Gomez, Rafael del Pan, Leon Ma. Guerrero, Pedro Paterno, Pablo Ocampo, and Rafael Palma, argued for early independence without any help or contamination from the United States in maintaining it. The distinction would appear to be significant; the Union Nacionalista was willing to wait for independence in order to make sure that it would be viable when obtained. In December 1906 its members contemplated merging with the Federalistas, provided the latter would agree to urge Congress to commit itself to ultimate independence. On the other hand, it is arguable that this distinction was of less importance in defining the two groups than was rivalry for office and power. Was Osmeña more radically committed to independence than Ocampo or Palma? The leaders of the Independistas were for the most part young men with a conspicuous association with the Revolution, whose power was based in the provinces. Quezon, Osmeña, and one wing of the Lukban family are cases in point. The Union Nacionalistas, although they included in their number young men such as Palma and revolutionaries such as Ocampo, clearly leaned at the leadership level toward hispanized men of more advanced age, many of whom were based in Manila. Men like Gomez, Paterno, and del Pan—different in many respects—were alike in refusing to be dominated by newly arisen provincials. They used the Union Nacionalista to improve their bargaining position. But circumstances did not favor them. At Taft's request, the Federal Party declined their merger bid. Three weeks later, merger talks were opened with the Independistas. In April 1907 the two independence factions were officially joined as the Partido Nacionalista, with a platform advocating "the immediate independence of the Philippine Islands

. . . under a democratic government without prejudice to the adoption in due time of any form of guarantee."[20]

Party platforms in the Philippines tell us approximately as much and as little about Philippine politics as their counterparts in this country tell us about American politics. It is important to know that the Nacionalista Party favored immediate independence, while the Federal Party favored prolonged tutelary retention followed ultimately by independence. And it is revealing that apart from this the two parties agreed about a great deal during the campaign to elect the first Philippine Assembly. Both wanted increased provincial and municipal autonomy, increased filipinization of the government, equal salaries for Filipinos and Americans in similar positions, economy in government, repeal or modification of most taxes, promotion of agriculture through science, education, and the improvement of credit facilities, and humane treatment of convicted criminals. Granted all this, how did they appeal to their constituents? What was the texture or tone of politics? How tight was the link between provincial and national party leaders, and which way did initiative usually flow between them? What was the relationship between the 3 percent of Filipinos who had the vote and the 97 percent who didn't? We are very much in the dark as to the answers to questions of this sort, but not entirely so.

We have, for example, a remarkable eyewitness account of the formation of the Partido Independista Inmediatista in the province of Tayabas, where Manuel Quezon, protegé of Pardo de Tavera and of prominent American Constabulary officials, was governor. Throughout the month of December 1906 Dr. Justo Lukban and an associate traveled around the province, holding rallies and organizing local committees. Lukban had a family connection with Tayabas, where one of the principal towns is named Lukban, but he was himself a resident of Manila; and he is described in various government documents as one of the national, Manila-based leaders of his party. Evidently, he had taken the trouble to win Governor Quezon's support in advance, for on at least some occasions the two of them spoke together. Lukban's theme in his public speeches was that the quest for immediate independence was legitimate. This legitimacy was of two types. On the one hand, Filipinos had earned the right to be free: the brothers and fathers of those in his audience had fought and died for the cause, and since the new government had been established, other Filipinos had shown by their management of high provincial and municipal offices that theirs was a people capable of governing itself. On the other hand, America itself wanted the Filipino people to be free. "America came here not to subjugate us but to protect us and give us liberty." The Americans had provided a peaceful method for achieving what in the past men had been compelled to fight for. The people need only take advantage of the opportunities that had been provided. Then Quezon spoke, reinforcing Lukban's assertion of legitimacy. He praised the United States and its intentions toward the Filipino people. He himself had come to the meeting, he continued, not to support immediate independence, but to assure the people by his official presence that advocacy of immediate independence was not incompatible with loyalty to the present government. "The Americans," he is quoted as having said, "came here to give us liberty, and independence, if we wish it, after we have proved ourselves capable. And the only reason we are not given our independence now is that the Americans do not think that we are yet capable, notwithstanding the fact that we do." Despite his protestations of benevolent neutrality, Quezon was unanimously elected chairman of the party's provincial committee and was nominated to be one of its candidates for the Assembly.

These guarded speeches were accompanied by allegorical dramas which filled out the emotional content of the party's message. In one, Francisco, eldest son of a noble lady, misguidedly gives the use of the family's lands to Don Anselmo, a powerful and rich man posing as a philanthropist. His younger brother, Salvador, upbraids him for being a dupe, and in long speeches addressed frontally to the audience proclaims the equality of races and the sacred right to one's patrimony. This meets with vigorous applause. When the lands begin to produce abundantly, Francisco, acting under the prodding of Salvador, asks Don Anselmo to return them, the act of philanthropy having been accomplished. Don Anselmo refuses, alluding to the family's inability to protect its property against others, and draws a revolver from his belt. The double meaning of this act is not lost either on Francisco or on the audience. Nevertheless, Francisco presses his request, which again is rejected, this time on the grounds that the family is disunited and the brothers themselves at odds with each other. Thereupon, the two brothers unite, and their manifest harmony and growing strength so impress Don Anselmo that he returns their land to them. The whole troupe is now on stage, and as one they cry aloud, "Hurrah for independence! Hurrah for justice!"[21]

After only one month of this, the Independistas had achieved a near monopoly of organized political activity in Tayabas.

In the meantime, the Federal Party, which in the course of the campaign changed its name to the Partido Nacional Progresista, was carrying its message to the voters in a more restrained way. There was no denying that Filipinos desired independence, and in explaining why the party opposed their having it at once Federalista campaigners were drawn into an attitude or tone that ranged from the cautionary to the deprecatory. Juan Sumulong, the party's chief tactician, told the newly established Sampaloc Federal Committee that Federalistas would promptly agree to an independent government were it not for the need to make the government democratic, as well. One could not have a successful democracy until "the individual should, in every respect, have attained his full development." Otherwise, citizens would encroach upon each other's rights, and government upon the freedom of all. Dictators and demagogues might arise; civil war would be a possibility. "We, the Federalists, want an independent and at the same time a democratic government," he concluded, "and if, in contending that the people may establish an independent government but not a democratic government at least at present, we attract unpopularity, we will face the consequences. We denounce as an error or a danger-ous imposture the policy of those who believe or pretend to believe that the function of political bodies or leading elements should be that of yielding to every kind of imposition by the masses."[22]

These were proud words, having about them something both of condescension and defiance. On the hustings, the language was even plainer. On March 10, 1907, the Progresistas held a rally in Pasay, an important suburb of Manila. Sumulong warned the crowd that inde-pendence would not bring affluence and ease, as some of its advocates had promised. It would bring enormous expenses for defense and heavy obligations. In his opinion, Filipinos had no proper complaint against the United States for running their government; Americans had a complaint against Filipinos for their lack of gratitude. Sumu-long was followed by Arsenio Cruz-Herrera, sometime mayor of Manila, who spoke of the danger an independent Philippines would face from Japan. Rather than wishing Americans away, the people should be "offering prizes for American settlers to come here and lend you that air of security and safety which are so essential to the up-building of the Philippines." Then came the governor of Bataan, who also depicted the danger of foreign aggression against an independent Philippines: "Have you ever stopped to consider that any Chinese junk could come in here, should America grant you immediate independence, without your being able to keep it off unless you think you could do it with a bamboo stick?"[23]

What the crowd's response was to all this we do not know. Doubtless, some among them knew that the Nacionalistas linked independence with an international treaty of neutralization; others would have recalled, perhaps bitterly, that Filipinos had defeated Spain and forced even the United States into a lengthy and costly war. It is unlikely that many of them went away with the sense of uplift and aspiration obviously conveyed by the Nacionalista campaign in Tayabas.

Taft was aware that the Federal Party faced an uphill fight. His correspondence for 1906, when the campaign for the Assembly was in its formative stage, shows concern over the party's disorganization and lack of initiative. It is doubtful, however, that either he or his advisers fully appreciated the handicap it operated under because of its overt and condescending elitism. Quite the opposite seems to have been the case; the elite quality of Philippine Federalism was considered a virtue. Testifying before the visiting congressional delegation in 1905, Pardo de Tavera had described sympathizers with the Federalista position toward independence as "the educated, cultivated, thinking classes, and quite a number of ignorant people who are gifted with sound common sense," while disposing contemptuously of the emerging Nacionalistas: "That party is composed, to a great degree, of ignorant people or designing men." Which, in a sense, is what Taft himself had meant when writing to his wife that "Filipinos of Manila having social aspirations" opposed Wright, and what Governor General James F. Smith was to say (in a different way) in analyzing the parties as of September 1906. "The Federal Party . . . is really composed of the most conservative, best educated and talented Filipinos in the Islands. When this body of men gets to work it usually makes itself felt."[24]

In fact, they did not make themselves felt. Despite rebaptism as the Partido Nacional Progresista and other steps designed to free it from the burden of its annexationist past and emphasize its evolutionary present, the party was roundly defeated in the 1907 elections for the first Philippine Assembly. With 98,251 out of a total of 104,966 registrants voting, Nacionalistas won 34,277 votes and Progresistas 23,234, the remainder scattering to independents and minor party candidates. Upon organization of the Assembly, 58 delegates declared themselves Nacionalistas, 16 Progresistas, and 6 Independents. This was the closest the Progresistas were ever to come to the Nacionalistas in the Assembly or elections for it. A party committed to obtaining immediate independence was in the saddle: by his own logic, Taft had suffered a stunning setback.[25]

In October, he journeyed to the Philippines to inaugurate the new Assembly. The tone of the event was ambiguous. In conceding an elected assembly less than a decade after its entry into the islands and only five years after the official end of the insurrection, the United States was acting magnanimously from a position of strength. On the other hand, its policy was stale; initiative had passed to the Filipinos. With the passage of time and the acquisition of new and greater responsibilities, Taft had lost much of his involvement and expertise in Philippine matters. He had nothing new to say in 1907 but had come out to the islands in the hope that by his presence he might somehow inspire the Assembly to a more conservative stance than that which it presumably would take if left to itself. There was a sort of helplessness about his position. He fully expected that whatever he said the Assembly would proceed in its initial acts to petition for immediate independence. The most that he hoped for was that its organization would be dignified and its officers responsible, and that in good time its members would get independence out of their systems and settle into absorption in economic matters and the current work of the existing government.[26]

At the inaugural ceremony, October 16, he spoke for over an hour, reiterating policies with which everyone was by then familiar, including the seemingly incongruous one of working slowly and open-endedly so as to preserve the possibility of evolving into a permanent relationship. Following this, an abridged translation was read and the roll of deputies called. From time to time, a name was greeted with applause. Finally, the clerk came to Sergio Osmeña, the 29-year-old former governor of Cebu, candidate of the dominant element in the Nacionalista Party for the post of Speaker; and a tumultuous ovation poured forth. That afternoon, at the Assembly's first business session, Osmeña was nominated by his friend Manuel Quezon and elected unanimously, Pedro Paterno and Dominador Gomez having withdrawn their candidacies in advance. In the evening, at the inaugural ball in Malacañan Palace, the Secretary of War upset all arrangements by handing down his appointed partner for the opening rigodon, Mrs. Pardo de Tavera, and taking the startled Mrs. Osmeña off the arm of Cameron Forbes.[27]

It was no coincidence that the broker in this transfer was Forbes, for of all the senior members of the government he alone was on personal terms with the leaders of the Nacionalista Party. The previous year, when Forbes had returned to the Philippines, the sole survivor of Pardo de Tavera's and Legarda's vendetta against Wright and his supporters, he had found himself all but isolated within the government. Wright's successor, Ide, who had been on the same side in the taxation controversy, proved to be no friend. Having been personally stung in the past by the work of Forbes' reorganization committee, he now used his brief months in power to take vengeance on both Forbes and his department. W. Morgan Shuster, who had been appointed to the vacancy in the Commission caused by Wright's resignation, had a similar grudge and was both a personal friend and a political ally of Pardo and Legarda. A colleague who met Forbes at the pier had candidly remarked that you could count on your fingers the number of people glad to see him back. Alienated and outvoted, Forbes needed friends. Taft had warned him in 1905 that it was part of his job to develop better relations with the Filipino people; and so, in 1906, Forbes had adapted this warning to his situation and set out like Wright before him to develop a relationship with politicians outside the ranks of the Federal Party. In the political context of 1906, this meant cultivating Nacionalistas. Like him, they needed to break through the alliance of Progresistas and Americans then dominating the government. In his inspection trips around the islands, therefore, Forbes patronized and, in some cases, formed real friendships with many of the young, provincial Nacionalista leaders. They, in turn, were gratified to receive the attentions of a member of the Commission. Relationships blossomed; each side needed the other.[28]

Among the friends Forbes made during those months were Sergio Osmeña and Manuel Quezon. Osmeña had first come to Forbes' attention some time before when, as provincial attorney of Cebu, he had taken the lead in rebuilding a portion of the city of Cebu that had been gutted by fire. Not content simply to see new buildings erected, Osmeña had replanned the burned out district so as to allow wide, straight streets, improved sanitation, and extensive beautification. As an example to others, he had ceded to the city some of his own property, to facilitate the widening of streets. Elected governor of Cebu, he had carried out his own plans and at the same time led a successful campaign against outlaws who had terrorized the province for years. These were acts of striking executive capacity, just the sort of thing Forbes valued. Before long Osmeña was turning up as a guest at

Forbes' houses in Manila and Baguio. As the elections approached, he emerged as the leading conservative in the ranks of the independistas. Quezon, the protegé of prominent Constabulary officers, may well have been recommended by them to their superior, the Secretary of Commerce and Police. Apparently, Forbes first met him in April 1906 during an inspection trip to Tayabas. Energetic and charming, Quezon won Forbes at once by his dynamic activism and his dazzling public speeches in defense of taxation as a means of improving the country.[29]

Forbes knew his men well, knew that their commitment to independence was not so urgent as their rhetoric suggested. In 1907, Osmeña had told Forbes in the presence of Quezon and two prominent Progresistas that Nacionalistas wanted to obtain offices and would not upset the government once they got them. Personally, he later added, he wanted the United States promptly to pledge itself to give the Philippines *eventual* independence. Armed with this knowledge, Forbes could afford to be complacent about the Nacionalistas' victory in the Assembly elections. In a sense, the result was personally gratifying. On the day after the election, when most resident Americans in the islands were ruminating bitterly about ingratitude and misguided liberality, Forbes jauntily noted in his journal: "Osmeña was elected, as I expected, and will be Speaker, I think. It means that I shall have great power with the Assembly, if signs do not fail."[30]

Knowing, as did everyone, Taft's expectation that the Assembly would open its first session by petitioning for immediate independence, Forbes decided on inauguration day to test his ties with Nacionalista leaders and probe the strength of their public commitment to immediate independence. On the morning of October 16, he drafted a resolution by which the Assembly would notify the President that it was ready to begin its work under the laws of the United States and the Philippines and thereby implicitly recognize American sovereignty. He took this draft—which was subsequently rewritten by Governor General Smith to make it a vote of thanks to the United States for having conceded a legislative voice to the Filipino people —to Quezon, who had once volunteered to secure passage of any bill Forbes wanted, and suggested it be made the Assembly's first act. Afterwards, both he and Smith began to worry that they had gone too far. Taft, when he was told, during a carriage ride, approved of their gamble but agreed that the chances of passage were slim. Forbes began to fear that he might have imperiled Osmeña's leadership. The more they talked it over, the more concerned all three of them became. In some agitation, they drove to the Ayuntamiento, Taft saying outright he thought the plan would fail. The Assembly had been in session behind locked doors for more than an hour when they reached there, and Forbes ran up the stairs to the second floor offices to seek word of what was happening. In the office of the Executive Secretary he found Osmeña, who told him that the resolution had been passed as drawn without opposition.[31]

What had happened was neither a freak occurrence nor a unique act performed out of friendship for Forbes. It was common sense, and it heralded the approach the Assembly's Nacionalista leaders were to adopt throughout its first session. More conservative by disposition than their political rhetoric suggested, Osmeña and Quezon were prepared to wait for independence. Both men perceived that independence could not be extracted from an unwilling America by force or obstruction. At least for as long as Taft and his agents controlled American policy toward the Philippines, they were ready to work constructively within the framework of American sovereignty. That meant avoiding unnecessary, pointless conflicts with the Commission, such as those which would result from the repeated passage of independence resolutions or from a major challenge to the Commission's legislative program. Therefore, although the Assembly passed many bills during its first session with which the Commission disagreed, and which it consequently rejected, Osmeña and Quezon prevented the occurrence of a standoff over basic issues. This was not easy. Osmeña, developing already the repertory of parliamentary maneuvers by which he was to dominate Philippine legislatures for fifteen years, blocked the introduction of explosive measures where possible and kept them from a vote if they got past his first defenses. Already, by January 1908 he had killed three attempts by assemblymen to introduce resolutions calling for immediate independence. In the meantime, Quezon acted behind the scenes. Learning in December 1907 that 46 of the Assembly's 80 members had decided to press an independence petition to a vote, he feigned agreement to win their confidence, and then, at a five and a half hour meeting in a private house, persuaded his colleagues to drop the plan. When several members announced their intention to call up an independence resolution for a vote on the last day of the regular session, Osmeña staged the first of his famous closing night carnivals, holding the Assembly in session until the members became dazed, while he and his lieutenants rammed through countless bills back to back, some of them popular, some of them not, everything the Speaker wanted passing in a great, confused train of motions. When it was all over, the Assembly still had not taken a stand on independence.[32]

All things considered, the Assembly seems not to have minded. The *quid pro quo* for the deputies was a special session, made necessary by the Commission's dissent, as upper house of the legislature, from key bills, among them the appropriation bill for the coming year, that came up in the last hours of the regular session. Osmeña's tactics had their compensation in the form of extra *per diems*. The Speaker, for his part, seems to have felt that his tactics were indispensable, given the nature of the Assembly. Late in May he told Forbes confidentially that the session had been a severe strain and that he had come to recognize that without steadying influences such as the Commission the Assembly would govern irresponsibly. The special session, too, went off in the leaders' chosen spirit of harmony. Pressed by the Progresistas and impelled by the logic of their own platform, the Nacionalistas passed an appropriation bill ₱4 million less than what the Commission wanted, then consented in conference to restoration of ₱3½ million of it. On the final day, with two independence petitions on the table, Osmeña finally spoke on the question. It was consistent and reasonable, he said, to be loyal to the United States and at the same time aspire to be independent. Filipinos were competent to maintain an independent government and desired to have one. The Nacionalista Party recognized, however, that in fact independence could come only by concession from the United States; and for this reason the Assembly, under its guidance, would cooperate with the Americans in the Commission to make the best government possible in the meantime. The Assembly approved his address unanimously as its own expression, with the sole exception of his contention that the people were competent to cope with independence. The Progresista minority dissented on this point, acknowledging that the people thought themselves prepared but stating that in fact they were not. "Assembly has been a blessing to the Government," Smith cabled Washington, "and will serve as an important factor in educating the people as to their responsibilities and benefits of modern government."[33]

The United States government, for its part, responded solicitously to this evidence that the Nacionalistas would be conservative and cooperative. On the very day of the Assembly's vote of thanks to the United States, Taft unexpectedly announced that the Speaker of the Assembly would henceforth be the second ranking officer of the government, taking precedence over the vice governor, the senior military and naval officers, and, of course, the Filipino commissioners. The following day, Forbes summoned the commander of the Constabulary "to conspire how we could help to keep harmony among Osmeña's following." Shortly thereafter, fearing for the Speaker's delicate constitution, Forbes had him examined by his own doctor for tuberculosis; nothing turned up, but for good measure Forbes sent Osmeña fresh milk from his own cow daily. Early in 1908 the Commission was expanded by one, and a Nacionalista of Osmeña's choice, Rafael Palma, was added over the strenuous objections of Pardo de Tavera.[34]

All this meant an end, of course, to Cameron Forbes' isolation. Shortly before Taft's arrival, Forbes' difficulties with Smith had ended abruptly when a friend leaked word to the governor that Forbes' brother secretly owned the pro-administration *Manila Times*. And Taft himself had been struck both by Forbes' influence with the Nacionalistas and by his achievements and plans for developing infrastructure and improving the city of Manila. He went away profoundly impressed. In the meantime, Luke Wright, whom Roosevelt proposed to appoint Secretary of War in order to free Taft for the forthcoming campaign, had advised the President that Forbes should be made vice governor. Roosevelt, who seems to have liked both Wright and Forbes personally, agreed. Pardo de Tavera, getting word, tried one last time to finish Forbes off: "Heard Forbes to be appointed Vice Governor," he cabled Taft. "Can not believe such nightmare." Pardo's day had passed, however. On June 30 Wright took office as Secretary of War and on the same day Forbes' appointment was announced. Forbes, at the time, was en route to the United States on leave; and upon reaching Washington, he consolidated his position still further. Informed by Roosevelt, Wright, and the Chief of the BIA that he would succeed Smith, Forbes dropped the word that he could not do so unless Pardo and Shuster were removed from the Commission. On March 1, 1909, both were allowed to resign.[35]

6

Declension

Forbes was inaugurated Governor General on November 24, 1909, after having served for half a year as acting governor. Although he had disagreed with Taft regarding the political tactics required to effect the government's policy, he was in full accord with the policy itself. Pursuit of prosperity and economic development and evasion of political definition were to be the hallmark of his administration. While still acting governor he had pledged Taft his adherence. "I have made material progress my slogan throughout the Islands ever since I first arrived here," he explained, "and it is one which meets, I find, the ready sympathy of the people. . . . I believe it is easier to divert their minds from political matters by giving them something to think of than by entering into arguments with them for the purpose of refuting their statements or by making promises which I am not in position to fulfill."[1]

The inauguration itself reflected this commitment. After Bishop Brent had prayed for the islands' deliverance from "the plottings of evil men" and for the unification of "us who are gathered from the ends of the world into one family," Speaker Osmeña had gracefully introduced the new governor as the apostle of prosperity. Forbes had then articulated his program. He would not waste his time, he said, in "unprofitable consideration and discussion of the future political status of the Islands." Rather, he would concentrate on things within his power to effect. His "principal object" would be "bettering the condition of the people," and he bade them follow his example: "To the Filipinos I say, turn your undivided attention to the material development of your country and rest confident in the good faith of

139

the United States." The administration would take for its goals improvement of transportation, increase of registered land ownership, promotion of irrigation projects and the drilling of artesian wells, suppression of rinderpest and locusts, extension of postal, cable, and wireless service, and steady filipinization of the government where this could be done without sacrifice of reliability. Within existing schools, vocational and agricultural education would be encouraged; but the extension of education would take second place to development of the islands' infrastructure. "The amount of education we shall be able to accomplish in ten years will be very much greater if we devote our first money toward increasing the wealth of the people and later use the resulting increase of revenue for extending our educational facilities." Above all, the administration would promote the investment of capital, the *sine qua non* of development and prosperity. Filipinos, he admitted, were wary of foreign capital, but they had no cause to be: "the advantages which flow from [it] will far more than offset any possible disadvantage due to the fact that some of the profits will leave the country or that some of the owners of the capital will endeavor to influence the administration of the Islands or their political status."[2]

Few would have denied that much of what Forbes spoke about on that day was potentially of great benefit to the Filipino people. However, the prospect of significant investments of foreign capital—everyone knew that it would be foreign, since Filipino capital was relatively limited and very conservative—made Filipinos apprehensive and raised questions as to the motivation behind other programs, such as those for improving infrastructure and sanitation. It was not that the advantages of capital were unappreciated. "We are not opposed to any capital coming into and properly developing the islands," said Quezon, speaking in the United States House of Representatives. "We are not living in the fifteenth century . . . . We are living in the world of today, and we want to see our country prosper and develop." His fellow Nacionalista Rafael del Pan once told a Congressional committee: "I do not believe there is any intelligent Filipino who is opposed to the honest investment of American capital." Rather, the uneasiness came from a fear that foreign capital, insufficiently regulated and restricted, would take from Filipinos that control of their own destiny to which they aspired.[3]

This theme is everywhere present in the Filipino press and politics of Forbes' period. It cut across all lines within the society of articulate people. The aging Pardo de Tavera wrote to an American investor that his kind were welcome, provided they were committed to helping the country become "great, happy, and the master of its own destinies." Tomas Confesor, then a young Filipino student at the University of California, proclaimed the mission of his generation: "To control our commerce and our industries and make use of and develop our natural resources." *El Ideal,* official organ of the Nacionalista Party, confessing its ambivalent reaction to a rumored American investment, explained: "We are not systematically opposed to foreign capital. We know that wealth in an inactive state does not bring any benefit to the collectivity and that its exploitation, whatever the capital employed may be, will have some influence on the general economic order . . . . And, notwithstanding this, our distrust and suspicions take deeper root. We are well aware of what we are, of the extent and measure of our forces, and, comparing them with the forces of the potentates from beyond the seas, we have become convinced that in rude competition we are the ones most exposed to be crushed." *El Renacimiento,* the radical newspaper whose life was later ended by a libel suit brought by Commissioner Worcester, pondered Wright's slogan "equal opportunity for all" and concluded that if the sovereign American people were finding it necessary to end *laissez-faire* in order to combat their own trusts, subject Filipinos would find it essential to fight being overwhelmed by these same trusts from without. "We fear absorption, monopoly, special privileges in perpetuity, the very death of our nationality." The *Renacimiento*'s successor, *La Vanguardia,* upbraiding Forbes for his repeated rhapsodies over the growth of commerce and the rise in prices, foresaw a day not more than 12 years distant when the resources of the Philippines would be in the hands of outsiders: "Wealth will be progressively augmented, agriculture, commerce, and industry will acquire greater impulse, and amid so much movement, activity and work, amid so much splendor and abundance in the production of material goods, will live a proletarian people."[4]

This fear of foreign capital was primarily a fear of American capital. To some degree this reflected simply the fact that investments in an American possession were more likely to come from the United States than from elsewhere. Beyond this, however, two considerations heightened Filipinos' alarm. For one thing, they could read during those Rooseveltian years of the awakening in the metropolis itself to the abusive and exploitative behavior of American big business. *El*

Renacimiento was by no means alone in drawing from this observation a lesson for the Philippines. In the same speech cited above, Quezon went on to explain why, despite his people's desire to "prosper and develop," they were wary of American investments: "The echo of the struggle in this country [the United States] between the American people and the trusts has gone beyond the seas and reached the ear of the Filipino people. We have learned that, in spite of the fact that the American people are self-governing . . . they have not yet succeeded in throwing off the heavy yoke of great corporate capital. What, then, can the Filipinos hope for in the undoubtedly forthcoming struggle between them and these powerful corporations in the Philippines . . . considering the fact that the Filipinos have no control of their government, which is in the hands of an alien people?" In addition, there was a fear that this exploitative capital, antagonistic in itself to the realization of Filipinos' economic and social aspirations, would be used by those in charge of America's Philippine policy to frustrate Filipinos' political aspirations. As we have seen, there was very good reason for their apprehension.

This latter concern took two forms. For some Filipinos, the chief worry was that American companies, having established interests in the Philippines, would lobby effectively in the United States for retention so as to protect their investments. For others, the danger was seen in the metaphysic of retention through promotion of mutually beneficial interests. This was not an idea confined to Taft and the governors general who served under him. Possibly because these prominent figures spoke their hopes in this respect aloud, it was an idea in the air; and few literate Filipinos could have been unaware of it. Thus the Manila *Cablenews–American* editorialized hopefully that agitators for independence would lose their following after infrastructure, education, and free trade relations had eliminated "discontent and unhappiness"; and a prominent American businessman from Manila, close to Forbes and the BIA, praising the growth of prosperity and the spread of infrastructure and urging the investment of American capital in the islands, told the Lake Mohonk Conference: "A splendid job is being done, and the influence of it on the Filipino is most marked. Where, a few years ago, the talk was all politics, the center of interest is shifting, and the Filipino is beginning to see what there really is ahead of him and is doing his best to take advantage of it." At the previous year's conference, John Hord had entreated the American public to insist that Philippine products be welcomed in good faith in the American market: "Just so long as a small minority of the American people here at home are willing and able to artificially cheapen or enhance the market value of tropical products . . . just so long will there be *independistas* in the Philippine Islands."[5]

The point was not lost on Filipinos. The *Cablenews–American*'s editorial was answered the following day in the Tagalog-language paper *Taliba,* by one entitled "The Jokes of the Jingoes." Among numerous witticisms of the Americans which make Filipinos "split with laughter," said *Taliba,* mentioning Taft's motto "the Philippines for the Filipinos" and Forbes' promises of rapid filipinization, there was a new one, the argument that "it is necessary for the Filipinos to be rich, for then they will cease to think of independence." "It was and still is believed that by promising the people wealth they would be silent and relegate to oblivion their longings for liberty and independence . . ." wrote *El Ideal* the following year: "We Filipinos are perfectly well aware of the responsibilities that are resting on us." So prevalent was Filipinos' awareness of the Taft strategy that evidence of it was seen even where none existed. When Forbes, with no ulterior motives, asked for congressional authority to issue insular government bonds to finance internal improvements, Benito Legarda, then one of the resident commissioners to the United States, volunteered confidentially to the governor that he understood it was a plan to reduce the likelihood of independence—and approved![6]

The politically active Filipinos of Forbes' period had lived through the revolution against Spain and the insurrection against the United States. Many of them had fought on the Filipino side in one or the other; most had sympathized. They were part of a generation that had rejected inferior status in their own islands and had struck blows against world powers in order to assert the racial self-respect and political equality of Filipinos. Whatever their view as to the advisability of independence, or the need for tutelage, almost all of them were adamantly in favor of eventual self-government and full mastery of their own economic house. Insofar as American reforms and developmental policies had a strong and clear potential for helping to achieve these ends or were of apparent altruism or simple, apolitical benefit, they provided a ground upon which Filipinos and Americans could unite. Open-ended reforms ranging from road building to reordering of the currency system fit this description. Investment of American capital did not, in the opinion of most Filipinos. The distinction, implicitly, was between public services and facilities, on the one hand, and private initiative, on the other. Paradoxically the former, controlled by the government, posed less of a threat of external domination than the latter. This was so because while there could be hope that political participation by Filipinos would in time deliver the government and its works into Filipinos' hands, there was no parallel commitment or acceptance of responsibility by private foreign investors to devolve even local control on Filipinos. Development by private foreign initiative, therefore, was not open-ended either politically or economically. At the least it posed a threat that major portions of the Filipinos' patrimony might be alienated, and at the worst it was an insidious agent for the total absorption of the Philippines into dependency.

This apprehension struck at the heart of the policy which Taft and Forbes were pursuing. True development, the sort that would result in prosperity for the Philippines and mutual benefit for Filipinos and Americans, could not be had simply by building roads and rectifying legal codes and the currency. Such acts removed obstacles to development, but a dynamic element was still needed to stimulate the economy and promote the effective use of these improved facilities. To the turn-of-the-century mind, that element was private capital. This meant that the realization or fulfillment of America's tutelary responsibility turned upon the introduction of capital; or, to put it another way, both the justification for having annexed the Philippines and the hope for permanently retaining them would be compromised if significant amounts of capital were not invested fruitfully in the islands. In effect, however, Filipinos were telling the Taft and Forbes administrations that American capital would be welcome only if their own political control of the islands was assured. The more resolutely Americans stuck to their policy of evading definition, the more suspect their advocacy of foreign capital investment became. In the end, this insistence upon intruding into the private sector of the Philippine economy without assurances of good faith broke the precarious accommodation between Forbes' Commission and Osmeña's Assembly.

The alliance between the Commission and the Nacionalista majority in the Assembly survived for a time on the strength of mutual conciliation. In the legislative session of 1908–09, Quezon and Osmeña once again secured passage of potentially troublesome government bills, even including one conceding a perpetual franchise to the Speyer interests for railroad development in Southern Luzon. For its part, the Commission greased wheels where it could by the use of pork barrel and patronage. At the Speaker's request, it agreed to creation of a joint standing committee, the assemblymen on which would be paid between sessions; Osmeña promptly filled the posts with his key committee chairmen. On the final night of the session, after producing an appropriation bill acceptable to the Commission, Osmeña spoke in favor of independence. This time his words were more radical than they had been the previous year, and after finishing his speech he carried a motion directing Quezon, newly elected one of the islands' two resident commissioners to Washington, to petition Congress for independence. Then he walked over to Forbes' office and calmly explained that he had had to give his backers something with which to campaign for re-election.[7]

Already, however, strains were developing. Osmeña himself had balked at the perpetual railroad franchise, arguing that the benefit of increasing railroad mileage did not outweigh the loss involved in permanent alienation of Filipinos' control. Forbes had appealed to Quezon, who persuaded the Speaker and secured unanimous approval in the Assembly. It had been wrong to argue with Osmeña logically, Quezon warned Forbes; he should have played upon a Filipino's sense of courtesy and obligation by putting it to Osmeña as a personal favor. Suggestive though it is, however, this near confrontation over a perpetual franchise was at the time an event of far less moment than the outright collision over tariff policy which took place in the same legislative session.

There were two tariffs in question between the United States and the Philippines, one on each side of the Pacific. Until 1909 the Philippine tariff was not an issue. The Treaty of Paris, which ended the Spanish American War, had provided that for ten years after its ratification Spain should receive the same treatment as the United States in the Philippine tariff. For this reason, it was impossible to reduce the rates on imports into the islands from the United States without correspondingly reducing the rates affecting Spain, thereby multiplying the insular government's loss of revenue. Accordingly, although various reforms and alterations were made in the Philippine tariff, basic changes affecting trade relations between the United States and the Philippines were postponed. In the meantime, however, the American tariff upon imports from the Philippines was very much an issue. The United States Supreme Court having ruled that the Philippines were not a "foreign country" subject automatically to the Dingley tariff but also were not subject to the uniform taxation provision of the Constitution or any of its other parts unless Congress should so legislate, there was no legal impediment to Congress' establishing a special tariff for import from the islands.

From the beginning, both Filipinos and the Americans connected either with the insular government or with trade from the islands pressed Congress for substantial reductions of the Dingley rates. All were agreed that preferential access to American markets was necessary to offset the disruption of pre-revolutionary export patterns and boost the islands out of their depression. When Taft had visited Washington earlier in 1902 to help draft and win passage of the Organic Act, one of his chief goals had been to secure a reduction of at least 50 percent in the existing tariff on Philippine products. Cables from Manila urged him to try for even more, a cut of 75 percent or outright free entry. The resulting act, subjecting Philippine products to a tariff equal to 75 percent of the Dingley rates, was an acute disappointment. Beginning later that year, with a BIA draft for a tariff fixed at 25 percent of the Dingley rates, energetic attempts were made every year until 1909 to lower the rates. These efforts had widespread—one is tempted to say unanimous—support from Filipinos. Dominador Gomez, on behalf of the principal labor union of the time; Juan de Leon, on behalf of the Agricultural Association of Panay; Francisco Reyes, on behalf of the Filipino Chamber of Commerce; T. H. Pardo de Tavera; Benito Legarda; Pablo Ocampo; and Sergio Osmeña were among the many who over the years petitioned Washington for drastic reductions or total free entry. When Taft visited the islands in the summer of 1905, public hearings were held in Manila and Iloilo, at which Filipino sugar and tobacco growers, and tobacco manufacturers, portrayed the depressed condition of Philippine agriculture and pleaded for reduction of the tariff on Philippine products to not more than 25 percent of the Dingley rates.[8]

In the background, but plainly discernible, in the arguments made by interested Americans for preferential treatment of imports from the Philippines, there were other considerations as well. In 1902 Taft braced up a Senate advocate of lowering the rates to 25 percent, with a view of the reciprocal advantages that would ensue in due course: "I predict fair and proper treatment to the Philippines at this time will eventually result in their being our most valuable possessions. The Eastern trade offers a great chance for our surplus manufactured goods and produce, as well as employment for American banks, capital, vessels, etc." Wright, testifying before Lodge's committee later that year, argued that increasing the volume and value of Philippine exports to the United States would awaken American businessmen and investors to the potential value of the islands and result in increased investments of American capital there.[9] And where would all this lead? For the answer, one turns once again to Taft's remarkably candid speech to the Harvard College Alumni Association in 1904:

> If we ultimately take the Philippines in behind the tariff wall . . . and give them the benefit for their peculiar products of the markets of the United States, it will have a tendency to develop that whole country, of inviting the capital of the United States into the islands, and of creating a trade between the islands and this country which can not but be beneficial to both. Now . . . is it wild to suppose that the people of the islands will understand the benefit that they derive from such association with the United States and will prefer to maintain some sort of bond so that they may be within the tariff wall and enjoy the markets, rather than separate themselves and become independent and lose the valuable business which our guardianship of them and our obligation to look after them has brought to them.[10]

No secret was made of this speech or of others only slightly less bald in announcing the hope that access to the American market would dissuade Filipinos from desiring to be independent. Taft himself suggested as much directly to the Filipinos in his speeches at Manila in 1905 and 1907. It is striking, therefore, to find that Filipinos did not shrink from, but actually pursued such links. The first session of the Philippine Assembly, acting upon a request from Adriano Hernandez, a deputy from the sugar producing and shipping region around Iloilo, passed on December 19, 1907, a resolution instructing the resident commissioners to appeal to Congress for free entry of 400,000 tons of Philippine sugar—that is, more than the total annual production of the islands at the time—3¼ million pounds of leaf tobacco, at least 150 million cigars, and unlimited quantities of cigarettes, cut tobacco, hats, native textiles, and manufactured hemp. Copra and unmanufactured hemp, the other chief exports of the Philippines, were on the American free list, regardless of source. Later in the session, this resolution was recast in a form subsequently considered definitive, increasing the amount of unmanufactured tobacco to be allowed duty-free entry to 7 million pounds. What obviously concerned the assemblymen was not the risk of being snared by the American market, but the threat that domestic Philippine development might be affected by a demand from the United States for reciprocity in the Philippine market. Both resolutions called for revision of the Philippine tariff to permit free entry of agricultural and road building machinery, among other things, from any source whatever, but laid down the general dictum that the preferential status sought in the American market was to be obtained "without special concessions" to the United States in the Philippine tariff.[11]

As the end of the decade of equal treatment for Spain approached, the question of reciprocity grew in importance and urgency. In the summer of 1908, Quezon leaked word to John Hord that influential Nacionalistas, fearing reciprocity, were beginning to oppose free trade. And *La Democracia,* organ of the Progresistas, warned that reciprocal free trade would lead to an American monopoly of Philippine imports, making the country "commercially tributary" to the United States and disrupting the natural growth of the islands' economy. Even the insular government began to have second thoughts. The loss of revenue that would ensue from the removal of tariffs on imports from the United States looked enormous, ₱3,000,000 directly and an estimated ₱2,000,000 more resulting from a predictable shift from European to American sources for many types of imports. However, opinion both in the BIA and in Congress was that free entry into the American market for Philippine products could by then be obtained only on a reciprocal basis. On March 17, 1909, Representative Sereno Payne introduced in the House of Representatives a tariff reform bill, section 5 of which provided for reciprocal free trade in articles that were the growth, product, or manufacture of the United States or the Philippines, subject to limitations upon the quantity of sugar and tobacco nearly the same as those suggested in the Assembly's resolution of December 1907. In effect, Filipinos were asked to choose between a long-desired economic stimulus and protection of their home economy.[12]

To the consternation of the insular government, they chose the latter. When news of Payne's bill reached Manila, a resolution was introduced in the Assembly declaring free trade detrimental to the interests of the Filipino people. Smith promptly got ahold of Osmeña and Quezon and secured, as he thought, their agreement to delay action on the matter. Then he left Manila for Baguio, the summer capital. The Governor General, however, was in no position to defend reciprocal

free trade. At the time, he was himself engaged in an agitated cable correspondence with the BIA, the gist of which was that the Philippines could not afford the loss of revenues that would follow from the Payne Act. The Speaker and Quezon came away from their conversation with Smith feeling that the governor was ambivalent about the matter and that they had leeway to oppose free entry of American goods without alienating the Commission. Osmeña's private thoughts are not known. We do know, however, that Quezon, a member of the committee which had reported favorably the resolutions requesting free access to the American market, believed that reciprocal free trade would create an alliance of interests on both sides of the Pacific committed to retention of the Philippines. Apparently, he decided not to allow the chance of ultimately achieving independence to go by default. On March 27 the Governor General and the Commission being out of the city, Quezon took the floor of the Assembly by pre-arrangement and spoke for two hours against the Payne bill. Placing heavy emphasis upon the revenue question, which he knew was Smith's weak point, and skirting the question of independence, which he knew would be counter-productive in the Assembly's efforts to appear responsible in the eyes of Americans, he focused on the economic implications. Filipinos had asked for free access to United States markets, not for reciprocal free trade. "We did not expect," he said, "that the United States would concede this advantage only on the condition that we conceded an equal and even greater one. When this question . . . has been spoken of [by Americans] it has always been treated as a matter not of commerce, but of humanitarianism." If free trade were to come in this way, it would cause dislocations in some parts of the Philippine economy, and subject the country to an invasion by American trusts and monopolies. After one other speech, a resolution reflecting Quezon's emphases was introduced and unanimously approved. Between the second and third readings a Progresista assemblyman amended it to state also that the links the bill would create were inimical to independence. This, too, was unanimously passed.[13]

Two days later a conference committee from the Assembly met with the Commission at Baguio. It was an awkward encounter. Smith, who had been double-crossed and embarrassed before both his colleagues and his superiors, did most of the talking. He and Forbes pointed out that the restrictions on the size of holdings that could be purchased by a corporation from the public lands (2,500 acres) precluded large-scale American capital investment in Philippine agriculture; they argued that prosperity would hasten, not retard independence; they scoffed at fears of insufficient revenue, claiming that if necessary Filipinos could easily afford to pay more taxes, and promising to seek financial assistance from Congress. The assemblymen, led by Quezon, were having their first face-to-face conflict of major proportions with men who had shortly before been the sole governors of the islands. Their behavior was respectful, but firm. Free trade would produce an inflow of American capital, they insisted, if not in agriculture then in manufacturing and commerce. This would take economic initiative out of Filipinos' hands and jeopardize the achievement of independence by creating new links to the United States. The question was not prosperity, but control. Agreement on this point proving impossible, the meeting adjourned under a face-saving formula. Afterwards, eager to mend his fences with the Commission, Quezon ebulliently told Forbes that the assemblymen had been converted. "Airy persiflage," said Forbes.[14]

Against unusual pressures, the Assembly stuck to its guns. Hord, who was in Washington, cabled his assistant in Manila, the acting collector of internal revenue, to solicit petitions favoring the Payne bill from "all important tobacco and sugar growers" and to use "all internal revenue officers" to launch an educational publicity campaign to stir public support. By April 3 messages and petitions were flooding into Manila from sugar and tobacco growers in nine provinces; twenty-two tobacco manufacturers had come out in favor of the Payne bill, as had newspapers in Iloilo and Pampanga. By April 7 petitions and cables containing approximately 2,100 signatures, including those of "all important sugar and tobacco planters," had been received. In the meantime, Smith had prepared an alternative resolution with some elements of compromise; and he, Forbes, Juan Sumulong, and Rafael Palma lobbied for its passage by the Assembly. Smith suggested to Quezon that the Assembly could reverse itself and still save face by basing its action on the expressed will of its constituents; Forbes met privately with Osmeña and Quezon, even visiting Osmeña twice in the latter's sickroom. The Filipino leaders were polite and conciliatory, never specifically saying no; but on April 7 the Assembly definitively rejected the Commission's alternate resolution.[15]

There was a tendency among the American commissioners to blame the Assembly's original action upon a misunderstanding of the revenue risks, and to chalk off its later refusal to change its stand to the assemblymen's need to save face. However, the Assembly's position in

1909 was consistent both with what it had previously held as to trade relations with the United States and with the apprehension widely expressed by Filipinos that the overt and direct involvement of American private interests in the domestic economy of the Philippines would stultify their aspirations. This was a question of self-interest, and naturally it was perceived differently by different people. The issue of reciprocal free trade was broad enough to touch upon many potentially sore points. Among the Assembly's supporters, for example, were the Filipino Chamber of Commerce and the principal manufacturers of cigars and cigarettes. Both the chamber and the tobacco companies were interested in the development of Philippine industries. Opening the American market would raise the price of leaf tobacco and other raw materials used by such industries, while at the same time the elimination of protection against American manufactured goods would decrease the competitive advantage of insular manufacturers.[16]

Most opponents, however, seem to have agreed that the chief danger in allowing establishment of trade relations from which Americans would reap profit was that this would lead to the investment of American capital. Thus the radical assemblyman Filemon Sotto warned in an Assembly speech that once American business got control of the Philippine market through its tariff advantage over foreign competitors, it would invest in the islands and lobby against their ever being separated from the United States. Pablo Ocampo, then one of the islands' resident commissioners to Washington, had worked diligently to win free access to the American market for Philippine products, and later, at the Assembly's order, to defeat reciprocal advantages for Americans in the Philippine market. In a farewell statement upon his retirement later in 1909, he predicted that free trade would lead to an inflow of American investments that in turn would prevent the development of an economy suited to the needs and redounding to the benefit of Filipinos. He exhorted his countrymen to form "small syndicates purposely organized to fight, even indirectly, the avalanche of American monopolies which I see hovering over our heads." A Spanish observer, noting that opposition to the Payne bill followed upon the heels of a rash of strikes against American-owned businesses in Manila, succinctly remarked: "The rabbits in the Filipino warren notice the approach of the dogs."[17]

None of this prevented Congress from adopting a slightly modified version of the reciprocal provision in Payne's bill. Over the years since the islands had been acquired, it had become clear that Philippine sugar and tobacco growers could not in the foreseeable future produce in volume sufficient to affect the domestic American market seriously, and with this discovery opposition to free entry for these items had declined. In December 1907 General Clarence R. Edwards, chief of the BIA, had arranged a deal with prominent Democratic opponents in the Senate whereby they would withdraw opposition in 1909 if the BIA would agree to let free trade fail in the election year 1908. By 1909, when Edwards' deal was scheduled to pay off, William Howard Taft was President. Taft, of course, had been an urgent advocate of free trade with the Philippines all along. He neutralized remaining congressional opposition by agreeing to compromises that fixed the maximum amount of Philippine sugar to be admitted duty free at 300,000 tons (with preference within this quota given to planters whose annual production did not exceed 500 tons) and set the permissible maximum value for foreign-grown or produced material in manufactured items of either the United States or the Philippines at 20 percent of their total value. With these qualifications, the Philippine provisions of the Payne bill passed handily and became law as part of the Payne-Aldrich Tariff in August 1909. For the President, it was the fulfillment of years of labor and hope. "I am confident," he wrote to his wife, "that it will greatly clear up the difficulties of Philippine politics and Philippine conditions."[18]

Economically, the Payne-Aldrich Act fulfilled the Administration's hopes. On the day after word of its final passage reached Manila, Forbes, who was then acting governor, noted in his journal: "Those fool Assemblymen who voted unanimously against free trade will have a chance to see practically what asses they have made of themselves. . . . Sugar jumped up like mad today, and orders for many millions of cigars are crowding in." Seven months later, things looked even better: "From all over the Islands comes the same story—better crops, more cultivation, better feeling, and more prosperity." In the five year period 1905–09, the average annual gross foreign trade of the Philippines (imports and exports, all countries, including the United States) had been $62,779,922; in the period 1910–14, it rose to $99,632,918. Average annual exports of sugar, 1905–09 had been 127,987 metric tons; for 1910–14, the figure was 184,285. As predicted, trade shifted to the United States. In 1905–09, the United States took 37 percent of Philippine exports and supplied 18 percent of Philippine imports, by value; in the ensuing five years, it took 42 percent of exports and supplied almost 44 percent of imports.[19]

The establishment of free trade did nothing to ease the political situation, however. In fact, in the years immediately after enactment of the Payne-Aldrich Act relations between Filipinos and the American government were worse than at any other time between the official end of the insurrection in 1902 and the outbreak of the cabinet crisis under Leonard Wood in 1923. There were many reasons for this, among them the tactics of the ostensibly pro-American Progresista Party. The Progresistas' position was mortifying. The Nacionalistas, having portrayed them in the campaign as less nationalistic and less trustful toward the Filipino people, behaved once they had won the elections just like Progresistas. They had contrived to be all things to all men, emotional partisans of Philippine nationality and Filipino competence on the stump and responsible partners in tutelage inside the government. The Progresistas, naturally, resolved to expose their rivals as two-faced. This, of course, embarrassed Osmeña and Quezon before both their constituents and their party colleagues and rendered cooperation with the government increasingly difficult. As early as April 1908 the Progresista paper in the Speaker's home province had written tauntingly: "Everyone recalls the fact that the Assembly has done nothing so far on behalf of the independence of the Philippines and it is because Osmeña has so decreed. It is because the much discussed Cebuan politician does not care to displease the American government." Later that year, when Commissioner Palma joined the rest of the Commission in sending a congratulatory cable to President-elect Taft, *La Democracia* ran a large picture of Palma beneath a headline reading: "El Progresismo Gana un Nuevo Proselito."[20]

The danger in this was not that Progresistas might defeat the Nacionalistas, but rather that they might so embarrass the party as to split it into factions and impair the ability of the Speaker to carry on cooperative government with the Commission. Ironically, this possibility was increased by the Nacionalistas' stunning victory in the Assembly elections of November 1909. On the one hand, with 62 out of 81 seats in the Assembly, but only 17 of these 62 in the hands of re-elected members of the previous legislature, the Nacionalistas were ripe for intra-party dissension. On the other hand, the Progresistas reacted to their defeat by moving to the left, thereby exerting pressure on the Nacionalistas to do likewise in order to maintain their advantage.

Following the example of their counterparts in the Partido Federal of 1904 and 1905, the regional committees and provincial representatives to the Progresistas' annual convention forced their central committee to agree to appeal for a prompt declaration of intent by the United States. The convention adopted and sent to Congress a resolution calling for an immediate pledge of eventual independence, basing its action largely upon the need for a guarantee that the investment of American and other foreign capital would not stultify hopes for Philippine freedom.[21]

Since few Nacionalistas supposed that independence itself could be had immediately, the two parties had come by 1910 to occupy almost identical positions as to future relations with the United States. For both, the essential point was that the United States define its intentions before continuing with tutelage and development. One recognizes and allows for the political motives involved in the presentation of demands apparently in excess of what many members of both parties thought desirable. Nevertheless, it is clear that immediate definition—as distinct from immediate independence—had become the common denominator in Philippine politics. Even Pardo de Tavera, who was in political retirement by 1910, agreed. "It is curious to observe how the separation, and more than separation,—the antagonism between Americans and Filipinos has been increasing here," he wrote to his former protégé Quezon. "I do not believe it can be said that we have a bad government; but the fact is that in spite of the establishment of the Assembly, and other advances in the interior political condition of the Philippines, not only has it failed to gain the affection and confidence of the people, but the strange thing is that it has lost much of what it had already gained. . . . It is simply through this persistence in not saying in a clear and frank manner that some day independence will be given. Naturally, upon seeing that there is a desire to elude making this declaration, it is understood that they do not wish to promise that which they do not wish to concede."[22] With both parties agreed as to the need for the United States immediately to pledge itself to the principle that the Philippines should in due course be independent, and the party in power committed by its platform to a far more radical position, the possibility of continued cooperative government by Americans and Filipinos within Taft's framework of indefinite retention and open-ended nation building was small indeed.

In spite of mounting obstacles, the cooperative relationship within the government survived for a while longer on the strength of personal links between the men holding the offices of Governor General and Speaker. Little by little, Cameron Forbes and Sergio Osmeña had come into what any Filipino would recognize as a relationship of mutual obligation, an amalgam in this case of official and unofficial hospitality at Baguio and Cebu, of executive and legislative give and take, and of growing personal affection. One need scarcely repeat what Osmeña had done for Forbes. The governor, for his part, responded with patronage and public works, and with marks of official esteem. At the Speaker's request, Forbes made Cebu the first province he visited after his inauguration; and he regularly allowed Osmeña the use of a Coast Guard cutter for even unofficial voyages of a personal or political nature.

The personal side of this relationship lasted for as long as Forbes and Osmeña lived; politically, its zenith passed in the year 1910. At the outset of that year both men needed a special session of the legislature; Forbes, because the long-range success of his road-building program depended upon the legislature's making permanent the double cedula tax by which most road revenues were raised; Osmeña, because until the newly elected members were organized and the Second Philippine Legislature begun, the position of Speaker was vacant and he had no patronage or appropriations with which to maintain his power. In February, therefore, they agreed to a special session, each undertaking to assure passage of the other's prime measures. From then on things moved with a kind of precision rare in legislative circles. Dominador Gomez, proclaiming himself "a patriot of steel" and Osmeña a "patriot of hojaldre,"* undertook to organize a coalition of radical Nacionalistas and Progresistas to make either himself or Pablo Ocampo Speaker. Forbes passed the word to Progresista leaders that were they to ally with radicals he would cut them off without executive patronage; and Osmeña, taking them on the rebound, coolly told them that he would win no matter what combination might be organized, and that their assignments to committees would depend upon their voting for one of their own, not for a rebel Nacionalista. The rebellion wilted, and Osmeña was elected Speaker with 56 out of 79 votes. He then returned Forbes' favor, burying the permanent double cedula provision deep in an omnibus bill entitled "An Act to amend Act Numbered Eighty-three, entitled 'The Provinical Government Act,' by further extending the powers of provincial governments

---

* *Hojaldre* is a pastry made in the southern islands. It was particularly associated with Cebu.

in certain particulars," and securing its passage. Finally, in an extraordinary act of personal good will, the Speaker rammed through at 4 o'clock in the morning during the last meeting of the session, an act ratifying after the fact Forbes' highly controversial deportation of twelve Chinese during the previous summer, a matter for which the government was then being sued in the courts.[23]

For Forbes, this was all very well. Within a week of the session's end, he wrote to the Secretary of War asking for authority to shift the government's patronage still further from Progresistas to Nacionalistas. Later that year, after Forbes had discreetly raised the issue with Taft himself, the President gave his approval. But for Osmeña the results of the special session were painful. The Speaker's domination of the Assembly had been so overwhelming as to raise hackles, and for those who were out of sorts the ratification of Forbes' deportations was an issue of emotional potency. Not only was it irregular (because after the fact), it was a precedent which, for all anyone knew, might be applied to justify high-handed executive acts against Filipinos. Above all, it seemed to symbolize that close relationship between the Speaker and the American government which was detrimental, in the eyes of some, to independence and, in the eyes of others, to their own political advancement. Less than a week after the session's close, Osmeña traveled to Malolos, the former capital of the Philippine Republic, where at the instigation of Teodoro Sandiko, a radical Nacionalista and former governor of the province, he was met by signs reading "Away with Osmeña" and was prevented on two occasions from speaking. At the end of the day, he was followed to his train by a crowd whistling and crying out "Kill the Assembly!" "Away with Osmeña!" and—sardonically—"Viva America!" Several nights later, the Speaker's name was booed at a mass meeting in Tondo, a district of Manila, apparently because of his role in pressing the deportation measure. And in the days that followed, both Osmeña and his wife were the objects of protest and personal discourtesies.[24]

Osmeña was a skilled political strategist, and he was not at a loss to know how to combat this turn of events. He moved to the left and escalated his rhetoric. At first the change was almost imperceptible. On May 7, at San Miguel de Mayumo, Bulacan, not far distant from Malolos, he proclaimed that war having failed, the Assembly was the agent for fulfillment of the people's revolutionary ideal: "Yesterday, it is true, we fell in the struggle, but that ideal, which did not fall yesterday, now stands and will stand." Slowly and carefully, as was his wont, he built upon this theme, until in July 1910 he openly avowed, to great applause from participants at a banquet in Manila, that should the Filipino people wish to revert to their former means of pursuing the ideal he would abide by their decision.[25]

The summer of 1910 was a turning point in many respects; for not only had cooperative relations between Forbes and the Speaker become an embarrassment to the latter, but the issue of capital investment and its effect upon the political and economic future of the Philippines, raised at the time of the Payne-Aldrich controversy, was coming into focus. As Filipinos had foreseen, American investors took a new look at the Philippine Islands after the establishment of reciprocal free trade. Prevented by law from acquiring blocs of more than 2,500 acres of public land per corporation—an amount much too small for efficient, mechanized agricultural production—they turned their attention to private holdings and to the former friar estates purchased by the government in 1903.

The friar estates had been purchased in order to remove a chronic social and economic irritant from Philippine life and avoid transference to the United States of the animosity felt by tenants toward the Spanish government because of its identification with the friar landlords. Wherever the lands in question were occupied, the government undertook to survey them and sell them to the actual tenants on a 25-year installment purchase plan. From the outset, the administration of the estates proved an economic burden. In the fiscal year 1907, for example, revenue from the friar lands was ₱226,627.63, as against administrative expenses of ₱657,083.78 and additional costs for irrigation and surveying of approximately $220,000. In September 1909 the chief of the BIA wrote sardonically to Acting Governor Forbes that it might be a saving to the government simply to give away the whole property. The Philippine legislature, in the hope of encouraging the purchase of unoccupied land by third parties, and thereby reducing expenses, specifically exempted such property from the limitations otherwise placed upon the sale of public lands, provided the purchaser was an individual rather than a corporation.[26]

In the first week of September 1909 a member of the New York law firm Cadwallader & Strong, of which Henry Taft was a partner, called at the BIA and talked with the assistant chief, Frank McIntyre, about the possibilities for the purchase of land for agricultural use in the Philippines. McIntyre informed him that the insular government could not sell large units of land from the public domain and apparently was not at the time prepared to do so from the friar estates. The attorney transmitted this to his clients, and there the matter rested until late October, when one E. L. Poole, who unknown to the BIA had been simultaneously negotiating in Manila with the insular government for the purchase of the large, virtually unoccupied San José estate on the island of Mindoro, told the insular authorities he had been informed such a sale would be illegal. Steps were taken to assure both Poole and the Cadwallader & Strong attorney that this was incorrect. No one in the government either in Manila or Washington as yet knew who the principal or principals might be. On November 22 the Washington *Evening Star* broke a story that "agents of the Sugar Trust" had purchased 55,000 acres of undeveloped Philippine lands; and the following day a new lawyer from a different firm appeared at the BIA to announce that he "thought" his clients were the purchasers alluded to in the *Star*, that they were, in any case, negotiating for the 58,000 acre San José estate, and that they wanted an opinion from the United States Department of Justice as to the legality of actually completing the purchase. He named his clients—Horace Havemeyer, of the family which controlled the American Sugar Refining Company, Charles J. Welch, and one Senff—and described their intention to build a modern sugar estate at a cost of more than "a million and a quarter." In the meantime, Poole, who was indeed the Manila agent of Havemeyer, Welch & Senff, had signed an agreement with the insular government to purchase the estate the following January.[27]

The matter was held in abeyance and submitted to the Secretary of War and the United States Attorney General, who decided respectively that there was no objection to such a purchase on grounds either of public policy or of legality. Taft himself was then consulted. The President considered the sale a windfall, a means of unloading what he had always supposed a relatively worthless estate. "I saw an opportunity to help the Government to $300,000," he was later to write, "and to increase the agricultural investment in a backward island by double that sum." He was convinced that Mindoro was not prime sugar land, and that even if the purchaser should prove to be the Sugar Trust, acquisition of an estate there could not prejudice the well-being of Filipino sugar producers in better locations. On this basis, approval of the sale was authorized. On December 30, after the decision had been made, the American Sugar Refining Company specifically denied having any interest whatever in the San José transaction. On January 4, 1910, the estate was officially purchased for ₱674,000, a gain of more than ₱76,000 over the price paid for it by the insular government.[28]

This seemed at the time to be an opening wedge, and capital conscious Americans in Manila were excited. In the next several months there were reports that large tracts in the Isabela and Calamba friar estates were being eyed by American investors and that private holdings in Pampanga and Nueva Ecija, as well, might be purchased. "There can be no doubt that the Payne Bill is responsible for the interest excited," one American paper exulted, "and that capital has only commenced to realize the possibilities for well directed investment here." Meanwhile, in the United States, anti-imperialists and others opposed to developing the Philippines under the auspices of American private capital, launched a counterattack. Under the prodding of the Anti-Imperialist League and a Colorado congressman with beet sugar-growing constituents, congressmen introduced a flurry of resolutions calling for information on the insular government's dealings and relations with private capital. In June 1910 a resolution was passed directing the Committee on Insular Affairs to make a complete investigation of the Philippine Department of the Interior in its operations having to do with land.[29]

The sale of unoccupied friar lands and the prospect of increased American investment in Philippine agriculture led to further clarification of the views of Filipino leaders toward capital and development. It is notable that as to the investments themselves, Filipino reaction was more complacent than that of American critics. Knowledgeable Filipinos were aware that more than 4/5 of the land area of the islands was in the public domain, where by common consent the congressional limitations applied. Of the rest, most was occupied by Filipinos. The amount of land to which the San José precedent applied was presumably no more than 200,000 acres.[30] Later, in 1911 and 1912, when their hands had been forced by the campaign of American opponents of the measure, Filipino politicians waxed eloquent over the need to make the standard limitations on the sale of public lands applicable to the friar estates. Quezon, in fact, became so aggressive in Congress that General Edwards threatened to have him removed as resident commissioner if he persisted in his course. In the summer of 1910, however, when the issue was new, the primary objection of Filipino political leaders was not to the investment of American capital in Philippine land, but to the fact that this investment took place without Filipinos' being in a position of political control.

It is true that when Secretary of War Jacob M. Dickinson visited the islands in August, Osmeña and the Progresista leader, Vicente Singson Encarnación, petitioned him jointly for application of the standard limits on the sale of public lands to the friar lands. Their request, however, was buried deep in a memorandum devoted primarily to a request that Filipinos be allowed to draft a constitution for the islands.[31] The views held by the hierarchy of the majority party are clear in the separate memorial of the Nacionalista Party composed by Osmeña and handed to Dickinson on September 1, 1910.

Osmeña's memorial, although overly long, is a brilliant piece of political analysis, a perceptive appeal to Americans to commit themselves to eventual Philippine independence and in the interval to lighten their tutelary direction, promote filipinization of the higher echelons of government, and aim for a government whose spirit and form would be Filipino, not American. "The American government," he wrote, "needs the cooperation of the people, it needs the support of the Filipinos [if it wishes] to convince the country of the generous and altruistic intentions that have prompted it to remain in the Islands. . . ." But so long as the Philippines' future was left undefined, American and Filipino residents of the islands would be in conflict: "Few of the Americans who associate with the Filipinos can listen calmly to the Filipinos' claims to independence, while many treat it with ridicule as an impossible thing. On the other hand, the Filipinos who trust in the good faith and sincerity of [the American] policy can, in view of these demonstrations by Americans, scarcely infuse a ray of hope in the minds of their countrymen." Cooperation in the development and modernization of the country was compromised as trust failed. The case of capital was illustrative:

All the Filipinos believe the development of the now unproductive natural resources of the land to be necessary and understand the need for the aid of capital from without; but at the same time they cry out against the policy of selling large tracts of land to corporations, against the granting of perpetual franchises to railway companies, against the great privileges granted to public-service companies, and against the preponderance of commercial communities and interests. This apparent inconsistence has its origin in the firm belief that the future of the people is threatened by the invasion of that capital, which, once invested here, will when the time comes be opposed to any change of sovereignty, because it will not consider itself to be sufficiently safe and protected, except under its own. If this government were the image and creature of the people, these fears would not be entertained, and the present cries of protest would be converted into shouts of praise and benediction, because the people would have complete faith and entire certainty that their interests and their future in the hands of such a government would be under the protection of such guarantees as to permit the development of native capital together with the foreign.

The time had come for a new initiative to restore the integrity and appeal of the original policy. "If it is presumed that the basis of the policy followed in the Philippines is the preparation of the Filipinos for the exercise of the powers of an independent government, we fail to see how under the present system such an end can be assured." The United States should pledge itself to Philippine independence and place Filipinos promptly in policy-making positions.[32]

Despite the obvious political motivation behind Osmeña's request for more and better jobs, this was advice which the Taft administration would have been well advised to take seriously. In retrospect, one perceives that it embodied the authentic Nacionalista insight: that actual independence ought to wait until development and reform had taken hold, that good will and mutual trust were essential in the interval and desirable at all times, and that instead of gradualism and trust there would be haste and recrimination unless Americans ended their apparent deceitfulness and spoke frankly to the issues raised by Filipinos' self-respect. Far from precluding evolution toward some sort of permanent association, the course recommended by Osmeña was, in the changed circumstances of 1910, the only one by which time could be gained in which mutually beneficial links might appear and flourish. The Secretary of War's visit made this strikingly clear.

Dickinson was an old friend of Taft, who knew him as a former attorney for the Illinois Central Railroad and a force of some potence in Tennessee politics. He had a careful, judicious mind, and little sympathy for Forbes' pursuit of results without regard for the nice points of means—"That is the trouble with Mr. Forbes," he once exclaimed to a Manila editor. "He is like Roosevelt; he wants to do the practical thing whether or not he has authority in law." Both the BIA and the insular government had been slightly concerned about what was taken to be a lack of sympathy in the secretary; and on the long voyage out to Manila in 1910, General Edwards did his best to indoctrinate him through "a mapped-out program of daily morning hours" of study. "Pouring over maps and seeing the area, the difficulties of communication, the different tribes and languages and the grand way the United States has started on the problems, really absorb him," Edwards reported. "For the first time he is getting infected, and the beckoning from the East rather than the call is in his blood. His visit, I am sure, will be a revelation."[33]

Throughout Dickinson's visit, Nacionalistas and other ostensibly radical Filipinos loudly proclaimed their desire for early independence. In most cases, however, independence was invoked for its symbolic and political value; what was sought was something appreciably less. Thus, a Nacionalista orator in Albay, who had praised American development efforts, but asked for independence even so, later sent an informal apology to the secretary, explaining that the latter part of his remarks had been politically expedient. What repeatedly shows through in such requests for independence is an intention to assert its desirability and force from Americans, not the thing itself, but recognition of Filipinos' right to it, with no strings attached. *La Vanguardia*, regretting that agitation for independence had "embittered" Dickinson's visit, justified the demonstrations he had encountered on the grounds that they were necessary to disabuse Americans of their assumption that Filipinos could, in effect, be bought off: "Remember that among other arguments of President Taft to justify to the American people the retention of the Islands, he said that in the measure they were Americanized, the Filipinos would forget their national ideals, preferring to live always under the banner of the U.S. Let the great American people see how twelve years of Americanization, instead of killing the Ideal in the soul of the Filipinos, have strengthened it through painful tests." When Dickinson, in a major speech, enunciated the customary Taft doctrine that Americans were not opposed to Filipinos' aspiring to be independent, but that for the time being Filipinos must eschew political agitation and, instead, cooperate "in all just and reasonable efforts to advance the material interests and prosperity of the people," *El Ideal* replied that for Filipinos to labor in good faith, certain assurances were necessary. Among these were reform of the schools to produce "Filipinized Filipinos" instead of "Americanized Filipinos," definition of the terms under which Americans would relinquish sovereignty to Filipinos, and adoption of a policy of favoring Filipino over American private interests whenever the two were in conflict.[34]

The reactions of Forbes and Dickinson to this cry for definition and for credible evidence of American good faith were quite different. On Dickinson's final night in the Philippines a large banquet was given in his honor by a committee of Filipinos. The speakers were blunt. A Spaniard complained of high taxes; a Progresista criticized the sale of the San José estate and warned of a danger from foreign trusts; Quezon and Osmeña spoke in behalf of independence. Forbes, stung, responded coldly. He ridiculed the first two speakers, and then, turning his attention to the remarks of Quezon and Osmeña, continued archly: "There has been some talk of politics, and the amount of the political agitation in the Philippine Islands today. Just so long as you Filipinos can continue to increase the business and trade of the Islands twenty-five percent annually, you can talk just as much as you want to about politics. All we want is that you do not let it reach a point that will disturb the public order, and interfere with the business of the country." After this thinly veiled threat by Forbes, Dickinson spoke. The secretary was no pushover. Only the day before, he had startled a petitioner for immediate independence by replying bluntly, "Well you won't get it, that's all." But he had a sense for the politic that Forbes lacked. He was out to soothe tempers and remove irritants. Earlier in his visit, he had orally passed the word to Forbes to be governed in future sales of friar lands by the standard limitations applicable to public lands and, beyond that, to sell friar lands only to Filipinos already in occupancy. Now, he set out to assure Filipinos that Americans recognized the legitimacy of their aspirations. While reiterating Taft's prediction that in time Filipinos might not wish to separate themselves fully from the United States, he added: "Voicing my personal views, I say without qualification, that I would not be here to represent or further any plan which contemplated the denial of ultimate Philippine independence, and that I would be glad if the conditions which would justify in the American mind Philippine independence existed today. It is a consummation devoutly to be prayed for."[35]

The Filipino press was delighted. Dickinson had shown a "noble desire to impel us upward," wrote *La Vanguardia*, whereas Forbes, by "certain insulting phrases" and a "lack of political tact," had been "discouraging and depressing." In Forbes' address, *La Vanguardia* continued, "Good will towards the Filipino people is conspicuous by its absence."[36]

This growing polarization of Filipino and American leaders over issues of capital investment, political definition, and administrative devolution was paralleled by the emergence of a pattern of hostility and recrimination in informal social and cultural relations of the American and Filipino communities in the islands. From the beginning, racial awareness had been high on both sides. For Filipinos, assertion of racial dignity and self-respect had been an important motive behind the revolutionary activities of the late 1890's. Article IV of Emilio Jacinto's *Teachings of the Katipunan* proclaims: "All men are equal, be the color of their skin black or white. One may be superior to another in knowledge, wealth and beauty but cannot be superior in being." For many Americans this was a difficult conclusion to accept: "We are advised that the army has alienated a good many of our Filipino friends . . . ," Taft wrote in 1900, "and given them the impression, which ladies of the army certainly seem to have, that they regard the Filipino ladies and men as 'niggers' and as not fit to be associated with. We propose so far as we are able to banish this idea from their mind." Taft fought overt racism as best he could, believing correctly that racial hostility would preclude the growth of shared interests: "The blind folly and weak viciousness of short-sighted Americans who yield to a small-minded prejudice . . . obstructs the progress of the policy of attraction which must be our fundamental hope for the success of the experiment we are making there." But even he, in appealing for a spirit of fraternity between the two peoples, condescendingly pronounced Filipinos Americans' "little brown brothers."[37]

There was almost infinite variety in the ways Americans expressed their condescension or contempt for Filipinos. Bishop Brent, dilating upon the American *mission civilisatrice* in the Philippines, wrote in *The Outlook* that Filipinos had been "awake" for some time: "What the Americans have done is to get the Filipinos out of bed. They are now instructing them how to dress themselves." Frederick O'Brien, editor of the *Cablenews-American,* told an American reporter: "The Filipinos have to be led by the hand. They have no initiative. . . . [O]nly by occidental civilization and leadership can they be lifted from the slough of ignorance and sloth, in which they have wallowed contentedly for centuries." Typically, Americans who married Filipinas were subject to social ostracism and, in the opinion of one such, discrimination in government employment. When General J. Franklin Bell, in a conciliatory public address, urged Americans to show better understanding and greater sympathy for Filipinos' points of view, a public outcry from resident Americans forced him later to clarify his remarks: he had not said that Filipinos were the racial equals of whites, General Bell insisted; that would be too broad a generalization.[38]

The appearance of Filipino politicians in positions of real power raised American hackles and resulted in additional expressions of scorn and outrage. *The Manila Times,* editorializing over the results of the 1908 elections for the Municipal Board of the city, exploded into capital letters: "THEY WOULD SET UP OVER US ALL, MEN WITH WHOM WE DECLINE TO EVEN BRUSH ELBOWS IN THE STREETS." Three years later in a fit of irritation, the same paper chalked off the second most powerful Filipino in the government as "little Manny Quezon." The *Cablenews-American,* referring to the Manila elections of 1908, pronounced haughtily: "The natives have befouled their own nest, and must pay the penalty."[39]

For the time being, we can only guess at how such attitudes were expressed in encounters between American and Filipino individuals. We do know, however, that even Forbes, whose personal courtesies and hospitality to Filipinos won him lifelong friends, was given to thinking in highly racial terms. The adjective "white" appears in countless places in his journal to signify decency, honor, and good bearing, as, for example, in the comment, "Smith, as I have many times noted, was a wholly white person." Or the following remark, which comes on the same page as a strong denunciation of the *Cablenews* for the "asininity of stirring up a race feeling that might as well lie": "The Egans are a constant source of delight, witty, white and she a marvel with the guitar." In times of crisis, Forbes was wont to confer privately with the American commissioners without the knowledge of their Filipino colleagues. And in a farewell letter, advising his successor to acquire a Filipino secretary, he added gratuitously, "He need not live in the house, and could be taken from among Filipinos who have been educated in the States."[40]

Filipinos' response to the elemental question of racial prejudice was compromised by their unwillingness to identify with American Negroes. In part, this may reflect the especially intense hostility felt between Filipinos and blacks during the fighting in the insurrection. But beyond that, it shows awareness that Filipinos had a higher status, ironically, as "wards of the nation" than Negroes did as citizens. This advantage is implicit in Taft's remark, quoted above, distinguishing "our Filipino friends" from what Army wives had called them, namely "niggers." It is further apparent in the tendency of Filipinos to refer to "the colored race" by the pronoun "they." The resulting ambivalence shows plainly in an editorial charging that Filipino doctors at the Philippine General Hospital had been discriminated against because of their color. "The eight Filipino doctors who are in the hospital now," the editorial expostulates, "work like veritable negroes."[41]

Be that as it might, there was no difficulty in recognizing and replying to the general tone of condescension. The Filipino press of the Forbes years is filled with commentaries and protests, some of which are bathetic or laughable, but some of which are stunning in both perception and style. "Fill your coffers with gold, stock your granaries with *palay*, in a word, be millionaires and you will be independent," a speaker at the annual Teachers' Assembly had advised Filipinos in 1911: "He who enters a house, not by the door but by some other way is a thief. To enter the temple of liberty you must not climb through the windows because you will be thieves, but you must enter through the door. And the only door is material wealth. There is no other except it." To which *El Ideal*, controlled by the Speaker and Commissioner Palma, replied in an editorial entitled "Sophisms—and nothing more": "He who enters his own house can do so through the windows, the roof, the walls, can even tear it down without thereby meriting the denomination of thief."[42] In August 1912 *La Vanguardia* in an editorial of admittedly hyperbolical qualities, turned the force of sarcasm on the whole American pretension:

I saw him this morning parading through the streets of Manila his imperious haughtiness as the man of a superior race. I looked at him, but only for a second, because his haughty attitude, his proud and humiliating gaze and his [harmonious?] elegance compelled me to desist from my contemplation of that bristly and intangible figure.

He is an interesting type because of his superiority, because he is exotic. He is no figment of a feverish fantasy. He is not a delirium of a fever patient. He is a real personage who plays the part of a protagonist in the great colonial comedy. He is the providential man of history who directs and guides events.

The people venerate that personage of an almost supernatural character. Destiny, the supreme dictator of the world, has surrounded him with a luminous aureole of prestige and glory. Privileges are for him, prerogatives for him also. And the people are compelled to recognize those distinctions of his. He is white, he is a dominator, he is rich, he is strong, he has war machines, he is wise and he is feared by the world. The people are colored, dominated, poor, weak, they have scarcely a bolo to kill their animals, ignorant and scorned by everybody. Does not this difference of conditions really give the former a relative superiority? The master goes to the club, the opera, the races. The people hide themselves in a suspicious shack and sit beside a table with a green cloth, they go to the cock-pit, which is not at all a decent place, and if they want to see theatrical performances they go to the humble *moro-moro* comedies. Therefore, the master thinks he has a right to do what he pleases with the people when they trouble him. Has one of the latter obstructed his passage on the sidewalk? Push him. Has one brushed his neat suit in the street-car? Push him. In fine, it is all reduced to pushes, if not to clubbings and kicks. After all, what consideration can a dirty and ignorant *tao*, whose intimacy with the spurred and crested "biped" has reduced him to the ranks of its most intimate friend, merit from decent persons? What treatment can a semi-savage, who eats rice with his fingers and talks a language which is not a language but a string of ill-sounding monosyllables which vex one's ears, expect? Why should one show any consideration for persons who belong to the lowest social scale, who have a flat nose, thick lips and simian aspect, with tattooing and breach-clouts, who eat raw meat, the last representatives of an inferior and primitive caste destined to disappear before the impulse of civilization?

Fortunately for the natives, the dominator is so paternal and good-hearted that it does not occur to him to treat them as they really merit, because of their low condition. Thanks that the master has the patience to instruct them.[43]

By the opening of the legislative session in November 1910 the lines had been drawn for a confrontation between the Nacionalista leaders and Governor General Forbes. The pressures upon Osmeña were obvious. In the first week of November, he frankly informed Forbes that people felt they were too much in accord, and that a conflict between them would be good strategy. Forbes, for his part, was under pressure from at least two and possibly three of the other four Americans on the Commission to end what they called "trafficking" with Osmeña: to call a halt to the creation of new *per diem* assignments for assemblymen between sessions, to the use by the Speaker of a Coast Guard cutter for his private business, and to the favoritism shown to Cebu in public works appropriations. Instead of lulling political agitation, open-ended government was intensifying anxiety and contentiousness over the eventual outcome, and men in the middle were being called upon to show their true colors.[44]

Two issues, the election of resident commissioners to Washington and the demand of both Filipino political parties that Filipinos be permitted to draft their own constitution, brought matters to a head.

Of these, the first was by far the more important; for while the Commission could and did simply table the Assembly's resolution requesting authority to prepare a constitution, agreement between the two houses was required for the election of commissioners to represent the islands in the United States, and the deadlock between them became a prolonged combat of rising emotional intensity. The problem in the election of resident commissioners was that the Assembly refused to re-elect Benito Legarda, who had held his post since 1907; and the Commission, acting on orders from President Taft, refused to consent to the re-election of Quezon, who had been a resident commissioner since 1909, unless the Assembly went along with Legarda. American observers were inclined to see in the Assembly's action a thinly veiled design on the Speaker's part to deprive Quezon of a post in which he had been gaining so much notoriety as to become a rival to Osmeña. And as the weeks went on and the deadlock continued, Quezon himself seems to have leaned toward this or a similar view. Apparently, however, Osmeña was dealing from a position of weakness, not of power, and was aiming by his leadership of the Assembly's fight against the Commission not to undermine Quezon but to improve his own standing in Filipino politics. The Speaker's close friend Jaime de Veyra assured Quezon that if necessary funds would be collected privately to maintain him in Washington.[45]

Osmeña had chosen his issue with great skill. Legarda was genuinely unpopular in the Assembly, and his opposition to independence made him a highly unrepresentative figure. De facto practice in the past had been for each house to select one of the two resident commissioners; now, to the astonishment of the Commission's conference committee, Osmeña pressed the logic of representation, arguing that the resident commissioners, unless they were to be redundant to the BIA, ought both to represent the Filipino people and therefore had to be acceptable to the elected house of the legislature. Osmeña himself felt that his basic position, the demand for a more truly representative form of government, went to the very heart of the differences between Americans and Filipinos. And rising young Filipinos such as de Veyra and Teodoro M. Kalaw were awed by the energy and perceptiveness with which he pressed the argument. The Commission, whose basic position was far less idealistic—namely, that the President wanted Legarda and that the Assembly should not encroach upon established powers of the upper house—showed to poor advantage. In January 1911 the conference between the two houses was broken off inconclusively; and the United States Congress subsequently extended the terms of the incumbents until 1912.[46]

Against this background, other deadlocks were also developing between the Commission and the Assembly. The Speaker wanted his newspaper, *El Ideal*, placed on an equal footing with *La Democracia* and certain others that received government advertising; the Commission refused. The Assembly wanted to lower the qualifications for Filipino surveyors in the government service. The Commission objected; and as a result, the cadastral survey bill failed. The Commission insisted on higher rates for water provided by government irrigation works than the Assembly would tolerate and held out for government ownership against an Assembly provision to turn the works over to property owners in due course; this bill, too, failed. Special appropriations for fighting rinderpest and locusts failed in the Assembly, at least in part because they were known to be of special interest to Forbes. Finally, after waiting for 85 of the 90 days in the session for the Assembly to pass a general appropriation bill, the Commission passed one of its own. The Assembly's Committee on Privileges ruled that in so doing, the Commission had encroached on the traditional right of lower houses to initiate money bills. Whereupon, the Assembly, over-riding Osmeña's floor leaders and committee chairmen, voted a bill slashing general appropriations by ₱2,000,000, but increasing the Assembly's own appropriation by ₱25,000. The Commission, aware of course that a provision of the Organic Act automatically renewed the previous year's appropriation in the event no bill should pass, stuck its ground. In conference, Forbes, tired and under great pressure from Commissioners Gilbert and Elliott to make an example of the Assembly's irresponsible action, ridiculed the Assembly conferees. Whereupon, the appropriation bill failed, as well. To finish things off, the governor denied the Assembly a special session, a financial bonus it had come to expect on the basis of previous years' events.[47]

While the Speaker was moving into confrontation with the insular government in Manila, Quezon was following a similar course in Washington. During his first year as resident commissioner, he had been relatively diffident, concentrating with his senior colleague Legarda on opposition to high taxes and on promoting structural changes such as separation of the executive from the legislative powers in the insular government. It was altogether a lackluster performance. Quezon didn't personally believe that Philippine taxes were too high; and Legarda, who was so conservative as to worry over even suggestions for an elective senate, usually kept him from asking for independence. Evidently, Quezon felt he was doing little more than keeping the Philippines before American public opinion. "My opinion is that we don't so much need to have delegates here as to have a press," he wrote to Jaime de Veyra; "and the money which has to be spent for the delegates ought to be spent on a publication."[48]

All this changed in December 1910 when Quezon, like Osmeña, moved visibly to the left. As in the case of the Speaker, one can only guess at his motives. The emergence of Democratic control in the House after the elections of 1910 made outright opposition to the Taft administration politically feasible for the first time; and Quezon alluded to this when attempting to stir up independence agitation in the Philippines in support of his new efforts. Moreover, he seems to have felt a need to become indispensable at just that time, when his re-election was stalemated. A letter to Jaime de Veyra in January 1911 argued his indispensability on the grounds that he had established close alliances with Democratic leaders for the promotion of independence resolutions.[49]

Beyond these plausible motivations there is the fact that Quezon, like Osmeña, was a man of the middle, neither a retentionist nor a true partisan of immediate independence. Apparently he believed that a firm commitment to independence by the United States would be a moderating force in Philippine politics. In March 1911 he wrote to Osmeña: "It's necessary to know once and for all if they are going to give us independence or not, and if they are going to give it to us, when they intend to give it to us. From here I see very clearly the tendency of our people, each day more hostile toward the Government and if our situation isn't resolved promptly and definitively I don't know where we're going to wind up. On the other hand, the Government ought to know in an unequivocal manner that our aspiration to be independent isn't fictitious." Despite Quezon's efforts, the Democratic caucus omitted Philippine independence from its list of measures to be taken up in the special session of Congress in spring 1911; and no legislation on the subject passed in the House. As the certainty of this outcome increased, a theme began to emerge in Quezon's correspondence: the present government is insensitive to Filipinos' interests and can no longer be suffered in peace; change and definition are essential; a policy of moderate and responsible opposition should be undertaken in the hope of emphasizing Filipino grievances and creating a condition in American public opinion that will force American political parties to make concessions to Filipinos. To associates in the islands, he wrote: "I advise you that by all legal means, and demonstrating always moderation and reasonableness, you make the Government see that the people of the Philippines is really and truly disgusted by the present state of things. A politics of op-position can't occasion you any injury, provided it be responsible, and I am convinced that it is the only way to obtain some concessions from the Government." Not only Filipinos seeking immediate inde-pendence, but also those wishing simply for continued evolution toward filipinization, had an interest in fighting for prompt congres-sional action, Quezon wrote to Osmeña: "I am convinced that if the conduct of the Philippines continues as [it has] up to now, not only will we not obtain independence[,] but what is worse, we will not obtain from the Government any other concession tending toward the Filipinization of the service."[50]

Wherefore, Quezon launched a vigorous lobby for Philippine in-dependence in the United States. By the end of May, after conferring repeatedly with Congressman William Atkinson Jones, Democratic chairman of the House Committee on Insular Affairs, he was pre-dicting that in the next session of Congress legislation would pass effecting major reforms in the Organic Act: an elective senate, separa-tion of executive from legislative powers, explicit extension of limits on land sales to the friar lands. The following month, in a letter sent to all congressmen, he argued that there were only two solutions to the Philippine problem "that will do justice to the Filipino people and honor to the United States." The first was to give independence within two years; the second to declare at once an intention to give independence within eight years by means of a shared transfer of power and responsibility. The campaign was a great success in at-tracting attention to the Philippine issue. The press in Manila was filled with reports of Quezon's doings, and plans which had been entertained in some circles to send the radical Nacionalista Teodoro Sandiko to supplement or replace him faded.[51]

The intensified polarization that characterized political and gov-ernmental relations during the legislative session of 1910–11 lasted for as long as Forbes remained Governor General. In July 1911 Osmeña warned Forbes once again that he would have to keep to the left of the administration. In the meantime, Forbes had been reinforced in his new position of firmness by word from Taft himself. "I know just how the Filipinos have been acting and they have got to be made to understand that there are limits beyond which they cannot go," the President had told Forbes' private emissary. "This ought to be made very clear to Mr. Osmeña and the others. I know how they have been crowding and trying to encroach and I know their pretensions. I know just how capable they are. I am fully prepared for a break with the Assembly . . . and please say to Mr. Forbes that I will firmly support him when it comes. Those people must be handled with firmness always." In such circumstances a new collision was all but inevitable.[52]

A clerical error by a member of Forbes' staff provided a *cause célèbre* around which hostilities arose. In January 1912 Forbes undertook to rearrange the allotment of funds within the general sum automatically reappropriated in the previous session upon failure of the appropriation bill. By mistake a subordinate's idea of changing certain of the Assembly's own funds and suppressing certain offices within the patronage power of the assemblymen was left in the executive order, despite Forbes' having disapproved it. The mistake was promptly rectified, but the Assembly, once engaged, went on to challenge the governor's power to effect any changes at all. Forbes, with a ruling from the BIA to support him, stuck to his ground. The issue swelled into a major confrontation which soured relations between the Commission and the Assembly. In February, at the end of the session, not only Forbes' cadastral survey bill and the general appropriation act remained unpassed, but even the special appropriation bill for public works. *La Vanguardia,* under the title "A Complete Failure," branded Forbes the worst American governor to date. But Osmeña in a confidential letter to Quezon the following month had a different evaluation: "With the lessons which are learned with experience, he is one of the best that we could have at the head of the government. . . . [T]he present uneasiness is more the son of the regime than of the men."[53]

Meanwhile, Quezon was scrambling to produce an independence bill in the House which he and his party could cite as certification of their credentials as independistas. Jones, the new Democratic chairman of the Committee on Insular Affairs, was a determined advocate of early Philippine independence and had been producing strong minority reports on that theme since 1902. Now, finding his party in power, he was eager to take definitive action. In conferences with Quezon he declared his intention to produce a bill setting a fixed date for the establishment of Philippine independence, making its realization automatic, regardless of the success of efforts to guarantee neutralization and of all manner of discretionary judgment in the American President. Jones, however, was slow moving. He thought the only way a Philippine bill of the sort he wanted could be passed was by careful cultivation of his fellow Democrats and submission to the party's caucus. Aging and in poor health, he put off the task even of drafting such a bill. Finally in March 1912, with an election approaching in the Philippines, Quezon took matters in hand and drafted the major part of a bill conforming to Jones' ideas. This bill, the so-called First Jones Bill, provided for the election of an upper house of the Philippine legislature, to be followed eight years later by Philippine independence, American troops to remain in the islands for twenty years to safeguard the new government against foreign threats.[54]

With the Republicans in control of the Senate and Taft in the White House, it was obvious that no independence bill, however moderate, would become law. The importance of the First Jones Bill was that it established a precedent for subsequent legislation and gave the Nacionalista Party a platform to run on in the Philippines. From this point of view, the more radical the bill, the better it would be. The Jones bill, a bold step toward independence by any pragmatic standard, and much the best that could be hoped for from Congress, was in fact the barest minimum a party of *inmediatistas* could safely present to its Filipino constituents. Quezon had in his possession a draft provision by Osmeña, which shows us what the party would have preferred to run on. It authorized independence six months after completion of the reorganization of the insular government, provided there was domestic tranquility and no unusual foreign threat. This, of course, was out of the question. But Quezon did contemplate trying to force Jones and his committee to shorten the period of gestation to four years. He decided against even that when it appeared that he would risk alienating Jones by doing so.[55]

Jones' bill was reported favorably by his committee on April 2, but never came to a vote in the House itself. The House docket was crowded, and a special rule would have been necessary to call up Philippine legislation. Democrats in general seem to have been reluctant to commit themselves on the Philippine issue just before a national election, and Wilson himself told Jones in April that the party had better issues and ought not to divert attention from them by raising the question of Philippine independence. In the meantime, the Bureau of Insular Affairs was leading a spirited opposition to the bill. Replying to a request for information from Representative Horace M. Towner, General Edwards pronounced that opinion among those who had served in Philippine government was unanimous "that the Filipino is at present utterly unfit to take over the government of the Islands." He continued: "This is the view also of most of the responsible Filipinos themselves. By responsible, I mean Filipinos of property or who by their ability have become prominent among their own people in any other capacity than that of professional politician." Filipinos' attempts at even local self-government under American supervision had frequently been "pathetic." These pressures so clearly ruled out passage that when Jones finally obtained time to call up Philippine legislation, in May, he used it to bring to a vote a bill specifically limiting sales of friar lands.[56]

The effect of the First Jones Bill upon the fortunes of the Nacionalista Party seems to have been negligible. On March 14, before its contents were known in Manila, Osmeña had written confidentially to Quezon that the party was going to win handsomely in the June elections. And so it did, once again taking 62 out of the 81 seats in the Assembly, and defeating the Progresistas in the popular vote 124,753 to 37,842. The role of the bill even in the campaigning was relatively inconsequential. No major candidates attacked the bill, of course: Progresistas couldn't do so, because it was consistent with their platform; Nacionalistas couldn't, because their champion had produced it. It is clear, however, that Osmeña felt at least some uneasiness about the Jones bill, for he solicited through Quezon an expression of approval for the party and the bill from the Anti-Imperialist League. The League's cable, once received, was improved upon spaciously by *El Ideal*, which portrayed it as an endorsement of Quezon's (and hence the party's) course by all men of good faith, true democrats, and strict constructionists in the United States—in effect, a certification of both the efficacy and integrity of the Nacionalistas' leadership of the independence struggle.[57]

Perhaps the true measure of Filipinos' reaction both to the bill and to the Nacionalista leaders' general policy of accommodation is to be found in the embarrassing predicament in which Quezon and Osmeña found themselves amid their party's triumph. In Tayabas, Quezon's choice for provincial governor, Primitivo San Agustin, lost to Vicente Lukban, the candidate of a more militant faction of the Nacionalista

Party. San Agustin himself attributed his defeat to Lukban's having been a general in the revolution and having told the electors that Quezon's highly paid labors in Washington would not bring independence, whereas action taken by themselves in the islands would. "Everyone has considered your defeat as mine," Quezon conceded to the loser, "and thus I also consider it."[58] Meanwhile Osmeña's leadership of the Assembly had been placed in jeopardy. Only 29 of the 81 assemblymen elected had been members of the Second Legislature; two more had been members of the First, but not of the Second. With an enormous majority and relatively little continuity in membership, the Nacionalista assembly delegation threatened to fragment and move to another choice for Speaker. Man of the middle that he was, Osmeña was attacked by both Progresistas and radicals: "the most ambitious Filipino yet known," a letter to *The Philippine Republic,* of Hong Kong, called him; "not even shooting will make him let go the udder." At the Speaker's request, Quezon cabled *La Vanguardia,* editorial voice of Osmeña's opponents within the Nacionalista Party, that re-election of the Speaker was "essential." Subsequently, he wrote personally to 19 assemblymen, arguing that failure to re-elect Osmeña would weaken the impression in the United States that the Assembly had been a success. By combining their forces, the two leaders prevailed. On October 14, Osmeña received the support of a caucus of 70 Nacionalistas and independents.[59]

Well before the election of Woodrow Wilson or his nomination of Francis Burton Harrison conditions in Philippine politics had become such as to preclude further successes for Taft's policy of attracting, reforming, and building open-endedly. America's early extension of political participation and free elections, her willingness to grant most civil liberties, including almost perfect freedom of speech and of the press, her toleration (often ill-humoredly) of independence parties— all the things which followed from Root's original apprehension that the United States government by its nature might not abridge certain basic human liberties and from Taft's strategy for conciliating a hostile people—made it impossible for the United States government to evade the issue of independence except at the cost of Filipinos' trust and good will. This was the rock upon which Taft's policies broke up. The United States could force its presence upon the Filipinos; that had been proven. But it could not have their confidence and cooperation, given the open quality of life it permitted, without speaking frankly to the issue which had come in the 1890's to link the most potent and emotional concerns of the Filipino people. Those who presided over the American-Philippine encounter felt that this was a path they could not take. Personally desirous of retaining the islands in some sort of lasting relationship, they were in the dilemma of having either to encourage expectations and further define a course which they opposed, or to risk losing everything by frankly avowing views that would alienate both American congressmen and their Filipino "wards."

Taft's policy of undertaking constructive reforms and modernizing Philippine economic and social life had seemed to offer a third choice. Since these goals themselves were presumably desirable—and indeed no one should underestimate the depth of belief in Taft, Wright, Forbes, and most of their colleagues in the essential goodness of what they were doing for the Filipinos, the Philippines, America, and the world—one might reasonably expect that Filipinos could be drawn, through shared involvement in their pursuit, to a recognition of the advantages that would flow from permanent association with so powerful, enlightened, and benevolent a nation. This was not wholly an illusion, as Filipinos' lasting affection for Americans has shown. Probably, it could not have been carried out in a political vacuum in any case, however; and surely it could not if spokesmen were to persist in announcing that political definition was being avoided in order to leave room for apostasy at some later date. There was something at once ingenuous, opportunistic, and deceitful in such a policy; and in the end it discredited everyone who adhered to it.

THREE

The Philippines and
the United States, 1913-1921

7

Ferment

In 1912 Woodrow Wilson was elected President of the United States. He had run on a platform denouncing American imperialism as "an inexcusable blunder" and pledging the Democratic Party to work for "an immediate declaration of the Nation's purpose to recognize the independence of the Philippine Islands as soon as a stable government can be established." This position was traditional in Democratic platforms, and the wording quoted above exactly duplicated that of the party's plank in 1908. Wilson himself was less perfectly within the anti-imperialist tradition. He had been a staunch annexationist in 1899; and as late as 1907, in an address at Columbia University, he had argued sophistically that the United States could not, in the nature of the thing, give Filipinos self-government. It could give them good, honest, altruistic government. But self-government "is a form of character and not a form of constitution. No people can be 'given' the self-control of maturity. Only a long apprenticeship of obedience can secure them the precious possession." As the possibility of his being nominated by the Democrats had grown, American anti-imperialists and Manuel Quezon, in his capacity as resident commissioner, had worked hard at convincing him that Filipinos possessed maturity and national cohesion, but with relatively little success. In March 1912 Wilson told Quezon that although he was open to persuasion, he believed the Filipino people lacked sufficient cultural homogeneity to live amicably and govern themselves responsibly. A month later as we have seen, he advised Jones that the party had better issues and ought not to divert the voters' minds by raising the Philippine question. In July, it is true, he changed his mind and informed Jones and Representative Oscar W. Underwood that the Jones bill was acceptable to him and that its passage would not harm his candidacy. But a week after this change had been made known, Quezon confidentially told the new chief of the Bureau of Insular Affairs, Frank McIntyre, that he still felt Wilson personally favored neither independence nor any other radical alteration of the status quo.[1]

Actually, this was quite acceptable to Quezon. He told McIntyre, in this the first of many disarmingly frank conversations the two were to have over the years, that the insular government had become so unpopular with so many Filipinos that a significant change of structure would be necessary to regain public confidence. The change he recommended, however, was not independence, but the creation of an elected upper house in the legislature. "He believes," McIntyre wrote to Acting Governor Newton W. Gilbert, "that if this could be brought about in ten years there would be no thought in the Philippine Islands of separation from the United States: he believes that independence is better than the status quo but by no means so satisfactory as a relationship with the United States government which could be brought about by an efficient and considerate Commission having executive duties only and a purely Philippine legislature." Quezon added, however, that he would not publicly espouse such views.[2]

In fact, as the summer of 1912 faded and a Democratic victory became predictable, he did exactly the opposite, toughening his stance. On September 5, he wrote to McIntyre that he had lost his faith in the members of the Commission; and in an article for the November issue of his American magazine, *The Filipino People,* he launched a brilliant attack upon the logic of retention through commercial ties and the spread of prosperity. The Philippines could be of real advantage to Americans only if Filipinos were convinced of the good faith of the United States, Quezon argued.

> From the very moment that the Filipino people are convinced that the United States are in the islands to remain there, the government in the Philippines as well as all the American businessmen in the Islands, will be confronted by difficulties whose nature will be such as to make it a very expensive task for the American government to govern the Islands . . . .
>
> It is a mistake to believe that whatever benefits might have been conferred upon the Filipino people by free trade between the United States and the Islands have in the least lessened the desire of the Filipino to be free and independent or made them more favorable to American sovereignty . . . .

No mere economic policy is adequate to the growing aspirations of such a race as the Filipino. There is something far more difficult to supply and that is a legitimate outlet for the restlessness and ambition of an awakened and aroused people.

Taft's logic had been turned upside down: instead of mutually beneficial links leading Filipinos to sacrifice independence, Quezon was suggesting that they might lead Americans to sacrifice retention! Beyond this, however, and far more important, Quezon had reasserted the complexity of the original revolutionary amalgam and proclaimed its vitality after a decade and a half of American rule. Public works and infrastructure had been built; prosperity of a sort had grown. "Yet this prosperity," Quezon warned, "is not a solution of the Philippine problem, nor do these economic successes, striking as they are, meet the real expectation of the people themselves." The "real social needs of the people" remained unmet.[3]

Having delivered himself of this strikingly accurate analysis, Quezon left for the Philippines, at the Speaker's request, to lend his support to efforts to preserve Nacionalista unity and define a strategy for the independence campaign in the forthcoming post-Taft period. To the Filipino people, he counseled restraint and discretion. The primary obstacles to independence, he warned, were the apathy of the American voter and the persistence of a hard-core retentionist minority. Filipinos could overcome this two-fold barrier by adhering to the established Nacionalista policy of conciliating the Americans. The insular government, he argued, had been the best ever known in the Philippines: Filipinos should gratefully acknowledge this, should cooperate with the administration wherever possible, and should endeavor to win over Americans to their side by suasion and by the force of their responsible conduct.[4]

In this spirit, Quezon himself engineered an end to the deadlock between the Commission and the Assembly over the election of resident commissioners. Calmly conceding to the Commission the constitutional point for which Osmeña had fought in 1910, he arranged for the Commission to elect as its resident commissioner not Legarda, but another wealthy and conservative Filipino businessman, Manuel Earnshaw. Forbes, on the Commission's side, had facilitated this compromise by securing Taft's consent in advance to dropping Legarda. From Quezon's point of view, this outcome had several attractions. For one thing, it ended an embarrassing stalemate over the office he himself held, for once the election of Earnshaw had been agreed upon,

Quezon's own election as the other resident commissioner went through, too. For another thing, it removed from American-Filipino relations an irritant that might have been harmful to Filipinos' campaign to demonstrate legislative responsibility. Beyond this, moreover, it established a pattern, to which Quezon remained attached for as long as he held office as resident commissioner, of yoking him with a colleague who was rich, personally dignified as a representative of the Filipino people, and politically impotent. The last thing Quezon wanted was a rival either in Filipino electoral politics or American legislative politics. Earnshaw was perfect. He had no interest in politics at all, but he did have, in his conservative way, a desire for independence. Unlike Legarda, who had been senior to Quezon in tenure and had a cordial personal relationship with the President, Earnshaw knew nothing about America and its politics. He did as Quezon advised him. En route to Washington in 1913 he told a San Francisco reporter, in a perfect one-sentence précis of his colleague's position: "The Filipinos admit the great work that has been done by the United States, but independence is essential to the real development of the country."[5]

Quezon, then, was hedging against any probable outcome of the forthcoming debate over the future relationship of the United States and the Philippines. Moderates in the BIA, anti-imperialists in Boston, the independence-minded chairman of the House Committee on Insular Affairs, and Filipino independistas all thought him their man. In fact, he was clearly his own. But what did he really believe, what did he personally want? It is unlikely that we are ever going to know with certitude, and there is a strong possibility that Quezon himself didn't know at the time. Dramatic, insightful, and mercurial, Quezon played upon men and issues with dazzling versatility and nimbleness. Rare indeed was the man he couldn't outmaneuver, the situation he couldn't manipulate. In 1907 when elected by the first Assembly to be Nacionalista majority leader and chairman of the Committee on Appropriations, he had sought advice from a scholarly colleague as to what books he should read to acquaint himself with the nature of his own and his committee's tasks. "You study?" the other had replied. "People like you have no need for books or authors. You could make up a theory of finance in a minute, and then write a whole book about it later on." Quezon's fertile mind had, however, an affinity for the expedient. "There is no place for consistency in government," he was to declare years later. And to Osmeña, who was very much concerned with consistency and logical coherence, he once remarked: "The trouble with you is that you take this game of politics too seriously. You look far behind you and too far ahead of you. Our people do not understand that. They do not want it. All they want is to have the present problem solved, and solved with the least pain. That is all." Opponents, naturally, thought him cynical and even unscrupulous. A friendly critic, Teodoro M. Kalaw, considered him "sincere, each time." Forbes liked to think Quezon couldn't help himself. "He is the most responsive little organism to outside influences that I know," he wrote in 1913. "I have likened Quezon to a wonderfully trained hunting dog run wild. He sees someone going hunting. Instantly the spirit of hunting rises within him. . . . If the hunter is a skilled one he will find Quezon the most useful and adept partner in his enterprise. The next thing he will see a shepherd trying to bring in his sheep, and Quezon will become a sheep dog, rounding up the sheep and bringing them in admirably. But alone or in bad company, he goes wrong and ends up by killing lambs and devastating hen yards and is absolutely beyond control."[6]

In 1912 and 1913 the tolerances within which Quezon was maneuvering were fairly well defined. Since at least the beginning of 1911 he had felt that liberalizing changes in both the insular administration and its philosophy were essential if a dangerous, potentially violent level of alienation between the government and the people were to be avoided. The minimum appropriate change was an increase in Filipinos' participation in the executive wing of the government and recognition by the United States of the Philippines' *right* to be independent. Whether that right ought to be exercised—immediately, eventually, or ever—was evidently a question on which his opinion fluctuated. Americans who had known Quezon well in the years prior to his election to the Assembly were of one accord in doubting his desire for early independence; some had formed the opinion that personally he opposed independence altogether, preferring the modernization and enrichment of his country that could best come through some form of link with the United States. As a young man, Quezon had been profoundly influenced by the regional Constabulary commanders in Tayabas, H. H. Bandholtz and J. G. Harbord; and it is apparently the case that under their spell and that, briefly, of Forbes he had taken unto himself the best and most altruistic part of their vision. Decades later, during World War II, he wrote in his memoirs:

The word "independence" never meant much to me except as a young revolutionary fighting in the hills of Pampanga and Bataan. I had learned something since those days. I had learned that there were countries nominally independent but which in effect were under foreign rule; and still others which had in theory as well as in fact national independence, but whose people knew no freedom except the freedom to starve, the freedom to be silent, the freedom to be jailed, or the freedom to be shot. None of these situations was I willing to see become the fate of my people. . . . And the reason why I chose to follow and adopt the policy of the Nationalist Party for immediate, absolute, and complete independence was because I had always thought . . . that it was easier to get freedom and liberty for the Filipino people through the road to independence which the average American understands than through the policy of Presidents Roosevelt and Taft . . . which, although known and practiced by the English in their relations with their white subjects, was entirely alien to the American mind.

Conceivably, it is not too much to say that what looks like either duplicity or else matchless strategic and tactical skill in Quezon's positions in 1912 and 1913, was in fact very largely ambivalence.[7]

Certainly, however, there was very little ambivalence in the public reaction of the Filipino people to Wilson's election. *La Vanguardia,* which on the day before the results became known had called the American elections "a matter of life and death" for Filipinos, pictured the President-elect as a modern Moses: "He will preside over our triumphal entrance into the Promised Land after redeeming us from the long captivity to which the imperial Pharaohs reduced us." Ten thousand persons paraded through the streets of Manila, and twice that number gathered on the Luneta to hear Osmeña, Quezon, and Aguinaldo speak of the historicity of the occasion. The Speaker, in the principal speech of the day, told the throng that they were beginning the second stage in the pursuit of their national ideal, the first having been the creation of the Republic and the Malolos constitution. Everything in between had been in the nature of preparation, indeed preparation under unfavorable conditions, for this event. It was time to change the principles of the regime to make it responsive to the people, that they might feel pride in their achievements and derive stimulus to greater labors. In agitation, Martin Egan, editor of *The Manila Times* and a close personal friend of both Taft and Forbes, cabled the Secretary of War in government code, warning of growing demoralization among resident Americans in and out of government and a rising tide of Filipino demands for immediate independence.

Would not the President give Wilson the benefit of his understanding of the situation and arrange with him cooperatively to reassure Americans and disabuse Filipinos of their illusions? "Authoritative general statements saying Democratic program constructive, changes evolutionary, not revolutionary, all interests protected, would help situation and simplify future dealing."[8]

The President needed little urging. Before the election he had told Forbes, who was then on leave in the United States, that he doubted the Democrats would really act upon their Philippine plank if elected. After Wilson's victory, he set in motion a plan to make sure. Calling Forbes to the White House, Taft announced that he was beginning a campaign to prevent any precipitate steps in the Philippines and specifically to defeat the Jones bill. He directed Forbes to take an active part, calling on influential persons, preparing publicity, and making public appearances. At the same time, he ordered Forbes not to submit his resignation to Wilson. "His view," Forbes wrote, "was that we should assume our jobs were in no sense political ones, and not to be affected by a change of administration, and let it be put squarely to the new President to inject politics into the situation if he should see fit." Thus, a variant on the tactic applied to Filipinos was now to be used against Democrats in the United States. The existing policy looking quite frankly toward retention of the Philippines was held up as constructive, altruistic, and apolitical; to fight for it was to fight for a just and honorable national goal. To oppose either in whole or in part its fulfillment was a mean political act based upon self-serving or misguided premises. It was apolitical for the Governor General of the Philippine Islands to campaign and propagandize while in office for the defeat of a policy to which Democrats and most Filipinos had been committed for years; it would be political—and therefore sordid —for the Democrats and Filipinos to respond by removing him for having done so.[9]

Forbes himself had always used this sort of double standard. While refusing to discuss independence with Filipinos, he had regularly supplied information and arguments to American retentionists, asking as he did so that his role be kept secret from the Filipinos and the general public.[10] In late 1912 he threw himself into Taft's plan with fervor. During the month following the elections, he took his case to cardinals O'Connell of Boston, Farley of New York, and Gibbons of Baltimore, and to the Irish Catholic mayor of Boston; to President Lowell of Harvard, Richard Olney, and even the anti-imperialist Josiah Quincy;

to prominent Democratic politicians such as Senator James O'Gorman of New York and Wilson's future Secretary of the Treasury, William McAdoo; and to officials of the Hearst chain of newspapers. The results were encouraging. The prelates, their minds filled with memories of anti-Catholic and anti-clerical abuses during the Philippine Revolution, responded eagerly. Cardinal O'Connell introduced Forbes to Boston Democratic politicians over lunch in his own home and assigned the rector of his cathedral to carry on what Forbes called "active propaganda." Gibbons wrote to every bishop and archbishop in the United States, pointing out the danger of "civic unrest and disturbances" if the Philippines were to become independent. In New York, J. G. White and Co., "who," as Forbes ingenuously put it, "are naturally very interested in the matter," presided over arrangements and invitations. From Cambridge, Lowell attempted unsuccessfully to arrange an interview for Forbes with the President-elect himself.[11]

In the meantime, Taft also was working on religious leaders. Early in November he was in touch with Cardinal Gibbons ("I am very anxious, as I know you are, to prevent the passage of any bill which will . . . create a chaotic condition out there") and the Reverend J. T. Roche of the Catholic Church Extension Society. To Roche, whom he saw personally and primed with retentionist arguments prior to a meeting of the society's board of governors, he subsequently wrote: "The Filipinos are not fit for self-government and . . . nothing will show it more clearly than their antagonism to the missionary efforts of the churches among the people and their disposition to confiscate any property which the churches may have in their Islands . . . . The truth is that the minute we leave the Islands, chaos will succeed, revolutions will follow and will cause stagnation and suffering among the people that can not be exaggerated." Taft also gave his attention to Protestant churchmen, among them missionary leaders in the Baptist, Presbyterian, Reformed Episcopal, and Methodist Episcopal churches. To Bishop Brent, the Episcopal bishop of the Philippines, he wrote in January 1913 urging him to circularize "all the Bishops of your Church . . . testifying that the people of the Philippines are not yet ready for self government."[12]

As in Forbes' case, the results were encouraging. Father Roche addressed his board of governors "using all of the arguments suggested by you in our conference" and won strong support. Cardinal Gibbons gave out an interview, in which he dilated upon the disabilities of the Filipino people and warned that reversal of the established policy would frighten away capital and doom the islands to stagnation and underdevelopment. Cardinal Farley gave a dinner for the Most Reverend D. J. Dougherty, Bishop of Jaro, the Philippine diocese which included Iloilo, inviting prominent Catholic laymen including Senator O'Gorman, and several congressmen, judges, lawyers, and newspapermen. Dougherty addressed them; and afterwards O'Gorman told him not to worry, that the party's Philippine plank pledged only to give the islands independence "when they are fit for it." The Right Reverend Samuel Fallows, Presiding Bishop of the Reformed Episcopal Church, whose son was just then founding the American-Philippine Company, informed the President that he would contact "representatives of all the leading Protestant Churches in the United States" in behalf of maintaining the status quo.[13]

On December 6 the President sent to Congress a special message on fiscal, judicial, military, and insular affairs, in which he undertook to expose the folly, as he saw it, in the Jones bill. The United States, he argued, was attempting to do something entirely new in the history of western nations' colonial dealings in Asia: "We are seeking to arouse a national spirit and not, as under the older colonial theory, to suppress such a spirit." He detailed the achievements of the past decade and a half in education, infrastructure, health, and filipinization of the government. Filipinos by 1912, he observed in connection with the last point, filled all municipal offices, 90 percent of provincial offices, and 60 percent of insular offices. But all this was only a beginning; there had not yet been time for roots to develop. Were the Americans to withdraw their supervision, their example, and their guidance, things would regress. Politics would become the domain of "an oligarchical and, probably, exploiting minority." The economy would stagnate, health and educational programs would lose their momentum. "Our true course is to pursue steadily and courageously the path we have thus far followed . . . . We should do all this with a disinterested endeavor to secure for [individual] Filipinos economic independence and to fit them for complete self-government, with the power to decide eventually, according to their own largest good, whether such self-government shall be accompanied by independence. A present declaration even of future independence would retard progress by the dissension and disorder it would arouse."[14]

It is evident that by 1912 this policy was bankrupt, that, in fact, the only way retention could have been pursued at the time would have been by throwing away the fine distinction to which Taft clung,

frankly pledging that the United States would grant Philippine independence some day and leaving unspoken the possibility that Filipinos
themselves might change their minds. To have persisted as Taft did
in the conceit that Filipinos could be attracted more successfully by
evading the issue of independence than by facing it was to ignore the
last two years of Philippine history. Filipino political leaders and
journalists—the voice, albeit self-appointed, of their people—took the
message as the final straw, and responded bluntly. It was absurd, wrote
La Democracia, to protect the people against a Filipino oligarchy by
subjecting them to an American oligarchy: of the two, the former was
preferable, "because it at least has popular sanction." Mincing few
words, *La Vanguardia* called the message "the supreme effort of his
bungling life," and added trenchantly, "Mr. Taft has disposed of a
piece of property which is not his." The Assembly, acting on a motion
by José Clarin, promptly passed a resolution asking for approval of the
Jones bill, as a means of ending "the indefinite, absurd, and notoriously
unpopular period of apprenticeship against which the people have
been protesting to this day." Surely "a present declaration of future
independence" would not more seriously have retarded progress or
sown "dissension and disorder" than persistence in the established
course.[15]

Nevertheless, the campaign had by this point a kind of relentless
singleness of vision. Taft and Forbes were precisely the opposite of
Quezon. Having committed themselves to a policy, they refused to be
budged from it even by the most manifest evidence that it would fail
to achieve its ends. In December 1912, just before returning to the
Philippines, Forbes had broached to Taft the need for a lobbyist and
coordinator "who can meet and deal with the dignitaries of the Church
and State and others and talk in a convincing manner and at the same
time direct the movement and prepare the documents to send about."
Martin Egan had struck him as the very man and when, upon reaching Manila, he found that Egan had sold his interest in *The Manila
Times* and was planning to return to the United States, Forbes signed
him up. He equipped Egan with letters to ten friends and interested
parties, among them James Speyer of Speyer Bros. and Thomas W.
Lamont of J. P. Morgan, asking each for $2,500 with which to establish
a permanent Philippine lobby. "I want him to get started on his campaign," the Governor General wrote to an uncle in Boston, "and as
what might almost be called my life's work hangs in the balance, I

propose to see the thing through though it cost a good deal of money."[16]

Taft, for his part, spoke and wrote prolifically, reiterating his familiar themes. In January 1913 he told the annual banquet of the Ohio Society that political aspirations interfered with Filipinos' betterment and enrichment, and urged Democrats not to "reverse a policy that has vindicated itself so completely in ten years, for mere purposes of conformity to cobwebbed planks in forgotten platforms." In a lengthy article appearing in the New York *Tribune* of March 1, he pronounced that "the mere advocacy" of legislation promising eventual independence "inspires false hopes, checks present progress, provokes dissention and makes for dissatisfaction among the Filipino people." Elected honorary president of the newly formed Philippine Society—whose goal, ostensibly apolitical, was to create "a more sympathetic interest between the people of this country and the people of the Philippines" and whose executive committee of thirteen included such disinterested figures as Taft, Forbes, Wright, Egan, Frederick H. Reed of J. G. White & Co., C. D. Palmer of the International Banking Corporation, Richard E. Forrest of the American-Philippine Company, three missionaries, a former Constabulary officer, and James Ross, attorney for the Manila Electric Railroad & Light Co. and the owners of the San José friar estate—he delivered the principal address at the society's banquet in New York that June. Hailing American achievements and praising Americans' unselfish motives, he rejected all thought of independence. America was the Filipinos' guardian. She would do for them, he frankly added, what she ought to have done for the Cubans had it not been for the Teller Amendment.[17]

It is difficult to gauge the effect either of the Filipino effort to obtain legislation or of the retentionists' campaign in opposition. Certainly, a great many arguments against independence found their way to the new administration. Some came from knowledgeable sources such as David P. Barrows, formerly director of education in the insular government and in 1913 a professor of political science at Berkeley, who reasoned that Filipinos should be encouraged in their pursuit of nationality, but not by means of the existing Jones bill. Others came from Kipling-quoting missionaries or businessmen. J. G. White, arguing that his investments in the islands made him solicitous of Filipinos' prosperity and general well-being, urged the Wilson administration to eschew independence and work instead for a dominion-style relationship after the Canadian model. "My own personal belief," he wrote, "is that if the Islands were freed entirely from American control they would within a few months, be in as bad condition as Mexico is at the present time." Business leaders in San Francisco told the *Chronicle* that retention was important on grounds of national honor, commercial profits, and international prestige; and Captain Robert Dollar speculated in public about curtailing steamer service should the Jones bill pass. Prominent newspapers on both coasts came out in opposition to the Jones bill. *United States Securities and Government Finance,* the newsletter of the National City Bank of New York, discreetly observed that good sense would lead the new administration to do no more than modify the existing Philippine policy. Martin Egan, for his part, carried the retentionist message personally to cabinet members, eliciting approval from Lane, Redfield, and McAdoo.[18]

In fact, there was no Philippine legislation in 1913, except for minor tariff changes removing the limits on free importation of Philippine sugar and tobacco. At the beginning of the year it had seemed likely that Democrats would pass the Jones bill during the special session of Congress called to revise the tariff; but as opposition rose, Democratic leaders elected not to complicate their tariff fight by simultaneously taking on the question of Philippine independence. This was highly embarrassing to Nacionalista leaders, who in the flush of Wilson's victory had predicted early action by the Democratic majority to make good its platform pledge. Responding to Quezon's advice that action on the Jones bill would be put over until 1914, Osmeña cabled that the political situation "is and will be for some time of great uneasiness and embarrassment."[19]

Meanwhile, the Forbes administration was nearing its end. The Governor General returned to the islands in January 1913 to find Filipinos in a cooperative, buoyant mood, and resident Americans, in many cases, in a state of near panic. "I gather," he wrote to Taft, "that Mr. Osmeña and Mr. Quezon have been impressing it on their people that their best plan now is to show how well they got along, how harmonious they are and how well they are fitted to American institutions." With the legislative session nearing its end and almost no laws yet passed, Forbes took hold and in a conciliatory vein secured passage of a cadastral survey bill and a bill making English the official language of the islands while retaining Spanish as an official language of the courts until 1920. In the last five days of the session, forty-two laws were passed. Even the general appropriation bill almost succeeded. A conference committee, with Forbes himself one of the members, hammered out a compromise giving the Assembly various changes in accounting it had sought and providing a year-round monthly expense allowance for assemblymen, while preserving discretionary funds for the Governor General and evading resolution of the dispute between the two houses over the Assembly's assertion of an exclusive right to originate money bills. For once, however, Osmeña's closing-night tactics backfired. A group of irreconcilables in the Assembly, desiring larger monthly allowances and hoping to embarrass the Republican administration in its last year, filibustered during the waning hours of the session and prevented the compromise bill from coming to a vote.[20]

In spite of this, January 1913 was a time of much optimism in government financial circles. A predicted decline of $400,000 in customs revenues for the fiscal year had thus far failed to materialize; after six months of the year, in fact, revenues were up over $663,000. Therefore, while the general appropriation bill was stalled, the legislature in an optimistic mood passed special appropriations amounting to almost $1,800,000. Precisely at this point, however, customs receipts collapsed with even greater drama than had originally been predicted. A good crop in the Philippines led to a major reduction of rice imports, and at the same time the cumulative effect of a shift from European to duty-free American imported textiles began to become apparent. In the first four months of 1913 customs revenues declined by just over $1,000,000. Internal revenue, it was true, had continued to rise; but in May, an embarrassed Forbes was compelled to inform his new Democratic superiors that according to current predictions, the insular government's reserves would fall from $1,540,000 to approximately $250,000, during fiscal 1913. By that time, moreover, even internal revenue had begun to decline. In June things looked so bleak that Forbes, the great champion of infrastructure, contemplated halting all public works; the complete elimination of the reserve seemed in sight.[21]

Such an outcome had always been a possibility, given Forbes' heady approach to nation building. A devotee both of infrastructure and of primitive pump-priming techniques, he had written to a cousin à propos the government's response to the depression in the islands at the time of his arrival: "I went on the theory that while the country was depressed and business poor, the imports decreasing and production less, the Government ought to put in public works and spend all of its revenues in order to circulate money and try to stimulate the people somewhat, and I suggested that when the time of affluence came that then we could increase our reserve and lay by a surplus." On the other hand, the borrowing power of the insular government having been limited by Congress to $5,000,000 exclusive of friar land bonds and the issues of municipal governments, most public works had to be financed out of current revenues. Once economic conditions looked up, Forbes could never resist spending the government's funds on much-needed projects. "We are now spending all of our increased revenues instead of laying by a surplus," he reported to the BIA less than a year after becoming Governor General, "believing that the money can do more good invested in public works than lying in the treasury." Partly as a result of uncertainty over revenues in the first years after the Payne-Aldrich Act went into effect, the legislature got into the custom during Forbes' administration of appropriating more money for public works than conservative budgetary estimates would have justified, hedging this by a proviso that the funds be spent only if released in writing by the Governor General. In this way, public works could be pressed to the limit, by authorizing the largest possible expenditures on the assumption that the governor would release only as much of the appropriation as financial circumstances at the time warranted. As it happened, however, from 1910 until the end of Forbes' administration, the insular government lacked a wholly competent accountant; and Forbes, in his enthusiasm, consistently overspent.[22]

In January 1913 then, the insular government, legislature and executive alike, had acted in a predictable manner, hoping to squeeze as much as possible out of an apparent windfall in revenues. When this had proved illusory, the government had found itself with only small reserves and with a large staff and many ongoing public works projects. In June Forbes issued an emergency appeal for economy in the government bureaus, halted the cadastral survey, and curtailed expenditures for irrigation and other infrastructure. He was reluctant, however, to take drastic steps such as halting his road-building programs, fearing that if he did the government would lose its experienced staff of technical men. By July it was known that revenues for the first six months of 1913 had been $1,500,000 below those for the comparable period of 1912; and Forbes imposed a 5 percent cut on all bureaus except constabulary and education in the fiscal year then beginning and appointed an "efficiency committee" to recommend governmental economies.[23]

This financial distress, embarrassing as it was to an administration being appraised by new superiors of a different political persuasion, was only the most obvious part of a general pattern of developments suggesting that, like its philosophy, the administrative competence of Forbes' government in the Philippines had passed its prime. In many respects, the government was operating ineptly. Irrigation, one of the governor's major goals, is a case in point. The first two systems built by the insular government washed out, owing to faulty design, the first time heavy rains struck them. One of these, the system built on Tabacalera's Luisita hacienda in Tarlac, had been conceived as a model project. Original estimates of the cost had run to ₱273,000; and in August 1909 the insular government had signed a contract with Tabacalera for eventual reimbursement and had begun work on a budget of ₱300,000. No hydrographic survey was made, however; and in July 1911 over ₱70,000 of damage was caused by the washout referred to already. Plans were redrafted to allow for a diversionary dam; and in 1912 a new appropriation of ₱606,000 was made for the project. At that point, however, it was discovered that the question of legal water rights had been investigated only superficially. The system threatened to exhaust the water supply of the O'Donnell River, and the governor of Tarlac protested so vigorously that work was halted while claims were sorted out and priorities established. The dispute was still unresolved when the Forbes administration left office.[24]

These difficulties and evidences of incompetence were not peculiar to irrigation projects. The Office of Consulting Architect, a particular protégé of Forbes, had no construction engineer on its staff. The Bureau of Public Works, however, did not know this; accordingly, even though it did have engineers on its staff, they were not assigned to review plans approved by the consulting architect. As a result, a number of buildings were constructed during the Forbes administration without their engineering aspects having been studied by anyone with expertise. Some of these proved faulty. Two large government warehouses erected on the filled land in the new South Port Area were built with inadequate foundations: piles had to be driven underneath them after they had been constructed, a costly and time-consuming operation. The aquarium in Manila was delayed over two years because the glass in its tanks broke when they were filled with water.

Even the administration of justice, whose vagaries under Spain Taft and other early American officials had so piercingly condemned, was characterized by inefficiency so pronounced as to be abusive. In May 1912 one of Forbes' closest friends and advisers wrote him:

> In many instances prisoners are kept from three to four years before their cases are decided and if they are finally sentenced to more than six years they get no allowance for the time they have served as detention prisoners. . . . In some cases . . . the decision of the court of first instance has been made, say, in April 1910, appeal is taken and eight months later the papers come to the Supreme Court. This delay seems to be the fault of the clerk of the court of first instance. In many cases he has a good excuse, but that does not help the prisoner, and by law or regulation he is required to send an appeal case up within thirty days. The Supreme Court at once appoints an attorney to defend this man or if there is an attorney retained for him he is required to file his brief within fifteen days, which period is usually extended and may draw out on occasions to two or three months. The Attorney-General should then file his answer within fifteen days; it is more often a case of four to five months. . . .
> There appears to be an entire lack of an inspecting system.[25]

At the same time, the progress of educational work through the schools had actually been reversed. The official faith in education as a means of preparing the Filipino people for responsible self-government and for self-respecting life in the modern world had not changed on either the American or the Filipino side. But in practice many Americans had come over the years to believe that education should have lower priority than it had originally been given. In 1908, for example, *The Manila Times,* the most respected and generally the most temperate English language paper in the archipelago, had launched a major attack on the school system as costly and unproductive: "Can the Islands afford this? Are the young men who leave the schools becoming producers? Are they paying back to the country in productive work the money extracted from it in its penury so that they might be bettered? Should not the money annually expended for education be cut in half? Would it not better be devoted to irrigation and good roads and in other ways in the nature of investment so that wealth would tend to create more wealth?" Such criticism generally made two points: that the money could better be spent on public works (or, a variant, not spent at all: taxes could be cut), and that the education being received by Filipinos was unsuiting them for "productive" work.

An editorial appearing in the *Times* on the same day as the article just quoted, arraigned the existing school system for "robbing the workshop and the farm" by raising the aspirations of the young people in its classrooms. As a corrective, the *Times* recommended that 75 percent of educational funds be spent on "agricultural schooling."[26]

There was a great deal of sympathy for this attitude in Governor Forbes and in prominent American commissioners such as Worcester and Elliott. We have seen already that in his inaugural address Forbes had pledged himself to stimulate agricultural and vocational education but had warned that overall educational expenditures should take second place to those for public improvements. In this he was warmly supported by Secretary of War Dickinson. In the fiscal year 1911 expenditures on education, which had risen steadily since the beginning of American civil government, leveled off; in the next two fiscal years they actually declined. The total number of public schools in the Philippines, which had risen to 4,531 by 1910, declined steadily for the next three years until at the end of the school year in 1913, the number was 2,934. Other indices confirm the reversal: in 1911, the peak year up to that time, 9,086 teachers instructed 484,689 students or 26 percent of the total school-age population; in 1913 the numbers had fallen to 7,671 teachers and 349,454 students, or 18 percent of the school-age population.[27]

It is clear that the intensity of this decline was greater than Forbes had desired. He himself claimed that diversion of funds from elementary to secondary schools, in response to agitation from prominent Filipinos, had increased cost per student and thus lowered the number of children that could be educated. Others maintained that the most precipitate decline, which occurred while Forbes was out of the islands on a protracted leave of absence, was part of a plot by educational authorities to force the governor's hand and make him give them a larger share of revenues. Discovering the extent of the decline in May 1913, Forbes angrily ordered that 1,000 new schools be opened within six weeks. Nevertheless, although one may absolve Forbes personally of blame for the measure of regression that occurred, it is plain that he had intended at least a relative decline and that one had begun within a year of his inauguration. Like the financial debacle of 1913 and the administrative deficiencies already alluded to, the reversal of educational momentum served to discredit both the policy of tutelary retention and its practice.[28]

Initiative in defining future Philippine policy lay, then, not with Congress or the i isular government, but with the Wilson administration. For some time, the new President was content to allow matters to remain as he had found them. He believed, as he had frankly told partisans of independence in 1912, that the issue was of relatively small importance and that bigger matters should be treated first. But beyond that, he was unclear as to how to act even when the time could be found for addressing Philippine concerns. Ambivalent himself and possessed of a cabinet whose opinions on Philippine independence ranged from William Jennings Bryan's fervent anti-imperialism to William C. Redfield's spread-eagled retentionism, Wilson needed guidance. Late in 1912, confessing his uncertainty, he asked Walter Hines Page for advice. Page suggested that Wilson send a personal confidant on an unofficial tour of the islands to provide him with fresh information from an uncommitted source. This was an idea that had also occurred to avowed retentionists; and in February 1913 Vice Governor Gilbert made the same suggestion in a letter to Redfield, then newly designated Secretary of Commerce in Wilson's cabinet. Redfield passed the advice along to Wilson with his own endorsement. By this time, however, the President had already dispatched Henry Jones Ford, his successor in the chair of political science at Princeton and an authority on Canadian government, on a secret mission of investigation and evaluation.[29]

Ford traveled around the islands for two months, probing numerous aspects of the insular government and American-Philippine relations, and eventually making his purpose known in confidence to Forbes. After only a month, he had seen enough to convince him that a change of policy was urgently needed; and by the end of May, when he left the islands, Ford had been persuaded that Filipinos were sincere in their appeals for independence and might conceivably rebel unless steps were taken promptly to change the personnel of the insular government and set the islands on the road to early separation from the United States. These views he made known to Wilson by letter while still in the Philippines. In the official report which he subsequently wrote, Ford argued that the American government had succeeded in the task Taft had set it of preparing the people and the country for self-government, and that the time had come to abolish the Commission and allow Filipinos to draft a constitution of their own to go into effect at the President's discretion. Continuation of the existing tutelary arrangement would actually be harmful. Racial hostility was rising, and Filipinos were overlooking the good work of the government in their alienation from it over political issues. He specifically rejected the customary arguments that tribalism or linguistic diversity were so troublesome as to prevent independence and questioned whether caciquism in the Philippines was notably different from class abuses elsewhere in the world. Ford did not recommend establishing a specific date for independence but did urge prompt creation of a domestically autonomous government and frank avowal of a national policy to promote independence as soon as possible.[30]

In the meantime, while Ford was studying the islands at first hand as presidential emissary, the new Secretary of War, Lindley M. Garrison, was clarifying his views with the help of the BIA. Although predictably inclined toward moderation and continuity, leading officers of the bureau differed in the specifics and emphases of their recommendations. The official position of the BIA was that of its new chief, General Frank McIntyre. For many years General Edwards' assistant, McIntyre was optimistic and laudatory in his appraisal of past achievements: "Briefly, the Filipino as distinguished from a small class [of ambitious caciques] has been given more power in his government than is exercised by any oriental people, and all the agencies which are supposed to work for the advancement of a people in popular self-government are being used to the greatest practicable extent for the Filipino." As for changes and future policy, he recommended five actions, economic in emphasis and ostensibly apolitical in character: the removal of Dickinson's suspension of friar land sales; an increase in the maximum size of the blocs of public land that could be sold to individuals from 40 acres to 1,235 acres (that is, from 16 hectares to 500); elimination of all remaining restrictions and limitations on reciprocal free trade; acquisition of congressional authority to issue $10,000,000 in new bonds to finance public improvements; and acquisition of authority from Congress to revise the complicated arrangement of currency reserve funds, so as to make them a liquid resource of the government.[31]

To supplement this characteristically economic analysis, Garrison turned to the law officer of the BIA, the young Felix Frankfurter, for recommendations regarding future political evolution. Frankfurter's advice was notably more conservative than that beginning to come in from Ford in the islands. In Frankfurter's view, the insular government was by virtue of the Organic Act *"pro tanto,* an autonomous government"; and the existing structure would therefore serve adequately for future evolution toward full Filipino self-government. Like McIntyre, he distinguished between the people as a whole and what he called "a small, masterful, highly educated, wealthy minority, who have on the whole, but little community of interest and little sympathy with the great masses." The responsibility of the United States was to the whole people, and therefore devolution of control into the hands of Filipinos must be slow enough to allow the emergence of a broad-based polity. Otherwise there would be unrepresentative, oligarchical government. Nevertheless, the government must be purposeful and energetic in meeting its responsibility; it must not allow further loss of momentum such as had recently occurred. As for the future, Frankfurter recommended that wholesale changes either in personnel or institutions be avoided, as compromising America's instruction of Filipinos in "the value of continuity and stability in political administration." Instead, the existing vacancy in the office of insular Secretary of Commerce and Police should be filled by a man in perfect agreement with administration policy, who in due course could be promoted to replace Forbes. In the meantime, the Wilson administration should clarify national policy toward the Philippines, ending the evasiveness of the past, but being careful to stress continuity and to avoid demoralizing American civil servants in the islands.[32]

By mid-April, Secretary Garrison had reached his own conclusions. Improving upon the advice of Frankfurter, he recommended to the President a four-point plan: first, appoint a new Governor General of exceptional vigor, judgment and insight; second, in commissioning the new governor, end the prevailing uncertainty and define clearly the administration's intentions; third, after the Governor General had been given an opportunity to break into his new office, appoint a Filipino majority on the Commission; fourth, avoid any commitment to a specific date for independence, so as to preserve flexibility to respond to unforeseeable circumstances. This plan, which was appreciably more adventurous than Frankfurter's, had the advantage of enabling the administration to act in highly visible ways to end the stalemate between the Commission and the Assembly without having to seek any additional congressional action. In late May or early June Garrison explained his ideas to Bishop Brent, then in the United States lobbying for retention, who in turn tried them out on Quezon. The resident commissioner found them acceptable and predicted they would satisfy Filipino public opinion. Garrison was heartened. He felt he had found a formula for dealing with a difficult situation, and for the rest of his tenure as Secretary of War he stuck to this view. When events passed him by in 1916, he resigned.[33]

Quezon, as usual, was playing the field. In November of the previous year, after Wilson's election, Quezon had confidentially told General J. Franklin Bell, Army commander in the Philippines, that he felt promotion of a member of the existing government would be preferable to appointment of a totally new, inexperienced man to be Governor General; and this information had made the rounds of highly placed officials. But in March 1913 he had written to Erving Winslow, the peevish, single-minded secretary of the Anti-Imperialist League, that "the administration should at once accept the resignation of every member of the present Philippine Commission, who are all avowed imperialists, and should appoint there a governor-general who is thoroughly in sympathy with the policy of speedy relinquishment of American sovereignty over the Philippine Islands" and a Commission composed entirely of Filipinos. Now, in June, he was receptive to the idea of a delayed grant of a simple majority on the Commission to Filipinos.[34]

It is clear, however, that some change of personnel on the Commission was the minimum Filipino desire. And in this, as in so many other instances, the inflexibility characteristic of Taft and Forbes exacerbated tensions. Ordered by the retiring President not to submit his resignation, Forbes fought the desire of other commissioners to do so, trying to preserve the fiction of an apolitical insular administration by keeping the Commission intact. To Vice Governor Gilbert, who voiced a desire to offer his resignation to President Wilson as a courtesy, he wrote: "To assume that with a change of administration the Commission should resign is to assume that the administration of the Philippine Islands is in politics which, to me, is directly opposite to the assumption we should take. . . . We none of us resigned when President Taft took his oath of office." With the office-holders from the old regime apparently determined to retain their places, the issue of appointments and personnel took on special point for Filipino political leaders. In March Rafael Palma submitted his resignation from the Commission, couched in terms designed to embarrass the holdouts. And throughout the spring and early summer, Osmeña and Quezon exchanged views as to potential Filipino replacements for the existing commissioners.[35]

The real prize, however, was not the Commission portfolios, but the governorship. It was understood that the position would go to an American; and the Filipinos' interest, therefore, was in working for the selection of one who would be receptive to their initiatives. For at least the first half of the year the right man seemed to Quezon to be W. Morgan Shuster, the former insular collector of customs and Secretary of Public Instruction, Forbes' *bête noir* among the American commissioners in the years of his isolation. Graceful, but drivingly ambitious—a self-made man—Shuster had always gambled on rising in the Philippine service on the strength of good personal relations with Filipinos. Up to 1907 this had led him to ally himself with Taft's favorites, the established Progresista leaders. Now in 1913 he was on good terms also with Quezon. In the interval, he had changed his views as to Filipinos' competence for self-government. In July, having received the endorsement of the vestigial Progresista Party, he wrote out his policy for the Philippines in a letter of acknowledgment. There should be but one Philippine political party, Shuster argued; and its platform should call for immediate total filipinization of the civil service and "*practical* education of the people in the art of self-government" in preparation for early "political independence." The United States Congress, he continued, ought promptly to recognize "the absolute right of the Filipino people to their independence" and define "the time, general conditions, or state of experience in administration" requisite for Philippine independence.[36]

Shuster, however, had plenty of competition. Speaker Osmeña, remembering his Progresista leanings in the past, preferred Adam C. Carson, a justice of the insular Supreme Court. Carson had the support of members of Congress from Virginia; and L. M. Southworth, a Manila attorney, had similar support from Missouri congressmen. Others favored Rhinelander Waldo, police commissioner of New York City, or George Curry, formerly chief of police in Manila. Rumor had it that Joseph E. Davies had actually been offered the post, only to have the tender withdrawn due to pressure from Secretary Garrison. "It is a cold day when we don't have a new Governor-General, either self or press-appointed," Forbes noted in his journal that June, proceeding to a personal evaluation in trenchant language of fifteen leading contenders. Meanwhile, Forbes himself was being strenuously championed for retention in office by Wright, Taft, and Brent, each of whom spoke personally to Garrison in his behalf. Apparently their efforts were of no avail. In June Quezon wrote to Pardo de Tavera that he had been authorized by Garrison to say that both Forbes and Worcester would be replaced.[37]

Finally, at the beginning of August, the President was ready to move. Once this was clear, the forces which had been latent since his inauguration came into focus and effectively canceled each other out. Forbes' retention was not seriously considered, but with the help of Redfield and Brent the Governor General helped block the nomination of Shuster. The latter, on the other hand, prejudiced Quezon against Garrison's personal choice, Oscar T. Crosby, on grounds of his being a former army officer and an employee of J. G. White & Co., and therefore presumably unsympathetic to independence. At the request of the Anti-Imperialist League, Quezon suggested its president, Moorfield Storey; but Wilson himself rejected Storey because of his advanced age.[38]

That effectively cleared the stage. On either August 14 or 15, Francis Burton Harrison, a congressman from New York City, who was the second-ranking Democrat on the House Committee on Ways and Means and a pronounced anti-imperialist, called upon Quezon in behalf of the candidacy of Crosby, his friend. Quezon, instead, was struck by the idea of winning the job for Harrison himself. His qualifications were right from the Filipino point of view; and, as a member of Congress, he was almost sure to be easily confirmed. Quezon broached the idea. Harrison asked whether he wasn't joking, but upon being assured that Quezon was serious, gave his assent. Quezon then revealed his idea to Jones, who, at his request, mentioned it to Secretary of State Bryan, as if it had been his own. On August 16 Bryan passed Harrison's name to Wilson, with his own and Jones' endorsement. That same day Quezon saw Bryan and gave Harrison his backing. Bryan asked him to put it in writing and on August 19, after having received a receptive acknowledgment of his first note from the President, forwarded this expression of support from the resident commissioner to Wilson. In the meantime, Quezon had stirred up Underwood, chairman of the Ways and Means Committee, and Senator Gilbert M. Hitchcock, chairman of the Senate Committee on the Philippines, both of whom added their voices in Harrison's behalf. That left only Garrison, who was out of town on a tour of army posts, to be heard from. The President sounded him out by cable, and received his agreement on August 19. The following day, Harrison's nomination was decided upon.[39]

8

Consensus

Francis Burton Harrison is a study in contrasts. Wealthy and socially prominent, with something of the playboy about him, he had a real commitment to reform issues ranging from anti-imperialism and tariff revision to anti-trust action and the redistribution of wealth and power at home. A Virginian and a Yale man by background, proud of his cavalier ancestors, he had for some years represented a Tammany-controlled district of New York City in Congress. He could be a charming man, his bearing graceful and his manners elegant; but at times his control would break and a stubborn, volatile, impetuous temperament would appear, much the way a treble crack will pop out in an adolescent boy's melodious baritone. In many respects, apparently, he was torn in different directions. He was devoted to the cause of Philippine independence and wished to be an instrument for benefiting the Filipino people. But he seems to have felt little personal interest in them or curiosity about them and was often ill at ease in dealing with Filipinos. It is true that his friendship for Manuel Quezon and a few other political associates among the accomplished leaders of the islands was deep and real; but he seldom ventured beyond them and their circle. Forbes had loved to ride and sail about the archipelago, dropping in unexpectedly at remote places to hold public audiences and meet the people. He had a special fascination with the non-Christian tribesmen of Mountain Province and the Moros of Mindanao. Harrison, by contrast, traveled around the islands less than any previous American governor. After Harrison's retirement in 1921, the governor of a non-Christian province recalled that he had visited the Igorot tribesmen of Northern Luzon only once during his seven and a half year administration, and that then he had carried with him a cake of carbolic soap and had washed himself whenever possible after shaking hands with an Igorot.[1]

Harrison's view of Philippine conditions is clear. He did not think that Filipinos were ready to maintain a fully independent government in 1913, but he believed they quickly could prepare themselves to do so if released from the heavy-handed grip Taft and Forbes had fastened upon them. It seemed to him of the greatest importance that they be permitted to try. Three months before his appointment, he had written to Erving Winslow: "Every year I become more earnestly impressed with the necessity of our severing our bonds with the Philippines at the earliest moment practicable; not only have we no justification for holding those people in bondage but I consider the Philippines our 'heel of Achilles' in time of war." Willing to grant that Forbes himself had been honest and sincere in his efforts, Harrison nevertheless believed that his predecessor had been lax in control of his subordinates and arrogant in his relations with Filipinos. When the BIA sent him for review a draft of the appreciative cable it proposed to send in Wilson's name to the retiring governor, Harrison emasculated it, striking out two references to Forbes' having worked for the benefit of the Filipino people, and substituting the adjectives "faithful and careful" for "patriotic and disinterested" in a description of Forbes' personal conduct.[2]

The tone of Harrison's administration, therefore, was not one of succession or continuity, but one of reform. On October 6, 1913, he stepped ashore in Manila to a tumultuous welcome and delivered a ringing message from Wilson:

We regard ourselves as trustees acting not for the advantage of the United States, but for the benefit of the people of the Philippine Islands.

Every step we take will be taken with a view to the ultimate independence of the Islands and as a preparation for that independence; and we hope to move towards that end as rapidly as the safety and the permanent interests of the Islands will permit. After each step taken experience will guide us to the next.

The Administration will take one step at once and will give to the native citizens of the Islands a majority in the appointive Commission, and thus in the Upper as well as in the Lower House of the Legislature a majority representation will be secured to them. We do this in the confident hope and expectation that immediate proof will be given in the action of the Commission under the new arrangement of the political capacity of those native citizens who have already come forward to represent and lead their people in affairs.

Speaking then for himself, Harrison added that he had come to the Philippines not for the glory, honor, or power inherent in his office, but to "hasten the coming of the day of your independence," "to serve as well as in me lies the people of the Philippine Islands," and to "become an instrument in the further spread of democratic government." In a dramatic peroration, he concluded: "People of the Philippine Islands, a new era is dawning. We place within your reach the instruments of your redemption. The door of opportunity stands open and under Divine Providence the event is in your own hands."[3]

Talk of this sort had never before been heard from an American Governor General. The response was immediate. "The political mind and attitude were evident in every phrase," the *Cablenews-American* sniffed the following day. "With its reference to the consent of the governed it might have been a fourth of July 'short talk' at Tammany Hall." To Filipinos, however, the message seemed quite otherwise. *La Vanguardia,* the irreconcilable critic of Forbes' administration, noting that previously Filipinos had felt suspicion and ill will toward Americans, wrote editorially that Harrison's address and Wilson's message had changed everything: "Never before in our mutual history have respect and consideration of American sovereignty been as firmly rooted in these islands as now." The Assembly, at the opening of its session, promptly adopted a resolution, saying, in part: "We believe that happily the experiments of imperialism have come to an end, and that colonial exploitation has passed into history. The epoch of mistrust has been closed . . . . Owing to this, few days have sufficed to bring about a good understanding between Americans and Filipinos, which it had been impossible to establish during the thirteen years past."[4]

Once in office, Harrison pressed ahead vigorously to give substance to what already was being labeled, in his own words, the New Era. Exposure to Philippine conditions confirmed him in his view that Filipinos had been burdened with an arrogant, wasteful, and often corrupt government, which had stultified their development as a self-governing people. The Forbes administration, he felt, had been "irresponsible and despotic." The government, "top heavy with Americans," had been subservient to private "financial interests." Filipinization had been "very largely a myth." The cast of the Forbes administration had cost it the confidence of Filipinos, and this in turn had led to the recent history of deadlocks between the Commission and the Assembly. The proper course now, he reasoned, was to simplify and streamline the government and bring it into harmony with Filipinos' aims. Specifically, this

meant relaxing American guidance and supervision, paring down unnecessary elaboration in offices and structures of government, and open-
handedly transferring to Filipinos as much initiative and power as they
could cope with.[5]

The symbol of the New Era was Harrison's rapid filipinization of
the government. "Wherever possible, I have been giving the Filipinos
a chance to fill the offices for which they were competent," he wrote to
the Democratic chairman of the Senate Committee on the Philippines.
"There is no other way by which we can find out so quickly or so surely
whether or not they are capable of self-government." He started at the
top, with the Commission itself. Secretary Garrison had proposed
creating a Filipino majority once Harrison had established himself in
office, but the governor was in no mood for delay. Informed during his
outward voyage that Acting Governor Gilbert had made several appointments to office, among them a new director of education, dis-
tributed certain appropriations, and raised some salaries, Harrison had
inferred that the American establishment in Manila was attempting to
prejudice his freedom of action. Outraged, he had cabled the BIA from
Kobe, urging immediate action to appoint a completely new Commission. In vain, McIntyre replied that Gilbert had acted to meet an
emergency. Harrison was adamant: "Understand no emergency Education appointment except office seeking."[6] Acting unilaterally, he requested and obtained the resignations of the remaining members of
Forbes' Commission during his first week in Manila.

Faced with a *fait accompli*, the War Department requested recommendations for new Filipino commissioners. Harrison, who had been in
the islands less than a week, put his philosophy to the test. Bypassing
present and former American officials, he asked the Speaker to supply
him with a suitable list. Osmeña, equal to the task, recommended
twelve Filipinos, deftly chosen so as to include a representative of most
political groupings in the islands while leaving the preponderance with
Nacionalista regulars.[7] Ever alert for ways of augmenting the Assembly's power, he suggested that this list be submitted to the lower house
for its approval. This proving unacceptable to Garrison, Harrison and
Osmeña narrowed the list to five after consultation with Quezon, Earnshaw, Chief Justice Arellano, and J. G. Harbord, chief of the Constabulary. The final nominees were Victorino Mapa, an aging justice of the
Supreme Court from Iloilo, for Secretary of Finance and Justice; and
for commissionerships without portfolio Rafael Palma, former commissioner and leader of one wing of the Nacionalista Party, a lawyer from

Cavite; Jaime de Veyra, a newspaper editor and former provincial governor of Leyte, a personal protégé of both Quezon and Osmeña; Vicente Singson Encarnación, leader of the Progresista Party, a wealthy attorney and landlord from Ilocos Sur and former classmate of Osmeña and Quezon in college; and Vicente Ilustre, an attorney and landowner from Batangas, representative of the so-called irreconcilable anti-American element. On October 27 these nominations were approved by the United States Senate; and until after the new year, when three American appointees reached Manila to join them, five Filipinos and the American Governor General comprised the Commission. Filipinos had achieved majority control of the legislature.[8]

At the same time, Harrison was taking steps to increase filipinization of lower levels of the insular government. The Schurman Commission had originally recommended that the government of the Philippines be staffed almost entirely by Filipinos: "It is a safe and desirable rule," the members had reported, "that no American should be appointed to any office in the Philippines [below the level of executive portfolios] for which a reasonably qualified Filipino can, by any possibility be secured. . . . The primary demand will be for honesty and integrity: then for intelligence, capacity, and technical aptitude or skill to perform the duties of the office to be filled." However, while never entirely lost, this vision had been compromised over the years. Thus, although required by McKinley's instructions to favor Filipinos for government employment when their qualifications were comparable to those of other applicants, the Taft Commission had also ordered that discharged American military and naval personnel be given preferential status and had encouraged appointment officers to exercise discretionary power in choosing between eligible Filipinos and Americans. Doubtless, it seemed necessary to make some such allowance, given the paucity of Filipinos capable of speaking English and given also Taft's low opinion of Filipinos' ethics. Whatever the reasons, however, the result had been to augment the inevitable corps of American supervisors and technicians at the top of the government with a body of American clerks and petty office holders in the lower echelons. Their number had for many years remained almost the same. In 1913, when Harrison arrived, there were 2,623 regularly employed Americans in the service of the insular government, more than there had been in 1907 or 1908 and only 154 fewer than there had been in 1903. Twenty-one of twenty-four bureau chieftaincies were in American hands, as were twenty-nine of thirty-five assistant chieftaincies.[9]

This is not to say that filipinization had been stalled. Rather, the number of Americans had remained constant, while the number of Filipinos had increased as government employments had grown more numerous. In 1903, 2,697 Filipinos had held 49 percent of all government posts; in 1913, 6,363 had filled 71 percent. For years, however, Filipino leaders had complained that this rate of filipinization was inadequate. For one thing, they argued, numerous Americans were being retained in lower-echelon offices for which there were competent Filipinos available. Even more important, Americans so totally controlled responsible, policy-making positions that Filipinos were, in effect, denied an opportunity to prove their capacities. The results of such a situation, Osmeña had complained to Secretary Dickinson in 1910, were stultification of Filipinos' individual talents and loss of the people's ability to shape institutions to their own, rather than American, expectations.[10]

Disposed as he was to believe not only that the American establishment was thwarting Filipinos' development but also that many members of the government were corrupt, Harrison began at once to clean house. The director of lands and the first assistant executive secretary, both of whom had been involved in the sale of friar lands, were promptly removed from office. The collector of customs, who doubled as Republican National Committeeman and had large interests in mining, was fired, as were the chief of police and prosecuting attorney of the city of Manila and the director of posts. The director and assistant director of printing appealed over Harrison's head to American political and labor union allies in an effort to ward off a rumored salary cut and were thereupon removed for insubordination. Other officials were transferred, to open up places for Filipinos. The collector of internal revenue, for example, was appointed director of posts and replaced by his Filipino assistant. The executive secretary, Frank Carpenter, who had for years exercised supervisory power over provincial and municipal governments with extraordinary competence and sensitivity, was appointed first civilian governor of Moro Province and was replaced by the former attorney general, a Filipino. Since it was not expected that the new executive secretary would equal Carpenter in energy or ability, this arrangement had the added attraction for Harrison of indirectly decentralizing power and increasing the autonomy of lower levels of government.[11]

Beyond this, a general reduction in American employees was made. Numerous offices held by Americans were consolidated or eliminated;

and the legislature, with the governor's approval, abolished two bureaus of the government. High-ranking American personnel suffered from the appropriation act of January 1914, which imposed a reduction of 10 percent on all government salaries over $5,000 and one of 5 percent on those over $3,000. Ostensibly a gesture toward governmental economy, this struck at a range of offices held almost entirely by Americans and was widely held to be designed to force senior American officials out of the government. Many American civil servants, senior and otherwise, did voluntarily resign their positions, acting variously for reasons of fear, pride, and disenchantment. Some quit rather than serve under newly appointed Filipino superiors. All this, of course, speeded the progress of filipinization. During the first year of the Harrison administration, the number of Americans employed by the insular government declined from 2,623 to 2,148, while the number of Filipino employees rose from 6,363 to 7,283 and the number of bureau chieftaincies in the hands of Filipinos increased from three to eight.[12]

Predictably, there were cries of outrage from many American residents of the islands. The *Cablenews-American,* reporting certain of Harrison's early removals, proclaimed its exasperation in its headline:

LEECH, HOGGSETTE AND WILSON
SURRENDER THEIR SCALPS TO
GOVERNOR GENERAL HARRISON

Three More Stalwart Upbuilders
of Philippine Prosperity Fall Before
Onward March of Reconstruction

Former Commissioner Worcester, speaking at a banquet given him by the Manila Merchants' Association, branded the new policy a "radical mistake" and hinted at an eventual backlash: "The Filipino politicians are like the horse-leech's daughters crying, 'Give! Give!' They will not cease constantly to demand powers which they are as yet wholly unfit to exercise until something has been taken away from them." American businessmen, concerned for the security of their investments, chimed in. Three weeks after his arrival, the *Times* addressed to the governor for comment a statement reading, in part: "The business community, irrespective of nationality, is suffering acutely from the unwholesome fear felt and expressed by employees of the government that their positions were neither secure nor permanent under the present administration." Although Harrison responded with assurances of security for existing employees, the scare continued to grow. "In business nearly everyone is marking time," the independent *Philippines Free Press* wrote in January 1914: "Everywhere retrenchment is the word." Two weeks later, an official of J. G. White & Co., writing to his principals from Iloilo, agreed: "No one at this time can predict just what attitude this Administration is likely to take toward American enterprises in the Islands, but the present indications are that no assistance or protection may be expected if political capital can be made out of an opposite course. . . . [A] large number of Americans of the better class not connected with the Government are so disheartened by the present prospect that they are making arrangements to dispose of their holdings at whatever price can be obtained and to leave the country as early as practicable." On the anniversary of the Governor General's arrival, *The Weekly Times* surveyed his first year in office in scathing terms—"today we find the civil service destroyed . . . . important positions held by incompetents . . . politics triumphant while public need is unregarded . . . depression, where there had been buoyant confidence"—and pronounced its verdict: "all that Mr. Harrison did was destructive—and a child might have done as well. . . . The need of the time was for a man of constructive ability, a man of resource, not a politician of purely negative attainments."[13]

Not all Americans, by any means, felt this way. For years, a considerable number of persons outside the government service had been arguing, like Filipinos, that definition was better than evasion. To be sure, most of them preferred that the definition in question look to permanent retention, or at least vigorous, authoritarian short-term measures; but if these were unattainable, then they were prepared to accept independence. Many who felt this way were former Army men, who had learned at first-hand the tenacity and capabilities of Filipinos and who had never forgiven Taft for denying them, as it seemed, a clear-cut victory over Filippinos by force of arms. Some, such as James Blount, went further. To them, Taft's condescension toward Filipinos and his refusal to take seriously the intensity of their will to be independent amounted to an imputation of incompetence or cowardice to the American forces that had fought the insurrection. Self-respect led such men to affirm the force and determination of their former enemies. If one could not squarely conquer them, there was a strong compulsion to avoid deceits and compromises.[14]

Beyond this, many businessmen, regardless of previous careers, believed that the Taft formulation had been indecisive and had retarded material development of the islands by pointlessly irritating Filipinos. A vice-president of the Atlantic, Gulf, and Pacific Company had told an American journalist in 1906: "What we ought to do is either to get in or get out; either get in the islands and develop them and so make them prosperous, or else get out and let the people make their own laws, establishing a protectorate to keep the peace." To which William H. Anderson, former Army major, and at the time one of the islands' most successful merchants, had added: "If the United States would only proclaim some sort of definite policy, we would be all right."[15]

To such men, the prospect of a Democratic administration was not in itself disturbing. Anderson, before the elections, predicted that a change of administrations would be "a Godsend to a large number of the present pessimists." And after Wilson's victory, such prominent business figures as Frank L. Strong, E. C. McCullough, and B. W. Cadwallader expressed confidence in the continued stability and prosperity of the islands. James Ross, a former Army officer and judge who had become the attorney for the Manila Electric Railway and Light Co. and the owners of the San José friar estate, hailed the event. Except for a "negligible" group of imperialists, he said, all Americans recognized the right of Filipinos ultimately to be independent. Although opposed to the Jones bill, he advocated immediate creation of an elective upper house in the legislature.[16]

When at the end of December the President-elect remarked in an informal speech that he hoped the United States "presently" would withdraw from the Philippines, many Americans in the islands had panicked, but this group had held its ground. The *Manila Daily Bulletin,* at this point in its history, spoke for men in the range from Anderson and McCullough to Blount, much as the *Times* spoke for the Forbes administration and the prosperous Republican lawyers and international merchants linked with Edward B. Bruce, William H. ("Ham") Lawrence, Maurice F. Loewenstein, and the Pacific Commercial Company, and the *Cablenews-American* spoke for and to a middle level of excitable, hard-line persons in and out of government who believed in permanent retention and racial superiority. In the aftermath of Wilson's statement, while the *Times* wrote loftily of the "selfishness" of early withdrawal compared with the existing "generous" attitude of the retentionists, and the *Cablenews* emotionally declared that independence would be a "calamity," the *Bulletin* proposed a simple take-it-or-leave-it solution: proceed at once to a territorial form of government, frankly avowing the corollary of permanent dominion-like status, or else grant immediate independence. Difficulties between Filipinos and Americans over politics and government, the *Bulletin* affirmed, had sprung from Taft's "spineless and un-American policy." For fourteen years, both sides had endured a "nerve-wrecking" drift; now it was time to clarify the future relations of the two peoples. Predictably, the proposal won strong endorsement from Anderson, Mc-Cullough, and a number of other businessmen.[17]

Improving upon this opening, Harrison acted to undercut the opposition to his administration in the American community. Personally, the governor was convinced of the importance of capital investment and a healthy business environment; and in January 1914 he began to leak these sentiments to the press. So long as capital sought no political voice, it would be not only welcomed but encouraged. As if to provide tangible evidence of his attitude, Harrison moved in the following months to rescue the hard-pressed owners of the San José estate, by depositing ₱600,000 of government funds with a Manila bank for use in loans to the estate. In April he responded to charges that he had isolated himself from Americans by inviting members of the business community to a smoker at Malacañan, where he beguiled them with expressions of good will and pledged himself to work for improved understanding and communication with them. By the middle of the year, his efforts were paying off. Criticism of the administration began to decline, and business leaders expressed optimism about economic prospects.[18]

For those who could not be won by the carrot, there was a stick. Some time in 1914 Harrison began using the secret service of the Constabulary to unearth the sources of unfavorable materials on his administration that were appearing in the American press. And in the last months of the year two leading critics of the governor, Charles Cohn and Edward Bruce, received warnings through third parties that if they continued in their course, their clients would be made to suffer. Quezon, for his part, stopped off in San Francisco en route to Washington the following year and advised investors there to transfer their Philippine interests from arch critics like Bruce to some other representative. The message was plain. The San Franciscans did as requested, and old-line retentionists in Manila mended their ways. "The struggle is over," wrote Newton Gilbert, who had moved from the vice governorship to Cohn's law firm. "It is simply now a question of being able to wait it out." That winter, Maurice Loewenstein informed Quezon that the *Times* would henceforth moderate its tone.[19]

The leaders of the Nacionalista Party found Harrison's early pace disturbing. They had wanted the United States to commit itself to give their country independence, and they had wanted brisker, more purposeful evolution toward filipinization of the government; but they had not supposed the country ready for immediate independence. During the interregnum in September 1913 Osmeña had predicted confidentially that were the United States to reverse itself and press early independence upon the Philippines, his people would actually draw back and hedge. Harrison's ingenuous devotion to independence and the vigor and speed with which he pursued it, produced exactly this result. Presented by the newly arrived governor with a list of government employees and asked to indicate the Americans who should be replaced by Filipinos, one prominent Nacionalista refused. Changes should be delayed until the governor could acquire personal knowledge of both men and conditions, he argued; were the efficiency of the government to be impaired by precipitate action, independence might actually be set back. Harrison was unmoved. Rapid filipinization was the administration's policy, he replied; and he intended to effect it. "Sometimes the Governor shows himself so impatient . . ." the Speaker told a friend, "that I myself have to caution him to be more moderate. But he says that since he has already started the job, it has to be thorough."[20]

Osmeña's reaction, mixing concern with bemusement, was less intense than that of Quezon. Harrison's personnel changes, extending as they did to Americans who were Quezon's personal friends and former patrons, sobered the resident commissioner; and when, on his return voyage to the United States after having accompanied Harrison to the islands, he was approached by Japanese who seemed eager to fill the vacuum in the Philippines once America had withdrawn, sobriety turned to alarm. Before leaving, he had received a draft bill from Osmeña, which, if passed by Congress, would have authorized the convening of a constitutional convention at an early date for the purpose of allowing Filipinos to create their own governmental structure and institutions. And he well knew Harrison's support of the existing Jones bill. Instead of backing either of these alternatives, however, Quezon sought out Frank McIntyre upon his return to Washington and, after ascertaining that the Wilson administration had not committed itself as yet on Philippine policy, volunteered a plan designed, as he put it, to postpone independence for at least 25 years. Under Quezon's plan, the President of the United States would continue to appoint the Governor General and the justices of the Philippines' Supreme Court, but all legislative authority in domestic matters would reside in a bicameral elected legislature. Power over public lands, natural resources, and tariff relations other than those with the United States would be exercised by the Philippine legislature, subject to the approval of the President; in ordinary legislation, the Governor General would have a reversible veto and the President an absolute one. As for independence, a census would be authorized in 1925 and every ten years thereafter; and whenever it appeared that 60 percent of adult males were literate in English, or 75 percent literate in any language, then, provided peace, good order, and financial responsibility prevailed, a referendum would be held on the question of independence, and a constitutional convention called if the outcome warranted one.[21]

This was a plan for increasing home rule, not obtaining independence; the literacy requirement and the impossibility of again raising the issue of independence before completion of the projected 1925 census made this clear. The political risk for Quezon in advocating such a course after having spent years as a spokesman for immediate independence was obvious. He himself told McIntyre that it would cost him his existing allies and constituents. He wanted to know whether the administration would support him if he were to make the move. McIntyre warily inquired whether Osmeña would. Quezon, saying nothing of the Speaker's draft, answered that he thought so, and that in any case Osmeña knew his views. Had Harrison been told? "My God, no," Quezon replied. "I think he believes in independence. He thinks he can turn us loose in about four years. He believes in it." McIntyre, professing doubt that the administration would support a plan to which its representative on the spot was opposed, nevertheless agreed at Quezon's request to draft a bill incorporating his ideas. During the third week of January, he circulated a detailed memorandum on Quezon's position and views to Garrison and Wilson, both of whom read it.[22]

On January 19 Quezon called upon Wilson to discuss the administration's Philippine policy. The President presumably had at hand McIntyre's memorandum, which had been sent over to the White House that day by Garrison. He may also have had in advance of the meeting some direct expression of the same views from Quezon himself. What transpired between the two men is not known, but out of their meeting there came agreement that the Jones bill was dead and that the administration would oppose immediate independence or any bill committing it to an inflexible schedule or succession of steps. On the other hand, the President expressed himself in favor of Philippine independence in principle and left open the possibility that the administration might back legislation in that session of Congress to increase Filipinos' participation in the government and declare eventual Philippine independence to be national policy. This, of course, was a framework well suited to the plan Quezon had been advocating. But in reporting the outcome of the meeting to Osmeña and Erving Winslow, he omitted all reference to his own efforts and to the existence of the plan he had disclosed to McIntyre, portraying the President as the initiator and arguing that it would be necessary temporarily to accept less than immediate independence in order to retain the administration's good will.[23]

Fortified with the argument that Wilson would accept nothing more radical, Quezon produced a draft bill embodying his plan. McIntyre, analyzing the draft for the War Department, judged it "apparently intended to provide for a permanent relationship of the Philippine Islands to the United States" and commented approvingly on many of its administrative provisions. He recommended, however, that the governor's power over appointments and removals be clarified in such a way as to strengthen his control of the executive departments. Osmeña, Governor Harrison, and Moorfield Storey, president of the Anti-Imperialist League, reacted critically. All three preferred legislation providing for a constitutional convention. Osmeña and Storey were particularly vigorous on this point, the former calling an elected Senate "an unnecessary delay" and the latter bluntly pronouncing Quezon's draft apparently "calculated to postpone rather than hasten independence."[24]

Stung, Quezon retreated toward independista orthodoxy. Blaming the character of his draft on the need to cooperate with Wilson, he portrayed himself as struggling against the bureaucracy for something more liberal. In fact, under pressure from the Speaker and Storey, he deftly edited his proposed bill, changing its tone, but not its substance, by deleting the census and literacy requirements and adding a vague statement, patterned after the Democratic plank on the Philippines, that it was American policy to grant independence when a stable government could be established. This mollified Storey, but not Osmeña. Far away in Manila, however, there was little the Speaker could do. At the end of February, Quezon cabled him bluntly that his bill was unacceptable and that the choice was between Quezon's revised draft and no legislation at all. Reluctantly, Osmeña gave his assent to the proposed bill.[25]

After securing the acquiescence of Storey and Osmeña, Quezon submitted his draft to Jones for revision. Delays ensued: Jones was old and in poor health; his revisions took time. Then the Democratic caucus, reluctant to borrow trouble in an election year, shelved Jones' finished bill. Quezon began to despair. Winslow and Storey, once they saw in detail the bill they had approved in principle, resumed their opposition. Taking Martin Egan, the retentionist lobbyist, with him, Quezon went to McIntyre and protested the administration's lack of support. If this bill failed, he warned, the sentiment of the Filipino people would never again permit him to back so conservative a measure. At the end of May, he saw the President himself and urged that the administration act to obtain consideration of Jones' bill at that session of Congress.[26]

Quezon's efforts revived the so-called Second Jones Bill. In the first week of June its outline was cabled confidentially to Manila for the Commission's comment. Three of the four American commissioners, including Harrison, promptly responded favorably. Secretary Garrison, who had been reluctant to take further action in the Philippines until the dust from Harrison's initial steps had settled, saw trouble coming and ordered McIntyre to try to strengthen the supervisory powers in Jones' bill and omit the pledge of eventual independence in the preamble. Jones agreeably added to his bill a provision for the President to appoint the vice governor and strengthened the hand of both the American and insular executives in various ways but stuck by his preamble. On July 6 he secured Wilson's approval to introduce the bill, though both of them agreed that passage was unlikely.[27]

This was all very well for Quezon, who had elected to risk his career in order to obtain moderate legislation, but it posed grave problems for Osmeña. As we have seen, the Speaker personally had opposed the Second Jones Bill; and although he had given in to Quezon when it appeared that there was no alternative, he remained unconvinced of the bill's merits. In June he had advised the resident commissioner that its nature was such that it would be difficult to defend before public opinion except on pragmatic grounds that it was the only thing that could be had; if, therefore, the bill was unlikely to pass at that session, it ought not to be introduced at all. Osmeña himself was still hankering after a law that would permit

Filipinos to restructure the government and create their own future governmental institutions. He urged Quezon to arrange the Jones bill so that, at the least, the Assembly might implement the new powers to be granted and the existing legislature reorganize the executive departments of the government.[28]

Sergio Osmeña was very different from his friend and rival Quezon. In background, he was a Chinese mestizo and practicing Catholic from the Visayas, Quezon a Spanish mestizo and a Mason from central Luzon. They had entered politics by different routes, Osmeña as a journalist and attorney, Quezon as a soldier and attorney. Osmeña could be warm and benign, and in his personal relations deeply loyal; in these respects he was perhaps more human, certainly more vulnerable than his mercurial, free-wheeling colleague. But in spite of this, most men found him the more remote of the two. He was punctilious in temperament, guarded and introspective in manner. Prizing logical rigor and consistency, he tried never to commit himself in matters of public policy until he had analyzed all the consequences and ramifications of the course he proposed to follow.

Industry and personal discipline propelled Osmeña to the pinnacle of Philippine politics, where, during the Forbes and Harrison administrations, he presided over the Assembly with deft and graceful tyranny. His dominance, almost absolute, rested partly on his dazzling mastery of parliamentary sleight of hand, partly on his control of patronage and appointments under the acquiescent Governors General of the time, partly on the effortless ease with which his composure enabled him to puncture the florid pretensions of hispanized colleagues. "I want you to know," announced an angry assemblyman, warming up to a full-scale assault on the Speaker, "that when I get angry, I send everybody to hell . . . my wife, my children, everybody . . . . " "Corpus," replied Osmeña, smiling benevolently, "that is terrible. But I never intervene in family quarrels." Beyond all this, moreover, there was his pursuit of excellence: "He worked far harder than any other member of the Assembly," wrote Joseph Ralston Hayden. "By sheer industry he made himself the master of every important problem to be dealt with. Chairmen of committees found that he knew more about their special fields of legislation than they themselves did."[29]

In order to controvert Americans' argument that Filipinos lacked the ability successfully to govern themselves, Osmeña made the Assembly a demonstration of his people's capacities, "an instrument of liberty," as he was wont to say. Partly for this tactical reason and partly because his own political strength was there, not in Washington, he preferred that the Philippines' evolution toward autonomy and eventual independence take place within the structure of Philippine politics. Repeatedly in the years leading up to the Jones Act, he urged Quezon to secure from the Americans not specific changes in the Philippine government but authority for the Assembly, or the full legislature, or a constitutional convention in the islands to make changes of its own choice. In this, he was concerned with far more than simple aggrandizement of his own power or fealty to his original tactical insight; he wanted Filipinos to evolve toward institutions appropriate to their own expectations and needs, not those of Americans. He had said this pointedly in the Nacionalista petition to Dickinson in 1910, and he was to demonstrate it in numerous ways throughout his life: in his preference for Spanish over English, for example, and his deeply felt opposition to the employment of American experts and technocrats in the Philippine government. This was the crux of his objection to the Second Jones Bill. As he argued to Quezon, opposing one of its provisions, the structure and practice of Philippine government "must be formulated when the time has come not in accord with theory obtaining in other countries, no matter how enticing it may look," but "through the light of what really suits the nation."[30]

Defense of the Second Jones Bill was not only odious to Osmeña, it was politically dangerous. In filipinizing the insular government Harrison had studiously sought the recommendations of Nacionalista leaders, thereby focusing upon the Speaker in particular both the clamor of those seeking office and the anger of those who were disappointed in their quest. In March 1914 the left wing of the party, under the leadership of Teodoro Sandiko, deserted and joined its interests with those of former revolutionary army officers in the new Partido Democrata Nacional. Through their organ, *Consolidacion Nacional,* the Democratas launched a bitter campaign of vituperation against Osmeña and the regular Nacionalistas, charging them with government by clique and with abandonment of the fight for independence.[31] The Second Jones Bill, lacking its predecessor's specificity as to independence, was grist for the Democratas' mill. *Consolidacion Nacional,* ridiculing Nacionalista pretensions to stand for immediate independence, announced that the New Era had become an "Era of Deceit"; and Democrata orators at a rally in Manila hinted

217

at a return to armed rebellion, winning wild applause. When Nacionalistas called a rally of their own, to endorse the bill, Democratas and Progresistas packed the meeting and carried a vote opposing it.[32]

Osmeña took it all in stride. He had asked Quezon in advance to provide him with strongly worded endorsements of the bill by American anti-imperialists if it was introduced; and Quezon, drawing upon his ally Jones and employing a go-between to pacify Storey, supplied messages certifying the bill as a step in good faith toward independence. Quezon himself drafted the Anti-Imperialist League's cable in support of the bill. In Manila, Harrison, who took Quezon at his word that the Jones bill was the best that could be obtained for the time being, issued a strong endorsement, calling attention to the pledge of independence in the preamble.[33] Meanwhile, the Speaker himself was regrouping his forces after the initial Democrata onslaught. It was easy to arrange public meetings in support of the bill, and rallies were held promptly both in Manila and in Cebu. But this did not end the opposition. The inadequacies of the Second Jones Bill became the rallying point for all manner of disaffected persons— Progresistas, Democratas, hispanophiles, Nacionalista back benchers, Veterans of the Revolution. The ostensible issue was hypocrisy, the support of a moderate reform bill with a vague pledge of eventual independence by a party whose platform called for immediate independence. In fact, the issue was the dominance of Philippine political life by Sergio Osmeña; the targets of the opposition were, in its own terms, Caesarism and nepotism. Coolly, Osmeña allowed the movement to have its day; as he was later to write to Quezon, he "left all the windows open to calumny." In the meantime, he circulated information about the Jones bill and prepared his organization. Once the hyperbolical rhetoric of his opponents had begun to grow tedious, he counterattacked. His political allies in the provinces, far away from the supercharged atmosphere of Manila, began passing and sending to the capital resolutions of support. Fortuitously, an abortive armed revolt by revolutionary romantics and the outbreak of the European war in August produced panic and a retreat to the security of proven leadership even among his critics. By October 9 resolutions in support of the Jones bill had been received from nine provincial councils, four municipal assemblies, 256 municipal councils, and 71 popular gatherings. At the opening of the Assembly, thousands of Filipinos gathered outside the Ayuntamiento, while the Alcalde of Manila presented a resolution of gratitude for the Jones bill in their behalf.[34]

In effect, an American Governor General pressing for early independence and a Filipino independista working for moderation had brought most of those involved in Philippine-American relations to a rough consensus behind the Second Jones Bill. Osmeña, emerging victorious from the political trials of mid-1914, seems to have felt a new identification with the bill he had so tenaciously defended. "In general," he wrote to Quezon, "the Jones Bill as it was approved by the House of Representatives is good"; he would not wish to imperil its enactment by pressing his own ideas upon it. In Washington, McIntyre and Garrison joined with Quezon to testify in the bill's behalf; and the President himself approvingly endorsed a memorandum from George Fairchild urging passage, and forwarded it to Senator John F. Shafroth.[35]

Backed this widely, the Jones bill passed the House comfortably in October. From there it went to the Senate committee, which amended it so as to clarify certain administrative features and strengthened American supervisory power by introducing provision for presidential appointment of the islands' vice governor, auditor, and director of civil service. None of this touched the parts of the bill deemed most important by Filipinos, however: creation of an elective senate, extension of the franchise to adult males literate in any language, provision for the Philippine legislature to restructure the executive departments and for the proposed Senate to confirm cabinet-level appointments. On these points there was so little criticism that the Republican members of the committee neglected even to file a minority report. There was, however, a hard core of from six to eight senators sufficiently opposed to the preamble to threaten a filibuster unless its pledge of independence were qualified or omitted. Quezon and Earnshaw, desperate for action, saw McIntyre by night at the latter's home to implore that, if necessary, the administration obtain passage by withdrawing the preamble altogether. But Jones and the Senate chairman, Gilbert Hitchcock, refused to pass the bill without any reference to independence; and none of them, Quezon included, would accept a compromised preamble. Before this riddle could be solved, the end of the session had come.[36]

By 1915, then, the hard-line retentionists were on the ropes. Eight senators might block a bill in the closing days of a hectic session, but presumably they could not prevent its passage the next time around. In the autumn of 1915, it is true, Taft, Forbes, and their chief congressional ally, Representative Clarence B. Miller of Minnesota, launched a last ditch campaign. Taft, speaking in San Francisco that September, charged Harrison with ignorant and malicious behavior in office and dilated upon his Tammany background. Miller, after returning from a visit to the Philippines, told the New York *Sun:* "Not Attila of the Huns nor Theodoric of the Goths ever laid such destructive hands upon human institutions. The result is complete governmental chaos." The extravagance of the attack, however, suggests the desperation of its authors. Their ranks had suffered serious losses, the most spectacular defection being that of Theodore Roosevelt. Beginning in the latter years of his own administration the former President had become uneasy about America's ability to defend the islands and fearful that they might become a cause of friction with Japan. When to this was added the testimony of his own former subordinates that the administration of the islands had become discreditable, he decided that the country should wash its hands of the whole affair.[37]

An even greater loss, albeit less prominent, was the support of the business community. This is not by any means to say that all, or even most, business and commercial interests approved of the Jones bill. The San Francisco Chamber of Commerce and the Merchants' Association of New York, for instance, propagandized strenuously against the bill and in favor of permanent retention. And other bodies, which did not oppose the bill or argue for retention, were not necessarily in favor of passage and independence. The significant point is that American firms with investments in the Philippines, which might have been expected to align themselves with Taft and other critics, in large measure failed to do so. Quezon, like Harrison, had been working to this end through a carrot-and-stick policy. "I have seen many people in New York," he reported in September 1914, "especially those who have money invested in the Philippines, and by using all kind[s] of arguments to suit their particular view, I am succeeding in getting them not to fight . . . the bill." And three months later he advised Osmeña to have the insular government withhold all aid to "big interests" until they had testified before Congress on Philippine legislation. To his friend James Ross, he had held up the threat of more radical legislation if the whole Jones bill, including the preamble, were not passed; and both Ross and his clients, who, as we have seen, were enjoying preferential treatment from Harrison and the Assembly, got the message and lent their support. As Charles J. Welch, a partner in the Mindoro Company, wrote to Jones, "No legislation that benefits the Philippine Islands can fail to help us, and nothing that adversely affects the Filipinos can fail to hurt us." Others, soured on Philippine investments, backed the bill for different reasons—J. G. White & Co. wanted the good will of Filipinos and the insular administration in the hope that it could unload its unprofitable Cebuan railroad lines on the government. The Speyers, who had already contracted to sell their lines on Luzon to the insular government, backed passage because the bill authorized the issuance of bonds necessary to consummate the purchase.[38]

For all these reasons—the moderation and wide appeal of the bill, the disintegration of the retentionist alliance, the successful mastery of Filipino political opposition by Osmeña, and the inheritance of legislative momentum from the near success of the previous session— hopes were high for quick, easy passage of the Senate version of the Jones bill early in 1916. Then, in the second week of January, the consensus upon which success depended was shattered by the announcement that Senator James P. Clarke of Arkansas would introduce an amendment directing the President to terminate American sovereignty within two years. Clarke, apparently, had been goaded into this action by Republican taunts that the Jones bill as it stood indicated tacit acquiescence by Democrats in the policy of preceding administrations. At Wilson's request, he modified his original amendment, fixing the time for transferring sovereignty at not less than two nor more than four years and allowing the President discretion to extend the time limit to the end of the next session of Congress after the expiration of four years, if he thought Congress ought to reconsider the question at that time. Provision was made, also, for the retention of naval bases and coaling stations and for neutralization of the islands or, failing that, a five-year guarantee of their integrity by the United States alone. This revised version Wilson cautiously declared himself willing to accept if Congress were to pass it.[39]

Presidential acceptance of the Clarke amendment produced shock waves in the War Department. Garrison, a basically conservative and judicious man, believed that having disrupted Philippine life in numerous ways, the United States was obligated to guide Filipinos safely to a viable and stable alternative to what had been left behind. That end, it seemed to him, was not yet in sight. Therefore, he had been uneasy even with the vague preamble to the Second Jones Bill, accepting it in time only because he was persuaded that an assurance as to America's ultimate purposes would have a settling effect in the islands. At a cabinet meeting on January 25, he argued forcefully from a memorandum written by McIntyre that four years was an inadequate amount of time for completing what had been started and that Filipinos themselves wished a more measured progress toward independence. Wilson responded that although he agreed Clarke's amendment was unwise, it was not his place to declare a fixed opposition before Congress had acted. On February 2, however, the Clarke amendment passed the Senate by the casting vote of the vice president. Garrison mulled over this sequence of events. For some time he had been at loggerheads with both the President and Congress over preparedness issues in general and the role of the National Guard in particular; perhaps the seemingly disingenuous reversal of his Philippine policy was the last straw. In any event, on February 10 he resigned his office, citing differences with Wilson concerning both military and Philippine policies.[40]

These developments ended all possibility of Quezon's continuing in the moderate, cautionary role he had taken toward Philippine legislation since December 1913. At that time he had frankly told McIntyre that the risks were too great to be borne unless the administration would stand behind him; this, in effect, it had done, allowing him to blame his advocacy of mere reform instead of immediate independence upon administration policy. Now, in 1916, the issue of independence was out in the open; and the President, for reasons which are still not clear today, but which smack of indecision and ambivalence, had spread abroad the impression that he would accept a radical bill were Congress to pass one. Quezon responded accordingly. Cabling news of the Clarke amendment to Osmeña, he invited the Speaker to reactivate his proposal for a constitutional convention, if he wished. "Nothing that you can do," he added, "will hurt the Bill."[41]

There was more than expediency to recommend the Clarke amendment to Nacionalista leaders. The measure was more conservative than at first glance it seemed, for it not only gave independence but assured the ensuing Philippine government of protection against external dangers for at least five years. Assuming that the United States would retain sovereignty for the full four years allowed in the revised version of the amendment, Filipinos could count on nine years in which to complete organization of a fully self-sustaining government. This would bring them to 1925, the year when independence might first have come under Quezon's earlier formula. The President appeared to favor this approach, at least tacitly, over that of the Second Jones Bill; and his support was essential for any legislation they hoped to pass. In a word, Nacionalistas had been asking for immediate independence for years; and this was the safest way they were likely ever to get it. Accordingly, the Assembly unanimously passed a resolution in support of the amendment, and Quezon, forwarding it to Wilson, added his personal endorsement.[42]

Then second thoughts set in. For one thing, the Senate, in passing the Clarke amendment, struck out of it all provision for neutralization or American protection after independence; and the closeness of the vote persuaded the resident commissioners, Jones, and Hitchcock that they dared not try to reverse this action unless they were prepared to lose the whole amendment. This sharpened the issue a great deal, making the Senate bill more truly an immediate independence bill. Principle and consistency still required that it be supported, but pragmatic considerations seemed to favor the Second Jones Bill. As Quezon cabled to the Speaker, emphasizing the need for a firm decision: "Is the desire for early independence paramount regardless of the consequences? If so, let us accept unqualifiedly Clarke amendment. Are we seriously concerned about possible injury to our material interest and the lack of safety from foreign aggression? Is this concern such that we would rather see our independence postponed ten or fifteen years or perhaps indefinitely? If so, let us insist on Jones Bill."[43]

This, of course, schematizes a matter which was in reality agonizingly personal and emotional for the men involved. In Washington, Quezon was briefly prostrated in bed by the tension; and in Manila, the ordinarily composed and inscrutable Speaker cast about in agitation for ways of slowing the juggernaut of virtually immediate divestment. Both were concerned about the danger of a revolution under the Clarke amendment. Nor were they alone. Harrison and Rafael Palma, it is true, announced themselves ready for independence even without neutralization or a guarantee of protection. But other leaders were less sure. Teodoro Kalaw went so far in the opposite direction as to draft a resolution by which the Assembly would have declared itself unwilling to accept independence unless subsequent negotiation of a guarantee was intended. In mid-February the consensus among Nacionalista leaders was that, while the Clarke amendment was perilous without a guarantee, they could not risk opposing it. But in fact, one wonders why not. Singson and Sandiko, leaders, respectively, of the Progresistas and the Democratas, also feared the omission of a guarantee; and public response to the amendment was conspicuously tepid.[44]

In these circumstances, tactical planning was chaotic. Osmeña was inclined to concentrate all efforts on restoring the guarantee and on amending the final bill so as to loosen up the inflexible schedule of steps toward full independence. In particular, he wanted the bill to prescribe what the Philippine government must have accomplished prior to receiving its independence, namely reorganization of insular, provincial, and municipal governments, creation of a constitution, adjustment of government finances to meet the requirements of nationhood, and establishment of a defense plan. Barring anything this specific, he recommended that the President be given increased discretionary power to delay final separation of the two countries.[45] At one point, Quezon, who had repeatedly advised Osmeña that any attempt to amend the Clarke amendment would kill it, himself urged the Assembly to appeal by resolution for its amendment to include a guarantee. But three days later, he had changed his mind. In the interval, he had become convinced that equivocation as to the Clarke amendment might kill not only that measure, but the Jones bill as well. On these grounds, he agreed with Jones and Wilson to try for passage of the Senate bill, including the Clarke amendment, in the House, relying upon the President's general treaty-making powers for subsequent protection.[46]

Not only Quezon, but the other authors of the original legislation, as well, found this a troublesome course. Jones, opposed both to the Clarke amendment and to a prohibition clause inserted into his bill by the Senate, would have preferred not to report the Senate version, but gave in rather than risk defeat of the whole bill by opening a Pandora's box of amendments. McIntyre, for his part, considered the independence and prohibition provisions so distasteful as to justify defeat of any legislation whatsoever.[47] Nevertheless, the tactic was followed through to the end. On March 1 Jones' committee reported out the Senate bill on a strict party vote; and on April 28, pressed by the President, Jones, and Quezon, the Democratic caucus in the House adopted the measure. However, twenty-eight Democrats, led by Tammany men from New York, refused to follow the caucus' vote. On May 1 this group, allegedly under the influence of the Catholic hierarchy, but probably in some cases answering a call from banking and textile interests concerned, respectively, for the security of Philippine government bonds and Philippine markets, joined with Republicans to defeat the Clarke amendment and substitute the Second Jones Bill for the Senate version.[48]

This served, as perhaps Quezon had foreseen it might, to restore in somewhat battered and weary form the consensus that had existed prior to January 1916. Ranks closed, and after some inevitable legislative delay, a conference committee reported essentially the Senate bill of 1915. This was easily passed, and on August 29, 1916, became law. With an air of relief, William Atkinson Jones announced that the right choice of provisions had been made.[49]

Reaction in Manila was jubilant. Forty thousand persons paraded through the streets, and the city bestowed upon President Wilson a silver tablet inscribed with a message of gratitude. Ceremonial cables of gratitude and congratulation crossed the ocean to and from Washington. Osmeña, in an official cable, declared to Quezon: "No other living Filipino could have fulfilled such a tremendous task with such a rare success in so short a time, and it should be here emphatically stated that your sincere and steadfast efforts have saved to your country centuries of sufferings which other less fortunate peoples have to go through on their way to final emancipation."[50]

9

Nationalizing
the
Economy

While taking steps to clarify American political intentions toward the Philippines, Harrison had also been acting to promote economic development in the islands. Like Forbes, he believed that economic growth depended upon the investment of capital; but unlike his predessor, he was an advocate of early Philippine independence and was unwilling to achieve economic development in ways that would retard progress toward that political goal. For Harrison, nation building and the pursuit of nationality were inseparable. His attitude toward capital and toward business in general was affected also by his sympathy for reform. Recent American history had convinced him that concentrations of economic power in the hands of private interests were likely to be both abusive and corrupt, quite apart from their influence upon the prospects for Philippine independence. For these reasons, Harrison's enthusiasm for foreign investment in general, and for American investment in particular, was guarded. He consistently welcomed American capital when it could be had without political strings attached, but at the same time he was determined to make the Philippine economy self-sustaining without it. In company with the Filipinos themselves, he believed that the inhabitants of the islands should control their own economic destiny.

The solicitude of earlier insular administrations and the fears of Filipino leaders notwithstanding, American investors had taken relatively little interest in the Philippines. American banks and investors purchased the insular government's bond issues, contributing in this way to the growth of infrastructure; and American and foreign individuals and firms invested in such fields as wholesale and retail commerce and newspapers. But up to the beginning of the Harrison administration relatively little American capital had been invested in production—in agriculture, mining, or manufacturing. In part, most authorities at the time agreed this resulted from Congressional restrictions such as that placed upon the amount of public land that could be purchased or leased. But in addition to this, investment was discouraged by the remoteness of the islands and the uncertainty of their political future. We have seen how, after an initial surge of enthusiasm, prospective investors backed away from involvement even in building Philippine railroads, leaving the government at the mercy of the Speyers and the White syndicate. "The truth is," Taft wrote in the midst of that negotiation, "that capital finds itself so profitably employed in this country [that is, the United States] that it is only after the greatest effort that it can be induced to go as far as the Philippine Islands."[1]

Partly for this very reason, however, American authorities in previous administrations had often been so attentive toward businesses that did involve themselves in the islands as to lend substance to Filipinos' suspicions of preferential treatment and fears of possible exploitation. Officially, it is true, the government had conceived its role in relation to private business simply as that of an enabling agent. "The Government can not make prosperity," Forbes once told the members of the Manila Merchants' Association, "the Government can not create wealth, it can only assist. . . . To use a figure of speech, the surface of the field is to be kept smooth by the Government: it is the merchants who play ball." Unofficially, however, it went much further. As Forbes later recalled: "My idea was that we should jealously guard the interests of people who came out to the Philippines and put up money, and make sure they made money if we possibly could, with the idea of giving Manila a good name among capitalists."[2]

Railroads are a case in point. The Manila Railroad Co. on Luzon and the Philippine Railway Co. in the Visayas were the largest foreign investments made in the islands during the first decade and a half of American rule. For this reason and because of the centrality of railroads to the government's plans for economic development, they were regarded as models; and the insular government had taken special pains to ensure their success, hoping that it would stimulate potential investors in other fields. To begin with, it had confined itself to guaranteeing a return of 4 percent on bonds issued by the railway companies to cover the costs of constructing certain specified routes. In practice, however, assistance in this form and extent quickly proved inadequate. Both companies had difficulty selling their bonds at a price even approaching par value, and this threatened their ability to build the systems upon which they and the government had agreed. Anxious both to speed construction of the railroads and to prevent any failure or compromise of the largest investment projects yet undertaken in the islands, the government had steadily increased its support of the two companies. In the case of the Philippine Railway, the weaker of the two, the insular government had itself bought the company's bonds and had taken a liberal and forgiving attitude toward its failure to meet certain requirements of its concession. In late 1908 bonds of the Philippine Railway were marketed through the offices of the BIA, at Taft's own insistence, in an attempt to stimulate sales by emphasizing the government's interest in the line's success; and New York banks were induced to support the issue by promises that funds of the insular government would be deposited with those that cooperated. This support brought Philippine Railway bonds into effective competition with those of the Manila Railroad, requiring an extension of the 4 percent guarantee to the latter's future bonds if they were to be sold. This was arranged in 1909, as part of a deal whereby the company, for its part, undertook to build a difficult 22-mile branch through the mountains to the summer capital at Baguio and a 135-mile line linking its existing branch in Albay with the rest of the Luzon system. This too proved inadequate to the railroad's needs; and so in 1911 as part of a reduction and recalculation of the currency reserve funds, 25 percent of the Gold Standard Fund was made available to the Governor General for short-term loans to help the line meet its construction costs.[3]

Each of these increases of government support had for its rationale the need to ensure rapid expansion of the railroad system and support investors who had thrown in their lot with that of the Philippines. This was a defensible position, given both the conviction of high government officials that private ownership of railways was infinitely preferable to public and the absence of other investors to take up the burden should those already involved in Philippine railroads grow discouraged. Evidence suggested, however, that considerable corruption existed in the railroad companies and that the government's largesse was serving in great measure to enrich private individuals rather than promote the public interest. Construction costs on the Philippine Railway, for example, ran approximately 50 percent in excess of original estimates; and it was noted bitterly, even within the government, that J. G. White & Co., organizer of the railroad syndicate, was itself the construction contractor for the line. White's syndicate had guaranteed White & Co. a profit of 15.5 percent on the cost of construction, and it was obviously to the contractor's advantage to run up expenses as high as possible. Feeling on the Commission and in the office of the supervising railway expert was that White was building honestly and well but was putting in a more costly line than was necessary to carry the anticipated level of traffic. The Manila Railroad, on the other hand, suffered from profiteering in its own right-of-way department. The head of that department, one José Robles Lahesa, transacted the company's business through his own bank account, paying for land purchased by the railroad in personal checks, then billing the company for much larger amounts. Moreover, he himself refused to deal directly with the original owners of the land in question, insisting instead upon buying through a clique of middlemen, who both squeezed the owners and inflated the price finally charged the railroad. An investigation in 1913 estimated that on account of this network of corruption approximately half of the ₱3,067,121.68 expended for acquisition of land "was disbursed unnecessarily by the company and went into hands other than those of the original proprietors of the land." All this was known both to the management and to the insular government.[4]

Unlike his predecessors, Harrison believed that railroads, as essential public utilities, ought ideally to be owned by the state. He could see no legitimate reason for the government to continue its expensive support of private corporations that had failed to sustain themselves; and he strongly suspected that the previous administration's persistence in doing so, despite knowledge of corruption in the companies, implicated the government itself in their misdeeds. Ethics and theory alike pointed toward reform and possibly eventual nationalization. As a first step, he abolished the existing Board of Rate Regulation and the office of supervising railway expert, replacing them with a Public Utilities Commission of his own choosing. This body promptly launched an investigation not only of the railroads' current state, but also of their relations with the Forbes administration. Harrison himself made it plain that certification of future bond issues for the insular government's guarantee of interest would be made only after a complete study of past as well as present procedures for acquiring right-of-way. Government solicitude toward investors in Philippine railways was over.[5]

Of the two companies, the Philippine Railway was the larger financial burden to the government. At the beginning of Harrison's administration, payment of the 4 percent on its bonds was taking around ₱600,000 annually. On the other hand, it posed no challenge to Philippine economic self-determination. Plagued by high construction costs and low traffic density, its owners convinced that it was unlikely ever to become consistently profitable, the line had been offered to the government for purchase as early as 1909; and in the opening months of Harrison's administration the offer was renewed.[6] The governor, confident that the Philippine Railway could be dealt with at leisure, concentrated his energies on the larger Manila Railroad. He did so at a time when the Luzon system was encountering serious financial difficulties. Although operating revenues continued to be high enough for the railroad to show a profit as a carrier, construction expenses were becoming unmanageable. Even with the government's guarantee, the company's bonds could be sold at no more than 70 percent of their par value. According to law, moreover, such bonds could be issued only against the security of completed sections of track 20 miles in length. This meant that in the case of the ruinously expensive 22-mile branch line being built to Baguio, virtually the entire estimated cost of $3,000,000 would have to be paid out prior to the issuance of even these depreciated bonds. Faced with this prospect, the company informed the BIA in July 1914 that it would have to halt all construction unless the government were to lend it funds with which to continue.[7]

This brought matters to a head. To Harrison, further support for the railroad seemed almost unthinkable. Opposition to its management, which included some of the most strenuous critics of the New Era, had become almost an *idée fixe* with him; and late in July his feelings were reinforced by disclosure that the railroad had been paying its construction contractor (which happened to be the parent Manila Railway Company in England) in bonds, thereby placing the insular government in the position of guaranteeing a return of 4 percent not only on construction costs, but on profits as well. Declaring his administration's lack of confidence in the company, Harrison urged that the government end its support of private interests and acquire ownership itself. "I am and have for some years been a strong believer in government ownership of railroads wherever that policy is feasible," the governor explained to Garrison. "The long series of scandals and frauds connected with the construction of the Manila Railroad Company certainly afford us an object lesson in how private ownership of railroads may not be ideal." Receiving no encouragement from Washington, he bided his time and then, when the company's financial position worsened, tried a new tack. On October 27 he unexpectedly notified the War Department that he would file for receivership of the railroad on the following day.[8]

The response in Washington was decidedly unfavorable. General McIntyre, who had been Edwards' assistant in the BIA during the Taft years, believed as a matter of principle that the Philippines ought to be developed by private capital; and he could conceive of no advantage whatsoever from hastily overturning the existing company. Completion of the Manila Railroad's routes was to everyone's advantage, he believed; and given the condition of world money markets following the outbreak of war, the government would have to finance at least part of the remaining construction, no matter what the ownership or management of the railroad might be. If the existing company survived, it could be expected to carry part of the burden; if it failed or was nationalized, not only would the whole cost rest with the government, but present and potential investors in other fields would be disheartened, to the general detriment of the islands' economic well-being. Consulting Charles Conant, chief architect of the Philippine currency system, McIntyre ascertained that the insular government could safely lend the railroad up to ₱2,500,000 more from the Gold Standard Fund. He recommended that it do so, on condition that the company undertake to provide an additional ₱2,200,000 from sources of its own.[9]

McIntyre's economic argument against nationalization or receivership was complemented by the political views of Garrison and Quezon. Both men felt that failure of the largest foreign investment in the Philippines would be taken as a sign that criticisms of the Democratic administration had been justified. This, in turn, could be expected to reduce or even eliminate the likelihood of passing either the Second Jones Bill or any other progressive legislation for the islands. Wherefore, both joined McIntyre in urging the insular government to suspend its plans, at least for the time being, and take steps to continue its support of the existing company. Garrison, for his part, seems also to have shared McIntyre's concern to avoid discouraging other private investors.[10] Quezon's position was more ambiguous. It was he, as we have seen, who had originally won Assembly approval for a perpetual franchise, over the objections of Osmeña; and in 1914, at the time this question was raised, he was trying to neutralize possible opposition to the Second Jones Bill by investors with interests in the Philippines. Hence his apparently sincere opposition to Harrison's desire for nationalization or a receivership. Finding, however, that not only Harrison, but Osmeña and a majority of the Assembly, as well, were disposed to end government support of the company, Quezon backed away from identifying himself with an unpopular cause. In mid-November, his cables to Manila begin to show signs of hedging, with allusions to eventual nationalization of the railroad; and by the latter part of December he was openly ambivalent.[11]

Harrison was a tenacious, even willful man. Ordered by the Secretary of War to scrap the idea of a receivership and proceed with obtaining the legislature's approval for additional loans of up to ₱2,500,-000 from the Gold Standard Fund, he complied; then he set terms so obstructive as practically to rule out the possibility of the railroad's accepting them. Negotiations for the actual loan dragged on until October 1915, Harrison doling out small amounts of money from time to time during the interval to prevent total cessation of construction.[12] Finally, the company gave up the fight. Unable to sell its bonds at an acceptable price and confronted by evident hostility in the insular government, it opened negotiations for sale of the railroad to the government at the end of October. Terms were easily arranged; and in December Harrison and the general manager of the line (whom he had banned from his presence since December of the previous year, because of alleged complicity in the company's corruption) signed a contract. Final acquisition occurred in 1917, following approval by the United States Congress of the necessary increase in the insular government's bonded indebtedness.[13]

The intense personal antagonism that characterized the confrontation between Harrison and the Manila Railroad ought not to divert one from recognizing that, at root, acquisition of the railroad was undertaken to help prepare the Philippine economy for the requirements of national independence. To Harrison, it was not enough that there be a railroad, even a well-managed one, in the islands; what mattered was that the railroad should be so governed as to make the well-being of the Philippine nation its primary goal. "I believe that the people of the Philippine Islands should own their greatest public utility," the governor declared in recommending legislative approval of the purchase. "This railroad is a public highway and should be operated for the benefit of those served thereby rather than for the financial benefit of private stockholders. . . . The conduct and operation of the Manila Railroad Company enters in one way or another, into almost every detail of your economic growth, and thus directly or indirectly affects and will continue indefinitely to affect the daily lives of the people of these Islands."[14]

Obviously, this logic could be applied not only to railroads, but to every pivotal aspect of the islands' economy. In particular, it was relevant to institutions that controlled the supply of capital and the availability of credit. During previous administrations, as we have seen, Filipinos had become acutely sensitive to the danger of their country's being exploited by foreign capital. Ironically, however, overseas capital had shunned the islands by and large, throwing them back upon their own resources for financing development and growth. By common consent, these had proved inadequate. Industrial development had been almost nonexistent during the administrations prior to Harrison's and repeatedly the government had been forced to intervene in the credit market by depositing its own funds in local banks for use in loans to sugar growers. At the end of the Forbes administration, interest rates in most parts of the islands ranged from a low of 25 percent to a high of 100 percent.[15] Determined to lay the foundation for a viable, truly national economy, Harrison needed a vehicle that could increase the supply of capital and credit in the islands without attendant risk of foreign exploitation or political intrigue. Not surprisingly, he decided upon a national bank.

The Philippine National Bank, established by act of the legislature in 1916, was a logical extension of earlier attempts to increase the availability of credit. Almost from the beginning of civil government, for example, there had been a broad consensus among both Americans and Filipinos that creation of an agricultural bank was essential. In 1903 the Commission had ordered preparation of a plan for establishing such a bank with government funds. But E. W. Kemmerer, upon whom the task devolved, disapproved of a government-owned bank and recommended instead that the Commission follow the example of the British in Egypt. To this end, he drafted a plan for a privately owned and managed institution, limited by its charter to agricultural banking and prohibited from charging interest in excess of 10 percent; in order to minimize risks and thereby encourage private interests to take on the job, the insular government would guarantee a return of 4 percent on capital invested in the bank and would facilitate its operations by permitting government employees to make collections and do certain other work for it. Kemmerer's draft, though attacked both by advocates of straight government ownership and by private bankers, impressed the Commission and the BIA. As a second report by Kemmerer demonstrated, the Egyptian bank had been a conspicuous success; and it seemed that conditions in the Philippines were nearly enough analogous to justify high expectations for such a bank there. Strongly advocated by Taft, a bill for a private agricultural bank along the lines recommended by Kemmerer passed Congress early in 1907 and was signed into law on March 4.[16]

As was so often the case with Philippine investment opportunities, private capital lacked interest: in Manila the Banco Español-Filipino rebuffed an inquiry from the Commission, claiming that the task was beyond its resources; and British and American bankers evaded the issue by referring it to their superiors overseas. Approached by the BIA, James Speyer declined on account of financial conditions in the United States. Other American bankers followed suit, citing lack of experience in agricultural banking and doubts about finding qualified personnel. For a while, it appeared that a syndicate of bankers in Kansas City might be interested; and one of them actually accompanied Taft to the Philippines in 1907 to investigate. This possibility was eliminated, however, when the bankers in question insisted upon a wide variety of special privileges, including a 25-year government guaranty of their principal and the right to issue national bank notes and engage in general as well as agricultural banking. Spurred on by urgent pleas from the islands for assistance to agriculture, Taft thereupon reverted to his original plan of government ownership. In June 1908, acting with his approval, the Philippine legislature created an insular agricultural bank with capital of ₱1,000,000, authorizing it to receive deposits from the public and to make loans of not less than ₱50 nor more than ₱25,000, at interest of 10 percent or less, on agricultural land or insured crops.[17]

At first, the new bank did a disappointing business. In 1908 the condition of land titles was little better than it had been under the Spaniards, and many persons who might usefully have borrowed from the bank could not provide acceptable security. But once the insular government's program for a general cadastral survey began to produce results, the number of loans increased markedly. By the second half of 1912 the end of the bank's original capital was in sight, and steps were taken to expand its operations. In December of that year the insular treasurer temporarily authorized the deposit of provincial governments' funds in the Agricultural Bank; and in February 1913 the legislature, approving his action, empowered the bank to receive deposits from all levels of government as well as from private sources and pay interest of up to 4 percent. Thus rejuvenated, the Agricultural Bank played a major role in the economy during the early years of the Harrison administration. In just the second half of 1913 it loaned more than its entire original capital; and by the end of 1914 it had more than ₱4,000,000 in loans outstanding. Moreover, through its branches, the bank established a system for transferring funds and collecting bills between different parts of the islands, thereby facilitating not only agriculture but commercial exchange as well.[18]

Beneficial though all this was, it soon threatened to exhaust even the augmented revenues of the Agricultural Bank. To help carry the burden, the legislature passed an act in February 1915 creating and regulating rural agricultural cooperative associations. But obviously this was only a stop-gap. That summer, therefore, the vice governor, Henderson Martin, drafted a bill for a government-owned "Insular Bank" with a capital of ₱10,000,000 and power to lend for agricultural purposes as well as for those of commerce and industry. And in October, at the opening of the new legislative session, Harrison recommended the establishment of a single, multi-purpose national bank, capable of sustaining all the government's developmental efforts.[19]

Not everyone welcomed this prospect. Frank McIntyre, for example, was reluctant to see the insular government involve itself further in the economy. Surely, he reasoned, it ought not to make commercial and industrial loans in competition with existing private banks. Indeed, when it became known that autumn that the National City Company had acquired control of the International Banking Corporation, McIntyre went so far as to suggest to Harrison the possibility of the government's getting out of all types of banking, including agricultural and international exchange operations and leaving the whole field to this powerful newcomer. In Manila, the Chamber of Commerce of the Philippine Islands evaded the issue of government ownership, upon which its members presumably were divided, but recommended that the draft be revised so as to allocate four times as much capital to agricultural loans as to industrial and commercial loans.[20]

The Nacionalista leaders found neither of these positions compelling. For them, as for Harrison and Martin, the special value of the proposed bank was its potential for becoming an engine of national development. It was the essence of the proposition that the funds of the insular government and the management of its developmental programs should be in the hands of a public, Filipino institution, not a private, American one. "We should make the Philippines financially independent of any outside corporation," Quezon cabled Osmeña in December 1915; to which the Speaker replied, "We are determined to have [a] Bank assuming commercial functions." Anxious that so important a measure be absolutely sound, Quezon had Martin's bill reviewed by the anti-imperialist economist H. Parker Willis, who subsequently drafted a lengthier, more sophisticated bill of his own. Willis' bank, capitalized at ₱25,000,000 and wholly government-owned, was to have had two divisions, a Division of Discount and a Division of Investment, each with its own capital. The Division of Investment was designed to carry on the work of promoting agriculture through the issuance of intermediate and long-term loans; the Division of Discount would deal in short-term, fluid, and commercial credit, issue circulating notes, and carry on open market operations in securities and paper of all types. The bank as a whole was designated fiscal agent of the Philippine government, and the Division of Discount was required to carry on the government's exchange operations and manage as much of the Gold Standard Fund as the Governor General should see fit to deposit with it. A copy of this bill was mailed to the Philippines in December, with Quezon's endorsement.[21]

In Manila, Willis' bill was merged with Martin's and both then altered in the legislative process, so as, in the end, to create an institution in which were ambiguously combined elements of central, developmental, speculative, and wildcat banking. Capitalized at ₱20,000,000, the new bank was made the exclusive depository of all levels of government and was empowered to conduct exchange operations for the government and the general public and to issue circulating notes which would be receivable by the government as legal tender. On the other hand, because of reluctance to increase the government's investment beyond the ₱10,000,000 originally suggested by Martin, ownership of the bank was thrown open to public subscription, provided only that the government retain 50.5 percent of its stock. This introduced an element of private profit into the scheme and even raised a remote possibility of the government's losing control of the bank, owing to the absence of any prohibition against its using its stock to raise funds. More important than this, however, the final act lacked the rigorous protections Willis had built into his bill: the distinction between types of accounts and uses of resources was both complicated and imprecise; the president, or, in his absence, the vice-president, was empowered to make loans on commercial paper unilaterally, without the advice of a discount committee; and the upper limit on the size of loans was raised markedly above the levels Willis had considered safe. In this form, the bill creating the Philippine National Bank, or PNB, was enacted and signed into law on February 4, 1916.[22]

These early efforts to filipinize the economy were contemporaneous with the beginnings of one of the greatest economic booms in Philippine history. World War I, with its vast mobilization of men and resources and its attendant economic demands, produced a marked improvement in the world market for Philippine staples. Happily, the islands were in a position to respond with profit. Although hampered somewhat by the inevitable risks of wartime commerce and by a shortage of ocean-going shipping, they had the advantage of being remote from the scene of the conflict; neither their productive patterns nor their labor pool was disrupted. Accordingly, the Philippine economy expanded rapidly during the war years. The average annual value of exports, which had been ₱98,111,508.50 in the four-year period 1911–14, rose to ₱177,274,487.50 during the years 1915–18. The table on page 238 shows the growth of the three largest items within this total figure.[23]

This growth of exports was accompanied by a general quickening of the islands' economic pace. The value of merchandise sold by merchants, manufacturers, and peddlers within the archipelago rose from ₱487,785,170 in 1915 to ₱1,327,206,302 in 1918. Between the same two years, the number of passengers carried on the two railroads increased from 5,592,317 to 8,403,006, and the amount of freight from 746,766 tons to 1,229,371 tons. In 1915, 114 new domestic corporations, nominally capitalized at ₱12,953,718, registered to do busi-

Export product	Year	Average annual weight in kilos	Average annual value in pesos
Abaca	1911–14	139,886,809	38,438,348
	1915–18	154,508,026	76,515,363
Sugar	1911–14	199,988,025	19,484,248
	1915–18	256,917,426	28,989,938
Coconut oil	1911–14	4,238,604	1,882,781
	1915–18	47,508,650	24,909,771

ness in the Philippines; in 1918, 299 corporations, having between them a nominal capital of ₱72,558,208, did so. The resources (and liabilities) of the islands' commercial banks, which had amounted to ₱63,745,929 in 1913, when Harrison succeeded Forbes, were ₱399,-807,942 at the end of the war in 1918.[24]

Through their government, Filipinos took numerous steps to assure themselves of leading roles in this drama. In February 1915 the legislature authorized the use of up to ₱3,000,000 from the Gold Standard Fund for loans to promote the development of sugar centrals (that is, modern centrifugal sugar mills) and factories for the manufacture of coconut and abaca products. At the same time, it created the Sugar Central Board, charged with encouraging cultivators to build cooperative centrals by such varied steps as guaranteeing their principal and interest, purchasing their bonds, and making them loans. A concurrent resolution, passed in conjunction with these two acts, declared it national policy to provide government support for the creation of cooperative manufacturing facilities not only by sugar growers, but by abaca and coconut producers. Looking ahead to the formation of the PNB, it called for enactment of "such banking legislation as may secure for the national industries ample, easy, and sure credit."[25]

In the following years, these beginnings were broadened out by the creation of various government agencies designed both to promote development and to ensure Filipinos' active participation. Among these, the Coconut Products Board, the National Cement Company, and the National Coal Company were addressed to specific needs of the islands, while the New Industries Board and the National Development Company aimed broadly to promote the growth of Philippine enterprise. The National Petroleum Company and the National Iron

Company, authorized by the legislature, were not in fact organized during the Harrison years.[26]

However, Filipinos' chief instrument for affecting the economy and maximizing their role in it was the PNB. With its mixed character, the bank was in a position to enter into every aspect of the islands' economic life and carry out the policies of the newly filipinized insular government. The importance of its being efficiently organized and effectively managed was, therefore, very great and was, if anything, heightened by the coincidence of the bank's creation with the debate over the Clarke amendment. Recognizing this, Quezon induced Parker Willis to become the first president. "One of the great difficulties that we will have in the Islands for the next few years . . ." he wrote to Harrison, "will doubtless be found in the handling of our finances, for it is well known that we have no experts on this subject, and I am sure that Dr. Willis will be of great help to us in this regard. I wish he could be induced to accept a contract with the Philippine Government for several years as financial adviser."[27]

Willis' credentials were impressive. At the time of his appointment, he was Secretary of the Board of Governors of the Federal Reserve System; and prior to assuming that post he had taught at Columbia and George Washington universities and had been a consultant in the framing of both the Underwood Tariff and the legislation creating the Federal Reserve. In addition to this, he was a dedicated anti-imperialist, the author of a book on the Philippines and the some-time editor of Quezon's American propaganda magazine, *The Filipino People*. In 1913 Harrison had recommended him for a post on the Philippine Commission. Willis' interests, however, were not wholly the same as those of Filipinos. Aware, naturally, of the PNB's role as a national and developmental institution, he brought to its presidency the perspective of a banking theorist and a booster of American foreign trade. Thus, although hopeful of lowering the cost and increasing the availability of credit, he was concerned also to improve the quality and professionalism of banking operations. He hoped that once the PNB had proven itself, links could be established between it and the Federal Reserve System, thereby increasing the use of American dollar drafts both in the Philippines and in the Orient-at-large and facilitating the growth of American export trade.[28]

From the outset, it was plain that Willis' professionalism and conservatism were out of place. The PNB was regarded by the Harrison administration and the majority of Filipino political leaders less as a bank than as a political and developmental tool of the government and the majority party. Accordingly, its loan policy was promotional and open-handed. Even before Willis' arrival, at a time when the presidency was effectively vacant, the administration committed the PNB to lend ₱1,500,000 to the Mindoro Development Company, owners of the San José friar estate, on incomplete security. And when Willis himself subsequently cautioned against the bank's succeeding to the government's role of making annual advances to sugar growers, pointing both to the lack of tangible security and the misuse of funds by many growers, he was dismissed in the press as bookish and impractical and was persuaded to postpone any cutback for at least one more year.[29]

A cornucopia of easy credit, the bank was also considered a vehicle for patronage. When Willis attempted to hire American experts to train his Filipino staff, he was blocked by the board of directors. Technical expertise was an irrelevant luxury, he was told; Filipinos already knew the banking needs of their country. As a result, during the first four years of its existence, the bank had only four officers trained in modern banking practice; of these there were never more than two employed at any one time, and one subsequently proved either incompetent or dishonest. There was no mistaking the meaning of these signs. When Willis expressed dismay at the slowness of people to purchase the bank's stock and open accounts, he was told by prominent Filipinos that the PNB was too political for them safely to invest or deposit their funds with it.[30]

Willis, who had taken a leave of absence from the Federal Reserve to launch the PNB, returned to the United States in September 1916 and eventually resigned the presidency of the bank in February 1917. He was succeeded by Samuel Ferguson, a former stenographic clerk in the insular Executive Bureau, who had risen abruptly to prominence by ingratiating himself with Harrison. Ferguson, proving erratic, was replaced in March 1918 by General Venancio Concepción, a director of the bank since its founding and a former deputy collector of internal revenue. A revolutionary general, Concepción was a protégé of Speaker Osmeña, whose life he once saved; he remained in office until November 1920. A fierce nationalist with a rhetorical temperament and a pronounced disdain for rigorous or specialized forms of knowledge, Concepción was the antithesis of Parker Willis. He it was who had led the fight in 1916 against the employment of trained

American bankers in the PNB. Bringing to office this temperamental set, an extraordinary network of personal links, a penchant for money making, and an impressive facility at intrigue and manipulation, he undertook to guide the bank, the economy, his friends, and his personal fortunes through the heady excitement and risks of the wartime boom.

The tone of the PNB's operations in these years is suggested by the response of its management to the disclosure in 1918 of abuses in the handling of agricultural loans. In May of that year, Archibald Harrison, brother of the Governor General and himself a director of the bank, began an investigation of rumored misdeeds. By July and August he was in possession of information showing gross violations both of accepting banking practice and of the PNB's charter. Agents working under Harrison's orders reported from Occidental Negros:

> Loans have been made for large amounts, for agricultural purposes, on mountain land 25 miles from the nearest market that has never been cultivated and, owing to its location and formation, can never be cultivated. Many loans were found to be in excess of the assessed value of the land and, in other cases, the owner had declared the land at several times its value for the purpose of getting a larger loan from the Bank. In other cases, it was found that the Bank has granted loans for more than would be required to buy equally good land adjoining the property mortgaged and in addition, a large crop loan is also granted. As might be expected, the mortgagor is in arrears in interest and amortization payments . . . .
>
> Of the 230 mortgages inspected, a great many have not complied with the terms under which the loan was granted . . . . Several of them have frankly admitted it. Others claimed that they did not know what reasons were stated in the applications, the bank's officials advised them to change the reasons given and suggested other purposes which the Bank's Directors favored and would, therefore, stand a better chance of being approved. In some cases, the money obtained from the bank for agricultural purposes had been diverted into commercial or industrial investments, and instances were found where the money had been loaned out to other farmers at the rate of 25% per annum.

Thirty-five specific irregularities were detailed in an accompanying document. And Harrison himself presented the bank's board of directors with a 59-page indictment of agricultural and crop loan operations in Negros alone.[31]

Harrison and his agents had discovered an extension of the conditions about which Willis had warned in 1916. Clearly, no bank could go on for long operating this way, especially not a bank which had responsibility for the funds of the government. To Harrison's charges, however, Concepción turned a deaf ear. Using numerous red herrings designed to discredit the investigation (for example, officiousness and indiscretion on the part of the agents, ignorance of Philippine agricultural conditions), he organized other members of the board of directors, all Filipino, and with the acquiescence of Quezon hastily voted an end to the appropriation for Harrison's investigation. Harrison, angry and humiliated, resigned from the board and left the islands.[32]

Once rid of this restraining influence, Concepción and the PNB elaborated their network of loans and credits. In part, they did so with the deliberate intention of shepherding the economy through the expected cycle of wartime boom and postwar bust. The case of hemp is illustrative. In 1917 and early 1918, under Ferguson's presidency, the bank lent erratically but munificently to hemp exporters, apparently with the dual intention of financing the movement of crops and making a speculative profit for itself. By July of the latter year an oversupply of hemp had accumulated in the United States, and prices began a steep descent. Instead of contracting its operations or taking other protective steps, the PNB expanded credit enormously in an attempt to buoy up the market and support Philippine producers and exporters. The Philippine Fiber and Produce Company, granted a ₱1,650,000 line of credit by the directors of the bank, was actually loaned ₱4,638,100 on the authority of the president; another firm, U. de Poli, authorized a line of credit amounting to ₱300,000, was loaned ₱1,175,000 by the personal action of Concepción and his American vice-president, J. Elmer Delaney. The hemp-exporting firm of G. Martini, Ltd., its credit with the bank having been terminated in January 1918 because of its apparent misuse of PNB funds, was haltingly reinstated on the bank's credit ledgers during the following months and finally granted a ₱2,000,000 line of credit in July. By October Martini was back for more. Concepción and Delaney, arguing that Martini had used his loans to break up combinations of buyers intriguing to lower prices and pointing out that "the matter refers to an important commodity of the country," recommended an extension to ₱3,000,000. Overruled by the board of directors, they went ahead anyway. By November the PNB had loaned or discounted bills for Martini in the amount of ₱4,610,000. Grossly overextended and apparently speculating in currency as well as in hemp, Martini was in desperate straits by the beginning of 1919; ultimately, the bank acquired his company, leaving him to manage it, after having extended a total of more than ₱8,500,000.[33]

Even this experience, involving expected losses of ₱3,000,000 each from the loans to Martini and Philippine Fiber and Produce, did not markedly sober the bank's management. In February and March 1919, after Martini had proven unsatisfactory as a support for the market, ₱2,638,700 in dummy loans were made to two of the bank's directors on the authority of Concepción. Ostensibly loans made against the security of hemp already owned by the directors, these were in fact used to purchase hemp on the market as a means of supporting the price. The dummy loan format was employed to hide the fact that the bank itself was the purchaser and thereby hopefully foster the impression of a naturally strong market. No interest was paid on these "loans," and somehow the hemp purchased in this way proved to be worth only about half the amount of money lent to the two directors. When an American bank examiner subsequently asked Concepión why this operation had been undertaken, the president replied that the PNB was a national institution and had been used in this as in other cases to promote the national interest.[34]

A similar condition existed with regard to investments in the sugar industry. In August and September 1918 the bank's New York agency warned it that a severe contraction lay ahead in the sugar market. Nevertheless, in the following months the PNB undertook a major program of capital investments in the construction of new sugar centrals. Between November 1918 and March 1919 approximately ₱22,000,000 in credit was authorized for nine projected centrals. When added to existing agricultural loans in other forms, this resulted in the bank's being committed to approximately ₱21,000,000 more than the statutory limit upon the amount of lending it could do in this category. In this field, as with hemp, there were numerous irregularities. The Bacolod Murcia Milling Company, having itself a paid-up capital of ₱1,039.50, was loaned ₱2,169,000 on the security of mortgages covering land of widely varying quality, whose value as collateral had been arrived at by averaging the value per acre of all the company's holdings. The Talisay Silay Milling Company, with paid-up capital of ₱1,450, was granted a credit of ₱2,568,000, of which it actually drew ₱1,076,600. Both Talisay Silay and Bacolod Murcia presented different collateral for their loans, inferior in value to that which they had offered at the time the bank's directors approved them.[35]

So it was, also, with the manufacture and marketing of coconut oil. The Philippine Vegetable Oil Company, authorized for credit of ₱3,597,000, received a total of ₱26,000,000 in loans and discounts at the personal order of Concepción. Against this, the company had offered mortgages amounting to ₱11,000,000; but these, in fact, had never been recorded, leaving the bank with a major capital loan virtually without security. The Cristobal Oil Company, with capital of ₱906,200 and fixed assets of ₱344,800, reorganized itself in 1918, inflating the paper value of its fixed assets and introducing a "good will" factor of ₱1,526,000; capitalized in its reorganized form at ₱4,000,000, it readily obtained a loan of ₱1,466,000 from the PNB, seven of whose directors and officers were among its stockholders.[36]

Besides acting in these ways to move the islands' crops and promote the construction of mills for preparing them for market, the PNB also financed the wartime sale of former German properties in the Philippines to Filipino and American purchasers. Approximately ₱16,000,000 in loans were made for this purpose, and an equivalent amount of money transferred to the United States for the account of the Alien Property Custodian. As in the cases mentioned above, loans tended toward generosity and security was minimal.[37]

Clearly, there was more to this extraordinary expansion of credit than simply heady nationalism and professional incompetence. Many of the loans issued in these years were grossly and obviously unethical. Directors of the bank authorized extravagant loans to companies in which they were themselves investors, and General Concepción subsequently was sent to jail for misuse of the bank's funds for his own advantage. Questionable or excessive loans were made to prominent political figures. Many loans were misappropriated by the recipients to finance personal consumption, instead of production or commerce. Plainly, the bank had become a vehicle for elitist profiteering and back-scratching, an institutional reflection of the dyadic and familial character of Philippine personal ethics.[38]

More significantly, the misuse of the PNB highlights the interpenetration of politics and economics inherent in the islands' dependent status. The centrality of the independence issue and the standing challenge of American control focused Filipinos' energies upon politics and made even the elementary pursuit of profit and gain a political act. Given the small size of the leadership cadre, its absorption in politics, and the limited sense of class conflict among the people at large, it was arguable that the elite's use of the bank to promote their own economic interests was a nationalist act. Who but the Americans would develop the islands, if not they? Who but the Americans would profit, if, having committed themselves, they failed? Hence the paradox that the use of the bank to develop and sustain the economy through the elite appeared an economic means to a political end, self-determination, while control of the bank's credit policy through the majority party was in fact, for some, a political means to an economic end, personal profit.

Even more important, in the short run, were the simple economic concomitants of this type of banking, carried out, as it was, by the fiscal agent and depository of the insular government. Thanks to the penchant of Concepción and others for filipinization even at the cost of competence, the PNB embarked upon its expansionist, developmental programs without officers or a staff experienced in modern banking. As the economy expanded and demands upon the bank grew, the administration of the PNB collapsed in bureaucratic confusion. An American clearing house examiner sent to the islands at the end of 1919 to investigate the bank discovered, for example, that no combined accounts were kept for the Manila home office and its 13 branches and 58 agencies, and that the bank's calculation of its own reserves was more than ₱22,300,000 in excess of their actual size. The foreign department, suffering from incomplete records, disparities of up to ₱5,000,000 between subsidiary ledgers and the general control ledger, and inconsistent practice in bookkeeping and categorization of accounts, was in the position of being literally unable to determine key balances and the amount of credit extended to various accounts. In one spectacular case, a company actually in debt to the bank was credited with a surplus of over ₱934,000, owing to the payment of proceeds from the sale of its hemp into the unmatured foreign bills account, while the bills covering the hemp in question were filed inexplicably as liquid assets in the account of the bank's New York agency. Elsewhere, it was found that the bank had out almost ₱7,000,000 in loans, for which there was no competent appraisal or other evidence of the value of the collateral.[39]

Misconstruing the provision of the act creating the PNB that required the insular treasurer to deposit government funds with the bank, the Treasury of the Philippine government deposited its currency reserve fund with the PNB during the early months of the bank's existence. In fact, by law the currency reserve could only be deposited properly in the insular Treasury or in such member banks of the Federal Reserve System in the United States as the Governor General might designate. The New York agency of the PNB had a relationship with the Federal Reserve System and thus seemed an acceptable depository for the government's reserves; but unknown to either the treasurer or the Secretary of Finance, the agency was prohibited by its charter from accepting any deposits whatsoever. Funds credited to it were in fact deposited to its account in other American banks. Ignorant of this fine point, the insular government transferred its reserve funds, as it thought, from various other depositories to the PNB agency in New York. Confusion within the bank led to these reserves' being carried on its books as funds deposited in various American banks to the account not of the New York agency, but of the PNB as a whole. In this way, they became merged with accounts maintained by the PNB for its own exchange operations in the same American banks. Because of the government's transmission of unusually large amounts of funds to the United States during the war, most of the currency reserve fund eventually wound up in this position.

In the meantime, the PNB, anxious to support the booming, but vulnerable Philippine economy, was inflating its note issue. To do this, it adopted the policy of reissuing pesos paid in at Manila for the purchase of foreign exchange in New York, instead of retiring them as the law and common sense required. By this process, the currency reserve fund was steadily paid out in New York in the course of ordinary exchange operations, while at the same time the amount of currency in circulation was increased. The effect was intensified by the PNB's miscalculation of its own reserves and consequent overissue of its circulating notes. In 1915, the year before creation of the PNB, there were ₱51,284,907 of all types of currency in circulation in the Philippines; by May 1920 the figure had risen to ₱163,428,638. This was the money which financed the bloated loans of the wartime and postwar periods.[40]

This condition was discovered quite by accident in December 1918, when the insular government, thinking itself temporarily squeezed for exchange because of trade conditions and the payment in the United States of Liberty bonds and APC revenues subscribed in the Philippines, asked the BIA to transfer part of the Gold Standard Fund and other insular deposits in the United States to the current account of the PNB. In Washington and New York puzzled men slowly tumbled to the fact that the government and the PNB thought the reserve fund was in America; in Manila baffled and incredulous men discovered that it wasn't. Over ₱82,000,000 had vanished without anyone's noticing more than a heavy movement in exchange.[41]

There ensued a two-year standoff, during which McIntyre and the United States Treasury regularly demanded retrenchment in Manila and a contraction of both the currency in circulation and the loans of the PNB. By no other means, McIntyre argued, could the reserves of the government be restored and the constant drain upon Philippine funds in the United States for exchange be ended.[42] In response, the bank vociferously and the insular government apologetically insisted that the first responsibility of both in the premises was for the well-being of the whole economy; restoration of reserves was secondary. Implored by Parker Willis, then advising the BIA and the New York agency, to end expenditures for sugar centrals, Concepción refused, arguing: "We must not lose sight of the fact that this bank, unlike the others, on account of its being national, is in some way subordinated to the policy pursued by the Government in the way of economic plans." In the first six months of 1920 the PNB's loans and discounts actually increased by approximately ₱8,000,000; and that August, contrary to all urgings from Washington, Harrison informed Concepción he would permit further issues of the bank's circulating notes.[43]

In the end, however, the plight of the bank could not be ignored. General Concepción resigned in November 1920 to be replaced at the beginning of the new year by two American bankers. Horrified at what they found, the new heads began a careful contraction, issuing few new loans and demanding payment of old ones where possible. Their task, however, was hydra-headed. In the last weeks of December, just before their arrival, the condition of the Bank of the Philippine Islands became critical; suspension was warded off on one day only by the concerted action of private investors, who came to the bank's relief. For years the BPI had been the chief purveyor of crop loans to sugar growers, and its failure would have had a ruinous effect upon agriculture. Not only for this reason, but also because the BPI was in debt to the PNB, the national bank was forced to come to its aid. During the first four months of 1921 it loaned ₱7,500,000 to the smaller institution. During the last week of January, moreover, it was discovered that the manager of the PNB branch in Shanghai had been speculating in currency with the bank's funds and had lost an estimated ₱10,000,000.[44]

Utter breakdown of the currency system and bankruptcy of the government seemed real possibilities; and in the first week of March exchange rates for telegraphic transfers to the United States rose to 14 percent. In order to provide funds for essential government expenditures in the United States, loans to cultivators were called in, raising the spectre of agricultural depression. In Manila there was dismay and confusion. "As far as I could learn," one of the new PNB officers later recalled, "not a single official really understood the fundamental principles of the [currency] system. Every one seemed to have been obsessed with the idea of building up the Philippine National Bank into an immense institution which was to be a panacea for all ills. When this institution finally became almost hopelessly tied up as the result of false theories and incompetent management everyone was up in the air." There was no plausible relief in sight—for the bank, the government, or the agriculture and commerce of the islands—unless the dream of the PNB as an engine for filipinizing the economy were laid to rest and appeal made to the United States government for massive measures of support.[45]

10

Stalemate

In March 1915, more than a year before the final enactment of the Jones bill, Frank McIntyre had drafted a cautionary letter to be sent to Harrison by the Secretary of War if and when passage occurred; and in August 1916 the letter was sent over the signature of Newton D. Baker, Garrison's replacement, ostensibly outlining the Wilson administration's wishes for the future government of the Philippines.[1] Speaking in terms of Garrisonian gradualism and ignoring utterly the near passage of the Clarke amendment, the letter enjoined the Governor General to insist vigorously and scrupulously upon the maintenance and exercise of his official prerogatives and the general supervisory powers of the United States. Filipinos should be confined to the fields opened to them by the Jones bill and should not be permitted to encroach upon the executive. Further filipinization of high offices should depend exclusively upon the capacity of the potential appointees; and approval of legislation by the Governor General, now armed for the first time with the power to veto acts, should depend upon its merit. No impairment of the governor's control of executive functions in the government and no act adversely affecting insular tariff relations, discriminating against American citizens, expanding the electorate to voters of questionable competence, or interfering with the independence of the American-appointed auditor should be tolerated. "We should give to the people of the Islands what Congress has given to them," the Secretary's letter warned, "but we should be particularly careful and not give them those powers which Congress has withheld." Failure to hold the line might afford an excuse for opponents of independence to seek retrogressive legislation.

The Philippines and the United States, 1913–1921

These instructions were not exclusively dictated by constitutional scruples. McIntyre wrote into the letter—and Baker allowed to stand —a suggestion that the Jones Act might, if carefully administered, become a new vehicle for the pursuit of the old goal of retaining the islands by indirect tactics. To some retentionists, like Taft and Worcester, the preamble of the Jones Act seemed an almost irredeemable error: promise a people independence, and you'll have to give it to them. To others, however, Filipinos' desire to be independent, and even their expectation that they would be, complemented the logic of open-ended reform. In 1910 even Forbes had written in his journal: "I rather like, and applaud inwardly, the almost universal desire for independence, and am trying to steer this desire into a motive force for progress and material development. I don't write or speak in favor of independence, as I don't believe in it for them. I believe in the desire for it." McIntyre, who was very different from Forbes in many respects, shared with him a desire to retain the islands indefinitely, at least partly for the good of the Filipinos. He took much the same attitude toward the Jones Act. "Congress has recognized the truth of a generally understood principle," he observed in explicating the act, and then quoted a British colonial jurist who had written: "The problem of colonial government is to keep the bonds of allegiance . . . taut and true. We believe that it can only be done by fostering the spirit of independence, so that . . . every colony should feel that it is a nation in embryo, capable if it will, of at least endeavoring to attain to that capacity of declaring its independence if the Mother Country neglect it or treat it improperly. Such success as we have attained is by the fearless recognition of this principle; and we foster it by self-reliance, by granting as much official and administrative independence as each is capable of exercising."[2]

This was not the interpretation given to the Jones Act by Harrison. Seeing in its passage congressional sanction for the policies of the New Era, he set out in 1916 not to confirm what had newly been received, but to build upon it toward early independence. Thus, in September 1916 he told participants in a banquet given in Quezon's honor:

Both in an economic and in a political sense, we have proven to the satisfaction of Congress that the islands are ready for these new concessions. . . . We have entered upon two great matters destined to work out the economic independence of this Archipelago. We have founded a great national bank which is destined to free commerce in the Philippines and we have entered upon . . . nationalization of the greatest transportation system in the Islands. We have laid the economic foundations for the future greatness of this country, and we have also made the basis of the political structure which is now about to be erected. How could anybody tell whether the Filipino people were ready for independence unless they had a chance to show their capacity in government? The question was not a new one. It had been enunciated substantially by all my predecessors in office here, but we have accomplished more in that respect in three years' time than they had in the fifteen years that went before. . . . These are the foundations that we have laid here in the Philippines. Upon these we are about to begin a new structure. My understanding of the mandate of Congress, as expressed in the Jones Law, is that the Filipinos shall be given an opportunity to demonstrate that they can set up a stable government. And one of the first steps which should be taken to give that demonstration should be the appointment of Filipinos to all positions for heads of departments within the power of the Governor General.

To Baker's official letter, the Governor General replied that suasion was more effective as a means of dealing with the people than rigor or legalism, and that further filipinization was essential to properly fulfilling the intention of the act, "to give the Filipinos a chance to show whether or not they could set up a stable form of government composed largely of Filipinos."[3]

Throughout the entire Harrison administration, there was a disparity sometimes verging on open conflict between the intentions and conduct of the Governor General in Manila and the policy and desires of the BIA in Washington. This was, perhaps, to be expected, in that the relative power and status of the insular executive and the chief of the bureau had never been conclusively defined. Up to 1913, the Governors General of the Philippines had a de facto pre-eminence resulting from Taft's personal knowledge of the islands and his tendency to make policy himself on the basis of exchanges with the men on the spot. In the Wilson administration, however, neither the President nor the Secretary of War approached the Philippines with independent knowledge or special personal interest. As a result, decision making regarding the Philippines shifted from the White House and the Cabinet to the BIA, making its chief, for all practical purposes, the Governor General's superior in Washington.

McIntyre, who succeeded Clarence R. Edwards in 1912, was the ideal man for the job. A career Army officer with a penchant for mathematics and a rigorously logical mind, he had an encyclopedic knowledge of the Philippines and an impressive mastery of the fine points of finance and legislation. This was balanced by a personality that was warm, low-keyed, and courteous. McIntyre had the respect of practically all the actors in the Philippine drama of the years, regardless of their stands on the various issues at stake. In spite of this, he was not in a position to force his will upon the Philippine government in the absence of support from his superiors; the lack of interest and commitment at the highest levels of American government that enlarged the power and influence of the BIA was also, in the end, a limitation upon its effectiveness. From the beginning, Harrison had been able to force the hand of the administration as in his replacing the sitting commissioners and acquiring the Manila Railroad by taking unilateral action on the spot; and once America had entered the war in 1917 and both the President and the Secretary of War were, perforce, absorbed in more pressing concerns than those of the Philippines, his freedom of action was in fact almost total.

This is, of course, only part of the story. It is not immaterial that both Wilson and Baker sympathized at least vaguely with what they took to be the aspirations of Filipinos. Besides this, it is obviously the case that a Governor General who defied or evaded orders from Washington in ways that attracted strong support from the Filipino people could justify his actions as necessary or expedient to maintain the good will of those for whom, ostensibly, American tutelage had been undertaken. It is noteworthy, however, that even in the worst depths of the PNB debacle, when the conduct of both the insular government and the bank was clearly wrong, the BIA could not elicit consistent or effective support from the Secretary. One infers from this that among explanations for Harrison's freedom of action, greatest importance should be attached to the absorption of the highest officials of the government in other matters.

During the first years after passage of the Jones Act, in any event, it was Harrison's view that shaped the course of Philippine government. Considering himself to be, in effect, a constitutional monarch presiding over a government of Filipinos, the Governor General deliberately surrendered initiative to elected officials. In practice, this led to an increasing measure of control by the legislature over the executive departments and even the judiciary. The so-called Reorganization Act is a case in point. Acting under authority of the Jones Act, the legislature restructured the executive departments of the insular government late in 1916, altering the existing allotment of responsibilities and creating two new departments. In doing so, it provided that all members of the Cabinet except the Secretary of Public Instruction (who, by law, had to be an appointee of the President of the United States) must be citizens of the Philippine Islands; that appointments, subject to the confirmation of the Senate, should be coterminous with the duration of each legislature; and that cabinet officers should be subject to the call of either house to account for their conduct of office, unless the Governor General should declare in writing that their appearance would be detrimental to the public interest. Having in these ways made the Cabinet an arm of the majority party, the legislature subsequently bolstered the power of the heads of departments vis-à-vis the Governor General, providing, among other things, that his supervisory control should be exercised only in "matters of general policy" and that under ordinary circumstances he should act in such matters as executive orders and proclamations only upon the recommendation of the relevant Cabinet members. In the meantime, filipinization of all levels of government went ahead lustily. By 1920 the number of American employees of the government, including teachers, had fallen to 582, while the number of Filipinos had risen to 12,561.[4]

The elaboration of Filipinos' role in the government culminated in the creation in 1918 of the Council of State. An informal body, established by executive order rather than by legislation, the Council united the Governor General, the Speaker, the President of the Senate, and the members of the Cabinet, "with the main purpose," as the Speaker put it, "of concentrating governmental responsibility especially in relation with the preparation of the budget and other important legislations."[5] Structurally, the Council reproduced to a certain extent the role of the original Commission as a forum in which legislative and executive functions overlapped. As we have seen, Taft's intention in uniting governor, Cabinet officers, and legislative members—American and Filipino alike—had been to encourage cooperation and eliminate any institutional bias toward confrontation. This was an effective technique while the Commission was all, and the Americans clearly dominant. But once the Commission had become only the upper house of a bicameral legislature, its mixed character may actually have intensified polarization, by committing the Governor General and his cabinet— and therefore, by implication, the American government—to a partisan role in legislative conflicts with the all-Filipino Assembly. Just how destructive and stultifying this could be—how inimical to the evolutionary tactics favored by the Nacionalista leaders—had become obvious during the Forbes administration. Now, with both houses of the legislature and all but one of the Cabinet portfolios in Filipinos' hands, it made sense to recreate Taft's original forum, in reverse, as a technique for absorbing the Governor General into a cooperative format institutionalizing Filipinos' initiative in the government.

In addition, the Council served to promote cooperation among Filipinos themselves. In view of the growth of Filipino participation in the highest levels of the executive branch and the creation of an upper house in the legislature under the presidency of Quezon, some such step had seemed necessary to preserve the effectiveness and coordination of policy making among Filipino leaders. Put in personal terms, the question to be answered in the first years after the passage of the Jones bill was whether Speaker Osmeña could continue to dominate and unify Philippine politics, and thereby give consistency and efficiency to Filipinos' governmental relations with Americans, once there were other Filipinos in positions of major responsibility. The Council of State was a temporary answer to this question. By bringing together all the potential centers of power in one body, it provided a forum for adjusting differences and enabled Osmeña to become *primus inter pares.* At the Council's first meeting, Quezon suggested and the other members agreed that the Speaker should be vice-president, the Governor General being president, *ex officio.*[6]

The executive and legislative branches of the government having been coordinated and the Speaker made, as it were, prime minister, Filipinos in effect enjoyed the prerogatives of domestic autonomy during the last two years of the Harrison administration. By act of the legislature, an increasing number of executive powers was made subject to the consent of either the Council of State or the Filipino holders of portfolios; and control of the stock in government owned companies was vested in a three-member Board of Control, on which the Governor General could be outvoted by the Speaker and the President of the Senate. Both by disposition and by philosophy, Harrison was content that this should be so. For his own part, he scrupulously consulted the wishes of the Speaker and Quezon in patronage matters and is even charged by a knowledgeable attorney with having assigned judges to suit the desires of Nacionalista leaders. Not that the Nacionalistas really needed help of the latter kind. Possessed of the independence issue, controlling appointments at every level of government from the Cabinet to the justices of the peace and the politically potent provincial fiscals, led by figures of unrivaled national stature, the Nacionalista Party was virtually invincible. The elections of 1916 gave it 22 of 24 seats in the Senate and 75 of 90 seats in the House of Representatives, the new name of the lower house; in 1919 it won 21 of 24 senatorships and 83 of 90 seats in the House. The outgrowth of steady filipinization was, in effect, what the mid-twentieth century calls a one-party democracy.[7]

Having obtained domestic self-government and recognition of their right to independence, Filipino leaders turned to strengthening their nation in fields other than politics. Hoping to win federal arms, training and financial support for the nucleus of a Philippine army and navy, the insular government volunteered to form a division of troops and build and man warships for use in World War I.[8] And after the war's end, buoyed by the belief that the PNB had secured Filipinos' mastery of their own economy, the government launched a major campaign to increase American trade and investment. In the case of investments, it is true, opinion in the highest circles of the government was divided. Speaker Osmeña and a few of his closest protégés, such as Secretary of Commerce Dionisio Jakosalem, resisted the campaign to attract American capital, arguing that there was sufficient capital lying dormant in the islands and that the proper task of the government was to activate what was already at hand. But not even Osmeña could resist an alliance of Harrison and Quezon, and with these two figures in the lead the campaign went forward.[9]

By 1920 the business press of the United States was resonant with the pleas of Filipinos for greater American involvement in the islands' economy. In some instances, the question of the islands' future governmental relationship with the United States was handled prudently: "American capital and American initiative are welcomed in the Philippines," wrote the manager of the government's commercial agency in New York, "and no matter what the political status of that country may be in the future, one thing is certain and that is, it will always find closer attachment with that nation to which it greatly owes the progress and the prosperity it now enjoys—the United States of America."[10] At times, however, independence seems to have been forgotten altogether. The manager of the commercial agency in San Francisco exhorted his readers: "Think of 120,000 square miles of rich tropical lands capable of producing all sorts of tropical raw materials, with cheap labor, natural facilities, and in the shadow of the stars and stripes. . . . The Filipinos realize that American brains, capital, and initiative constitute a great factor in the development of their resources. . . . That is why they are very anxious to see the Americans take advantage to the utmost of the principle that 'trade follows the flag.' "[11]

There were some persons who, contemplating this campaign and other evidences of Filipino contentment with American links, inferred that early independence was indeed no longer desired. Erving Winslow, by now 79 years old and eager for imperialism to end while he could still rejoice, was among them. The Nacionalistas, he wrote to Secretary Baker, had "executed a 'volte-face' " and were mincing words about independence while actually courting investments. Cameron Forbes, acting as toastmaster at a luncheon in honor of the Independence Mission of 1919, caustically advised its members not to press too hard for independence, lest they actually get it.[12]

It would appear, however, that at least in 1918 and 1919 the Nacionalista leaders were prepared at last honestly to welcome independence. Agitation of the issue had been out of the question during the World War, and in the course of that enforced interlude a credible Filipino government had unfolded in the islands. By the end of hostilities, most responsible American officials in the Philippines felt that Filipinos had met the terms of the preamble of the Jones Act and that a stable government capable of an independent existence had been achieved. Writing to Wilson in November 1918, Governor General Harrison declared that the time had come when America's pledge could safely be fulfilled:

> Most of the doubts and fears expressed by critics of our progressive concessions to the Filipinos have been relegated to the past, and while it would be difficult to assert that any government ever set up by man is perfectly satisfactory in every respect, I will be glad to have the operations and achievements of the Filipinos in public office subjected to the most severe scrutiny without any fear of the judgment of any impartial observer as to their general integrity, patriotism, self-control and wisdom in the disposition of public matters. From a close association with the Filipinos and their representative men over a period of more than five years, I have no hesitation now in stating that I consider the Filipino people capable of conducting an independent government and that I believe that the concession to them of independence would best promote their own happiness and welfare.

In this recommendation, he was seconded by Frank Carpenter, Forbes' old executive secretary; even Vice Governor Charles E. Yeater, no advocate of haste in the matter of independence, placed on record his admiration for Filipinos' achievement.[13]

Confident in their own minds, supported by their American tutors, stimulated by Wilsonian rhetoric of national self-determination, the members of the legislature created a Commission of Independence in November 1918 and prepared to send a subsidiary group under its auspices to the United States to seek agreement upon a fixed date for Philippine independence. Their timing was bad. The war had just ended, and men in Washington were thinking about the future of Europe and the world, not about Philippine independence. The President, whom the mission would have wanted to see, was about to leave for Versailles. Therefore, with the concurrence of the resident commissioners, the Secretary of War requested the mission to postpone its visit.[14] The reaction in Manila was bitter. The purpose of the proposed mission, although not candidly announced, had been divined by the Philippine press; and in America the Republicans had won control of Congress in that autumn's elections. For both these reasons, postponement involved risks. The Nacionalistas felt they had conducted themselves with restraint during the war and were entitled to special consideration as a result. Quezon, in a rage, talked of breaking relations with Washington, even starting a revolution; a mass resignation by the entire government was considered. In the end, however, reason prevailed and a temperate statement written by Osmeña was cabled to Washington: The mission would be delayed as requested, in the "firm conviction that the President already has a plan that will satisfy the National aspirations of the Filipino people . . . and that the execution of such plan in so far as the Government of the United States is concerned is assured, during the present administration."[15]

When a mission finally did go to the United States, somewhat over three months later, its visit was conducted with a sobriety suggestive of high purpose. Publicity concerning both the mission and its goals was kept to a minimum, so as not to alienate officials in Washington; and at every stage, gratitude for America's accomplishments in the islands and hope for a future of mutually beneficial non-governmental links were emphasized. Despite Republican control of Congress, the mission's leaders seem to have felt that there was cause for optimism. Secretary Baker told Quezon privately that he and the President approved of the mission and hoped for definitive action to settle the question of Philippine independence; and the chairman of the Senate Committee on the Philippines gave Quezon to understand that if the Filipinos could win enough Catholic Democrats to give an independence bill a fighting chance, there would be a sufficient number of Republican crossovers, himself included, to pass it.[16]

Evidently, however, the administration had not yet arrived at a final decision as to Philippine policy. Receiving the full mission on April 4, Baker read the members a warm, graceful, non-committal letter from

Wilson (who was then in Europe) and added a hesitant, uncertain expression of his own good will: "I know that I express the feeling of the President; I certainly express my own feeling—I think I express the prevailing feeling in the United States—when say that we believe the time has substantially come, if not quite come, when the Philippine Islands can be allowed to sever the mere formal political tie remaining and become an independent people." Two months later, when sounded out by the ranking Democrat on the House committee concerning the administration's wishes for legislation, the Secretary was still in the dark. Personally, he replied, he favored granting Philippine independence in 1925, provided the Filipino people had in the meantime prepared and adopted a constitution acceptable to the President; what Wilson desired, he simply did not know. In the absence of a strong lead from the administration, whatever chance there might have been for prompt passage of an independence bill was lost. By late summer of that year, the League of Nations and other politically potent issues had the stage, and the Republican chairman of the House committee, Horace M. Towner, was declaring himself unwilling even to consider Philippine legislation.[17]

There things remained for the duration of the Wilson administration. Filipinos and their supporters, it is true, tried in various ways to reignite the issue of independence, but always without success. Harrison and Quezon alike tried to arrange, at least, for the appointment of a Filipino as either Governor General or vice governor and for the creation of a Filipino majority on the insular Supreme Court. They won a sympathetic ear from Baker, but little more.[18] In November 1920, fully aware that Towner had publicly ruled out passage at that session of a bill granting or promising independence, the resident commissioners persuaded Joseph P. Tumulty to ask the President to recommend such a bill anyway, in order to place on the record his certification that Filipinos had met the requirements of the Jones Act. Wilson did, but nothing came of the recommendation. No one had really supposed anything would. "Things will come out all right in good time," a sympathetic congressman advised Quezon, "and patience is a good thing to cultivate."[19]

Although Congress or the new Harding administration might refuse to consider Philippine independence, no one in a responsible position proposed retrogression from the level of filipinization achieved under Harrison. Harding, in a private conference with Forbes, described himself as "a mild imperialist," reluctant to lower the flag, but he showed no interest in doing more than holding on, reforming things where necessary, and presumably reaping whatever commercial advantage was to be had. John W. Weeks, his Secretary of War, confessed himself uncertain whether the United States ought to remain in the islands at all. Even Cabot Lodge, aging and worn, thought the Philippines an awkward situation.[20]

Cameron Forbes had reached much the same conclusion. Earlier, in 1915, he had hoped that Harrison could be followed by an outright reactionary: "From one point of view . . . it is advisable they should make as big a mess of things as they can. It is well they should make a demonstration of it. If they can set everything back ten years, they may set them forward fifty by making the restoration of a permanent and more direct control imperative. . . . What I had feared more than any other thing was they would go just far enough to let dry-rot in and not far enough to bring about a crash, which would compel a reorganization." But by January 1921 he had changed his mind. Neither the islands nor their inhabitants were prepared for independence, he advised Harding; and a strengthened American control would be necessary. Nevertheless, there had been great gains made in some respects and the President-elect ought not to allow himself to be misled by "the calamity howlers." Asked by Harding for his own recommendation as to policy, Forbes advocated bolstering American control through the strategic placement of American inspectors and supervisors at various levels of the government but making no attempt whatsoever to deprive Filipinos of the concessions made to them during the previous administration. He was supported in this by Taft, Luke Wright, General Pershing, and prominent businessmen. Leonard Wood, rumored to be Harding's choice for Governor General, hinted to Resident Commissioner Jaime de Veyra that he, too, considered the Jones Act and the filipinized government elaborated under it to be permanent parts of the Philippine scene.[21]

Predictably, this disposition to retain and reform without notably or visibly retrogressing informed the conclusions of the Wood-Forbes Mission, sent to the Philippines by Harding later in 1921 to advise him on future policy. Arriving in Manila early in May and devoting itself first to an investigation of the financial crisis and then to exhaustive tours of the provinces, the mission had reached a tentative evaluation of Philippine conditions by the end of July. The interlude under the control of Harrison and leading Nacionalistas had produced mixed results, the members concluded. Support of the government and the general level of public order were both high; education had flourished. Facilities for transportation and communication had been adequately maintained. On the other hand, public health, the land title program, and the efficiency of the civil service had all suffered; agriculture was depressed; and the administration of justice and the government's finances had been serious failures. Cabling these views to Weeks, Wood and Forbes concluded: "Economically, the Filipino people are unable to maintain an independent government under present conditions. From the standpoint of organization and preparation, they are not prepared to defend successfully their independence if attacked. The struggle in the minds of the people is between their aspirations for independence and their judgment. There is a substantial body of citizens of all classes, men and women, who are opposed to any separation from the United States. There is strong feeling of appreciation of what the United States has done. People as a whole are contented and happy and living with more freedom, less taxation and less responsibility than the great majority of peoples of [the] earth." There were more reports to come, including a written final one detailing the plusses and minuses of the insular government, pointing to various needs for continued American tutelage, support, or protection and declining, in keeping with Forbes' established tactic, to address itself at all to the question of how and when Filipinos' aspiration to be independent might be fulfilled. None of these, however, altered the perception of the problem already substantially agreed upon even before the mission's departure. Upon receipt of the preliminary report quoted above, Weeks officially requested Wood to accept appointment as Governor General.[22]

These developments were not unexpected by knowledgeable Filipinos. Recognizing that the criteria used by Wood and Forbes would be more rigorous than those employed by Harrison, and understanding that the PNB debacle had at least temporarily destroyed their argument that a stable Filipino government had been established, Quezon and Osmeña had taken the bull by the horns at the outset of the mission's visit and quietly asked Wood and Forbes to be discreet about disabusing the people of their faith that independence was almost at hand. Privately, Quezon wrote to McIntyre: "I do not know what kind of a report they will submit, and it may be that I shall not agree with their conclusion, but my present feeling is that they are trying to be absolutely fair. . . . What they may say about the Philippine National Bank will not surprise me. I think if I were the investigator . . . very likely my criticism [would] be strong not only against the managers of the Bank but against the Board of Control itself, including the President of the Senate, for not having interested himself enough to know what was going on in the Bank." Release of the mission's final report brought forth a flurry of criticism from Filipino leaders, it is true; but privately, Osmeña, Quezon, and Palma, the foremost powers in the Nacionalista Party, all confessed that the conclusions seemed generally fair.[23]

But what of the future? Accepting the need for a temporary delay and for the achievement of specific reforms was not the same thing as reconciling oneself to permanent foreign sovereignty. Filipinos had grated under the deliberate evasiveness of American policy during the Taft and Forbes years; and they wanted to know in 1921, at the outset of a new period of Republican hegemony, what the prospects were, what they would have to accomplish and how, in order to become independent. Maximo Kalaw, in an incisive critique, protested that the Wood-Forbes report, though descriptive and remedial in form, had nowhere defined its authors' criteria for the successful maintenance of nationality. Suppose that the efficiency of the government had fallen off in certain respects, as the report charged: was that in itself just cause to deny a people independence? Suppose it to be true, as the report maintained, that Filipinos could not by themselves defend their islands against certain foreign powers: did anyone maintain that the French, twice overrun within the past fifty years, were not entitled to their independence? That there were inferences to be drawn from the report as to the desirability and practicality of early Philippine independence, no one would have denied. Why had they not been articulated clearly, so that Filipinos would know where they stood?[24]

Quezon, anxious to know the answers to such questions as these, had hastened to Washington in August 1921, while Wood and Forbes were still in the Philippines. The President and the chairmen of the House and Senate committees willingly assured him that no backward step would be taken. No one in a position of power would talk about independence or the future.[25]

In fact, of course, there was a policy or at least a set of expectations, concerning such matters. American policy toward the Philippines, Weeks and McIntyre agreed in an exchange of memos in May 1922, was the preparation of the Filipino people for independence, particularly by means of fomenting prosperity and economic development through the investment of private capital. Whether the Filipinos would indeed want independence after this had been done, was another question altogether. "I can imagine a continued progress," the President later told that year's independence mission from the islands, "which will make our bonds either easier to sever, or rivet them more firmly because you will it to be so. We must await that development."[26]

By 1921 a stalemate had been reached in Philippine-American relations. The evolution of Philippine politics, the initiative of Nacionalista leaders, especially Sergio Osmeña, and the liberality of Francis Burton Harrison had led to the devolution upon Filipinos of a large measure of domestic autonomy. No responsible person could entertain notions of depriving them of this degree of self-determination. As Henry L. Stimson was to observe at the end of the decade: "We have gotten beyond the caveman age in regard to colonial development. We do not and cannot now hold colonies by force."[27] On the other hand, various motives—nostalgia, prudence, pride, *noblesse oblige,* dreams of commercial advantage, analyses of strategic responsibilities—led influential Americans who were part of the Harding administration or had access to it to oppose any further loosening of American control. The PNB debacle and the allegedly usurpative character of Filipinos' enlargement of their role in the government during Harrison's final years strengthened their hand by enabling them to argue that Philippine conditions required a period of consolidation: "We are convinced," wrote Leonard Wood and Cameron Forbes in 1921, "that it would be a betrayal of the Philippine people . . . and a discreditable neglect of our national duty were we to withdraw from the islands and terminate our relationship there without giving the Filipinos the best chance possible to have an orderly and permanently stable government."[28]

CONCLUSION

The Philippines and
the Imperialism of Suasion

From the beginning, there was a special complexity and subtlety of tone in the relationship of the American government and people to the inhabitants of their island empire in the Philippines. This arose partly from the disrupted and often dysfunctional character of Hispano-Philippine society and culture and partly from the ambivalent and domestically vulnerable character of American imperialism.

Neither traditional nor modern, western nor eastern, Hispanic nor Malay in any rigorous sense, the social and cultural patterns of the Philippines in the nineteenth century were transitional. Like the islands themselves, their modern configuration was the result of interplay and strain between residual matter and external forces. With varying intensity and effect, tides of alien influence—Spanish, Muslim, Chinese, even Anglo-American—had washed against and sometimes over the indigenous customs and institutions of Filipino, or indio, society. As with the breaking of waves upon a coast, the balance between the force and persistence of the assault and the mass and integration of the resistance determined the result: as it happened, the waves were erratic, almost random, and the resistance that of sand rather than that of rock.

This was pointedly so in the case of Spain. The Spanish conquest rolled over the islands with disruptive force. Lacking the cultural sophistication and integration of the Chinese or the Indians, the Filipinos were forced to give way. Violence, labor drafts, evangelization, demographic changes, the increase of unproductive aliens, and the introduction of new legal premises and practices all took their toll of pre-Hispanic customs and institutions and altered, in important particulars, the functional goals of barangay society. Still, the limited aims and declining power of Spain, the shallowness of Spanish settlement, and the geographical remoteness and topographical ruggedness of the islands afforded the people a great deal of protective insulation; and the Spanish reliance upon indirect rule provided an institutional vehicle for social and political continuity. The Filipino family remained intact, and the local community relatively free of non-clerical Spanish influences. There was leeway to adapt and adjust. The result was the emergence of an eclectic, often dysfunctional culture, located at the intersection of Spanish initiative and Filipino resilience. So long as the islands remained isolated and men lived deductively from inherited wisdom, this precarious accommodation sufficed.

The modern world came to the Philippines, haltingly, with the penetration of western commerce toward the end of the eighteenth century. When it did, it produced new social and economic conditions that, in turn, created new perspectives and perceptions among at least some residents of the islands. The resulting clarification of goals exposed the inadequacy of the existing Hispano-Philippine culture and its institutions. Uprooted from the Malay past and incoherent by the measure of western logic, it could neither sustain nor mediate. For a people faced with the challenge of modernity, it was stultifying. As commerce and contact spread, people in increasing number demanded that the Hispano-Philippine inheritance be adapted or replaced.

Had the Spanish government reconciled itself to this demand and encouraged the evolution of Philippine social and political culture toward liberal, secular, and rationalist forms, there would not have been a Philippine revolution at the time, or of the type, that there was. But that would have been to ask the impossible. Mired in an impotent traditionalism of its own, how was Spain to lead a colony to the modernization and cultural integration that eluded it at home? To their credit, certain individuals and ministries tried; and the general drift of governmental administration in the Philippines during the nineteenth century was toward rationalization of structure. But the progress was faltering and trivial, measured against the magnitude of the problem. To the end, the Spanish community and the church-state through which Spain ruled remained the chief support of the status quo and the foremost obstacle to major change. Across the spectrum of reform and discontent, advocates of economic development, improved government services, racial dignity, class interest, and political and educational liberalization all found in the Spanish regime a common target.

Broadly speaking, what ended the Spanish empire in the Philippines was a modernizing convulsion. Its goals were as varied in substance and intensity as the perspectives from which men criticized the status quo; and nationalism was its connective, not its cause. Wherefore, the elimination of Spanish sovereignty, rather than fulfilling the Philippine Revolution, exacerbated its internal tensions and contradictions. For once the obstacle to change had been removed, it was necessary to thrash out what kind of changes to make. From conservative reformers demanding, essentially, recognition of their de facto pre-eminence and increased opportunities to reap its benefits, to working- and lower middle-class radicals, desiring a social revolution, the spectrum of opinions was impressively broad.

The appearance of a new imperial overlord and the clumsy viciousness with which the insurrection was suppressed might have postponed this fragmentation. Clearly, that is what Aguinaldo and Mabini hoped for in first wooing the ilustrado elite and later establishing a temporary dictatorship: social discipline and political unity might be forged in the furnace of a defensive war against foreign aggressors. In limited measure, something of this sort actually occurred; but the centrifugal forces of regionalism, tribalism, language, religion, and class interest proved stronger than the centripetal power of nationalism, racial identification, and revolutionary fervor. The revolution fragmented, and the Americans won both a military and a psychological victory.

This was so partly because of the overwhelming strategic power of the United States, partly because of the personal limitations of Aguinaldo and the administrative inadequacy of his harried, fledgling government, and partly because of the depth and potency of the divisions in question. The disadvantages under which Filipinos labored, however, had their compensations. The enormity of the imbalance in regular forces, for example, forced the early abandonment of conventional campaigning and the adoption of guerilla tactics that proved far more vexing and punishing for the invader. Concomitantly, the expendability of the central government and the diffuse character of social and political organization deprived the Americans of convenient targets and sustained the spread of a guerilla, or people's war. In the circumstances, a conventional military victory—which it was clear the United States could achieve—might still have left a combustible polity, governable only by the recurrent overt use of force. Had it come to this, after so much expenditure of American blood, so many shameful atrocities, and so much rhetoric of duty and responsibility, the domestic political cost to McKinley and his successors of retaining the Philippines would have been insupportable.

Years before Hannah Arendt gave it theoretical legitimacy, the United States had stumbled, unawares, to the pragmatic discovery that, of all forms of government, the modern nation-state based upon consent is the least suited to empire. The character of the Philippine insurrection and the politics of imperialism at home required that victory be complemented by accommodation—that Filipinos be not merely defeated, but converted. Wherefore, the forebearance of Filipinos being essential to the very survival of the American empire in their islands, conquest did not produce subjugation; and the people of the islands retained significant leverage, or bargaining power, with which to affect their future.

This was the origin of the policy of attraction. Almost from the beginning, guided by ilustrado defectors, American civilian officials in the islands perceived both the divisions within Filipino society and the loose consensus for structural modernization and cultural integration that transcended them. Needing Filipino consent and support, they acted upon both fronts, detaching the elite by drawing them into the political process, and appropriating the modernization issue through programs of reform and nation building. The American conception of what a modern, libertarian state should be provided a common ground between the two peoples; and the joint pursuit of shared goals served far better than bullets to justify and to perpetuate American sovereignty. The subsequent Americanization of the schools, economy, popular culture, and governmental institutions of the Philippines and the pervasive neo-imperialist web of sympathy, influence, and control that survived formal independence are traceable to this tactical response by Americans to a Filipino initiative.

There was, of course, tactical and conceptual opposition to the policy of attraction on both sides of the Pacific. Filipino radicals and nationalists and American anti-imperialists attacked it from one extreme; militarists, some racists, and holdovers from the "days of empire," from the other. Even among adherents of the policy, there was division and contention. Attraction might lead to any number of possible outcomes—anything from cultural affinity or preferential economic relations to permanent American sovereignty; and although territorial, or dominion, status for the Philippines became the most popular of these, there was never any consensus as to the end in view. By the close of the Forbes administration, evasive open-endedness had become an irritant, not only in Fil-American relations but even between Americans.

Nevertheless, attraction worked. The American program of liberalization, secularization, and modernization overlapped with the goals of the revolution; and the congressional restrictions upon landholding, mining, and franchises—a product not of the policy of attraction but of anti-imperialism and domestic progressivism—ensured the islands against gross or overt exploitation. True, the Americans talked a better game than they played in most of these respects; true also, they had no effective answer to the demands of nationalism and racial dignity. Still, nation building and the imperialism of suasion were enough by themselves, in most cases, to neutralize hostility and promote confidence. As Theodore Friend has observed, "The worst was over at the beginning."[1] After the suppression of the Cavite uprisings in 1905, most of the insular government's intrusions into the life of the ordinary Filipino were at least superficially beneficent. It provided security of person and property more effectively than at any time in living memory. It built roads and bridges, dug artesian wells, provided elementary education and a modern curriculum for children whose parents could spare their labor; it did something in the way of sanitation and public health, made a start at agricultural education, and broke the oppressive hegemony of the friars. In many years the most powerful cause of opposition to the American government was the failure or misfiring of enlightened, well-intentioned programs—faulty inoculation of animals against rinderpest, for example, or arrogant, authoritarian behavior by public health and quarantine officials. This is not the stuff of which revolutions are made.

But attraction had its costs as well. It sacrificed initiative for the sake of accommodation; and in the process of broadening the Fil-American base, it not only co-opted much of the Philippine revolution but also stultified the most far-reaching reformist and modernizing goals of the Americans. At its loftiest, Taft's vision soared beyond efficiency and stability—out of the realm of currency, tariffs, and infrastructure—to a concern with democracy, due process, and the dignity of the individual. The secular, libertarian state, political participation, economic development, a modern curriculum, improved public health were his structural prescription to achieve the humane functional goal of freer and better lives for the Filipino people. This, not simply roads or schools, would be the cement of American-Philippine relations. Such a program was inherently disruptive, however; and its rewards long deferred. It was not to be achieved by attraction and accommodation.

That is the significance of Taft's opportunistic use of the ilustrados as his partners in attraction. The ilustrados, being the best equipped members of their society to lead and function in the modern world, were in one sense the natural mediators between the American government and the Filipino people. Yet their vested interests as the landed and professional elite of the islands, their social and economic dominance in their communities, and their determination to buttress this eminence with commensurate political power—in a word their presumption to unitary leadership of society—invalidated them as agents of social reform. For them, modernization and secular liberalism were means of legitimizing and extending the scope of their own de facto hegemony. Their network of influence and control, upon which Taft relied as a vehicle for reaching the masses, was in fact one of the logical targets of democratizing reform.

The politics of attraction wed the United States to the class interests of the Philippine elite. Preferential patronage and a 3 percent franchise confirmed the wealthiest and best educated members of the society in control both of the local communities and the filipinized offices of the insular government. After the creation of the Assembly in 1907, their values informed both administrative and legislative practice. There was no tackling the core problems of land, tenancy, labor, and the distribution of wealth without alienating them and subverting the process of attraction. This being the case, it made little sense to expect that education and infrastructure would crack the multi-faceted hierarchy of deference, reciprocity, and power. In the absence of correlative reforms, the gains of economic growth went disproportionately to those already in a position to reap them, and the social value of education was often lost in diffusion.[2]

This tension was less embarrassing to American officials at the time than one might at first suppose. For one thing, Americans like Taft, Forbes, and Harrison operated themselves from conservative-deferential premises, in which social and economic mobility and a free electorate coexisted compatibly with elitist patterns of leadership and hierarchies of deference. To elevate and liberate the masses, by their standards, one didn't have to end the class system or make people equal beyond the ballot box. Beyond this, they were whiplashed by the dynamic of insular politics they themselves had set in motion. The early appearance of an immediate independence party altered Americans' conception of what it was to be radical, conservative, reformist —and a host of other things—in the Philippine context. For most people, the hallmark became one's attitude toward the independence issue.

Independence meant different things to different people. Americans of the time simply missed the point in ridiculing Filipinos for their frequent lack of a clear definition. Behind the amorphousness of the idea lay the pluralistic, many-sided nature of the thing itself: independence could seem at times to mean nothing, because potentially it might mean anything or everything. That was its strength as a popular ideal and its weakness as a basis for programmatic action. It had a capacity temporarily to obscure alignments and interest groupings within the polity.

Debating the issue in the medium of Philippine politics, Americans found themselves awash in a sea of elites. Did they sympathize, like Francis Burton Harrison, with the "radical" aspirations of Filipino independistas? The appropriate course, in the context of Philippine politics, seemed to be speedy devolution of authority to the elected representatives of the Filipino people, the Nacionalista elite headed by Osmeña and Quezon. Did they perceive, like Taft and Dean C. Worcester, the elitist, anti-reformist implications of immediate independence—its likelihood of perpetuating the existing socio-political pattern and precluding American *noblesse oblige?* In that case, one's appropriate allies seemed to be the "conservative" aristocrats and retentionists, Pardo, Legarda, and Arellano. For all his arrogance and personal limitations, Cameron Forbes came closest to seeing the artificial polity of the period in its true light. Ignoring platforms and labels altogether and relying frankly upon personal relations and elitist self-interest to keep politics moderate, he simply tied up in ad hoc co-optation with the men who had the votes. To escape the tyranny of the independence issue and make politics responsive to the diversity of Filipinos' social and economic interests, one would have had to reach outside the whole existing structure of political participation.

The structure of official politics and the pivotal role of the elite were at least partially the result of conscious choice by the Americans.

The primacy of the independence issue and the resulting centrality of politics clearly were not. They arose partly because of the unexpected depth and resilience of Filipino nationalism, aggravated by recurrent examples of American arrogance, racism, and evasiveness; partly because of an ironic misfiring of the programs of attraction and nation building instituted, in part, as an alternative focus to independence and politics.

Nation building, modernization, and economic development were indeed attractive policies. Under ideal circumstances they might have combined with secularization and liberalization to channel men's energies and aspirations away from politics toward economics and social service. There were two obstacles, however. For one thing, despite its commitment to modernization and prosperity, the insular government achieved relatively little except in the fields of education and public health. Certainly this was the case with economic development. Infrastructure lost much of its bloom with the removal of Forbes and the embarrassment of the railroads. Economy and devolution mattered more to Harrison, public health and social services to Wood and Murphy. In 1931 Governor General Dwight F. Davis would return from a tour of neighboring colonies, confessing the Philippines' relative poverty of roads and physical plant.[3] In the private sector, restrictive legislation, combined with the availability of richer opportunities elsewhere, held down the investment of foreign capital and deprived the islands of a critical stimulus to growth and innovation. The result was a technically unsophisticated economy, dependent as ever upon a handful of vulnerable export staples, incapable of absorbing usefully the graduates of the public schools.[4] Simply put, the rewards were not adequate to divert social energies from powerful, emotional magnets such as nationalism, race, and the exhilaration of politics.

The other obstacle, paradoxically, was the politicization of economic development and cultural integration. To desire such things was not necessarily to ignore their cost. As it happened, the costs were impressive. At the elementary level, the internal revenue act of 1904 and the Payne-Aldrich tariff of 1909 revealed that the financial burden of development, American-style, would be borne by the islands' established industries, particularly breweries and tobacco manufacturers. More significantly, the candid pronouncements of the islands' highest officials—Taft, Wright, and Forbes among them—placed the whole subject of prosperity and modernization in the context of attraction and co-optation. In the circumstances, it became increasingly difficult to subsume ends in means and to maintain the fiction that nation building was an apolitical good.

Attempting to evade independence and co-opt politics, Americans had mistakenly supposed that they could isolate certain aspects of the social matrix and make them, in effect, independent variables. Try as they might, however, they could never separate social, cultural, and economic change from political questions of purpose and control. Accordingly, the system of political participation originally sanctioned by Taft as a vehicle for pacifying the islands and translating American policies to the people, came in time to have a life of its own. Even men who shared the American vision of mutually beneficial development and men for whom full independence was personally threatening, found themselves impelled by the nature of the polity and the issues and by the dynamic of personal and class interest to enlarge their political role and measure their achievements against popularly recognized criteria. Of these criteria, at once the most elemental and inclusive was independence. It became in time, as Joseph Ralston Hayden wrote, "synonymous with national honor and personal happiness."[5] Still, after years of attraction and co-optation, the connective tissue of Philippine aspirations, independence ceased to be the means of achieving social, cultural, and economic goals only to become, instead, the means of legitimizing them.

It would be difficult to exaggerate the importance of this outcome. At the obvious level, it doomed the formal American empire in the Philippines, foreclosed the prospect of territorial or dominion status as the ultimate relationship between the two countries, and foreshadowed the ambivalence with which the Filipino people have regarded the United States during most of the ensuing years. To desire and appreciate what was done, while acting from the premise that the control of which such benefits were a function was inadmissible, was, in practice, a source of repeated embarrassments and inconsistencies.

More important, the centrality of politics and the independence issue reinforced and legitimized the elitist, hierarchical character of the Philippine polity. It drew Filipino talent into the lawyer-politician mould typical of dependencies and skewed the perception of most other aspects of public life so as to make them, arguably, means to a political end. The Americans and the insular government being at once the sanction and the target of most public endeavor, and access to office being strictly limited to the economically and intellectually accomplished, the hierarchical structure of government in effect institutionalized the primacy of the established elite. In the circumstances, it was often difficult to separate the class interests of the elite from the national interest in realizing the ideal, independence. Examples abound: given the limited resources of the Philippines, it was narrowly elitist, as the Americans maintained, for Filipino officials to demand the diversion of funds from primary schools to the more expensive higher levels of education. Given the need for revenue with which to finance roads, schools, public health, and the like, it was irresponsible, as Americans charged in 1905, for established manufacturers to resist effective taxation. Given the magnitude of the stakes for the commonweal, it was viciously corrupt and self-serving, as Americans perceived, for several dozen prominent families to misappropriate the public funds of the Philippine National Bank for a personal gamble on wartime prosperity. Yet in each of these episodes, as in so many others, the structure of politics and the dynamics of nationalism led to the identification of a class or group interest with the cause of self-determination. The strengthening of a corps of leaders, the prosperity of those few entrepreneurs with a leg up on modern commerce and manufacturing, control of the marketing and processing of their own agricultural staples were all aspects of Filipinos' struggle to control their own lives. All the more so, since the principal actors were also the political spokesmen of the nation. Monopolizing both the initiative and the capacity to lead in the context of modernization, the elite became, as David Steinberg has observed, not just a class but "the very foundation of the state."[6] To defeat, contest, or repudiate them in any field was, by extension, a political act subversive to their realization of the ideal.

The goal of independence being at once the cement of unity and the sanction of class rule, Philippine politics assumed the outward form of a structure of advocacy, the Newtonian counter to America's imperialism of suasion. Thus the Assembly became, in Osmeña's formulation, an instrument of liberty; and "party policies," to quote Hayden, "were shaped primarily with reference to the overshadowing issue of independence rather than to the normal problems of Philippine life."[7] Privately, many of the practitioners had their doubts. Genuinely attracted to the United States—its vision, its markets, its protective shield, and its capacity to impose law and order within the islands—they were themselves far down the road to binationalism. Repeatedly, they wavered and hedged when actually faced with the prospect of early independence. Even in the late 1930's, after inauguration of the commonwealth and congressional enactment of a schedule for achieving independence, Quezon and other members of the elite dallied with the idea of permanent dominion status. Yet the period that created binationalism also prevented its consummation. As the Forbes years had tarnished attraction, so the Harrison interlude had braced up backsliders and discredited evasion. Events of the ensuing decades were to show that only the "discipline of the independence movement" could preserve the unity of the elite and forestall the nation's reckoning with basic and inevitable problems of equity and integration.

For Filipinos, nation building and the imperialism of suasion served, paradoxically, to expose the interdependence of modernization and nationalism. For Americans, they symbolized the impossibility of this nation's playing a major role in the territorial imperialism of the late Victorian and Edwardian years. The Philippines were almost a perfect test case. Arguably of major strategic and commercial value for their relation to the Asian continent; a receptive market in themselves for investors in banks, railroads, and all the paraphernalia of development; populated by a people eager and grateful for American education and political culture; they even came with the conscience-salving assurance that acquisition had been an unsought responsibility, a by-product of the humane war to free Cuba. Yet neither the geopolitics of Mahan, the Schumpeterian/Darwinian calculus of Roosevelt, nor the Hobsonian analysis of Charles Conant and a legion of others could persuade Congress frankly to defend, develop, and exploit the islands for the United States' own interests. Within a few years of the establishment of a civil government, the American presence had become essentially neo-imperialist. By the end of the Harrison years, almost nothing stood between retentionists and defeat except the shambles of the PNB and the personal ambivalence of certain Filipino leaders.

Briefly, it seemed that this might suffice. The PNB debacle, after all, had been a chastening experience; and the need for economic reconstruction was widely recognized. Privately, most Nacionalista leaders were prepared to acknowledge that this precluded early independence. The Quezon wing of the party went still further. Admitting the failures of the Harrison years, Quezon appropriated the islands' plight as a public issue, to legitimize his successful challenge to Osmeña's leadership. In the elections of 1922, the Nacionalista party split; and the Democratas won approximately 29 percent of the vote, with 5 out of 24 seats in the Senate and 26 of 93 in the House. The discipline of the independence movement had cracked, and the islands seemed on the road to a fragmentation of the elite. For the first time in years, retention was once again a real possibility. American policy and performance reinforced Filipinos' growing ambivalence. With a dignified and effective soldier-statesman reconstructing the islands' administration and the revitalization of hopes for Asian commerce attracting American money to the islands' depressed economy, the advantages of an American link seemed to many compelling.

But the moment passed. For one thing, the fragmentation of the elite re-emphasized its dependence upon nationalism and the independence issue as a vehicle of social and political control. In 1923, unable to assure his own ascendency, his party's hegemony, and the unity of his class without those issues, Quezon broke dramatically with Wood. Leading the reunited Nacionalistas into opposition to the American administration, he rallied the electorate and strengthened his own hand by discrediting the Democratas with the charge of pro-Americanism. The majority party having reaffirmed militant nationalism and the tactics of confrontation, consciousness of the issue was raised; and the possibility of a drift toward co-optation all but vanished. Moreover, the hardening of political relations between the two peoples was complemented by a faltering of the American economic drive in Asia, a major element in the calculus of mutual attraction. As Akira Iriye has brilliantly shown, the dislocation of markets, the political instability, the intensified nationalism, and the repeated challenges to the treaty system that accompanied the Chinese revolution frustrated the economic diplomacy of the Washington treaties.[8] As the bloom of the China market faded and rivalry with Japan intensified, initiative in the shaping of East Asian policy passed increasingly to strategic planners; and American perception of the Philippines altered accordingly. In 1931 the Secretary of War inquired of the Army, the Navy, and the departments of Commerce and State whether the Philippines were an asset or a liability. Military and naval authorities, who had realistically neither plan nor capacity to defend the islands, replied nevertheless that they were "a *positive* asset"; and State, which had nothing directly to do with the Philippines apart from Henry Stimson's personal service there, pronounced them "an enormous asset," whose abandonment would be considered by other nations "a demonstration of selfish cowardice and futility on our part." Commerce replied tepidly that it was a "fair conclusion" that the islands were more asset than liability.[9] To those who lived by the symbols of national power and purpose, an imperial presence in the Western Pacific was of manifest value. To those concerned with trade and investment, it was of only marginal advantage.

Most Americans—certainly most congressmen—were even less bullish. To people confronting depression at home and Japanese aggression abroad, the Philippines appeared increasingly a strategic liability, an economic competitor, and a source of unwanted immigration. By the early thirties, prompt divestiture of the islands had become an American goal—legitimized by the ongoing tradition of anti-imperialism and opposed only by special interests, a few officers and putative proconsul-stewards, and handful of moralists. Wherefore the American Congress, in perhaps the most notable of all the ironies attaching to the Philippine-American encounter, seized the initiative and, unmoved by the trembling of the co-opted, the cynical brutality of Nacionalista infighting, or the spurious theatrics of Quezon, rid itself of what had finally been identified as simply a burden.

Whence the unusual spectacle of conservative and radical historians agreeing that America's insular empire in the Philippines was only an anomalous sport: an aberration from our anti-imperialist norm, as a distinguished diplomatic historian would have it, or merely a link in the chain of island stepping stones to the real, open door "empire" in China, as numerous revisionists now assert.[10] Certainly there is justification for this. The encounter was brief and without issue; overseas colonialism, in any rigorous sense of the word, has been the exception not the rule in our history; economic expansion, in general, and infatuation with that elusive pillar of cloud and fire, the China market, in particular, have far more affected our Asian policy than territorial possession of the Philippines ever did.

All this notwithstanding, it is misguided to minimize or dismiss the Philippine-American encounter. For Filipinos, as I have attempted to show, it has been a major determinant of political, social, cultural, and economic development. Possession of sovereignty—even a sovereignty markedly circumscribed in practical application—permitted Americans to affect Philippine life directly, whether by shooting revolutionaries, eradicating cholera, building roads, establishing curricula, defining political and economic structures, or sanctioning power relationships. Indeed, the imperialism of suasion required it.

Conclusion

The goals, broadly speaking, were stability and development, pursuits which our subsequent experience suggests may be mutually exclusive. And since development or modernization, in the Philippines as elsewhere, was a disruptive and in some instances punishing process, American success in promoting stability through the imposition or sanction of one interest or structure over others had implications for almost every facet of Philippine social and economic life. In human terms, America's impact upon the Filipino people has been qualitatively different from her indirect effect upon the lives of, let us say, the Chinese or the Brazilians. This, in itself, commends to us the study of Fil-American history.

The more intensely and perceptively we pursue the question, I believe, the more clearly we shall see not just the peculiarities of the encounter but its typical character, as well. With its origins in the bloody suppression of a popular revolution, the Philippine empire was as far as the United States ever went toward orthodox, territorial imperialism.[11] As such, it locates the right wing in the spectrum of American influence and involvement in other people's countries. Only partially a separate account—or a road not taken—it became also in retrospect, an exemplar, a controlled experiment of sorts, for dealing with the lightly developed colonial and post-colonial parts of the world. Development, liberal reform, and the appropriation of modernization, their roots deep in the American experience, fared better as vehicles of attraction and influence than as blinds for political retention. For ironically, their use as means to a politico-diplomatic end sanitized and legitimized them when that end failed. Thus the defeat of American retentionists became at last the triumph of attraction.

Notes
Bibliography
Index

Notes

1. Society and Culture

1. William Henry Scott, *A Critical Study of the Pre-Hispanic Source Materials for the Study of Philippine History* (Manila, 1968), is the indispensable guide. The quotation is from Horacio de la Costa, *The Jesuits in the Philippines, 1581–1768* (Cambridge, Mass., 1961), p. 14.

2. Quoted, *ibid.*, p. 20.

3. *Ibid.*, p. 637.

4. J. Gayo Aragón, "The Controversy over Justification of Spanish Rule in the Philippines," in *Studies in Philippine Church History*, ed. Gerald H. Anderson (Ithaca, 1969), pp. 3–21. De la Costa, *Jesuits,* and John Leddy Phelan, *The Hispanization of the Philippines: Spanish Aims and Filipino Responses, 1565–1700* (Madison, 1967), are perceptive introductions both to this subject and, more broadly, to the first two centuries of the Spanish period. Nicholas P. Cushner, *Spain in the Philippines* (Rutland, Vt., 1972), is now the standard authority on the whole of the Spanish period.

5. William L. Schurz, *The Manila Galleon* (New York, 1939), is the standard authority. See also Benito Legarda, Jr., "Foreign Trade, Economic Change, and Entrepreneurship in the Nineteenth Century Philippines" (Ph.D. diss., Harvard, 1955), pp. 27–68, 80–84.

6. Concerning the pivotal role of the Chinese, see Edgar Wickberg, *The Chinese in Philippine Life, 1850–1898* (New Haven, 1965), pp. 6–15.

7. Horacio de la Costa, "Episcopal Jurisdiction in the Philippines during the Spanish Regime," in *Studies in Philippine Church History*, ed. Anderson, pp. 44–64. The Viana quotation is from Emma Helen Blair and James A. Robertson, *The Philippine Islands* (Cleveland, 1903–1909), L, 49.

8. The Más quotation is from *ibid.*, LII, 45; Villegas' testimony is in *Report of the Philippine Commission* (1900), pp. 25–26.

9. The population statistics are found in Blair and Robertson, *Philippine*

Islands, LII, 115n. Feodor Jagor, *Travels in the Philippines* (Manila, 1965), p. 109.

10. The structure and role of local government are treated exhaustively in Eliodoro Robles, *The Philippines in the Nineteenth Century* (Quezon City, 1969).

11. James A. LeRoy, *Philippine Life in Town and Country* (New York, 1905), p. 107; the complaint concerning isolation was made by Apolinario Mabini, quoted in Cesar Adib Majul, *The Political and Constitutional Ideas of the Philippine Revolution* (Quezon City, 1957), p. 109.

12. John Bowring, *A Visit to the Philippine Islands* (Manila, 1963), pp. 113, 130; *Census of the Philippine Islands* (1903), II, 49–52; Josefa Saniel, *Japan and the Philippines, 1868–1898* (Quezon City, 1963), pp. 314–315. It is generally agreed that the differentiation of dialects had begun before the Spanish conquest.

13. De la Costa, *Jesuits*, ch. 7; Phelan, *Hispanization*, pp. 23–24, 53–61, 72–81.

14. José Rizal, *The Social Cancer*, trans. Charles Derbyshire (Manila, 1912), p. 382.

15. The number of friars in the islands is reported in Phelan, *Hispanization*, p. 41, and *Report of the Philippine Commission* (1900), p. 23; the quotation is from Frederick H. Sawyer, *The Inhabitants of the Philippines* (London, 1900), p. 67. Criticism of the friars abounds in the travelers' accounts of the nineteenth century; and Teodoro M. Kalaw recalls, in *Aide-de-Camp to Freedom* (Manila, 1965), p. 6, that even in prosperous and worldly Lipa, at the end of the century, the *cura's* birthday celebration culminated in his coronation by beautiful girls with a crown of heavy gold, decorated with jewels lent by local notables. The case for the friars is set forth one-sidedly in Eladio Zamora, *Las corporaciones religiosas en Filipinas* (Valadolid, 1901).

16. Pizarro's comments are in Blair and Robertson, *Philippine Islands*, LI, 202; Sawyer, *Inhabitants*, p. 231.

17. Bowring, *Visit*, p. 114; Jagor, *Travels*, p. 48; John Foreman, *The Philippine Islands*, 2d ed. (New York, 1899), pp. 263–268. The classic account of the Spanish system in its later years is *Census* (1903), I, 398–407. A more recent treatment, somewhat more charitable, is Robles, *Philippines in the Nineteenth Century*, pp. 117–123, 132–136, 160, 188–189, 195–196, 201–202, 215–216.

18. The quotation from de la Matta is in Blair and Robertson, *Philippine Islands*, LII, 99; Jagor, *Travels*, p. 26.

2. The Turmoil of Change

1. The most useful accounts of this process are Legarda, "Foreign Trade," pp. 104–173 *passim;* Wickberg, *Chinese*, pp. 21–30, 45–47; *Early American-Philippine Trade: The Journal of Nathaniel Bowditch in Manila, 1796*, ed. Thomas R. and Mary C. McHale (New Haven, 1962); and M. L.

Díaz-Trechuelo, "The Economic Development of the Philippines in the Second Half of the Eighteenth Century," *Philippine Studies, 11* (1963), 195–231.

2. The standard sources on the role of foreigners are Legarda, "Foreign Trade," esp. chs. 4–6; and Benito Legarda, Jr., "American Entrepreneurs in the Nineteenth Century Philippines," *Explorations in Entrepreneurial History, 9* (1957), 142–159. The quotation is from "Foreign Trade," p. 434.

3. Statistics are from *Statistical Bulletin No. 3 of the Philippine Islands* (1920), pp. 125, 171, 176–177, 182–183; the quotation concerning hemp is from Legarda, "Foreign Trade," p. 455. As the century progressed, a high degree of product concentration came to characterize Philippine exports. In the years 1875–1895 the four leading agricultural exports—sugar, abaca, tobacco, and, usually, coffee—never comprised less than 71.94 percent of total exports; and for thirteen of those years they amounted to 90 percent or more. There is reason to believe that the flourishing export trade and its accompanying imports destroyed a burgeoning internal diversification of the islands.

4. Wickberg, *Chinese*, pp. 48–55, 61–64, 67–80; the quotation is from p. 78.

5. The quotations are from Rizal, *Social Cancer*, pp. 127 and 129, and José Rizal, "Old-Time Municipal Politics," in *Rizal's Political Writings*, ed. Austin Craig (Manila, 1933), p. 266. The literature on the subject is mountainous. See esp. *Report of the Philippine Commission* (Schurman), I, 17–18, 31–35; testimony of Felipe G. Calderón, *ibid.*, II, 258–266; *Census* (1903), II, 77–89, and III, 578–604, 613–621, 626–632; LeRoy, *Philippine Life*, pp. 202–210, 233–235; and Robles, *Philippines in the Nineteenth Century*, pp. 211–212, 217–229. Cf. the revisionist view, particularly Henry Frederick Fox, "Primary Education in the Philippines, 1565–1863," *Philippine Studies, 13* (1965), 207–231; Frederick W. Fox, "Some Notes on Public Elementary Education in Iloilo Province, 1885–1899," *Philippine Studies, 2* (1954), 5–19; and Frederick W. Fox and Juan Mercader, "Some Notes on Education in Cebu Province, 1820–1898," *Philippine Studies, 9* (1961), 20–46.

6. The Dominican quote is from *Census* (1903), III, 632; Rafael Comenge, *Cuestiones filipinas*, cited in Wickberg, *Chinese*, p. 133n.

7. Foreman, *Philippine Islands*, p. 290; the Russian is quoted in Blair and Robertson, *Philippine Islands*, LI, 40n.

8. Captain Andrés Novales, a Mexican mestizo, led a revolt of the King's Own Regiment in 1822, in protest against the replacement of creole and mestizo officers by newly arrived peninsulares. The quotation from de la Matta is from Blair and Robertson, *Philippine Islands*, LII, 95–96; Jagor, *Travels*, p. 16.

9. The plight of the Spanish community, as perceived at the time, is evident in Blair and Robertson, *Philippine Islands*, LI, 39–45, and LII, 32–40, 95–96, 100–102. For turn-of-the-century analyses, see James A. LeRoy, "The Philippines, 1860–1898," *ibid.*, LII, 117–128, 169–175; and T. H. Pardo de Tavera, "History," in *Census* (1903), I, 374–379. For an introduction to

modern scholarship on the subject see Robles, *Philippines in the Nineteenth Century*, pp. 36–43, 170–174; and David Joel Steinberg, ed., *In Search of Southeast Asia* (New York, 1971), pp. 158–161.

10. Wickberg, *Chinese*, pp. 128–132, 143; Legarda, "Foreign Trade," pp. 363–368.

11. Wickberg, *Chinese*, p. 135. The Chinese had a somewhat different structure of ethnic government: *ibid.*, pp. 182–184, 195–196. Cf. John A. Larkin, *The Pampangans: Colonial Society in a Philippine Province* (Berkeley, 1972), 54, 84–87.

12. Rizal, *Social Cancer*, p. 77. A recent study suggests that reform and rationalization of the government may actually have worsened the lot of lower officials: Robles, *Philippines in the Nineteenth Century*, pp. 61, 64–67, 84–87, 205–210, 238–242, 249–250.

13. LeRoy, *Philippine Life*, pp. 34–38, 65–68, 186–195; Wickberg, *Chinese*, pp. 134–145.

14. Robert MacMicking, *Recollections of Manilla and the Philippines During 1848, 1849, and 1850* (London, 1851), p. 148; Foreman, *Philippine Islands*, p. 182. The aphorism is given in Bowring, *Visit*, p. 185. Wickberg, *Chinese*, pp. 150–151; Sawyer, *Inhabitants*, pp. 163, 227; testimony of Horace Longwood Higgins, *Report of the Philippine Commission* (Schurman), II, 322.

15. The quotation is from Saniel, *Japan and the Philippines*, p. 332. Wickberg, *Chinese*, pp. 94–123, 146–153, 237–238.

16. *Ibid.*, pp. 38, 168, 177–199, 203–206. The quotation is from p. 196.

17. Más' recommendations are in Blair and Robertson, *Philippine Islands*, LII, 44–67; the physician's testimony is from *Report of the Philippine Commission* (Schurman), II, 407; Rizal, "The Indolence of the Filipino," in *Political Writings*, p. 194.

18. The best modern introductions to clerical nationalism are Horacio de la Costa, "The Development of the Native Clergy in the Philippines," in *Studies in Philippine Church History*, ed. Anderson, pp. 65–104; and Cesar Adib Majul, "Anticlericalism during the Reform Movement and the Philippine Revolution," *ibid.*, pp. 152–171. The quotation is from the former, pp. 99–100.

19. Beyond this level of generalization one moves with great hesitancy, for the rhetoric of the issue is highly charged and the truth not always evident. See Marcelo H. del Pilar, *Monastic Supremacy in the Philippines* (Quezon City, 1958), *passim*, esp. pp. 31–35, 87–93; José Rizal, "Land Politics," in *Political Writings*, pp. 273–279; *Report of the Philippine Commission* (1900), pp. 27–28, 30; and testimony of friars and Filipinos in Senate Document No. 190, 56 Cong., 2 sess.

20. The quotations are from José Rizal, *The Reign of Greed*, trans. Charles Derbyshire (Manila, 1912), p. 266; Rizal, *Social Cancer*, p. 377; and Majul, *Political and Constitutional Ideas*, pp. 78 and 75, respectively.

21. In addition to Majul, the standard authorities are Teodoro A. Agoncillo, *Revolt of the Masses: The Story of Bonifacio and the Katipunan* (Que-

zon City, 1956); Maximo M. Kalaw, *The Development of Philippine Politics, 1872–1920* (Manila, 1926); and John N. Schumacher, "The Filipino Nationalists' Propaganda Campaign in Europe, 1880–1895," (Ph.D. diss., Georgetown University, 1965). See also, Horacio de la Costa, "Nascent Philippine Nationalism, 1872–1896," *Philippine Historical Review, 3* (1970), 154–170. The quotation is from Foreman, *Philippine Islands,* p. 522.

3. Conciliation

1. Felipe G. Calderón, *Mis Memorias sobre la Revolucion Filipina: Segunda etapa,* quoted in Teodoro A. Agoncillo, *Malolos: Crisis of the Republic* (Quezon City, 1960), p. 308.

2. Testimony of Trinidad H. Pardo de Tavera, in *Report of the Philippine Commission* (Schurman), II, 391. Torres is quoted in James A. LeRoy, *The Americans in the Philippines* (Boston, 1914), I, 409n. The standard authority on the role of the ilustrados is Agoncillo, *Malolos.* See also, Majul, *Political and Constitutional Ideas, passim,* esp. pp. 61–62, 176–185; LeRoy, *Americans,* I, 141–144, 290–292, 382.

3. United States Adjutant General's Office, *Correspondence Relating to the War with Spain,* II, 719. LeRoy, *Americans,* I, 292, 400–401. For a revealing example of ilustrado condescension toward the republic and dissociation from it, see the testimony of Benito Legarda, in *Report of the Philippine Commission* (Schurman), II, 377–388.

4. W. Cameron Forbes, *The Philippine Islands* (Boston, 1928), I, 118–119. See also, concerning the tensions within the Commission, Dean C. Worcester, *The Philippines Past and Present* (New York, 1914), pp. 301–324.

5. *Report of the Philippine Commission* (Schurman), II, 68, 352.

6. Carl Landé, *Leaders, Factions, and Parties: The Structure of Philippine Politics* (New Haven, 1965), *passim,* esp. ch. 4; Mary R. Hollnsteiner, *The Dynamics of Power in a Philippine Municipality* (Quezon City, 1963); Jaime C. Bulatao, "Hiya," *Philippine Studies, 12* (1964), 424–438; Charles Kaut, "Contingency in a Tagalog Society," *Asian Studies, 3* (1965), 1–15, and "Utang na loob: A System of Contractual Obligations among Tagalogs," *Southwest Journal of Anthropology, 17* (1961), 256–272.

7. LeRoy, *Americans,* I, 378–382, 407; II, 236–240. The punctuation of the quotation has been altered.

8. *Report of the Philippine Commission* (Schurman), II, 60–67; Kenneth E. Hendrickson, Jr., "Reluctant Expansionist—Jacob Gould Schurman and the Philippine Question," *Pacific Historical Review, 36* (1967), 410–411.

9. *Report of the Philippine Commission* (Schurman), pt. 4, ch. 2: "Governmental Reforms Desired by Filipinos"; the quotations are from I, 84, 85, 82–83, and 91 respectively.

10. Philip C. Jessup, *Elihu Root* (New York, 1938), I, chs. 16 and 18; the quotations are from pp. 346–347, 345, 332 and 343–344, respectively.

11. The instructions may be found in Forbes, *Philippine Islands,* II, app. 7, pp. 439–445.

12. Henry F. Pringle, *The Life and Times of William Howard Taft* (New York, 1939), I, 23, 35; Archie Butt, *Taft and Roosevelt: The Intimate Letters of Archie Butt* (New York, 1930), I, 38.

13. Pringle, *Taft*, I, 159–162.

14. Taft to Root, cable, August 21, 1900 (Papers of William Howard Taft, series 3, box 63). Taft's papers, hereinafter cited as TP, are deposited in the Library of Congress.

15. Taft to E. B. McCagg, April 16, 1900 (TP, series 3, box 62); Oscar M. Alfonso, "Taft's Early Views on the Filipinos," *Solidarity, 4* (June 1969), 52–58; Taft to John M. Harlan, June 30, 1900 (TP, series 3, box 62).

16. Taft to Root, October 1, 1900 (TP, series 8).

17. Taft to Howard C. Hollister, October 15, 1900 (TP, series 3, box 63); Taft to Root, January 13, 1901, and January 18, 1901 (TP, series 8).

18. Taft to Root, July 14, 1900 (TP, series 8); Taft to Harlan, June 30, 1900, and to Henry Cabot Lodge, March 21, 1903 (TP, series 3, boxes 62 and 76); Daniel Roderick Williams, *The Odyssey of the Philippine Commission* (Chicago, 1913), pp. 82–83.

19. For the comment on Paterno, see Taft to Root, October 21, 1900 (TP, series 8).

20. Buencamino to Taft, November 1, 1900 (TP, series 3, box 64); Taft to Root, cable, November 4, 1900 (Bureau of Insular Affairs, National Archives, Record Group 350, file 364, enclosure 10). All future citations of this source will follow the form BIA 364–10.

21. Dapen Liang, *The Development of Philippine Political Parties* (Hong Kong, 1939), pp. 56–59, 61.

22. *Ibid.,* pp. 59, 61–65; Joseph Ralston Hayden, *The Philippines: A Study in National Development* (New York, 1942), pp. 316–317.

23. Forbes, *Philippine Islands,* I, 169, and II, 108. The following two paragraphs are drawn largely from an unusual public testament made by Pardo upon his retirement from active political life: "Address of Dr. T. H. Pardo de Tavera at the Farewell Banquet given him in Manila by his Friends on the Night of the 17th of April, 1909," of which there is a copy in box 42 of the Papers of Francis Burton Harrison, Library of Congress; and from a speech quoted in *La Vanguardia,* July 29, 1911, found in the Papers of W. Cameron Forbes, Houghton Library, Harvard University (fMS Am 1192.1, XII, 3353–4). Quotations are from the former.

24. Pardo de Tavera to Arthur MacArthur, May 14, 1901 (BIA 364–23); Pardo de Tavera to Taft, January 15, 1902 (TP, series 3, box 68).

25. Taft, undated memorandum (TP, series 3, box 68); Taft to Root, April 3, 1901 (TP, series 8) and to José M. de la Viña, *et al.*, November 7, 1902 (TP, series 3, box 74). Among the organizers of the Partido Democrata were Sergio Osmeña, Rafael Palma, Alberto Barreto, and Leon Ma. Guerrero.

26. Taft to Theodore Roosevelt, May 12, 1901 (TP, series 4, box 681); Hayden, *Philippines,* p. 317; Taft to Marcus A. Hanna, September 14, 1903 (TP, series 3, box 79). The subsidy for *La Democracia* is treated in a col-

lection of documents filed in TP, series 3, box 79, under the date of September 17, 1903, on pages numbered 13245–13252, inclusive.

27. Ironically, while local and provincial governments were steadily filipinized, malfeasance and incompetence at those levels led after 1903 to growing centralization of real authority in the insular government at Manila. See Michael Cullinane, "Implementing the 'New Order': The Structure and Supervision of Local Government During the Taft Era," in *Compadre Colonialism: Studies on the Philippines under American Rule,* ed. Norman G. Owen (Ann Arbor, Michigan Papers on South and Southeast Asia, No. 3, 1971), pp. 13–75.

28. Taft to Root, February 24, 1901 (TP, series 8); Arthur W. Fergusson to Taft, February 15, 1902 (TP, series 3, box 69).

29. This analysis draws upon Rōyama Masamichi and Takéuchi Tatsuji, *The Philippine Polity: A Japanese View,* ed. Theodore Friend (New Haven, 1967), pp. 52–53, 70. Cf. Bonifacio Salamanca, *The Filipino Reaction to American Rule, 1901–1913* (Norwich, Conn., 1968), pp. 54–60.

30. Taft to Root, January 9, 1901, and April 3, 1901, with postscript dated Iloilo, April 12 (TP, series 8); Taft to Root, April 12, 1901 (TP, series 3, box 65). Within the limits of what he called "the general rules which have been prescribed," Root gave the Commission free rein to work out "the form and machinery of government" in the Philippines. See Root to Taft, January 21, 1901 (TP, series 21, vol. 2); Jessup, *Root,* I, 299, 361–362.

31. Pringle, *Taft,* I, 169–170. The most recent study of the suppression of the insurrection and the tension between civil and military authorities is John Gates, *Schoolbooks and Krags: The United States Army in the Philippines, 1898–1902* (Westport, Conn., 1972).

32. This point is made at enormous length by a former member of MacArthur's staff, James H. Blount, in *The American Occupation of the Philippines, 1898–1912* (New York, 1912). The Taft and MacArthur quotations are from *Report of the Philippine Commission* (1900), p. 17, and *Report of the War Department* (1900), I, pt. 5, 61–62.

33. Taft to Root, April 3, 1901 (TP, series 8).

34. Taft to Root, August 25, 1901 (TP, series 8), postscript dated September 3; Williams, *Odyssey,* pp. 318–319.

4. Nation Building

1. Williams, *Odyssey,* p. 110.

2. *Ibid.,* p. 321.

3. Taft to Luke E. Wright, January 24, 1903 (TP, series 3, box 75). For more detailed treatment of these questions, see Frank T. Reuter, *Catholic Influence on American Colonial Policies, 1898–1904* (Austin, Texas, 1967), chs. 2, 4–7; and two articles, Peter G. Gowing, "The Disentanglement of Church and State Early in the American Regime in the Philippines," and Sister Mary Dorita Clifford, "*Iglesia Filipina Independiente:* The Revolutionary Church," in Anderson, *Studies in Philippine Church History,* pp. 203–

222 and 223–255, respectively. The evolution of policy toward the friar lands may be followed in BIA file 1644.

4. Taft to Root, April 21, 1900 (TP, series 8); Taft to Fred W. Atkinson, May 8, 1900 (TP, series 3, box 62). Hayden, *Philippines*, pp. 465–466. Forbes, *Philippine Islands*, I, 420–425.

5. Charles B. Elliott, *The Philippines to the End of the Commission Government* (Indianapolis, 1917), pp. 224–225.

6. The best introduction to the subject remains Hayden, *Philippines*, chs. 18–20. See also James A. LeRoy, *Philippine Life*, pp. 213–226.

7. The quotation is from *Report of the Philippine Commission* (1903), III, 701. Concerning the English language, see Hayden, *Philippines*, pp. 589–604, and Williams, *Odyssey*, pp. 54–55, 132–133. On vocational training, see Hayden, *Philippines*, pp. 519–527, and Forbes, *Philippine Islands*, I, 429, 449–454.

8. The Quezon quotation is from Maximo M. Kalaw, *The Case for the Filipinos* (New York, 1916), pp. vii–viii. Daniel R. Williams, *The United States and the Philippines* (Garden City, N.Y., 1924), p. 125. Forbes' observations are in the journal of W. Cameron Forbes, III, 377, 381–382, and I, 56–57, respectively. Copies of the journal—hereinafter cited as Forbes, Journal—are deposited in the Houghton Library, Harvard University, and in the Library of Congress.

9. *Report of the Philippine Commission* (1900), pp. 48–61; *Senate Document No. 432*, 56 Cong., 1 sess., pp. 29–30; Taft to Root, August 11, 1900 (TP, series 8).

10. Taft to J. G. Schmidlapp, June 15, 1900 (TP, series 3, box 62). An extract from Wright's speech is filed as BIA 1956–12.

11. Taft to John C. Spooner, November 30, 1900 (TP, series 3, box 64).

12. Concerning the delay, see Lodge to Taft, October 25, 1900 (TP, series 3, box 63) and Root to Taft, January 21, 1901 (TP, series 3, box 64). For Root's role, see Jessup, *Root*, I, 358–360. For the ethical motivation of congressmen, see Taft to Lodge, May 12, 1901 (TP, series 3, box 65).

13. Williams, *Odyssey*, pp. 163–164; Taft to Roosevelt, May 12, 1901 (TP, series 4, box 681); Taft to Root, March 17, 1901 (TP, series 8). I have found little indication that Lodge had initiative in shaping Philippine legislation. Many of his ideas, such as retention of a high tariff on Philippine sugar and tobacco, were directly opposed to those of Taft and Root. Lodge frequently introduced legislation of his own; but the Roosevelt and Taft administrations generally worked through Cooper and Payne in the House. Taft's correspondence with Lodge on legislative matters is devoted for the most part to arguments in support of bills already prepared in the BIA or introduced in the House.

14. Lodge to Taft, June 17, 1901 (TP, series 3, box 66); Jessup, *Root*, I, 361–362; Taft to Lodge, October 22, 1901 (TP, series 3, box 67); Taft to Root, November 17 and December 9, 1901 (TP, series 8).

15. The decline of support for territorial imperialism is discussed in Ernest R. May, *American Imperialism: A Speculative Essay* (New York,

1968), ch. 9. Concerning the limitation on land holdings, see Taft to Nelson W. Aldrich, May 6, 1902 (TP, series 3, box 71).

16. Garel A. Grunder and William E. Livezey, *The Philippines and the United States* (Norman, Okla., 1951), pp. 79–82; Dale Hardy Peeples, "The Senate Debate on the Philippine Legislation of 1902" (Ph.D. diss., University of Georgia, 1964). Taft to Wright, February 21, 1902 (TP, series 3 box 70); Taft to Legarda, February 14, 1902 (TP, series 3, box 69).

17. Sawyer, *Inhabitants*, p. 297. Concerning the ports in general and Manila in particular, see *Report of the Philippine Commission* (1900), pp. 57–58, 76–77; Foreman, *Philippine Islands*, pp. 398–400, 466–467; and Max L. Tornow, "A Sketch of the Economic Condition of the Philippines," *Senate Document No. 62*, pt. 2, 55 Cong., 3 sess., pp. 617, 623.

18. *Report of the Philippine Commission* (1900), p. 76. Frank McIntyre, Report to the Secretary of War, March 1, 1913 (BIA 119–72) gives a detailed account.

19. *Report of the Philippine Commission* (Schurman), I, 142–149, testimony of Bernancio Balbas, Edwin H. Warner, H. D. C. Jones, and A. Kuensle in *ibid.*, II, 152–154, 191–192, 209–212, 215, 225–227; Legarda, "Foreign Trade," pp. 206–207. For a scale of the depreciation of Mexican silver, see the tables of its average annual value in U.S. gold coin, in BIA, *Monthly Summary of Commerce of the Philippine Islands* (December 1904), p. 607, and Benito Legarda, Jr., "The Colonial Economy," in *Philippine Perspective: Lectures on the Pre-history and History of the Philippines* (Manila, 1964), sess. 1, pt. 2, ch. 6, table 4.

20. Legarda's testimony is in *Report of the Philippine Commission* (Schurman), II, 176–177; for complementary testimony from other businessmen and financiers, see *ibid.*, II, 185, 203, 211, and 338. Cf. Legarda, "Colonial Economy," *Philippine Perspective*, sess. 1, pt. 2, ch. 6, pp. 31–35. The quotation from Warner is in *Report of the Philippine Commission* (Schurman), II, 193, 197–198. The effect upon imports and exports is described in testimony of Bernancio Balbas, Charles Ilderton Barnes, Edwin H. Warner, A. Kuensle, J. T. B. McLeod, and Harold Ashton, *ibid.*, II, 154–160, 182–187, 191, 193–198, 226–227, 306–307, 338–340; and in Legarda, "Foreign Trade," pp. 207–208. The surplus of exports over imports ranged from a low in 1884 of ₱1,426,592 in a total trade of ₱43,919,074, to a high in 1895 of ₱11,256,929 in a total trade of ₱62,054,525; the average annual surplus for the entire period amounted to just over ₱6,330,000. Foreign trade statistics are from *Statistical Bulletin No. 3 of the Philippine Islands* (1920), pp. 125ff.

21. *Report of the Philippine Commission* (1900), pp. 85–90.

22. *Report of the Philippine Commission* (1903), pt. 3, 281–290; Wright to Root, cable, May 22, 1902, and Root to Wright, cable, May 31, 1902 (TP, series 3, box 72, copies filed with letter from Root to Taft, June 9, 1902); Taft to Root, November 22, 1902, and January 25, 1903 (TP, series 8).

23. *Report of the Philippine Commission* (1900), p. 91; Taft to Root,

December 27, 1900 (TP, series 8). The commissioners may have been influenced by observing that during the summer of 1900 British Indian silver dollars of the same weight and fineness as the Mexican were 2–4 percent less valuable in exchange in Manila than Mexican dollars. The Commission toyed with the idea of making British Indian silver receivable at par with Mexican as a way of freeing the government from its difficulties. Taft to Root, August 11, 1900 (TP, series 8).

24. Taft to Wright, February 21, 1902 (TP, series 3, box 70).

25. Taft to Cooper, September 15, 1902 (TP, series 3, box 73); Manila Chamber of Commerce to Lodge, cable, January 27, 1903 (copy, TP, series 3, box 75). Currency matters are discussed in the reports of the Commission; in Edwin W. Kemmerer, *Modern Currency Reforms* (New York, 1916); and in Charles A. Conant, "The Currency of the Philippine Islands," *Annals of the American Academy for Political and Social Science, 20* (November 1902), 44–59. For amplification: Taft to William B. Allison, May 21, 1902 (TP, series 3, box 72); Taft to Conant, November 23, 1902 (TP, series 3, box 74); Conant to Taft, March 2, 1903 (TP, series 3, box 76).

26. The evolution of Taft's thought under the impact of the crisis is shown in Taft to Henry A. Cooper, September 15, 1902 (TP, series 3, box 73); Taft to Root, August 25, 1902, and October 4, 1902 (TP, series 8); Taft to Lodge, October 4, 1902 (TP, series 3, box 73); Taft to W. B. Allison, November 24, 1902 (TP, series 3, box 74); Taft to Theodore Roosevelt, November 9, 1902 (TP, series 4, box 681); and Taft to Clarence R. Edwards, June 5, 1903 (TP, series 3, box 77).

27. Bowring, *Visit*, p. 144; Foreman, *Philippine Islands,* p. 239.

28. *Ibid.,* pp. 301–307, 378ff.; Tornow, "Sketch," pp. 608, 624; Victor Clark, *Labor Conditions in the Philippines* (Washington, 1905), pp. 792–794; *Report of the Philippine Commission* (1900), pp. 71–73. For a general survey, see Legarda, "Colonial Economy," *Philippine Perspective,* sess. 1, pt. 2, ch. 6, pp. 33–36.

29. BIA memorandum, May 1901 (BIA 2893–0); Forbes, *Philippine Islands,* I, 369–370; Forbes, Journal, III, 285; Forbes to Leonard Wood, October 5, 1921 (Forbes Papers, Houghton Library, Harvard University—hereinafter cited as FP—fMS Am 1366.1, vol. 4).

30. Forbes, Journal, V, 348–349.

31. Forbes, Journal, I, 98, 233.

32. Forbes, Journal, series 2, I, 377–378; Journal, I, 2.

33. *Ibid.,* I, 5–7; William James to Forbes, February 21, 1904 (FP, fMS Am 1364).

34. Forbes, Journal, I, 32–36; Forbes, *Philippine Islands,* II, 387n; Forbes to Olney, September 8, 1904 (FP, fMS Am 1366, vol. 1).

35. The quotation and the statistics are from Forbes, *Philippine Islands,* I, 376n and 383, respectively. For Forbes' analysis, see also Forbes, Journal, II, 279–281; III, 285n; IV, 335n; and Forbes to Wood, October 5, 1921 (FP, fMS Am 1366.1, vol. 4).

36. Wright to Carmack, cable, April 26, 1904 (BIA 4325–with 25); Forbes, Journal, I, 41.

37. The quotation is from Forbes, Journal, I, 65. For an introduction to the problem, see *Report of the Philippine Commission* (1900), pp. 71–75; *ibid.* (1901), pp. 60–66; Taft to Root, July 14, 1900 (TP, series 8); Wright to Taft, December 26, 1902 (TP, series 3, box 74); "Powerful Interests Behind Philippine Railway Project," *Washington Post,* January 26, 1906 (BIA 9057–37).

38. Contacts with prospective investors are treated in BIA 6805 and BIA 5012; S. M. Felton to Taft, January 30, 1904 (TP, series 3, box 91); Forbes to Taft, November 12, 1904 (TP, series 3, box 93); Edwards to Taft, September 20, 1904 (TP, series 3, box 91); and "Powerful Interests . . ." (BIA 9057–37).

39. For the narrowing of bidders, see cables from Taft to Wright, April 27 and May 5, 1905 (BIA 5012–after 112 and 113). For the Commission's opposition to the existing line, see Wright to Taft, cables, February 26, 1904 (BIA 5012–60), March 28, 1904 (BIA 749–75), and April 21, 1904 (BIA 4325–24); for its change of heart, see Wright to Taft, cables, March 22, 1905 (BIA 5012–111), April 22, 1905 (BIA 5012–112). The final acceptance of bids is covered in a variety of documents: BIA 12939–13/16. The Speyers formed an American holding company, the Manila Railroad Company, and transferred both the franchise and their stock in the English company to it.

40. The quotations are drawn, respectively, from *Congressional Record,* 56 Cong., 1 sess., p. 704; FP, fMS Am 1192.1, XVI, 4526 over; Lodge to Taft, November 22, 1900 (TP, series 3, box 64); Forbes, Journal, I, 14; *Annual Report of the Lake Mohonk Conference on the Indian and Other Dependent Peoples* (1911), pp. 113–119 (BIA 14840–40).

41. Carpenter to Leonard Wood, July 30, 1921 (BIA 22639–A–57 [B–1a]); *Mohonk Report* (1910), pp. 80–85.

42. Taft to Bellamy Storer, March 23, 1902 (TP, series 3, box 76); *Manila Cablenews,* August 8, 1907; Forbes, Journal, V, 145; Forbes to Charles W. Eliot, September 13, 1916 (FP, fMS Am 1366.1, vol. 3).

43. The examples of the official rhetoric are from *Message of the President of the United States to the Two Houses of Congress,* 56 Cong., 2 sess., p. 41, and *ibid.,* 58 Cong., 3 sess., pp. 44–45. The private views are from Roosevelt to Taft, March 12, 1901 (TP, series 4, box 681); Taft to Aaron A. Ferris, April 25, 1901 (TP, series 3, box 65); Taft to Root, August 25, 1901 (TP, series 8); Forbes to Eliot, August 13, 1910 (FP, unfiled, awaiting disposition in Houghton Library or the Harvard University Archives); *Boston Evening Transcript,* May 29, 1909.

44. Psychological dependence is suggested in Rōyama and Takéuchi, *Philippine Polity,* p. 73.

45. Taft to William Lawrence, February 14, 1904 (BIA 364–58). This was considered a model statement of American policy, and copies were sent

to Governor General Wright and former Secretary Root for their guidance. For the Alumni Association speech, see BIA 3862–72, pp. 35–36. Hepburn's remarks are reported in the *Manila Cablenews,* August 13, 1905. Opponents of retention understood the argument perfectly. Senator Thomas M. Patterson wrote to Taft reprovingly: "Once American capital becomes largely invested in the Islands those who oppose the policy of retention might as well retire from the field." (April 4, 1904, TP, series 3, box 85). Senator Newlands told Forbes in 1905 that he opposed free trade with the Philippines, because he didn't want ties that would be difficult to break. (Forbes, Journal, I, 295).

46. Hord is quoted in BIA 7488–42. Forbes' statement is in FP, fMS Am 1192.4, VII, 2295. *Manila Times,* March 16, 1910; Forbes to Ford, May 2, 1913 (FP, fMS Am 1366.1, vol. 2).

47. Concerning the tendency of progressivism to confuse means and ends, see Robert H. Wiebe, *The Search for Order* (New York, 1967), ch. 6, esp. pp. 154–155.

5. Alliances

1. Bourns to Taft, January 31, 1904 (TP, series 3, box 82); Liang, *Development,* pp. 62–66, 75. Concerning the nature of Philippine politics, see Landé, *Leaders, Factions, and Parties.*

2. *Manifesto of the Federal Party* (Manila, 1905), p. 5 (BIA 2833–6); Pardo to Taft, August 18, 1904 (TP, series 3, box 89); Taft to Wright, November 12, 1904 (TP, series 8, Sec War semi-official, vol. 42).

3. For the quotation from Roosevelt, see Roosevelt to Taft, July 13, 1908 (TP, series 4, box 686). Concerning the slogans, see the draft speech by Forbes (FP, fMS Am 1192.1, p. 239).

4. Concerning strained relations, see LeRoy to Fred (Carpenter), February 25, 1902 (TP, series 3, box 70) and Pardo to Taft, January 30, 1902 (TP, series 3, box 69). The reception: Pardo to Taft, May 4, 1903, and Legarda to Taft, May 2, 1903 (TP, series 3, box 77). Worcester to Taft, October 11, 1903 (TP, series 3, box 80).

5. *Official Gazette,* February 3, 1904 (BIA 26618); Pardo to Taft, February 9, 1904, and Alemany to Taft, February 10, 1904 (TP, series 3, box 83).

6. John S. Hord, *Internal Taxation in the Philippines* (Baltimore, 1907), pp. 10–16; *Report of the Philippine Commission* (1900), pp. 101–104, and (1901), pp. 39–40; *Report of the Philippine Commission* (Schurman), II, 67.

7. Ide to Taft, June 26, 1903 (TP, series 3, box 78).

8. Legarda to Wright, April 21, 1904 (TP, series 3, box 85); Pardo de Tavera, *et al.,* to Taft, July 28, 1904 (BIA 6830–3).

9. Wright to Taft, June 15, 1904 (TP, series 3, box 87).

10. Passage of the law is glowingly described by its co-author in Hord, *Internal Taxation,* pp. 19–45. For the reaction, see Taft to Legarda,

August 22, 1904 (TP, series 8, Sec War semi-official, vol. 41); Araneta to Taft, September 14, 1904 (TP, series 3, box 90); miscellaneous newspaper items and interpolated comments by Forbes in FP, fMS Am 1192.1, pp. 25–31; Alemany to Taft, November 14, 1904 (TP, series 3, box 93).

11. Taft to Legarda, August 22, 1904 (TP, series 8, Sec War semi-official, vol. 41); Legarda to Taft, October 14 and December 14, 1904 (TP, series 3, box 92 and 94); Pardo and Legarda, memorandum, undated (BIA 3777–15).

12. Hord, memorandum, undated (BIA 3777–16); Forbes, Journal, I, 51 and 62; Hord to Ide, October 27, 1904 (TP, series 3, box 92).

13. Pardo to Taft, February 19, 1905 (TP, series 3, box 98). The escalating conflict may be followed in Pardo to Taft, February 7, March 3, and May 19, 1905 (TP, series 3, boxes 97, 99, and 103); and in Legarda to Taft, February 28 and April 14, 1905 (TP, series 3, boxes 98 and 101).

14. Araneta to Taft, September 14, 1904 (TP, series 3, box 90); Alemany to Taft, November 14, 1904 (TP, series 3, box 99); Pardo to Taft, March 3, 1905 (TP, series 3, box 99). The quotation is from Pardo to Taft, February 7, 1905 (TP, series 3, box 97). One of the Filipino commissioners, Luzuriaga, voted some of the time with the American majority. A prominent sugar producer from Negros, his interests were in the export trade. From the official perspective, he was practically a model Filipino. He wanted peace, order, infrastructure, and free trade with the United States.

15. Concerning taxes, see Hord to Ide, August 3, 1905 (BIA 1228–39); Wright to Taft, September 17, 1905 (BIA 1239–53); and "Minutes of the Executive Session of the Philippine Commission and the Secretary of War and the Members of the Congressional Party . . . August 11, 1905," pp. 37–40 (BIA 1239–56). Taft ordered continuation of the taxes by cable, October 28, 1905 (BIA 1228–39). For the constabulary question, see Daniel Williams to Taft, August 31, 1905 (TP, series 3, box 107) and Taft to Helen Taft, September 24, 1905 (TP, series 3, box 108).

16. The text of the speech, delivered August 11, 1905, is filed as BIA 12277–50.

17. For the Wright-Forbes analysis, see "Minutes of the Executive Session . . . August 11, 1905," pp. 47–52 (BIA 1239–56); Forbes, Journal, I, 266–268; Wright to Forbes, May 22, 1906 (FP, fMS Am 1364). As to patronage and popularity, see Pardo to Taft, September 4 and September 25, 1905 (TP, series 3, box 108); Forbes, *Philippine Islands*, I, 147, and II, 108–109.

18. Legarda to Taft, September 2, 1905, and Pardo to Taft, September 4, 1905 (TP, series 3, box 108). Pardo to H. A. Cooper, September 8, 1905, filed with Pardo to Taft, September 15, 1905 (TP, series 3, box 108).

19. Taft to Helen Taft, September 24, 1905 (TP, series 3, box 108); miscellaneous cables collected as BIA 3038–26.

20. The early evolution of the independence parties has been studied surprisingly little. Standard sources are Liang, *Political Parties*, pp. 70–75;

Kalaw, *Philippine Politics,* pp. 287–306, *passim;* Salamanca, *Filipino Reaction,* pp. 160–161. I have supplemented these with official American sources, particularly James F. Smith to Taft, September 24, 1906 (BIA 3427–1); Henry T. Allen to Taft, October 31, 1906 (TP, series 4, box 683); two BIA memoranda, dated April 24, 1907, and May 1, 1907, filed with BIA 3427–2; V. Albert, "The Native Press on the Philippine Assembly," (BIA 6830–8). For the merger attempt between the Union Nacionalista and the Partido Federal, see Smith to Taft, cable, December 24, 1906, and Taft to Smith, cable, December 27, 1906 (BIA 364–88).

21. B. L. Smith, Captain of Constabulary and senior Inspector for Tayabas, to Adjutant, Second District, Lucena, December 31, 1906 (copy: FP, fMS Am 1192.1, pp. 299–303).

22. *La Democracia,* July 9, 1906, as quoted in a memorandum filed with BIA 6830–8.

23. Unidentified newspaper item in English dated March 12, 1907 (FP, fMS Am 1192.1, p. 398).

24. For Pardo's views, see "Minutes of the Executive Session . . . August 11, 1905," p. 58 (BIA 1239–56). Smith to Taft, September 24, 1906 (BIA 3427–1).

25. Statistics: Forbes, *Philippine Islands,* II, 118n, 119n. In the provincial elections, later in 1907, the Progresistas did much better, losing 44,288 to 38,153 in the popular vote, but obtaining the same number of governorships as the Nacionalistas. Liang, *Political Parties,* p. 88n.

26. Memorandum, August 20, 1907 (BIA 3427–3).

27. Forbes, Journal, II, 317–320; *Cablenews-American,* October 17, 1907 (FP, fMS Am 1192.1, pp. 844–846).

28. Concerning Forbes' isolation, see Forbes to [Wright], undated handwritten letter, addressee identified only as "Governor"; Forbes to Wright, August 10, 1906 (both FP, bMS Am 1364.1); and Forbes to Wright, unsent (FP, fMS Am 1192.4, I, 407). Forbes' cultivation of the Nacionalistas may be followed step by step in his journal for 1906 and 1907. For amplification, see Forbes to Wright, July 16, 1907 (FP, bMS Am 1364.1); Forbes' notation, written circa 1921, in FP, fMS Am 1192.4, IV, 1382; and *Philippines Free Press,* January 9, 1909 (FP, fMS Am 1192.4, V, 1568).

29. Forbes, *Philippine Islands,* I, 163. Concerning Osmeña, see also Forbes to Dickinson, February 1, 1910 (BIA 12940–28); Henry T. Allen to Taft, October 31, 1906 (TP, series 4, box 683); Forbes, Journal, II, 200. For Quezon, see Forbes, Journal, I, 416.

30. Forbes, Journal, II, 200, 282; the quotation is from *ibid.,* II, 269–270.

31. *Ibid.,* II, 319–324.

32. Smith to Edwards, cable, January 7, 1908 (BIA 17073–6); Forbes, Journal, II, 363–364; Smith to Edwards, cable, May 23, 1908 (BIA 17073–17).

33. Forbes, Journal, III, 27; Smith to Secretary of War, cable, June 19, 1908 (BIA 364–106).

34. Forbes, Journal, II, 326, 344. Concerning the new seat on the Commission, see cable correspondence BIA 387–34/50, inclusive; especially Smith to Secretary of War, April 17, 1908 (BIA 397–41). Legarda, misreading the signs, suggested that Roosevelt take the occasion to promote Pardo to a portfolio: Legarda to Roosevelt, February 26, 1908 (TP, series 4, box 685).

35. Concerning the *Times*, see Forbes, Journal, II, note 111; Forbes to Martin Egan, March 18, 1916 (copy: Forbes, Journal, series 2, I, 319). Taft's improved opinion is treated in Forbes, Journal, II, 321, 334, 336, 338–340; and in Taft to Forbes, November 30, 1907 (FP, bMS Am 1364). For the appointment to the vice governorship, see Wright to Forbes, February 29, 1908 (FP, bMS Am 1364); Pardo to Taft, cable, March 7, 1908 (BIA 3239–36). Forbes' consolidation emerges in Forbes to Wright, November 27, 1908 (FP, bMS Am 1364.1); Forbes, Journal, III, 56–57; and Forbes' memorandum from an interview with Roosevelt (FP, fMS Am 1192.4, V, 1578½).

6. Declension

1. Forbes to Taft, October 12, 1909 (FP, fMS Am 1366.1, vol. 1).

2. "Inauguration of Honorable William Cameron Forbes" (BIA 9892–111).

3. *Congressional Record*, 62 Cong., 2 sess., May 1, 1912, p. 5701; *The Manila Times*, February 21, 1911 (FP, fMS Am 1192.1, XI, 3078–3079).

4. *The Manila Times*, November 3, 1911 (FP, fMS Am 1192.1, XIII, 3585); Tomas Confesor, "The Battle We Have to Fight," *The Filipino Student*, I, no. 1, quoted in *ibid.*, January 8, 1913 (FP, fMS Am 1192.1, XIX, 5211); *El Ideal*, December 17, 1912 (FP, fMS Am 1192.1, XVIII, 5007–5008); *El Renacimiento*, November 13, 1908 (FP, fMS Am 1192.1, VI, 1411–1412); *La Vanguardia*, October 20, 1910 (FP, fMS Am 1192.1, X, 2756).

5. The quotations are from the *Cablenews-American*, October 9, 1910 (FP, fMS Am 1192.1, X, 2739); Edward B. Bruce, "The Economic Side of the Philippine Problem," in *Report of the Twenty-ninth Annual Lake Mohonk Conference of Friends of the Indian and Other Dependent Peoples* (1911), p. 94; and John S. Hord, "Shell or Substance of Free Trade—Which?" in *Report of the Twenty-eighth Annual Lake Mohonk Conference* (1910), p. 120.

6. *Taliba*, October 10, 1910 (FP, fMS Am 1192.1, X, 2740); *El Ideal*, August 30, 1911 (FP, fMS Am 1192.1, XIII, 3474–3475); Forbes, Journal, IV, 238–239.

7. Forbes, Journal, III, 151–155; Forbes to Dickinson, cable, May 1, 1909 (BIA 17073–39); Forbes to Taft, November 13, 1909 (FP, fMS Am 1366.1, vol. 1); Frank McIntyre, memorandum for the Secretary of War, January 6, 1917 (BIA 17073– after 158).

8. For a general discussion of the tariff in these years, see Pedro E.

Abelarde, *American Tariff Policy toward the Philippines, 1898–1946* (New York, 1947), pp. 36–49. Concerning the early emphasis upon tariff reduction as a recovery measure, see Taft to Root, cable, February 26, 1903 (BIA C.1250–18); Wright to Taft, cable, February 4, 1902 (TP, series 3, box 69); and Wright's testimony before the Senate Committee on the Philippines, December 9, 1902 (BIA C.1250–14). Filipino petitions for reduction or free entry are scattered through BIA files C.1246 and C.1250. *Public Hearings in the Philippine Islands upon the Proposed Reduction of the Tariff* . . . *August, 1905* (Manila, 1905), *passim*, esp. pp. 1–25, 79–89, 94–136, 148–171 (BIA 1239–55).

9. Taft to J. B. Foraker, February 17, 1902 (TP, series 3, box 70); Wright's testimony, December 9, 1902, is filed as BIA C.1250–14.

10. BIA 3862–72, pp. 35–36.

11. Joint Resolution No. 6, 1 Phil. Leg., 1 sess., December 19, 1907 (BIA C.1250–213); Joint Resolution No. 11, 1 Phil. Leg., 1 sess., May 19, 1908 (BIA C.1089–94).

12. John Hord, Memorandum for General Edwards, August 12, 1908 (BIA 7488–31); *La Democracia*, August 26, 1908 (BIA C.1246–77). For the insular government's fears see cables from Smith to Edwards, November 20, 1908 (BIA C.1250–70), January 8, 1909 (BIA C.1089–96), and March 19, 1909 (BIA C.1250–73). For Washington's insistence upon reciprocity: cables Edwards to Smith, November 17, 1908, and March 22, 1909 (BIA C.1250–after 69 and–after 73); Pablo Ocampo to Osmeña, cable, March 24, 1909 (BIA C.1250–after 73). The Payne bill—H.R. 1438, 61 Cong., 1 sess.—prescribed limits of 300,000 tons of sugar, 300,000 tons of mixed wrapper and filler tobacco, 3,000,000 pounds of filler tobacco, and 150,000 cigars. See Abelarde, *American Tariff Policy*, pp. 76–100.

13. Joint Resolution No. 36, 1 Phil. Leg., 2 sess., March 27, 1909. For Quezon's views, see Hord, memorandum for General Edwards (BIA 7488–31). His speech is quoted in *The Cablenews-American*, March 28, 1909 (FP, fMS Am 1192.1, VII, 1610–1612). In addition this account draws upon Forbes, Journal, III, 128–131; Forbes to Taft, November 13, 1909 (FP, fMS Am 1366.1, vol. 1); and cables from Smith to Edwards, March 19, 25, and 30, 1909 (BIA C.1250–73/75). The emphasis is my own. Cf. Manuel L. Quezon, *The Good Fight* (New York, 1946), pp. 107–108, 142–143, which claims he was wary of the snare of the American market. Evidence from the period suggests he feared the American market only if Filipinos had to grant reciprocity to get it.

14. Forbes, Journal, III, 130–131; Smith to Edwards, cable, March 30, 1909 (BIA C.1250–75). I am grateful to Glenn E. May for allowing me to see his detailed notes on this encounter from the copy of the Journal of the Commission, March 29, 1909, in the papers of James F. Smith at the Washington State Historical Society and Museum, Tacoma. Cf. Salamanca, *Filipino Reaction*, pp. 130–132.

15. This campaign may be followed in BIA C.1250–74/81, and in

Forbes, Journal, III, 130–131. For Hord's initiation of it, see Hord to Cromwell, in Edwards to Smith, cable, March 29, 1909 (BIA C.1250–after 74).

16. The Commission's interpretation is summarized in Salamanca, *Filipino Reaction,* pp. 127–132. Concerning the Assembly's supporters, see cables Smith to Edwards, April 7, 1909 (BIA C.1250–81); Fernandez to Taft, April 5, 1909 (BIA C.1250–83); and Gilbert to Edwards, June 30, 1909 (BIA C.1250–119). It is commonly held that Philippine cigars are an acquired taste for Americans. The major tobacco companies—Tabacalera, Insular, Yebana, Oriente, Germinal, Commercial, Paz y Buen, and Viaje—had their established markets in Europe and the Philippines; and they expected little gain from free entry to the American market.

17. *El Renacimiento,* April 13, 1909 (FP, fMS Am 1192.1, VII, 1635–1638); Pablo Ocampo de Leon, "Speech . . . at a Popular Banquet given in his honor . . . October 2, 1909" (pamphlet); *El Mercantil,* April 12, 1909 (FP, fMS Am 1192.1, VII, 1632–1634).

18. Taft to Helen Taft, July 11, 1909 (TP, series 7, folder 1). The tariff account is based upon Abelarde, *American Tariff Policy,* pp. 76–100; cables from Edwards to Smith, December 28, 1907 (BIA C.1250–after 61), November 17, 1908 (BIA C.1250–after 69), April 10, 1909 (BIA C.1250–after 83), and April 12, 1909 (BIA C.1250–after 84); BIA Memorandum, July 9, 1909 (BIA C.1250–122); Frank McIntyre, memorandum for the files, July 26, 1909 (BIA C.1250–after 130); and Stanley D. Solvick, "William Howard Taft and the Payne-Aldrich Tariff," MVHR, 50 (1963), 424–442.

19. The quotations are from Forbes, Journal, III, 245 and IV, 21–22. The statistics are based upon Forbes, *Philippine Islands,* I, 244, and *Report of the Collector of Customs* (1921), p. 21 and (1925), p. 71. The computation is my own.

20. The quote concerning Osmeña is taken from *The Cablenews-American,* April 22, 1908 (FP, fMS Am 1192.1, V, 1146). *La Democracia,* November 9, 1908 (FP, fMS Am 1192.1, VI, 1406).

21. Concerning the embarrassment of the Nacionalistas: Forbes to Dickinson, October 26, 1909 (BIA 3427–4); Forbes, Journal, III, 336–337, and IV, 26. Election statistics: Forbes, *Philippine Islands,* II, 119n. For the evolution of the Progresistas, see *The Cablenews-American,* February 2, 1910 (FP, fMS Am 1192.1, VIII, 2064); V. Singson Encarnación to Legarda, February 19, 1910 (BIA 364–117); Singson to Quezon, March 1, 1910 (Quezon General Correspondence File). The Papers of Manuel L. Quezon are housed in the National Library, Manila; hereinafter this file will be abbreviated QGCF. The subject file and the major correspondents' file will be cited as such.

22. Pardo to Quezon, February 10, 1910 (BIA 18073–19).

23. Forbes, Journal, III, 425, and IV, 27–28, 38–39; *The Cablenews-American,* March 29, 1910 (FP, fMS Am 1192.1, VIII, 2147); *La Vanguardia,* April 22, 1910 (FP, fMS Am 1192.1, VIII, 2196–2197). For background concerning the deportation, see Forbes, Journal, III, 272–273.

24. Concerning the shift of patronage, see Forbes to Dickinson, April 26, 1910 (FP, fMS Am 1366.1, vol. 1); Forbes to Taft, July 14, 1910 (TP, series 6, file 44); Forbes, Journal, IV, 221–222. For examples of the abuse of Osmeña, see *La Democracia*, April 28, May 7, and May 9, 1910 (FP, fMS Am 1192.1, IX, 2102, 2221–2223); unsigned Constabulary report, May 5, 1910 (FP, fMS Am 1192.1, IX, 2215–2218); unidentified copy of a confidential report, dated Manila, April 27, 1910 (QGCF).

25. *El Mercantil*, May 12, 1910 (FP, fMS Am 1192.1, IX, 2230); the *Cablenews-American*, August 28, 1910 (FP, fMS Am 1192.1, X, 2533–2534, quoting earlier reports.

26. *Report of the Philippine Commission* (1907), II, 184 ff.; Edwards to Forbes, September 27, 1909 (BIA 1644–after 104).

27. "Memorandum on the San José Friar Estate," April 19, 1910 (BIA 1644–after 121); Edwards to Forbes, September 27, 1909 (BIA 1644–after 104); Forbes to Edwards, cables, October 22 and November 29, 1909 (BIA 1644–106/107).

28. Taft to M. E. Olmstead, March 5, 1911 (TP, series 6, file 267); Dickinson to Taft, December 2, 1909 (BIA 1644–after 107); Taft to Dickinson, December 3, 1909 (BIA 1644–108). The sugar trust's disclaimer: E. F. Atkins to Secretary of War, December 30, 1909 (BIA 20494).

29. The quotation is from the *Cablenews-American*, February 25, 1910 (FP, fMS Am 1192.1, VIII, 2104). Congressional opposition may be followed in BIA 1644–120/124, and in BIA files 2914 and 212, *passim*.

30. "Memorandum on the San José Friar Estate," April 19, 1910 (BIA 1644–after 121).

31. Translated copy: FP, fMS Am 1192.1, X, 2566.

32. BIA 364–125/126.

33. Martin Egan to Forbes, February 5, 1910 (FP, bMS Am 1364); Edwards to Taft, June 3, 1910 (TP, series 7, folder 65).

34. Forbes, Journal, IV, 172–173; *La Vanguardia*, August 19, 1910 (FP, fMS Am 1192.1, IX, 2474–2475); *El Ideal*, August 17, 1910 (FP, fMS Am 1192.1, IX, 2457–2459).

35. Texts of the Forbes and Dickinson speeches are in FP, fMS Am 1192.1, X, 2605–2620. Forbes, Journal, IV, 188–189.

36. *La Vanguardia*, September 5, 1910. Three days after the banquet, a curious conversation took place between Quezon and Forbes. Six weeks earlier, upon his return from the United States, Quezon had told Forbes that he had devoted his maiden speech before Congress as resident commissioner to a plea for independence, knowing it would produce no effect in Washington but would help his career in the Philippines. (Forbes, Journal, IV, 146–147) When Quezon called upon the governor after the Dickinson banquet, Forbes told him that his talk of independence had been "disquieting" and might produce precisely the opposite effect from what Filipinos desired. "Well," Quezon replied, "but I think we do want it." Forbes eyed him intently and asked, "An adverse declaration?" "Yes," Quezon responded,

"it would stop agitation." (Forbes, Journal, IV, 192) Whether this is to be taken at face value or in a context of one-upsmanship is anybody's guess. Would an adverse declaration have ended independence agitation or increased its political payoff for Filipino politicians?

37. Jacinto is quoted in Agoncillo, *Revolt of the Masses*, p. 84. The quotations from Taft are from Pringle, *Taft*, I, 174 and Taft to Ide, March 21, 1906 (TP, series 8, Sec War semi-official, vol. 49).

38. *The Outlook*, October 25, 1913; *Oregon Journal*, August 13, 1909 (BIA 1239–67). For discrimination against squaw men, as they were branded, see John T. Pickett to Woodrow Wilson, November 11, 1912 (BIA 19861–16). The Bell episode is reported in *The Cablenews-American*, October 5 and October 8, 1911.

39. *Manila Times*, August 12, 1908 (FP, fMS Am 1192.1, VI, 1350); *ibid.*, May 19, 1911 (FP, fMS Am 1192.1, XII, 3231–3232); *Cablenews-American*, August 15, 1908 (FP, fMS Am 1192.1, VI, 1355).

40. The quotations are from Forbes, Journal, II, 437; *ibid.*, III, 141; and Forbes to Frank W. Carpenter, August 25, 1913 (FP, fMS Am 1366.1, vol. 2).

41. *El Ideal*, April 19, 1911 (FP, fMS Am 1192.1, XII, 3153) is an example of distinction by pronoun. This is an editorial predicting that in time "the colored race . . . will surge from everywhere to defend jointly the question of honor." Concerning the doctors, see *La Democracia*, July 7, 1911 (FP, fMS Am 1192.1, XII, 3326).

42. *El Ideal*, May 15, 1911 (FP, fMS Am 1192.1, XII, 3215–3216).

43. *La Vanguardia*, August 20, 1912, trans. in FP, fMS Am 1192.1, XVI, 4418–4420.

44. Forbes, Journal, IV, 238; Forbes to Dickinson, November 29, 1910 (BIA 17073–71).

45. Concerning the cause of the deadlock, see Forbes, Journal, IV, 244; Forbes to Edwards, cable, November 29, 1910 (copy: TP, series 6, file 44). For Osmeña's alleged motivation, see James G. Harbord to Quezon, December 2, 1910 (Quezon Major Correspondents' File); Quezon to Jaime de Veyra, January 12, 1911 (QGCF); de Veyra to Quezon, December 7, 1910, and March 4, 1911 (QGCF).

46. Osmeña to Quezon, December 24, 1910 (QGCF); Teodoro M. Kalaw to Quezon, January 3, 1911 (QGCF); de Veyra to Quezon, December 7, 1910, and February 14, 1911 (QGCF).

47. Forbes, Journal, IV, 277–280; Forbes to Dickinson, February 12, 1911 (BIA 17073–79). *The Manila Times*, February 7, 1911 (FP, fMS Am 1192.1, XI, 3060–61) summarizes the session. The Assembly rejected 28 bills passed by the Commission, and the latter more than 70 of the Assembly's bills. The session was by no means a total failure: Numerous useful bills were passed, including special appropriations for public works and the University of the Philippines. For additional perspective, see Frank Jenista, Jr., "Conflict in the Philippine Legislature: The Commission and the Assembly from 1907–1913," in Owen, ed., *Compadre Colonialism*, pp. 77–101.

48. Quezon to Jaime [de Veyra], January 12, 1910 (QGCF).

49. Kalaw, *Aide-de-Camp*, p. 92; Quezon to de Veyra, January 12, 1911 (QGCF).

50. Quezon to Osmeña, March 9, 1911 (QGCF); Quezon to de Veyra, April 6, 1911 (QGCF); Quezon to Osmeña, April 21, 1911 (QGCF).

51. For the prediction of reform legislation, see Quezon to Singson, May 25, 1911 (QGCF); Quezon to Erving Winslow, May 17, 1911 (QGCF). The letter to congressmen is in QGCF, dated June 21, 1911. For Manila reaction, see de Veyra to Quezon, April 28, 1911 (QGCF).

52. Forbes, Journal, IV, 423–424. Martin Egan to Forbes, February 5, 1910 (FP, bMS Am 1364); internal evidence establishes that the date should be 1911.

53. Forbes, Journal, V, 98–105; Quezon to Winslow, February 26, 1912 (QGCF); *El Ideal,* January 12, 1912 (FP, fMS Am 1192.1, XIV, 3691–3698). *La Vanguardia,* February 13, 1912 (FP, fMS Am 1192.1, XIV, 3789–3790). Osmeña to Quezon, March 14, 1912 (QGCF).

54. Quezon to Winslow, January 16, March 9, and March 20, 1912 (QGCF); Quezon to Osmeña, March 21, 1912 (QGCF); Winslow to Quezon, January 22, 1912 (Quezon Subject File: Anti-Imperialist League). The First Jones Bill was H.R. 22143, 62 Cong., 2 sess.

55. "Proposed Section 30 by Speaker Osmeña" (Quezon Subject File: Jones Bill). Quezon to Winslow, March 21 and 22, 1912 (QGCF); Winslow to Quezon, March 21, 1912 (QGCF); Quezon to Osmeña, March 21, 1912 (QGCF).

56. Quezon to Winslow, April 5, May 12, and May 18, 1912 (QGCF); Edwards to Towner, April 1, 1912 (BIA 364–159); Marlin E. Olmsted to Forbes, June 6, 1912 (FP, bMS Am 1364.1).

57. Osmeña to Quezon, March 14, 1912, and cable, March 26, 1912 (QGCF); Quezon to Winslow, May 18, 20, and 21, 1912 (QGCF); Winslow to Quezon, May 20, 1912 (QGCF). *El Ideal,* May 21, 1912 (FP, fMS Am 1192.1, XV, 4122–4123). Election statistics: Forbes, *Philippine Islands,* II, 118–119.

58. San Agustin to Quezon, June 24, 1912; Quezon to San Agustin, August 8, 1912 (both Quezon Subject File: Elections).

59. The udder quote is reproduced in *El Mercantil,* June 22, 1912 (FP, fMS Am 1192.1, XV, 4200). For Quezon's endorsement of Osmeña, see cables La O. to Quezon, June 14, 1912, and Quezon to *La Vanguardia,* June 14, 1912 (both QGCF). The letters to assemblymen, dated July 3, 1912, are in Quezon Subject File: Philippine Assembly. Osmeña's victory is reported in *Manila Times,* October 15, 1912 (FP, fMS Am 1192.1, XVII, 4676).

7. Ferment

1. The quotations are from Forbes, *Philippine Islands,* II, 568–569, and appendix XXVI. Winslow to Quezon, August 16, 1911, and January 30,

1912 (QGCF); Quezon to Winslow, August 17, 1911, and March 5, April 5, July 22, July 23, and July 27, 1912 (QGCF); McIntyre to Newton W. Gilbert, August 1, 1912 (BIA 364–after 182).

2. McIntyre to Gilbert, August 1, 1912 (BIA 364–after 182).

3. Quezon to McIntyre, September 5, 1912 (BIA 18428–32); "Philippine Independence and American Commercial Success," *The Filipino People*, vol. 1, no. 3 (November 1912), pp. 10–11.

4. *Cablenews-American*, October 10, 1912 (FP, fMS Am 1192.1, XVII, 4650–4652); *Manila Times*, October 16, 1912 (FP, fMS Am 1192.1, XVII, 4681–4683).

5. Forbes' role is evident in his memorandum of a conversation with Taft in October, 1912 (FP, fMS Am 1192.1, XVII, 4600). Earnshaw is quoted in the Manila *Daily Bulletin*, April 12, 1913 (FP, fMS Am 1192.1, XX, 5483).

6. The quotations are taken, respectively, from Kalaw, *Aide-de-Camp*, p. 62; Claude A. Buss, "Charismatic Leadership in Southeast Asia: Manuel Luis Quezon," *Solidarity, 1* (July–September 1966), 7; Kalaw, *Aide-de-Camp*, p. 271; *ibid.*, p. 268; and Forbes to Brent, July 21, 1913 (FP, fMS Am 1366.1, vol. 2). The most recent biography of Quezon is Carlos Quirino, *Quezon: Paladin of Philippine Freedom* (Manila, 1971). See also, Manuel L. Quezon, *The Good Fight* (New York, 1946), and my own sketch of him in the forthcoming *Dictionary of American Biography*, supp. 3.

7. For an example of the views of an American friend, see J. G. Harbord to Quezon, April 22, 1911, and July 22, 1911 (QGCF). Quezon, *The Good Fight*, pp. 142–143. Evidence from various sources is summarized in Salamanca, *Filipino Reaction*, pp. 168–177.

8. *La Vanguardia*, November 5 and November 7, 1912 (FP, fMS Am 1192.1, XVII, 4752, 4761–4764); *El Ideal*, November 12, 1912 (FP, fMS Am 1192.1, XVII, 4803–4806); Egan to Secretary of War, cable, November 12, 1912 (BIA 364–190).

9. Forbes, memorandum of private discussions with Taft (FP, fMS Am 1192.1, XVII, 4588); Forbes, Journal, V, 164–165.

10. See, for example, Forbes to Henry L. Stimson, August 11, 1911 (BIA 364–175) and May 26, 1912 (BIA 364–177), the latter enclosing material for Congressman Redfield.

11. Forbes, Journal, V, 166; Forbes to Taft, November 27, 1912 (TP, series 6, file 44c); Frederick H. Reed to Forbes, December 2, 1912 (FP, bMS Am 1364.1); James Cardinal Gibbons to Forbes, December 6, 1912 (FP, bMS Am 1364.1).

12. Taft to Gibbons, November 13, 1912 (TP, series 7, folder 398); Taft to J. T. Roche, November 20, 1912 (TP, series 6, file 44c); Taft to Brent, January 31, 1913 (TP, series 7, folder 522).

13. Roche to Taft, November 14, 1912 (TP, series 6, file 44c); Dougherty to Taft, January 3, 1913 (TP, series 6, file 44c); Fallows to Taft, December 6, 1912 (TP, series 6, file 44c). Gibbons' interview is reproduced as *House Doc.* no. 1446, 62 Cong., 3 sess.

14. *Message of the President of the United States on Fiscal, Judicial, Military and Insular Affairs . . . December 6, 1912* (BIA 15261–26).

15. *La Democracia,* December 9, 1912 (FP, fMS Am 1192.1, XVIII, 4964–4965); *La Vanguardia,* December 9, 1912 (FP, fMS Am 1192.1, XVIII, 4966–4968); Assembly Resolution No. 61, 3 Phil. Leg., 1 sess. December 10, 1912 (BIA 364–216).

16. Forbes to Taft, December 9, 1912 (FP, fMS Am 1366.1, vol. 1); Forbes to N. H. Stone, January 26, 1913 (FP, fMS Am 1366.1, vol. 2).

17. Taft's remarks to the Ohio Society are quoted in Manila *Daily Bulletin,* March 7, 1913 (FP, fMS Am 1192.1, XIX, 5452–5455). The Philippine Society is the subject of miscellaneous clippings and documents: FP, fMS Am 1192.1, XX, 5599–5607, 5612; its banquet is described in New York papers, June 11,1913.

18. Barrows to Redfield, June 6, 1912 forwarded to Wilson, January 2, 1913 (BIA 364–225); J. G. White to Garrison, May 8, 1913 (BIA 364–228). The *Chronicle* article is reproduced in Manila *Daily Bulletin,* January 2, 1913 (FP, fMS Am 1192.1, XVIII, 5110–5111); for Dollar, see *ibid.,* December 27, 1912 (FP, fMS Am 1192.1, XVIII, 5081). A copy of the bank newsletter, March, 1913, is filed as BIA 364–220. Egan to Forbes, March 13, 1913. (FP, bMS Am 1364).

19. Osmeña to Quezon, cable, June 28, 1913 (QGCF, filed with Quezon to Osmeña, May 20, 1913).

20. Forbes to Taft, February 11, 1913 (FP, fMS Am 1366.1, vol. 2); Forbes, Journal, V, 176–185.

21. Forbes to Lindley M. Garrison, May 19, 1913 (BIA 1998–88); Forbes, Journal, V, 239; Forbes to Garrison, June 21, 1913 (BIA 9892–211).

22. Forbes to Charles E. Perkins, September 30, 1907 (FP, bMS Am 1364.1); Forbes to Edwards, June 28, 1910 (BIA 364–121). Concerning overspending and the lack of a competent accountant, see Forbes to Stimson, August 1, 1911 (BIA 9892–136); Forbes, Journal, IV, 433; Forbes to McIntyre, April 22, 1913 (BIA 9892–201).

23. Forbes to Garrison, June 21, 1913 (BIA 9892–111); Forbes to Garrison, July 9, 1913 (BIA 4429–51); Forbes, Journal, V, 278, 282.

24. Elliott, *Commission,* pp. 364-369; Forbes to Stimson, December 14, 1911 (FP, fMS Am 1366.1, vol. 1). Concerning the debacle on the Luisita estate, see "San Miguel Irrigation System," memorandum, Papers of Francis Burton Harrison, box 38. The Harrison papers, hereinafter cited as HP, are deposited in the Library of Congress.

25. Forbes to Garrison, June 21, 1913 (FP, fMS Am 1366.1, vol. 2, pp. 313-317); Edward Bowditch to Forbes, May 5, 1912 (FP, bMS Am 1364.3, box 1).

26. *Manila Times,* April 27, 1908 (FP, fMS Am 1192.1, V, 1161–1168).

27. Concerning attitudes: Dickinson to Forbes, February 21, 1910 (BIA 9892–after 111); Forbes to Gilbert, March 12, 1912 (FP, fMS Am 1366.1,

vol. 1). Statistics are from Forbes, *Philippine Islands*, I, 448n, 472; McIntyre, Report to the Secretary of War, March 1, 1913 (BIA 119–72).

28. Forbes to Wilson, May 19, 1913 (BIA 3725–48); Forbes, Journal, V, 238–239; Elliott, *Commission*, 248n.

29. Roy W. Curry, *Woodrow Wilson and Far Eastern Policy, 1913–1921* (New York, 1957), pp. 65–69; Forbes, notation in FP, fMS Am 1192.1, XIX, 5170; Gilbert to Redfield, February 14, 1913, filed with Redfield to Wilson, March 24, 1913, Papers of Woodrow Wilson, series 4, file 44. The Wilson papers, hereinafter cited as WP, are deposited in the Library of Congress.

30. Curry, *Wilson*, p. 72. Forbes believed, erroneously, that Ford had been won over to the insular government's point of view: Forbes, Journal, V, 235–236; Forbes to Ford, May 2, 1913 (FP, fMS Am 1366.1, vol. 2). Ford's report was never printed. It is filed as BIA 364–295/296. The report was submitted after Wilson had already made the appointment of Francis Burton Harrison, and apparently was never read by him. Presumably, he knew Ford's views from the latter's letters and from personal contacts early in the summer, when Ford returned from the Philippines.

31. McIntyre, Report to the Secretary of War, March 1, 1913 (BIA 119–72).

32. BIA 141–76.

33. Garrison to Wilson, April 24, 1913 (BIA 141–78); Garrison to Wilson, June 13, 1913 (WP, series 4, file 44).

34. Bell to Forbes, November 20, 1912 (FP, bMS Am 1364.1); Quezon to Winslow, March 10, 1913 (QGCF). See also Gilbert to Quezon, November 22, 1912 (QGCF), which shows the vice governor answering questions put to him by Quezon in an apparent attempt to ascertain his suitability for the governorship.

35. Forbes to Gilbert, April 22, 1913 (FP, fMS Am 1366.1, vol. 2). Osmeña to Quezon, March 12 and April 9, 1913; Quezon to Osmeña, July 12, 1913; Osmeña to Quezon, July 15, 1913 (QGCF).

36. Concerning Shuster's candidacy, see the large number of cables and letters in the 1913 Quezon Major Correspondents' File: W. Morgan Shuster; and also Quezon to Shuster, April 10, 1913, and Quezon to Osmeña, June 20, 1913 (QGCF). The quotations are from Shuster to Quezon, July 4, 1913.

37. For Osmeña's views, see Osmeña to Quezon, cable, April 30, 1913 (Quezon Major Correspondents' File: Osmeña); Osmeña to Quezon, cable, June 3, 1913 (QGCF). Concerning the variety of contenders, see *Manila Times*, April 12, 1913 (FP, fMS Am 1192.1, XX, 5482); Egan to Forbes, March 13, [1913] (FP, bMS Am 1364); Forbes, Journal, V, 260. Quezon to Pardo de Tavera, June 2, 1913 (Quezon Major Correspondents' File: Pardo de Tavera).

38. Shuster to Quezon, August 2 and August 5, 1913 (Quezon Major Correspondents' File: Shuster); Forbes, Journal, V, 291–292; Quezon to

James Ross, August 5, 1913 (Quezon Major Correspondents' File: Ross); Quezon to Storey, August 12, 1913, draft letter not sent (Quezon Subject File: Anti-Imperialist League); Quezon to H. Parker Willis, August 5, 1913 (QGCF).

39. The key documents for understanding this much misunderstood episode are Quezon to Storey, August 22, 1913 (QGCF); Quezon to Willis, August 23, 1913 (QGCF); Bryan to Wilson, undated, received at White House August 16, 1913 (WP, series 4, file 44); Wilson to Bryan, August 18, 1913 (WP, series 4, file 44); Bryan to Wilson, undated, received at White House August 19, 1913 (WP, series 4, file 44); Garrison to Wilson, cable, August 19, 1913 (WP, series 4, file 44); Quezon to Osmeña, cable, August 20, 1913 (QGCF).

8. Consensus

1. Forbes, Journal, series 2, II, 77.

2. Harrison to Winslow, May 8, 1913 (Quezon Subject File: Governor General). The draft with Harrison's revisions is filed with an unsigned covering letter to Harrison, August 21, 1913 (WP, series 4, file 44).

3. Francis Burton Harrison, The Corner-stone of Philippine Independence (New York, 1922), p. 50; Cablenews-American, October 7, 1913 (FP, fMS Am 1192.1, XX, 5703–5704).

4. The quotations are taken from Cablenews-American, October 7, 1913; Harrison, Corner-stone, p. 73; BIA 141–85.

5. Harrison to Andrew J. Peters, November 4, 1913 (HP, box 31); Harrison to Garrison, October 24, 1913 (BIA 12940–42); Harrison to Ollie M. James, December 15, 1913 (HP, box 31); Harrison to Oscar W. Underwood, November 4, 1913 (HP, box 31).

6. Harrison to Hitchcock, December 5, 1913 (HP, box 31); Harrison to McIntyre, cables, September 30 and October 2, 1913 (BIA 397–62).

7. Harrison to Garrison, cable, October 11, 1913 (BIA 397–65). Those named, in order of preference, were Rafael Palma, Victorino Mapa, Jaime C. de Veyra, Vicente Ilustre, Vicente Singson Encarnación, Alberto Barretto, Dionisio Jakosalem, Espiridion Guangco, Francisco Ortigas, Leon Ma. Guerrero, Rafael Corpus, and Galicano Apacible.

8. Harrison to Garrison, cable, October 13, 1913 (BIA 397–66); Harrison, Corner-stone, pp. 64–65; El Comercio, January 2, 3, and 5, 1914 (BIA 13285–40).

9. Report of the Philippine Commission (Schurman), I, 112–113; Report of the Philippine Commission (1900), pp. 20–21; Forbes, Philippine Islands, II, 167, 230. Cf. Onofre D. Corpuz, The Bureaucracy in the Philippines (Manila, 1957), pp. 163–184.

10. Forbes, Philippine Islands, II, 167; Petition of the Nacionalista Party, September 1, 1910 (BIA 364–125/126).

11. Harrison to Garrison, December 4, 1913 (BIA 141–86½); Report of the Governor-General of the Philippine Islands (1914), pp. 15–23; Harrison, Corner-stone, pp. 77–80; Forbes, Philippine Islands, II, 221–224.

12. Harrison, *Corner-stone*, pp. 80–86; Forbes, *Philippine Islands*, II, 222–228, 231. For a Harrisonian's eye view of the reorganization of the Bureau of Customs, see B. Herstein to Harrison, February 9, 1914 (BIA C.567–39).

13. *Cablenews-American*, October 16, 1913 (FP, fMS Am 1192.1, XX, 5719); *Manila Daily Bulletin*, October 14, 1913 (FP, fMS Am 1192.1, XX, 5714–5715); *Manila Times*, October 27, 1913 (FP, fMS Am 1192.1, XX, 5754); *Philippines Free Press*, January 17, 1914 (FP, fMS Am 1192.1, XXI, 5840); William B. Poland to Frederick H. Reed, February 2, 1914 (BIA 1239–104); *The Weekly Times*, undated clipping (FP, fMS Am 1192.1, XXI, 5890–5891).

14. Blount's book, *The American Occupation of the Philippines, 1898–1912* (New York, 1912) is the classic statement of this position.

15. *Manila Times*, January 19, 1907 (FP, fMS Am 1192.1, 331–334).

16. *Cablenews-American*, December 5, 1911 (FP, fMS Am 1192.1, XIII, 3628); *Manila Times*, November 27, 1912 (FP, fMS Am 1192.1, XVIII, 4884–4888). Ross' comments are reported in the *Times*, November 11, 1912 (FP, fMS Am 1192.1, XVII, 4796–4798).

17. *Manila Times*, December 31, 1912 (FP, fMS Am 1192.1, XVIII, 5101–5102); *Cablenews-American*, January 3, 1913 (FP, fMS Am 1192.1, XVIII, 5124–5127); *Manila Daily Bulletin*, January 6, 1913 (FP, fMS Am 1192.1, XVIII, 5163–5164). The endorsements are reported in the *Bulletin* of January 9, 1913 (FP, fMS Am 1192.1, XIX, 5220). Ross was not an advocate of territorial government.

18. *Manila Weekly Times*, January 16, 1914; *Far Eastern Review*, January, 1914 (BIA Harrison "P"). Ross to Quezon, March 17 and May 12, 1914 (Quezon Major Correspondents' File). Concerning the smoker, see *Cablenews-American*, April 5, 1914 and *Far Eastern Review*, April 1914 (BIA Harrison "P"). The warming of the business community is described in Samuel Ferguson to McIntyre, June 1, 1914 (BIA Ferguson "P"), and *ibid.*, July 4, 1914 (BIA C.1247–47); Report of the American-Philippine Company, July 14, 1914 (BIA 26391–30A). The *largesse* toward the Mindoro Company reflected several changes in its policy and personnel since 1910. George Fairchild, by 1914 a partner of Havemeyer and Welch and the Manila agent for the company, had ingratiated himself with Harrison by defending his regime and testifying for the Jones bill. His arrival and the departure of Poole, the original purchaser, made the company more attractive. Moreover, Ross, its attorney, headed one wing of the insular Democratic Party and was a force for moderation among Manila businessmen. Once Quezon's superior in the government, he was on a Jimmie and Manolo basis with Harrison's original sponsor and had come out on the same ship with the new governor and Quezon in 1913. It was Ross who asked Harrison to deposit the funds. Finally, by 1914, the company was contemplating selling its land to Filipino cultivators and concentrating entirely on the milling of sugar.

19. Concerning the use of the secret police: Harrison to Garrison, Sep-

tember 30, 1914 (BIA 1239–123). Letters dealing with the threat to Cohn and Bruce are filed as BIA 13931–A–355. Quezon's activity in San Francisco is reported in Quezon to Harrison, cable, November 23, 1915 (Quezon Subject File: Sugar Trade), and Quezon to Harrison, December 6, 1915 (HP, box 36). Gilbert to Forbes, June 2, 1915 (FP, fMS Am 1364.1). Quezon to Harrison, Oct. 14, 1915 (HP, box 33).

20. Forbes, Journal, V, 326–327; Hayden, *Philippines,* pp. 100–101; Kalaw, *Aide-de-Camp,* p. 105.

21. This discussion of Quezon's position is based upon Frank McIntyre's memoranda of nine private conversations between Quezon and himself in late December 1913 and early Jaunary 1914, filed together as BIA 4325–158, and is supported by a report from the American consul general in Yokohama, filed as BIA 364–260. I have found no copy of the Osmeña draft. Its contents are described in cables from Osmeña to Quezon, February 19 and 22, 1914 (QGCF).

22. The quotation is from McIntyre's memorandum of December 29, 1913. For the circulation of Quezon's ideas, see McIntyre, memorandum, January 17, 1914; Garrison to Wilson, January 19, 1914; and Wilson to Garrison, January 21, 1914 (BIA 4325–158).

23. Quezon to Osmeña, January 20, 1914; Quezon to Osmeña, cable, February 7, 1914; Quezon to Erving Winslow, January 19, 1914 (QGCF). There is an undated draft letter from Quezon to Wilson in the QGCF, January 1914. Internal evidence suggests composition toward the end of the second week of January. The letter proposes substantially the same plan described above, except for the omission of the referendum, and asks the President to make it the administration's policy.

24. Quezon's draft: BIA 4325-56. McIntyre, memorandum, February 21, 1914 (BIA 4325–57); Storey to Quezon, February 9, 1914 (QGCF); Osmeña to Quezon, cable, February 22, 1914 (QGCF).

25. Quezon to Storey, February 12, 1914; Quezon to Osmeña, cable, February 25, 1914 (QGCF). Storey to Quezon, February 16, 1914 (QGCF). Quezon to Osmeña, cable, February 25, 1914; Osmeña to Quezon, cable, March 4, 1914 (QGCF). I have found no indication that Quezon ever tried out Osmeña's plan on an official of the administration.

26. Winslow to Quezon, May 6, 1914; Storey to Quezon, May 15, 1914 (QGCF). McIntyre, memorandum, May 13, 1914 (BIA 4325–158). Quezon to Winslow, May 27, 1914 (QGCF); McIntyre, memorandum, May 26, 1914 (BIA 4325–158). Wilson had not even known of Jones' bill until Quezon appeared to ask his support for it.

27. McIntyre to Harrison, cable, June 5, 1914 (BIA 4325–64); Harrison to Garrison, cable, June 8, 1914 (BIA 4325–66). Garrison to Wilson, June 9, 1914 (BIA 4325–70/71); McIntyre, memorandum, June 19, 1914 (BIA 4325–74). Quezon to Osmeña, cable, July 6, 1914; Quezon to H. Parker Willis, July 7, 1914 (QGCF).

28. Osmeña to Quezon, cables, June 18, June 20, and June 22, 1914 (QGCF).

29. Kalaw, *Aide-de-Camp*, p. 96; Hayden, *Philippines*, pp. 170–171.

30. Osmeña to Quezon, cable, June 18, 1914 (QGCF). At present, there is no biography of Osmeña, although a work is in preparation by Vicente Pacis.

31. Liang, *Political Parties*, pp. 96–99, 113–116; Quezon to Winslow, January 17, 1914 (QGCF); McIntyre, memorandum, July 9, 1914 (BIA 59–55); *Consolidacion Nacional*, December 18, 1914 (BIA Harrison "P").

32. *Consolidacion Nacional*, June 13, 1914 (HP, box 32). Confidential Constabulary reports, June 12 and June 13, 1914 (HP, box 32). De Veyra to Quezon, September 21, 1914 (QGCF).

33. Concerning the anti-imperialists' endorsements, see Osmeña to Quezon, cable, June 23, 1914 (QGCF); Jones to Osmeña, July 10, 1914 (HP, box 34); Quezon to Storey, July 22, 1914 (QGCF); Quezon to Osmeña, July 23, 1914, and cable, July 27, 1914 (QGCF). Harrison to McIntyre, cable, July 17, 1914 (BIA 4325–89).

34. Osmeña to Quezon, cable, July 14, 1914; de Veyra to Quezon, September 21, 1914; Osmeña to Quezon, October 29, 1914; Kalaw to Quezon, cable, October 9, 1914 (QGCF).

35. Osmeña to Quezon, October 29, 1914 (QGCF); miscellaneous documents BIA 4325–139/142; Wilson to Shafroth, February 3, 1915 (WP, series 4, file 44).

36. Jones to Harrison, March 10, 1915 (HP, box 35); Hitchcock to Harrison, March 8, 1914 (HP, box 35); McIntyre, memorandum (BIA 4325–after 155). Cf. Quezon to Harrison, March 1, 1915 (HP, box 35), which elevates Quezon's importance and omits mention of the nocturnal visit to McIntyre.

37. For Taft's attack, see the *San Francisco Chronicle*, September 7, 1915. *The Sun*, November 9, 1915. Concerning Roosevelt, see Charles E. Neu, *An Uncertain Friendship: Theodore Roosevelt and Japan, 1906–1909* (Cambridge, Mass., 1967), pp. 141–143, 148–149; and the correspondence between Roosevelt and Forbes, collected in Forbes, Journal, series 2, I, 536–552.

38. Quezon to Harrison, September 21, 1914; Quezon to Osmeña, cable, December 15, 1914 (QGCF). Ross to Quezon, July 14, 1914 (Quezon Major Correspondents' File); Ross to Quezon, August 31, 1914 (Quezon Subject File: Jones Bill); Quezon to Ross, October 31, 1914 (Quezon Major Correspondents' File); McIntyre to Harrison, cable, February 1, 1915 (BIA 4325–after 148). Welch to Jones, February 1, 1916 (QGCF). Concerning the railroads: W. A. Kincaid to McIntyre, December 23, 1915 (BIA 4325–186); Richard Schuster to McIntyre, May 31, 1916 (BIA 13931–A–506).

39. Manuel Earnshaw, memorandum, March 1916 (HP, box 40). Hitchcock to Joseph P. Tumulty, January 11, 1916; Tumulty to Wilson, radio, January 22, 1916; Wilson to Tumulty, January 23, 1916 (all WP, series 4, file 44). Wilson to Garrison, January 25, 1916 (BIA 4325–204A).

40. McIntyre, memorandum, January 25, 1916 (BIA 4325–215A). Mc-

Intyre, memorandum, February 8, 1916 (BIA 4325–220B); McIntyre to Harrison, February 14, 1916 (BIA 1239–135). Curry, *Woodrow Wilson and Far Eastern Policy*, pp. 91–92; Arthur S. Link, *Wilson: Confusions and Crises, 1915–1916* (Princeton, 1964), pp. 15–18, 37–39, 50–54.

41. Quezon to Osmeña, cable, January 11, 1916 (QGCF).

42. Osmeña to Quezon, cables, January 12 and 15, 1916 (QGCF); Quezon to Wilson, January 25, 1916 (WP, series 4, file 44); Quezon to Osmeña, cable, February 13, 1916 (QGCF). For political reasons, Osmeña would have preferred that the instrument of independence be a bill of Nacionalista authorship, rather than the Clarke Amendment; but he favored a bill that would provide conditions similar to those explained here.

43. Earnshaw, memorandum, March 1916 (HP, box 40); Quezon to Osmeña, cable, February 11, 1916 (QGCF); Quezon to Osmeña, cable, February 13, 1916 (QGCF). The quotation is from the latter.

44. Concerning the reaction in Manila, see Osmeña's cables to Quezon, February 6, 8, 11, 13, 16 and 23, 1916 (QGCF); and Kalaw, *Aide-de-Camp*, pp. 112–113. For the American end, see McIntyre to Harrison, February 14, 1916 (BIA 1239–135); Quezon to Osmeña, cable, February 19, 1916 (currently in Quezon Subject File: 1916 undated).

45. Osmeña to Quezon, cables, February 6, 14, and 15, 1916 (QGCF).

46. Quezon to Osmeña, cable, February 16, 1916 (QGCF); Quezon to Osmeña, cable, February 19 and 22, 1916 (currently in Quezon Subject File: 1916 undated).

47. Concerning Jones, see McIntyre to Harrison, February 24, 1916 (BIA 4325–after 217); Jones to Harrison, March 13, 1916 (HP, box 40). McIntyre's views are set forth in his memorandum, March 16, 1916 (BIA 4325–225). His objection to prohibition was that it would cost the insular government tax revenues. As for the Clarke amendment: "The objection . . . is not that it recognizes the right of the Filipinos to independence, but that it gives them this in a manner in which it was not desired by them . . . and in the face of the evidence from our own witnesses . . . that what we offer them is something from which they can not possibly profit."

48. Quezon to Osmeña, cables, April 28 and May 2, 1916 (QGCF); McIntyre to Harrison, cable, May 2, 1916 (BIA 4325–after 234). It is widely held that Catholic influence accounted for the defeat of the Clarke amendment: Curry, *Wilson and Far Eastern Policy*, pp. 94–95; Link, *Confusions and Crises*, p. 354; Harrison, *Corner-stone*, pp. 193–194; Grunder and Livezey, *Philippines and the United States*, pp. 154–155. It is notable, however, that before the vote Jones omitted all reference to the church in describing the opposition, emphasizing instead bankers, cotton manufacturers, and persons with investments in the islands. After the vote, he specifically denied that William Kincaid, the church's chief lobbyist on this occasion, had influenced Democratic defectors: Jones to Harrison, March 13, 1916 (HP, box 40); Jones to Harrison, September 7, 1916 (HP, box 39).

49. Curry, *Wilson and Far Eastern Policy*, pp. 95–96; Grunder and Live-

zey, *Philippines and the United States*, p. 155. McIntyre to Harrison, September 1, 1916 (BIA 4325–after 263).

50. Osmeña to Quezon, cable, August 21, 1916 (QGCF).

9. Nationalizing the Economy

1. Taft to Ide, January 22, 1906 (TP, series 8, Sec War, semi-official, vol. 48). See also McIntyre to Harrison, January 10, 1914 (BIA 14791–15). Statistics on investments in the early years of the century are primitive. In August 1911 the collector of internal revenue estimated total American capital invested in the islands at ₱110,245,000, plus ₱30,250,000 in government bonds. This included the railroads, the Manila Electric Railway and Light Company, and numerous commercial concerns such as the Pacific Commercial Company (BIA 23908–1). In 1913, the total capital invested in manufacturing from all sources, including Filipinos, was ₱36,853,444.40. Much of this, apart from the ₱7,390,654.60 attributed to Americans, must have originated prior to the beginning of American government (*Daily Consular and Trade Reports*, October 18, 1913, p. 352 [BIA 23908–3]). In the period 1900–19, a total of fifteen American corporations, with a nominal capital value of $10,575,000, registered in the islands to engage in agriculture, mining, or lumbering, along with eight other foreign corporations capitalized at approximately ₱5,000,000. (Bureau of Commerce and Industry, *Statistical Bulletin No. 2 of the Philippine Islands*, 1919, p. 149). Investment in manufacturing rose sharply during the Harrison years, owing to investments in sugar centrals and coconut oil mills.

2. Forbes' address to the Merchants' Association, July 27, 1911, is filed as BIA 9892–125½. His recollection is found in FP, fMS Am 1192.2, III, 550–551, 554.

3. For background, see Forbes, Journal, III, 75–81, and materials grouped as BIA 13931–101/105. The 1909 arrangements are described in Edwards to Smith, cable, January 7, 1909 (BIA 13931–A–1); Forbes to Edwards, April 7, 1909 (BIA 13931–A–97); and Forbes to Dickinson, cable, May 19, 1909 (BIA 13931–A–34). Act No. 2083, 2 Phil. Leg., 2 sess., December 8, 1911.

4. Concerning the Philippine Railway, see Smith to Taft, cable, October 30, 1906 (BIA 14221–54); McIntyre to C. Lewis, October 30, 1906 (BIA 15058, p. 3); McIntyre to Smith, cables, October 30 and November 8, 1906 (BIA 14221–after 54); Forbes, Journal, II, 159, 163, 168–169, and note 90, pp. 440–441. Corruption in the Manila Railroad is described in D. R. Williams to Gilbert, June 24, 1913 (Quezon Subject File: Manila Railroad Company).

5. The evolution of Harrison's views may be followed in Harrison to Garrison, January 8, 1914 (BIA 15505–19); Harrison to Garrison, February 19, 1914 (BIA 1239–110); Harrison to Garrison, September 30, 1914 (BIA 1239–123); Garrison to Harrison, January 20, 1915 (BIA 1239–125); Mc-

Intyre, memorandum for Secretary of War, May 16, 1914 (BIA 13931–A–245).

6. For the 1909 offer, see BIA 14221–109; for the company's approach to Harrison, see Harrison to Garrison, February 19, 1914 (BIA 1239–110).

7. McIntyre, memorandum for Secretary of War, June 19, 1914 (BIA 13931–A–258); Richard Schuster to McIntyre, July 16, 1914 (BIA 13931–A–267 and 272).

8. Harrison to Garrison, August 1, 1914 (BIA 13931–A–288/289); Harrison to Garrison, cable, October 27, 1914 (BIA 13931–A–294).

9. McIntyre to Harrison, cable, October 27, 1914 (BIA 13931–A–294); McIntyre to Harrison, cable, October 31, 1914 (BIA 13931–A–296); McIntyre, memorandum, November 5, 1914 (BIA 13931–A–309); McIntyre to Harrison, cable, November 11, 1914 (BIA 13931–A–315).

10. McIntyre to Harrison, cable, November 3, 1914 (BIA 13931–A–297); McIntyre to Harrison, cable, November 11, 1914 (BIA 13931–A–315); Quezon to Osmeña, November 9, 1914 (QGCF); Quezon to Osmeña, cable, November 11, 1914 (BIA 13931–A–after 315); Garrison to Forbes, December 10, 1914 (FP, bMS Am 1364.1).

11. Quezon to Osmeña, cable, November 15, 1914 (QGCF); Quezon to Osmeña, cable, December 15, 1914 (QGCF). For Osmeña's reluctance to continue supporting the company, see Osmeña to Quezon, cables, November 14 and 21, 1914 (QGCF); Harrison to Garrison, cable, November 4, 1914, (BIA 13931–A–306).

12. BIA 13931–A–319/395 *passim.*

13. McIntyre, memorandum, December 14, 1915 (BIA 13931–A–434). The memorandum of agreement between the company and the insular government, November 23, 1915, is filed as BIA 13931–A–429; subsequent revisions and details are treated in BIA 13931–A–432 and BIA 13931–A–435/478 *passim.* The Philippine government purchased the railroad company's outstanding capital stock for $4,000,000 and consolidated its bonds in a new issue at lower interest.

14. *Manila Times,* January 11, 1916 (BIA 13931–A–471).

15. Hugo H. Miller, *Economic Conditions in the Philippines* (Boston, 1913), p. 343.

16. E. W. Kemmerer, "An Agricultural Bank for the Philippines," *Yale Review* (November 1907), pp. 262–279. *Report of the Philippine Commission* (1905), pp. 75–76; *ibid.* (1906), pp. 50–51, 645–695; *Annual Report of the War Department* (1906), I, 86–87. The Egyptian analogy was emphasized in an article prepared by the BIA for circulation in the press (BIA 6769–57).

17. For the Manila response, see Smith to Edwards, cable, March 14, 1907 (BIA 6769–69). American reactions: Speyer to McIntyre, March 15, 1907 (BIA 6769–70); William Salomon to Edwards, March 22, 1907 (BIA 15196–34); Thomas H. Hubbard to Edwards, March 22, 1907 (BIA 6769–71). The Kansas City interest may be followed in BIA 6769–73/79 and BIA 16651–1/7.

18. Carpenter to McIntyre, January 16, 1913 (BIA 6769–103), and June 5, 1913 (BIA 6769–109); Provincial Circular No. 60, Executive Bureau, December 29, 1913 (BIA 6769–115); *Report of the Philippine Commission* (1914), p. 243. Elliott, *Commission,* pp. 371–372.

19. Act No. 2508, Phil. Leg., February 5, 1915; Martin to McIntyre, September 2, 1915 (BIA 6769–123B). For Harrison's recommendation, see BIA 17073–144.

20. McIntyre to Harrison, November 3, 1915 (BIA 7454–after 29); McIntyre, undated memorandum (BIA 6769–with 123). *La Democracia,* September 16, 1915 (BIA 6769–A–2).

21. Quezon to Osmeña, cable, December 8, 1915 (QGCF); Osmeña to Quezon, cable, December 10, 1915 (Quezon Subject File: Banks). Willis' draft: BIA 6769–128. Quezon to Osmeña, cable, December 8, 1915 (QGCF).

22. Act. No. 2612, Philippine Legislature, February 4, 1916 (BIA 6769–139); Willis to McIntyre, April 23, 1916 (BIA 6769–143).

23. *Statistical Bulletin No. 3 of the Philippine Islands* (1920), pp. 125, 176–179, 182–183. The averages are my own calculation.

24. These statistics have been taken, respectively from *ibid.,* pp. 208–209, 260, 250–251, 297.

25. Acts No. 2465 and 2479, Phil. Leg., February 5, 1915; Samuel Ferguson to McIntyre, September 11, 1915 (BIA 4122–101); Concurrent Resolution No. 13, 3 Phil. Leg., 3 sess., February 5, 1915.

26. Exhibit G, accompanying the papers of the Wood–Forbes Mission, details the funds appropriated and spent by these companies and boards prior to June, 1921 (BIA 22639–A–57 [D–3]).

27. Quezon to Harrison, March 23, 1916 (HP, box 39).

28. Willis to F. A. Delano, May 31, 1916 (BIA 6769–149A); Willis, "The New Philippine Bank and Our Trade with the Islands," *The Nation's Business,* November 1916 (BIA 6769–A–16); Willis, speech to the Boston chapter of the American Institute of Banking, January 16, 1917 (BIA 6769–A–22); unsigned article, presumably by Willis, in the New York *Journal of Commerce and Commercial Bulletin,* February 19, 1917 (BIA 6769–A–with 20).

29. Willis to McIntyre, April 23, 1916 (Quezon Subject File: PNB); Willis to Harrison, June 15, 1916 (BIA 6769–152); Willis to Harrison, August 9, 1916 (BIA 6769–153); *El Tiempo* (Iloilo), August 5, 1916 (BIA 6769–A–11).

30. Willis to Harrison, June 15, 1916 (BIA 6769–152).

31. G. Seaver to Archibald Harrison, August 9 and 12, 1918, both filed with covering letter Harrison to Quezon, August 16, 1918 (Quezon Subject File: PNB); the quotation is from the former. Report by the Chairman of the Investigating Committee on Conditions Affecting Agricultural Property in the Island of Negros which is Mortgaged to the Bank, August 10, 1918 (HP, box 42).

32. Concepción to Quezon, July 16, August 31, and September 14, 1918;

Concepción, confidential memorandum, August 18, 1918; A. Harrison to Concepción, September 13, 1918 (Quezon Subject File: PNB).

33. Francis Coates, Jr., *Report of an Examination of the Philippine National Bank, Manila, P.I., as of at Close of Business November 30, 1919* (BIA 6769–565A), folios 18–40.

34. *Ibid.*, folios 59–62.

35. *Ibid.*, folios 85–92, 94, 283.

36. *Ibid.*, folios 114–116 and 52–57, respectively.

37. BIA, memoranda, December 30, 1919, and September 1, 1920 (BIA 26697–D–481); Secretary of War to Secretary of Treasury, March 21, 1921 (BIA 808–after 500); *Alien Property Custodian Report* (Washington, 1919), pp. 171–172. For examples of PNB lending of this type, see the Coates Report, folios 111–114. The details of APC sales in the Philippines may be followed in BIA 26697–D.

38. For examples of significant loans involving a possible conflict of interest, see Compañía Naviera (Coates, Report, folios 44–48); Compañía Mercantil de Filipinas (Coates, Report, folios 48–52); Cristobal Oil Company (Coates, Report, folios 52–58); La Cooperativa Naval de Filipinas and Puno y Concepción (Coates, Report, folios 63–64); Tutuban Mills (Coates, Report, folios 62–63); and Binalbagan Sugar Company (Coates, Report, folios 95, 284–286). *Manila Daily Bulletin,* June 25, 1921 (BIA 6769–A–40); *La Vanguardia,* June 24, 1921 (BIA 6769–A–39). For loans to political figures, see, for example, Nieva, Ruiz and Company (Coates, Report, folios 121–122); and the extraordinary network of Araneta and Singson holdings.

39. Coates, Report, folios 7–8, 65–84, 162–163, 185–186.

40. *Statistical Bulletin No. 3 of the Philippine Islands* (1920), p. 296. This description of the PNB's role in the loss of the reserve fund and the inflation of the currency is based upon BIA files 808, 6769, and 6769–F, *passim,* especially McIntyre, memorandum for Quezon, June 10, 1919 (BIA 6769–after 282); Charles C. Walcutt, Jr., memorandum for the Secretary of War, May 26, 1919 (BIA 6769–after 261); Charles E. Yeater to Walcutt, August 14, 1919 (BIA 6769–319) and McIntyre's undated memorandum for the record concerning this letter; McIntyre, memorandum, March 28, 1921 (BIA 808–504); and Willis to Harrison, April 17, 1919 (BIA 6769–245A).

41. BIA 6769–F–2/9 and 62/79; BIA 6769–202/319 *passim.*

42. See, for example, McIntyre to Harrison, August 1, 1919 (BIA 6769–after 306); McIntyre to Harrison, June 10, 1920 (BIA 6769–459); McIntyre to Harrison, August 12, 1920 (BIA 6769–after 494); S. P. Gilbert, Jr., to McIntyre, June 27, 1921 (BIA 808–525).

43. Concepción to Willis, June 17, 1919 (BIA 6769–282); McIntyre to Harrison, September 30, 1920 (BIA 6769–525); Quezon to Osmeña, August 17, 1920 (Quezon Subject File: Officials and Employees).

44. Concerning the BPI, see Harrison to McIntyre, cable, January 1, 1921 (BIA 6769–522); Harrison to McIntyre, March 17, 1921 (BIA 6769–

588); Yeater to McIntyre, May 1, 1921 (BIA 808–513). Concerning the Shanghai branch, see International Banking Corp. to BIA, cable, January 28, 1921 (BIA 6769–567); Wilson to Kopp, January 31, 1921 (BIA 6769–570); Harrison to McIntyre, cable, March 18, 1921 (BIA 6769–589).

45. Wood-Forbes to Weeks, cable, June 29, 1921 (BIA 808–526); Yeater to McIntyre, cable, July 2, 1921 (BIA 808–530). The quotation is from Ben F. Wright to McIntyre, August 11, 1921 (BIA 6769–666). In the summer of 1921, the opinion of the insular auditor was that final PNB losses would exceed ₱45,000,000, wiping out the bank's capital and surplus. The Secretary of Finance, Alberto Barretto, learning this, demanded that the bank be liquidated and was prevented from pressing his point only with the greatest difficulty. See Yeater to McIntyre, cable, July 26, 1921 (BIA 6769–646); William T. Nolting to McIntyre, June 17, 1921 (BIA 808–534).

10. Stalemate

1. Baker to Harrison, August 18, 1916, mailed September 15, 1916 (BIA 141–after 91); McIntyre's draft is filed as BIA 4325–after 155.

2. *Ibid.;* Forbes, Journal, IV, 147.

3. Text of speech, September 28, 1916 (HP, box 39); Harrison to Baker, November 10, 1916 (BIA 141–93).

4. Act No. 2666, Philippine Legislature, November 18, 1916; Act No. 2803, February 28, 1919; Forbes, *Philippine Islands,* II, 467.

5. Osmeña to Quezon, cable, June 4, 1917 (QGCF).

6. The Council was created by Executive Order No. 37, October 16, 1918. For a fuller discussion, see Maximo M. Kalaw, *Self-Government in the Philippines* (New York, 1919), pp. 24–38; Harrison, *Corner-stone,* pp. 210–215; Liang, *Political Parties,* pp. 116–123.

7. Hayden, *Philippines,* pp. 322–328; Liang, *Political Parties,* pp. 96–127; Forbes, *Philippine Islands,* II, 260–266. Election results: Forbes, *Philippine Islands,* II, 119n.

8. Quezon to Osmeña, cable, July 1, 1917 (QGCF); Ralph W. Jones to Harrison, memorandum, June 20, 1918, and Jones, memoranda for the Militia Commission, July 7 and November 14, 1918 (Quezon Subject File: Philippine National Guard); José Santos to Quezon, June 28, 1918 (Quezon Subject File: Philippine National Guard). For a more altruistic evaluation, see Harrison, *Corner-stone,* pp. 161–167, 185–186.

9. Osmeña to de Veyra, for Quezon, cable, January 30, 1919 (QGCF); Conrado Benitez to Maximo Kalaw, cable, February 2, 1920 (QGCF); *The Sun* (New York), February 4, 1919 (BIA 3432–A–13).

10. Arsenio N. Luz, "Philippine Economic Development Under American Sovereignty," undated clipping from *The Bankers Magazine* (BIA 27417–A–6).

11. M. J. de la Rama, writing in *The Commercial* (New York), April 24, 1920 (BIA 27416–A–8). An article by the same author in the issue of January 17, 1920, had invoked Cuba as a model for the type and volume

of American investment desired by Filipinos. File 27416–A contains various examples of government-sponsored publicity of this type.

12. Winslow to Baker, March 14, 1919 (BIA 26480–38). Forbes, *Philippine Islands*, II, 379; Varona to *El Debate*, April 23, 1919 (QGCF).

13. Harrison to Wilson, November 13, 1918 (HP, box 43). Carpenter to McIntyre, November 13, 1918 (BIA Carpenter "P"); Yeater to Walcutt, cable, February 10, 1919 (BIA 17073–188).

14. Harrison to Walcutt, cable, November 9, 1918 (BIA 364–338); Harrison to Baker, cable, November 11, 1918 (BIA 26480–11); Walcutt to Harrison, cable, November 15, 1918 (BIA 26480–13).

15. Harrison to Baker, cable, November 19, 1918 (BIA 364–339); Kalaw, *Aide-de-Camp,* pp. 128–129; Osmeña and Quezon, confidential memorandum for Governor General, November 19, 1918 (BIA 364–342A).

16. Quezon to Osmeña, cables, March 10 and March 25, 1919 (QGCF).

17. Baker's statement: BIA 364–348B. Baker to Finis J. Garrett, June 8, 1919 (BIA 364–379); H. M. Towner to Fairchild, August 28, 1919 (Quezon Major Correspondents' File: Fairchild).

18. Harrison to McIntyre, cable, November 13, 1920 (BIA 3038–89); Quezon to Baker, January 2, 1920 (QGCF); Harrison, *Corner-stone,* p. 287; Harrison to McIntyre, September 5, 1920 (copy in Quezon Subject File: Supreme Court).

19. De Veyra to Osmeña and Quezon, November 30 and December 3, 1920 (QGCF); James A. Frear to Quezon, December 29, 1920 (Quezon Major Correspondents' File).

20. Forbes, Journal, series 2, II, 27–30, 32, 320–324.

21. *Ibid.;* Forbes to Victor G. Heiser, March 31, 1915 (copy in Forbes, Journal, series 2, I, 198–199); Forbes to Harding, January 20 and February 7, 1921 (copies in Forbes, Journal, series 2, II, 33–34 and 313–319). Concerning Wood, see Michael P. Onorato, "The Wood-Forbes Mission," in his *A Brief Review of American Interest in Philippine Development and Other Essays* (Berkeley, 1968), p. 45.

22. Wood-Forbes to Weeks, cable, July 25, 1921 (BIA 22639–A–13); Weeks to Wood, cable, July 28, 1921 (BIA 22639–A–13). The administration had been urging Wood informally to accept the post for several months.

23. Onorato, "Wood-Forbes Mission," pp. 50–56; Quezon to McIntyre, May 16, 1921 (QGCF); Wood to Weeks, cable, December 7, 1921 (BIA 22639–A–37); Bowditch to Forbes, December 9, 1921 (FP, bMS Am 1364.3, box 2).

24. *Congressional Record,* 67 Cong., 2 sess., January 5, 1922, pp. 13265–13268.

25. Quezon to Osmeña, cable, August 28, 1921 (QGCF); memorandum of Harding's views as expressed to Quezon, August 19, 1921 (BIA 364–409A); Quezon to Harrison, undated letter from Vancouver, 1921 (HP, box 44).

26. McIntyre, Memorandum for the Secretary of War relating to Philip-

pine Policy, May 24, 1922 (BIA 364–after 429); the text of Harding's statement is filed with BIA 364–after 433.

27. Quoted in Theodore Friend, *Between Two Empires: The Ordeal of the Philippines, 1929–1946* (New Haven, 1965), p. 69.

28. Quoted from the Wood-Forbes Report, in Forbes, *Philippine Islands,* II, 543.

Conclusion

1. Friend, *Between Two Empires,* p. 9.

2. The Philippine government spent proportionately more of its revenue on education than any other Asian dependency, or than the independent government of Japan. By the Commonwealth period, 45 percent of school-age children and 10.7 percent of the total population attended the public schools. Social utility is harder to measure. Thirty-eight percent of those who attended school never got beyond second grade, a level which, in the words of the Monroe Survey report, gave them "practically nothing of permanent value." Less than half made it to fourth grade, the level considered the basic minimum by both the Monroe commission and the Commonwealth's National Council of Education. After four decades of American emphasis upon the centrality of English to success in commerce, government, and reform, only 26 percent of the population was capable of speaking it; the number who actually *used* it was much smaller. Even so, the job market was glutted with school-trained Filipinos. Hayden, *Philippines,* chs. 18–20, esp. pp. 469–480, 523–528, 600–604.

3. Friend, *Between Two Empires,* p. 6.

4. Hayden, *Philippines,* pp. 523–528.

5. *Ibid.,* p. 397.

6. David Joel Steinberg, *Philippine Collaboration in World War II* (Ann Arbor, 1967), p. 172.

7. Hayden, *Philippines,* p. 324.

8. Akira Iriye, *After Imperialism: The Search for a New Order in the Far East, 1921–1931* (Cambridge, Mass., 1965).

9. Friend, *Between Two Empires,* pp. 77–79.

10. There have been exceptions, of course. Theodore Friend's supple characterization of the triangular Philippine-American-Japanese relationship of the thirties is rich with implications for modern American history. William S. Pomeroy's *American Neo-Colonialism: Its Emergence in the Philippines and Asia* (New York, 1970), which I have criticized elsewhere for its excessive reliance upon Leninist theory, faulty factual basis, and innocence of Philippine history, is nevertheless perceptive and suggestive in identifying the neo-imperialist character of our Philippine experience.

11. I except the continental empire, because it was fully integrated into the national polity. I recognize that students of Indian history may reasonably object to this.

Bibliography

The following list includes all the items mentioned in the text and the footnotes, along with a limited number of other materials that were of special importance in the preparation of this book. It is by no means an inclusive bibliography of the subject. For an appreciation of these materials, the reader is referred to my historiographic essay, "The Forgotten Philippines, 1790–1946," in Ernest R. May and James C. Thomson Jr., eds., *American-East Asian Relations: A Survey*, pp. 291–316.

Throughout the book, my citations of the Quezon Papers are based upon the arrangement of the collection in the second third of the year 1968, when I did my research in Manila. In August of that year a major earthquake overturned most of the collection, jumbling its order and destroying a number of documents that had been in poor condition.

Manuscript Sources

Archives of the Bureau of Insular Affairs. National Archives. Washington, D.C.
W. Cameron Forbes Papers. Harvard University. Cambridge, Mass.
Francis Burton Harrison Papers. Library of Congress. Washington, D.C.
Henry Cabot Lodge Papers. Massachusetts Historical Society. Boston, Mass.
Manuel Luis Quezon Papers. The National Library. Manila, Republic of the Philippines.
Theodore Roosevelt Papers. Library of Congress. Washington, D.C.
Elihu Root Papers. Library of Congress. Washington, D.C
William Howard Taft Papers. Library of Congress. Washington, D.C.
Woodrow Wilson Papers. Library of Congress. Washington, D.C.

Bibliography

Books and Journals

Abelarde, Pedro E. *American Tariff Policy towards the Philippines, 1898–1946.* New York: King's Crown Press, 1947.

Abella, Domingo. "A Brief Introduction to the Study of Western Cultural Penetration in the Philippines," *East Asian Cultural Studies,* 6 (1967), 176–189.

Achutegui, Pedro S. de, and Miguel A. Bernad. *Religious Revolution in the Philippines,* 2nd ed. Manila: Ateneo de Manila, 1961.

Adams, Brooks. *America's Economic Supremacy.* New York: Macmillan, 1900.

"Administration of Philippine Lands." *House Report,* 61 Cong., 3 sess., no. 2289.

Agoncillo, Teodoro A. *Malolos: Crisis of the Republic.* Quezon City: University of the Philippines Press, 1960.

—————— *Revolt of the Masses: The Story of Bonifacio and the Katipunan.* Quezon City: University of the Philippines Press, 1956.

Alfonso, Oscar M. "Taft's Early Views on the Filipinos," *Solidarity,* 4 (June 1969), 52–58.

Alien Property Custodian Report. Washington: Government Printing Office, 1919.

Alzona, Encarnación. *A History of Education in the Philippines.* Manila: University of the Philippines Press, 1932.

Anderson, Gerald H., ed. *Studies in Philippine Church History.* Ithaca, N.Y.: Cornell University Press, 1969.

Annals of the American Academy of Political and Social Science, 30 (July 1907). Special issue on American Colonial Policy and Administration.

Annual Report of the Lake Mohonk Conference on the Indian and Other Dependent Peoples, 1910 and 1911.

Apostol, José P. *The Economic Policy of the Philippine Government: Ownership and Operation of Business.* Manila: University of the Philippines Press, 1927.

Barrows, David Prescott. *A Decade of American Government in the Philippines, 1903–1913.* Yonkers, N.Y.: World Book Company, 1914.

Beadles, John A. "The Debate in the United States Concerning Philippine Independence, 1912–1916," *Philippine Studies,* 16 (1968), 421–441.

Beale, Howard K. *Theodore Roosevelt and the Rise of America to World Power.* Baltimore: The Johns Hopkins Press, 1956.

Benda, Harry J. "Political Elites in Colonial Southeast Asia: An Historical Analysis," *Comparative Studies in Society and History,* 7 (1965), 233–251.

Benitez, Conrado, and Austin Craig. *Philippine Progress Prior to 1898.* Manila: Filipiniana Book Guild, 1969.

Bertin, Jacques, Serge Bonin and Pierre Chaunu. *Les Philippines et la Pacifique des Ibériques, XVIe–XVIIe–XVIIIe Siècles.* Paris: S.E.V.P.E.N., 1960.

Bibliography

Black, C. E. *The Dynamics of Modernization: A Study in Comparative History*. New York: Harper and Row, 1966.

Blair, Emma Helen, and James A. Robertson. *The Philippine Islands*. 55 vols. Cleveland: Arthur H. Clark, 1903–1909.

Blount, James H. *The American Occupation of the Philippines, 1898–1912*. New York: Putnam, 1912.

Blum, John Morton. *The Republican Roosevelt*. Cambridge, Mass.: Harvard University Press, 1954.

Bowditch, Nathaniel. *Early American-Philippine Trade: The Journal of Nathaniel Bowditch in Manila, 1796*, ed. Thomas R. and Mary C. McHale. New Haven: Yale University Southeast Asia Studies, monograph no. 2, 1962.

Bowring, John. *A Visit to the Philippine Islands*. Manila: Filipiniana Book Guild, 1963.

Bulatao, Jaime C. "Hiya," *Philippine Studies, 12* (1964), 424–438.

Buss, Claude A. "Charismatic Leadership in Southeast Asia: Manuel Luis Quezon," *Solidarity, 1* (July–September 1966), 3–8.

Butt, Archie. *Taft and Roosevelt: The Intimate Letters of Archie Butt*. Garden City, N.Y.: Doubleday, Doran & Company, 1930.

Carroll, John J. *Changing Patterns of Social Structure in the Philippines, 1896–1963*. Manila: Ateneo de Manila, 1968.

Casambre, Napoleon J. "Francis Burton Harrison: His Administration in the Philippines, 1913–1921," Ph.D. diss., Stanford University, 1968.

Census of the Philippine Islands, 1903. 4 vols. Washington: Government Printing Office, 1905.

Census of the Philippine Islands, 1918. 4 vols. Manila: Bureau of Printing, 1920–21.

Clark, Victor. *Labor Conditions in the Philippines*. Bureau of Labor, Bulletin No. 10. Washington: Government Printing Office, 1905.

Cloghessy, James F. "The Philippines and the Royal Philippine Company," *Mid-America, 42* (1960), 80–104.

Conant, Charles A. "The Currency of the Philippine Islands," *Annals of the American Academy of Political and Social Science, 20* (November 1902), 44–59.

———— *The United States in the Orient: The Nature of the Economic Problem*. Boston: Houghton Mifflin, 1901.

The Congressional Record.

Corpuz, Onofre D. *The Bureaucracy in the Philippines*. Quezon City: University of the Philippines Institute of Public Administration, Study No. 4, 1957.

———— *The Philippines*. Englewood Cliffs, N.J.: Prentice-Hall, 1965.

———— "Western Colonisation and the Filipino Response," *Journal of Southeast Asian History, 3* (1962), 1–23.

Correspondence Relating to the War with Spain. 2 vols. United States Adjutant General's Office. Washington: Government Printing Office, 1902.

318

Bibliography

Costa, Horacio de la. *The Jesuits in the Philippines, 1581–1768*. Cambridge, Mass.: Harvard University Press, 1961.

———— "Nascent Philippine Nationalism, 1872–1896," *Philippine Historical Review*, 3 (1970), 154–170.

Curry, Roy W. *Woodrow Wilson and Far Eastern Policy, 1913–1921*. New York: Bookman, 1957.

Cushner, Nicholas P. *Spain in the Philippines*. Rutland, Vt.: Tuttle, 1972.

Díaz-Trechuelo, María Lourdes. "The Economic Development of the Philippines in the Second Half of the Eighteenth Century," *Philippine Studies*, 11 (1963), 195–231.

———— *La real compañía de Filipinas*. Seville: Escuela de Estudios Hispano-Americanos de Sevilla, 1965.

Dickinson, Jacob M. "Special Report on the Philippine Islands to the President of the United States." *House Document*, 61 Cong., 3 sess., no. 1261.

Elliott, Charles B. *The Philippines to the End of the Commission Government*. Indianapolis: Bobbs-Merrill, 1917.

———— *The Philippines to the End of the Military Regime*. Indianapolis: Bobbs-Merrill, 1916.

Emerson, Rupert. *From Empire to Nation: The Rise to Self-Assertion of Asian and African Peoples*. Cambridge, Mass.: Harvard University Press, 1960.

Espiritu, Socorro C., and Chester L. Hunt, eds. *Social Foundations of Community Development: Readings on the Philippines*. Manila: R. M. Garcia, 1964.

Fernandez, Leandro H. *The Philippine Republic*. New York: Columbia University Press, 1926.

Fieldhouse, D. K. *The Colonial Empires*. New York: Delacorte, 1967.

Fischer, Georges. *Un Cas de décolonisation: Les États-Unis et les Philippines*. Paris: Pichon et Durand-Auzias, 1960.

Forbes, W. Cameron. *The Philippine Islands*. 2 vols. Boston: Houghton Mifflin, 1928.

———— "Reply to Jones." Pamphlet. Manila: n.p., 1913.

Foreman, John. *The Philippine Islands*, 2nd ed. New York: Scribner's, 1899.

Fox, Frederick W. "Some Notes on Public Elementary Education in Iloilo Province, 1885–1899," *Philippine Studies*, 2 (1954), 5–19.

Fox, Frederick W., and Juan Mercader. "Some Notes on Education in Cebu Province, 1820–1898," *Philippine Studies*, 9 (1961), 20–46.

Fox, Henry Frederick. "Primary Education in the Philippines, 1565–1863," *Philippine Studies*, 13 (1965), 207–231.

Fox, Robert B. "The Study of Filipino Society and its Significance to Programs of Economic and Social Development," *Philippine Sociological Review*, 7 (January–April 1959), 2–11.

Friend, Theodore. *Between Two Empires: The Ordeal of the Philippines, 1929–1946*. New Haven: Yale University Press, 1965.

Bibliography

Garraty, John A. *Henry Cabot Lodge*. New York: Knopf, 1953.

Gates, John. *Schoolbooks and Krags: The United States Army in the Philippines, 1898–1902*. Westport, Conn.: Greenwood, 1972.

Golay, Frank H., ed. *Philippine-American Relations*. Englewood Cliffs, N.J.: Prentice-Hall, 1966.

Griswold, A. Whitney. *The Far Eastern Policy of the United States*. New York: Harcourt, Brace, 1938.

Grossholtz, Jean. *Politics in the Philippines*. Boston: Little, Brown and Company, 1964.

Grunder, Garel A., and William E. Livezey. *The Philippines and the United States*. Norman, Okla.: University of Oklahoma Press, 1951.

Gwekoh, Sol H. *Manuel L. Quezon: His Life and Career*. Manila: University Publishing Company, 1954.

Hagedorn, Herman. *Leonard Wood: A Biography*. 2 vols. New York: Harper & Bros., 1931.

Harrison, Francis Burton. *The Corner-stone of Philippine Independence: A Narrative of Seven Years*. New York: Century, 1922.

Hartendorp, A. V. H. *Short History of Industry and Trade of the Philippines from Pre-Spanish Times to the End of the Roxas Administration*. Manila: American Chamber of Commerce of the Philippines, 1953.

Hayden, Joseph Ralston. *The Philippines: A Study in National Development*. New York: Macmillan, 1942.

Healy, David F. *The United States in Cuba, 1898–1902: Generals, Politicians, and the Search for Policy*. Madison: University of Wisconsin Press, 1963.

———— *U.S. Expansionism: The Imperialist Urge in the 1890s*. Madison: University of Wisconsin Press, 1970.

Hendrickson, Kenneth E., Jr. "Reluctant Expansionist—Jacob Gould Schurman and the Philippine Question," *Pacific Historical Review*, 36 (1967), 405–421.

Hofstadter, Richard. "Manifest Destiny and the Philippines," in *America in Crisis*, ed. Daniel Aaron. New York: Knopf, 1952.

Hollnsteiner, Mary R. *The Dynamics of Power in a Philippine Municipality*. Quezon City: University of the Philippines Press, 1963.

Hord, John S. *Internal Taxation in the Philippines*. Johns Hopkins University Studies, series 25, no. 1, 1907.

Hoyt, Frederick Gilman. "The Wood-Forbes Mission to the Philippines, 1921," Ph.D. diss., Claremont Graduate School, 1963.

Ireland, Alleyne. *The Far Eastern Tropics: Studies in the Administration of Tropical Dependencies*. Boston: Houghton Mifflin, 1905.

Iriye, Akira. *After Imperialism: The Search for a New Order in the Far East, 1921–1931*. Cambridge, Mass.: Harvard University Press, 1965.

Jagor, Feodor. *Travels in the Philippines*. Manila: Filipiniana Book Guild, 1965.

Jessup, Philip C. *Elihu Root*. 2 vols. New York: Dodd, Mead, 1938.

Kalaw, Maximo M. *The Case for the Filipinos*. New York: Century, 1916.

Bibliography

―――― *The Development of Philippine Politics, 1872–1920.* Manila: Oriental Commercial Company, 1926.

―――― *Self-Government in the Philippines.* New York: Century, 1919.

Kalaw, Teodoro M. *Aide-de-Camp to Freedom,* trans. Maria Kalaw Katigbak. Manila: Teodoro M. Kalaw Society, 1965.

―――― *The Philippine Revolution.* Manila: Manila Book Company, 1925.

Kaut, Charles. "Contingency in a Tagalog Society," *Asian Studies,* 3 (1965), 1–15.

―――― "Utang na loob: A System of Contractual Obligations among Tagalogs," *Southwest Journal of Anthropology,* 17 (1961), 256–272.

Kemmerer, Edwin W. "An Agricultural Bank for the Philippines," *Yale Review,* 15 (1907), 262–279.

―――― *Modern Currency Reforms.* New York: Macmillan, 1916.

Kirk, Grayson L. *Philippine Independence: Motives, Problems, and Prospects.* New York: Farrar & Rinehart, 1936.

Koebner, Richard, and Helmut Dan Schmitt. *Imperialism: The Story and Significance of a Political Word, 1840–1960.* Cambridge, England: Cambridge University Press, 1964.

Kuhn, Delia, and Ferdinand. *The Philippines Yesterday and Today.* New York: Holt, Rinehart and Winston, 1966.

LaFeber, Walter. *The New Empire: An Interpretation of American Expansion, 1860–1898.* Ithaca, N.Y.: Cornell University Press, 1963.

Lala, Ramon Reyes. *The Philippine Islands.* New York: Continental Publishing Company, 1898.

Landé, Carl. *Leaders, Factions, and Parties: The Structure of Philippine Politics.* New Haven: Yale University Southeast Asia Studies, monograph no. 6, 1965.

―――― "The Philippines," in *Education and Political Development,* ed. James S. Coleman. Princeton: Princeton University Press, 1965.

Larkin, John A. *The Pampangans: Colonial Society in a Philippine Province.* Berkeley: University of California Press, 1972.

Legarda, Benito, Jr. "American Entrepreneurs in the Nineteenth Century Philippines," *Explorations in Entrepreneurial History,* 9 (1957), 142–159.

―――― "Foreign Trade, Economic Change, and Entrepreneurship in the Nineteenth Century Philippines," Ph.D. diss., Harvard University, 1955.

LeRoy, James A. *The Americans in the Philippines.* 2 vols. Boston: Houghton Mifflin, 1914.

―――― *Philippine Life in Town and Country.* New York: Putnam's, 1905.

Leuchtenburg, William E. "Progressivism and Imperialism: The Progressive Movement and American Foreign Policy, 1898–1916," *Mississippi Valley Historical Review,* 39 (1952), 483–504.

Liang, Dapen. *The Development of Philippine Political Parties.* Hong Kong: South China Morning Post, 1939.

Liao, Shubert S., ed. *Chinese Participation in Philippine Culture and Economy.* Manila: Bookman, 1964.

321

Bibliography

Link, Arthur S. *Wilson: The New Freedom*. Princeton: Princeton University Press, 1956.

―――― *Wilson: The Struggle for Neutrality*. Princeton: Princeton University Press, 1960.

―――― *Wilson: Confusions and Crises, 1915–1916*. Princeton: Princeton University Press, 1964.

Lodge, Henry Cabot, ed. *Selections from the Correspondence of Theodore Roosevelt and Henry Cabot Lodge, 1884–1918*. 2 vols. New York: Scribner's, 1925.

MacMicking, Robert. *Recollections of Manilla and the Philippines During 1848, 1849 and 1850*. London: Richard Bentley, 1851.

Majul, Cesar Adib. "The Historical Background of Philippine Nationalism," *Asia*, 9 (Fall 1967), 51–66.

―――― *Mabini and the Philippine Revolution*. Quezon City: University of the Philippines Press, 1960.

―――― *The Political and Constitutional Ideas of the Philippine Revolution*. Quezon City: University of the Philippine Press, 1957.

May, Ernest R. *American Imperialism: A Speculative Essay*. New York: Atheneum, 1968.

―――― *Imperial Democracy: The Emergence of America as a Great Power*. New York: Harcourt, Brace and World, 1961.

―――― and James C. Thomson Jr., eds. *American–East Asian Relations: A Survey*. Cambridge, Mass.: Harvard University Press, 1972.

McCormick, Thomas J. *China Market: America's Quest for Informal Empire, 1893–1901*. Chicago: Quadrangle, 1967.

McHale, Thomas R. "A Critical History of Economic Development in the Philippines," *University of Manila Journal of East Asiatic Studies*, 9 (April–July 1960), 1–52.

Merk, Frederick. *Manifest Destiny and Mission in American History: A New Interpretation*. New York: Knopf, 1963.

Messages from the President of the United States to the Two Houses of Congress [The Abridgement]. Washington, D.C.

Miller, Hugo. *Economic Conditions in the Philippines*. Boston: Ginn & Company, 1913.

Minger, Ralph Eldin. "Taft, MacArthur, and the Establishment of Civil Government in the Philippines," *The Ohio Historical Quarterly*, 70 (1961), 308–331.

Montero y Vidal, José. *Historia general de Filipinas desde el descubrimiento de dichas islas hasta nuestros días*. 3 vols. Madrid: M. Tello, 1887–95.

Monthly Summary of Commerce of the Philippine Islands, December 1904. Bureau of Insular Affairs. Washington: Government Printing Office, 1904.

Moore, Barrington, Jr. *Social Origins of Dictatorship and Democracy: Lord and Peasant in the Making of the Modern World*. Boston: Beacon, 1966.

Morison, Elting E. *Turmoil and Tradition: A Study of the Life and Times of Henry L. Stimson*. Boston: Houghton Mifflin, 1960.

Bibliography

———— and John M. Blum, eds. *The Letters of Theodore Roosevelt.* 8 vols. Cambridge, Mass.: Harvard University Press, 1951–1954.

Neu, Charles E. *An Uncertain Friendship: Theodore Roosevelt and Japan, 1906–1909.* Cambridge, Mass.: Harvard University Press, 1967.

Noyes, Theodore W. *Oriental America and Its Problems.* Washington: Judd & Detweiler, 1903.

Ocampo de Leon, Pablo. "Speech of the Hon. Pablo Ocampo de Leon at a Popular Banquet given in his honor . . . on the occasion of his return from the United States by members of the Various Political Parties and Mercantile Organizations." Pamphlet. Manila: n.p., October 2, 1909.

Onorato, Michael P. *A Brief Review of American Interest in Philippine Development and Other Essays.* Berkeley: McCutchan, 1968.

———— "Governor General Francis Burton Harrison and His Administration: A Re-appraisal," *Philippine Studies, 18* (1970), 178–186.

Osias, Camilo. *The Filipino Way of Life.* Boston: Ginn & Company, 1940.

Owen, Norman G., ed. *Compadre Colonialism: Studies on the Philippines under American Rule.* Ann Arbor: Michigan Papers on South and Southeast Asia No. 3, 1971.

Pardo de Tavera, Trinidad H. *Reseña Historica.* Tr. as "History," *Census of the Philippine Islands, 1903,* I, 309–388.

Peeples, Dale Hardy. "The Senate Debate on the Philippine Legislation of 1902," Ph.D. diss., University of Georgia, 1964.

Perkins, Whitney T. *Denial of Empire: The United States and Its Dependencies.* Leyden: A. W. Sythoff, 1962.

Phelan, John Leddy. *The Hispanization of the Philippines: Spanish Aims and Filipino Responses, 1565–1700.* Madison: University of Wisconsin Press, 1959.

Philippine Perspective: Lectures on the Prehistory and History of the Philippines. Pt. 1: *Lahi.* Pt. 2: *Hispanidad.* Manila: Ateneo de Manila, 1964.

Pilapil, Vicente R. "The Cause of the Philippine Revolution," *Pacific Historical Review, 34* (1965), 249–264.

———— "Nineteenth Century Philippines and the Friar Problem," *The Americas, 18* (1961), 127–148.

Pilar, Marcello H. del. *Monastic Supremacy in the Philippines,* trans. Encarnación Alzona. Quezon City: Philippine Historical Association, 1958.

Pomeroy, William S. *American Neo-Colonialism: Its Emergence in the Philippines and Asia.* New York: International, 1970.

———— "Pacification in the Philippines, 1898–1913," *France Asie/Asia, 21* (1967), 427–446.

Pratt, Julius W. *America's Colonial Experiment.* Englewood Cliffs, N.J.: Prentice-Hall, 1950.

———— *Expansionists of 1898.* Baltimore: The Johns Hopkins Press, 1936.

Pringle, Henry F. *The Life and Times of William Howard Taft.* 2 vols. New York: Farrar and Rinehart, 1939.

Quezon, Manuel Luis. *The Good Fight.* New York: D. Appleton-Century, 1946.

Bibliography

Quirino, Carlos. *Quezon: Paladin of Philippine Freedom*. Manila: Filipiniana Book Guild, 1971.

—— *The Young Aguinaldo: From Kawit to Biyak-na-bato*. Manila: Bookmark, 1969.

Report of the Governor General of the Philippine Islands. 1916–1921. Manila.

Report of the Philippine Commission (Schurman). Washington, 1900.

Report of the Philippine Commission. 1900–1916. Washington, D.C.

Reuter, Frank T. *Catholic Influence on American Colonial Policies, 1898–1904*. Austin, Texas: University of Texas Press, 1967.

Reyes, José S. *Legislative History of America's Economic Policy toward the Philippines*. New York: Columbia University Press, 1923.

Rizal, José. *The Reign of Greed* [*El Filibusterismo*], trans. Charles Derbyshire. Manila: Philippine Education Company, 1912.

—— *Rizal's Political Writings*, ed. Austin Craig. Manila: Oriental Commercial Company, 1933.

—— *The Social Cancer* [*Noli Me Tangere*], trans. Charles Derbyshire. Manila: Philippine Education Company, 1912.

Robles, Eliodoro. *The Philippines in the Nineteenth Century*. Quezon City: Malaya, 1969.

Rodríguez Baena, María Luisa. *La Sociedad Económica de Amigos del País de Manila en el Siglo XVIII*. Seville: Escuela de Estudios Hispano-Americanos de Sevilla, 1966.

Rōyama, Masamichi, and Takéuchi Tatsuji. *The Philippine Polity: A Japanese View*, ed. Theodore Friend. New Haven: Yale University Southeast Asia Studies, monograph no. 12, 1967.

Russell, Charles Edward. *The Outlook for the Philippines*. New York: Century, 1922.

Salamanca, Bonifacio. *The Filipino Reaction to American Rule, 1901–1913*. Norwich, Conn.: Shoe String Press, 1968.

Saniel, Josefa. *Japan and the Philippines, 1868–1898*. Quezon City: University of the Philippines Press, 1963.

Sawyer, Frederick H. *The Inhabitants of the Philippines*. London: Sampson, Low, Marston and Company, 1900.

Schumacher, John N. "The Filipino Nationalists' Propaganda Campaign in Europe, 1880–1895," Ph.D. diss., Georgetown University, 1965.

—— and Nicholas P. Cushner. "Documents Relating to Father José Burgos and the Cavite Mutiny of 1872," *Philippine Studies, 17* (1969), 457–529.

Schurz, William L. *The Manila Galleon*. New York: E. P. Dutton, 1939.

Shenton, James P. "Imperialism and Racism," in *Essays in American Historiography: Papers Presented in Honor of Allan Nevins*, eds. Donald Sheehan and Harold C. Syrett. New York: Columbia University Press, 1960.

Solvick, Stanley D. "William Howard Taft and the Payne-Aldrich Tariff," *Mississippi Valley Historical Review, 50* (1963), 424–442.

Bibliography

Statistical Bulletin of the Philippine Islands. No. 2, 1920. No. 3, 1921. Manila: Bureau of Commerce and Industry.

Steinberg, David Joel, ed. *In Search of Southeast Asia: A Modern History.* New York: Praeger, 1971.

—————— *Philippine Collaboration in World War II.* Ann Arbor: University of Michigan Press, 1967.

Storey, Moorfield, and Marcial P. Lichauco. *The Conquest of the Philippines by the United States, 1898–1925.* New York: Putnam's, 1926.

Taft, Mrs. William Howard. *Recollections of Full Years.* New York: Dodd, Mead, 1914.

Taylor, George E. *The Philippines and the United States: Problems of Partnership.* New York: Praeger, 1964.

Tignor, Robert L. *Modernization and British Colonial Rule in Egypt, 1882–1914.* Princeton: Princeton University Press, 1966.

Valenzuela, Jesus. *A History of Journalism in the Philippine Islands.* Manila: privately printed, 1933.

Weinberg, Albert K. *Manifest Destiny: A Study of Nationalist Expansionism in American History.* Baltimore: The Johns Hopkins Press, 1935.

Wells, Henry. *The Modernization of Puerto Rico: A Political Study of Changing Values and Institutions.* Cambridge, Mass.: Harvard University Press, 1969.

Wernstedt, Frederick L. and J. E. Spencer. *The Philippine Island World: A Physical, Cultural, and Regional Geography.* Berkeley: University of California Press, 1967.

Wickberg, Edgar. *The Chinese in Philippine Life, 1850–1898.* New Haven: Yale University Press, 1965.

—————— "The Chinese Mestizo in Philippine History," *Journal of Southeast Asian History,* 5 (March 1964), 62–100.

Wiebe, Robert H. *The Search for Order, 1877–1920.* New York: Hill and Wang, 1967.

Williams, Daniel Roderick. *The Odyssey of the Philippine Commission.* Chicago: A. C. McClurg, 1913.

—————— *The United States and the Philippines.* Garden City, N.Y.: Doubleday, Page, 1924.

Williams, William Appleman. *The Tragedy of American Diplomacy.* Cleveland: World, 1959.

Willis, Henry Parker. *Our Philippine Problem: A Study of American Colonial Policy.* New York: H. Holt and Company, 1905.

Wolff, Leon. *Little Brown Brother.* Garden City, N.Y.: Doubleday, 1961.

Worcester, Dean C. *The Philippine Islands and Their People.* New York: Macmillan, 1898.

—————— *The Philippines Past and Present.* 2 vols. New York: Macmillan, 1914.

Wurfel, David. "The Philippines," in *Governments and Politics of Southeast Asia,* ed. George McTurnan Kahin. Ithaca, N.Y.: Cornell University Press, 1959.

Bibliography

Young, Marilyn B. "American Expansion 1870–1900: The Far East," in *Towards a New Past: Dissenting Essays in American History*, ed. Barton J. Bernstein. New York: Random House, 1967.

———— *The Rhetoric of Empire: American China Policy, 1895–1901*. Cambridge, Mass.: Harvard University Press, 1968.

Zaide, Gregorio F. *Philippine Political and Cultural History*. 2 vols. Manila: Philippine Education Company, 1949.

Zamora, Eladio. *Las corporaciones religiosas en Filipinas*. Valladolid: A. Martin, 1901.

Index

Index

Bacalod Murcia Milling Company, 243

Baker, Newton D., 249–250, 251, 252, 256, 257–258

Banco Español-Filipino (Manila), 234

Bandholtz, H. H., 183

Banks, Philippine, 94, 96; nationalization of, 233–237; resources of, by close of World War I, 238. *See also* Philippine National Bank

Barangay, 4

Barretto, Alberto, 128

Barrows, David P., 189

Basco y Vargas, José de, 25

Bell, J. Franklin, 164–165

"Benevolent assimilation," American policy of, 54, 58, 65, 89

Beveridge, Albert J., 89, 106

BIA, *see* Bureau of Insular Affairs

Blount, James, 209

Bonifacio, Andres, 46, 56

Boston Evening Transcript, 109

Bourns, Frank S., 56, 69, 115–116, 117

Bowring, Sir John, 11, 14, 21, 97

Brent, Rt. Rev. Charles H.; condescension of, toward Filipinos, 107, 164; and inauguration of Forbes, 139; and retention, 186, 198; his support for Forbes, 200; and Shuster, 201

Bruce, Edward B., 210, 211

Bryan, William Jennings, 64, 65, 196, 201

Buencamino, Felipe, 54, 68–69, 72

Bureau of Insular Affairs (BIA), 138, 142, 180, 203; and the railroads, 105, 228, 230; on Dickinson, 161; tariff draft by, 146; on free trade, 148–149, 152; on friar estates, 157–158; and resident commissioners, 168; opposition of, to Jones Bill, 174; and insular finance, 192; policy of, regarding Philippines, 197; and appointments to Philippine Commission, 205; and Agricultural Bank, 234; and PNB, 246, 247; conflict between Harrison and, 251; power of, 252

Burgos, José, 45

Butt, Archie, 62

Cabecillas (wholesale merchants), 28–30

Cabezas de barangays, 13–14, 37–38

Cablenews, The, 107

Cablenews-American (Manila), 164; on independence, 142, 143, 210; on 1908 elections, 165; on Harrison's speech upon arrival in Philippines, 204; on filipinization, 208

Caciquism, 67, 125, 197

Cadwallader, B. W., 210

Cadwallader & Strong (law firm), 157–158

Calderón, Felipe G.: on education, 32; and Malolos Constitution, 53; on need for Americans to show "actual deeds," 55–56, 58, 81; his plan for a municipal council, 73–74

Canada, bond between England and, 125

Capital investment: Filipino reaction to foreign (American), 140–144, 159, 233; fear of free trade leading to American, 151; effect of, on Philippine political and economic future, 157; Harrison's view of foreign (and American), 226–227; campaign to attract American, 255. *See also* Banks; Tariffs

Carpenter, Frank, 107, 207, 256

Carson, Adam C., 200

Casas, Bartolomé de las, 6

Catholicism: history of, 10–13; efforts to convert Philippine pagans to, 15–19; decline of, among Chinese, 42. *See also* Clergy; Clerical nationalism; Friars; Religion

Cavendish, Thomas, 9

Cavite uprisings, 45, 269

Census, first Philippine (1903), 90

Charles III (King of Spain), 25, 36

China, importance of retention of Philippines to U.S. trade with, 106, 109, 276, 277

Chinese community in Philippines, 5; economy of, 9–10; expulsion of Christian and non-Christian from, 24; domination of new distribution system by, 28–30, 94; agitation against, 41–42; separation of, from Philippine society, 42; Forbes' deportation of twelve persons from, 156; influence on Philippine society of, 265. *See also* Mestizos, Chinese

Index

Index

Egypt, 108; educational reform in, 83; Agricultural Bank of, 233–234

Elections: of 1907, 127–128, 132–133, 135; of 1909, 153; for Manila Municipal Board (1908), 165; of 1912, 174; of 1916 and 1919, 254–255; of 1922, 276

Eliot, Charles W., 109

Elliott, Charles B., 169, 195

Emerson, Ralph Waldo, 99

Encomenderos, encomienda, 3, 5–6, 7, 9

England, 83, 108, 125; occupation of Manila by (1762 to 1764), 24–25

English, as a *lingua franca,* 84–85, 190

Epidemics, 34, 96–97

Evangelization, 15–19, 21, 265

Exports/imports, 25, 26; growth of, in nineteenth century, 27–29; effect of Philippine currency on, 93–94; effect of free trade on, 152–153; growth of, during World War I, 237–238

Fairchild, George, 219

Fallows, Samuel, 187

Farley, Cardinal John M., 185, 187

Federal Reserve System, 239, 240, 245–246

Federal/Federalista Party, Federalistas, *see* Partido Federal

Ferguson, Samuel, 240

Filipinization: position of political parties on, 129; as goal of Forbes administration, 140, 143; Osmeña on, 160; Quezon on, 171; efforts by Harrison to increase, 204, 205, 206–212, 217; effects of and reactions to, 207–212; BIA caution concerning, 249

Filipino People, The (American magazine), 180–181, 239

Finance, insular, 191–193. *See also* Currency; Tariffs; Taxation

Flores, Ambrosio, 69, 75

Forbes, John Murray, 99

Forbes, W. Cameron (Governor General 1909–13), 126, 176; on Pardo de Tavera, 70; on Americanization of Filipino children, 86; characterized, 99–101; on Philippines and Filipinos, 101–102; road and rail-road policy of, 102–104; on retention of the Philippines, 106, 107–108, 109, 112, 113; his friendship with Quezon, 134, 135, 183; his friendship with Osmeña, 134–138, 155–157; and Philippine Assembly, 135–138, 169; appointed Vice Governor, 138; appointed Governor General, 139; Philippine policy of, 139–140; and foreign capital, 140–144, 227; and free trade, 149–150; and friar estates, 157; Jacob Dickinson on, 161; reaction of, to Philippine request for evidence of American good faith, 162–163; racism of, 165; conflict between Osmeña and, 167; and polarization of political and governmental relations, 171–172; and dispute over election of resident commissioners, 181; on independence, 185–186, 188–189, 250, 256, 259; end of administration of, 190–191; and finances, 191–193; inefficiencies in administration of, 193–194; on education, 195; inflexibility of, 199; possible replacements for, 200–201; compared with Harrison, 202, 203, 204, 226, 275; and Second Jones Bill, 220; and Wood-Forbes Mission, 259–261, 262; on elevating the masses, 270–271; analysis of Philippine polity by, 271

Ford, Henry Jones, 113, 196–197

Foreman, John: on friar abuse, 19; on Philippine law under Spain, 20, 21; on Spanish commercial houses, 34; on indolence of natives, 40; on Filipino revolt against Spanish government, 46–47; on conditions of roads, 98

Forrest, Richard E., 189

Frankfurter, Felix, 197–198

Friar(s): role of, in Philippine government, 9, 10–13; efforts of, to convert Filipino pagans to Christianity, 15–19; conflict over replacement of, with Filipino priests, 43–45

estate(s): conflict over ownership of, 43, 45; government purchase of, 82, 157; efforts by American investors to pur-

Index

chase, 157–160; San José, 158–159, 163, 211; Dickinson's limitations for future sales of, 163, 197

Friend, Theodore, 269

Garrison, Lindley M.: Philippine policy of, 197, 198–199; resignation of, 199, 222; and replacement for Forbes, 200–201; on Filipino majority on Commission, 205; and Quezon's plan for postponing independence, 213; on Second Jones Bill, 215, 219, 221–222; and public ownership of railroads, 231–232; replaced by Baker, 249

General Order No. 15 (on transportation), 98

General Order No. 40 (municipal code), 74

General Order No. 43 (plan for a municipal council), 73–74

Gibbons, Cardinal James, 185, 186–187

Gilbert, Newton W., 169, 180, 196, 199, 205, 211

Gobernadorcillo (captain), 13–14, 37–39, 42

Gold Standard Fund, 228, 231, 232, 236, 238, 246

Gomez, Dominador, 128, 133, 146, 155

Gómez, Mariano, 45

Government, local: role of friars in, under Spanish rule, 10–13; rejection of traditional offices of, by new elite, 37–39; organization of municipal and, 73–76

Government, organization of central civil, 76–77, 79; secularization of, carried out by Americans, 82. *See also* Indirect rule

Gremio de Chinos, 42

Gremio de Chinos de Binondo, 42

Gremios (municipal corporations), 37–38, 39–40, 42

Guaranty Trust, 105

Guerrero, Fernando Ma., 128

Guerrero, Leon Ma., 128

Harbord, J. G., 183, 205

Harding, Warren G., 258–259

Harriman, E. R., 105

Harrison, Archibald, 241–242

Harrison, Francis Burton (Governor General 1913–21), 107, 259, 270–271, 275; nomination of, for Governor General, 175, 201; characterized, 202–203; on independence, 202, 203–204, 213, 223, 250–251, 256, 258, 271; on Forbes administration, 203, 204; Philippine policy of, 203–205; and appointments of Filipinos to Commission, 205–206; efforts by, to increase filipinization, 205, 206–212, 217; and Quezon's plan for postponing independence, 214; on Second Jones Bill, 215, 218, 219, 220, 249; on nationalization of railroads, 229–233; and Agricultural Bank, 233, 235; and government ownership of banks, 236; and PNB, 239–240, 247; conflict between BIA and, 251, 252; on American capital investment, 255; liberality of, 262; importance of economy to, 272

Hart, Albert Bushnell, 109

Havemeyer, Horace, 158

Hayden, Joseph Ralston, 216, 273, 274

Hemp, *see* Abaca

Hepburn, Peter, 111–112

Hernandez, Adriano, 147

Higgins, Horace L., 41

Higginson, Henry Lee, 101

Hill, James J., 105, 106

Hispanization, 42, 43

Hitchcock, Gilbert M., 201, 219, 223

Honorary Commission to the St. Louis Exposition, 116, 120, 121

Hord, John: and free trade, 112, 142–143, 148, 150; and dispute over taxation, 119, 120, 121–122

Humboldt, Alexander von, 108

Ide, Henry C. (Governor General 1906): and Taft Commission, 63, 77; and Cameron Forbes, 101, 134; preparation of new system of taxation by, 119, 120, 121; succeeds Wright as Governor General, 127

Index

Ideal, El (organ of Nacionalista Party), 141, 143, 162, 166, 169, 174

Igorot tribesmen, Harrison's visit to, 202–203

Ilocanos, 3–4, 15

Ilustrados (Filipino intelligentsia): conflict with friars over control of parishes, 44–45; and Philippine Revolution, 48; used by Taft for policy of attraction, 52, 270; role of, in shaping U.S. Philippine policy, 52–57; dissent of, from Taft policy, 127

Ilustre, Vicente, 206

Imports, *see* Exports/imports

Independence, Philippine, 143; Filipino ambivalence toward, 102, 184, 274–275, 276; Taft policy on, 111–112, 124–126, 162; Federal Party's platform on, 123–124; rise of political parties for, 124, 127–133 *passim;* petitions for, in first Philippine Assembly, 135–137; position of Nacionalistas and Progresistas on, 154; Osmeña's memorial on, 160–161; Quezon on, 170–171, 179–181, 183–184; rising demand of Filipinos for, 184–185; American opposition to (1912), 185–190; steps toward, during Harrison administration, 202, 203–204; Quezon's plan for postponement of, 212–215; question of desirability of, 255–256; Commission of, 256–258; Wood-Forbes Mission on, 259–261; American policy on (1922), 261–262; lack of clear definition of, 271; American evasion of, 272–275. *See also* Jones Bill; Retention

Independence Mission of 1919, 256

Independistas, *see* Partido Independista Inmediatista

India, 108; educational reform in, 83; Cameron Forbes on, 99–100

Indios, 5

Indirect rule, Spanish reliance upon, 13–14, 15, 24, 266; effect of, 22–23

"Insular Bank," government-owned, proposed, 235

International Banking Corporation, 189, 235

Iriye, Akira, 276

Irrigation systems, 193

Isolation, Philippine, under Spanish rule, 14–15, 20, 21, 22–23, 24

Jacinto, Emilio, 164

Jagor, Feodor, 13, 21, 22–23, 27

Jakosalem, Dionisio, 255

James, William, 101

Japan: currency of, as model for Philippines, 95; danger from, for independent Philippines, 131, 212; U.S. rivalry with, 276

Jenks, Jeremiah W., 95

Jesuits: role of, in Philippine education, 31, 32; expulsion and return of, 44

Jones, William Atkinson: and First Jones Bill, 171, 172–174, 179, 201; and Second Jones Bill, 215, 218, 219, 221, 223–225

Jones Bill:

First, 188; provisions in, 173; Wilson's position on, 173–174, 180; opposition to, 174, 185, 187, 189–190, 210; Harrison's support for, 212; shelving of, 214, 215

Second, 231, 252, 254, 256; response to, 215–219; passage of, by House, 219; controversy over preamble of, 219–221; Clarke amendment to, 221–225; passage of, 225; opposition to, 232; McIntyre on, 249–250; Leonard Wood on, 259

Kalaw, Maximo, 261

Kalaw, Teodoro M., 168, 183, 223–224

Katipunan (revolutionary secret society), 46, 56, 76, 164

Kemmerer, E. W., 233–234

Kipling, Rudyard, 99

Lahesa, José Robles, 229

Lamont, Thomas W., 188

Lane, Franklin K., 190

Index

Index

Index

Index

Shipping, regulation of, 91
Shuster, W. Morgan, 134, 138, 200, 201
Singson Encarnación, Vicente, 160, 206, 224
Smith, James F. (Governor General 1906–09), 107, 135, 138, 165; succeeds Ide as Governor General, 127; on the Federal Party, 132; on the Philippine Assembly, 137; succeeded by Forbes, 138; and free trade, 148–150
Social class, Philippine: emergence of new, upon nineteenth century expansion of commerce, 30–31, 36–47 *passim;* changes in Spanish, 33; divisions in, 52–54, 55–58, 132
Sotto, Filemon, 151
Southworth, L. M., 200
Spain: arrival in Philippines (sixteenth century), 3; impact on Philippine culture and society of, 4–10, 21–23, 47–48, 265–267; insularity of Philippine provincial life under, 14–15, 20, 21, 22–23, 24; Philippine response to introduction of Spanish law, 19–21; increase of immigrants from, to Philippines, 34–35; declining role in economy of, 34–36; policy of governing Philippines, 37–39, 46; Filipino revolution against, 46–47, 48
Spanish-American War (1898), 51, 145
Spanish community in Philippines: peninsulares of, 33, 35–36; creoles of, 33, 35–36; mestizos of, 33, 35, 36, 39–40; economic decline of, 34–36, 47–48
Spanish language, 84; requirement to teach, in Philippine schools, 31–32; retention of, as official language of the courts until 1920, 190
Speyer, James, 188, 234
Speyer Brothers, 105–106, 144–145, 188, 221, 227
Spooner, John C., 76; Spooner bill, 76, 87–89, 95
Steinberg, David, 274
Stimson, Henry L., 262, 276
Storey, Moorfield, 201, 214–215, 218
Strong, Frank L., 210

Suárez, Hernán, 5
Sugar, 112; exports of Philippine, 25, 27, 152, 237–238; production of, 28; and tariff changes, 146, 147, 148, 190; and Payne bill, 150, 152; PNB investments in, 243
Sugar Central Board, creation of, 238
Sumulong, Juan, 116, 131, 150
Syncretism, 17–19
Synod of Manila, 7

Taft, Henry, 157
Taft, William Howard (Governor 1901–04), 66–67, 181, 199, 259, 273; and policy of attraction, 52, 67, 269–271; and Second Philippine Commission, 61, 62–64; characterized, 61–62; on Philippine Insurrection, 63–64, 65; attitude of, toward Filipinos, 64–65, 66–67, 75, 172, 206; Philippine policy of, 64–67, 80, 139, 143, 154, 175–176, 211, 259; and Partido Federal, 68–69, 72, 115–117, 128, 132; and Pardo de Tavera, 72, 123; attitude of, toward opposition parties, 72–73; on organization of civil government, 76–77; relations of, with MacArthur, 77–79; and educational reforms, 83; and economic reforms, 87; on Spooner bill, 87–89; and Organic Act, 90; and currency crisis, 95–96; and railroad construction, 104; on retention of Philippines, 107, 108, 111, 112, 113, 162; succeeded by Wright, 117, 118; and dispute over taxation, 120, 121; on independence, 124–126, 162, 185–189, 209–210; visit of, to Philippines, to deal with challenge to strategy of, 124–127; and first Philippine Assembly, 133, 135–136, 137–138; and Cameron Forbes, 134, 138, 200; and foreign capital, 144, 227; and reduced tariffs, 146–147; on free trade, 152; and friar estates, 158; and Jacob Dickinson, 161; on racism, 164, 165; and resident commissioners, 168; opposition to, 170; and Second Jones Bill, 220, 250; his sup-

Index

Index

Wood-Forbes Mission, 259–261, 262

Worcester, Dean C., 56, 57, 195; and First Philippine Commission, 55; and Second Philippine Commission, 63; on appointment of Wright as Governor, 117–118; libel suit brought by, 141; replacing of, 201; on filipinization, 208; and Jones Act, 250; on independence, 271

World War I: expansion of Philippine economy during, 237–238; Philippine troops and warships volunteered for, 255; impact of, on Philippine efforts toward independence, 256, 257

Wright, Luke E. (Governor 1904; Governor General 1905), 100, 101–102, 141, 176, 259; and Taft Commission, 63, 77; and Pardo de Tavera, 70; on education, 87; on Filipino ambivalence toward independence, 102; on railroads, 103–104; and Partido Federal, 116, 118, 126; succeeds Taft as Governor, 117–118; and dispute over taxation, 120, 121; and brutality by Constabulary, 122–123; replaced by Ide, 127; opposition to, 127, 132, 134; on appointment of Forbes as Vice Governor, 138; on American investments in Philippines, 147; and Philippine Society, 189; on retention of Forbes as Governor General, 200

Yeater, Charles E., 256

Zamora, Jacinto, 45
Zobel family, 121

Harvard Studies in American-East Asian Relations